Entropy, Information, and Evolution

Entropy, Information, and Evolution

New Perspectives on Physical and Biological Evolution

edited by Bruce H. Weber, David J. Depew, and James D. Smith

A Bradford Book
The MIT Press
Cambridge, Massachusetts
London, England

This book was set in Palatino by Asco Trade Typesetting Ltd., Hong Kong, and printed and bound by Halliday Lithograph in the United States of America.

Library of Congress Cataloging-in-Publication Data

Entropy, information, and evolution.

Based on papers presented at a conference on evolution, entropy, and information, held at California State University, Fullerton, May 1985, and sponsored by the University's School of Natural Science and Mathematics.
  "A Bradford book."
  Includes bibliographies and index.
  1. Evolution—Congresses. 2. Entropy—Congresses. 3. Entropy (Information theory)—Congresses. 4. Cosmology—Congresses. I. Weber, Bruce H. II. Depew, David J., 1942–. III. Smith, James D., 1940–. IV. California State University, Fullerton. School of Natural Science and Mathematics.
QH359.E57 1988   575   87-3822
ISBN 0-262-23132-8

Contents

List of Contributors

Daniel R. Brooks
Department of Zoology
University of British Columbia
Vancouver, Canada

John H. Campbell
Department of Anatomy
School of Medicine
University of California
Los Angeles, CA 90024

John Collier
Department of Philosophy
Rice University
Houston, TX 77001

D. David Cumming
Department of Oceanography
University of British Columbia
Vancouver, Canada

David J. Depew
Department of Philosophy
California State University
Fullerton, CA 92634

C. Dyke
Department of Philosophy
Temple University
Philadelphia, PA 19122

Steven Frautschi
Department of Physics
California Institute of Technology
Pasadena, CA 91125

Lionel G. Harrison
Department of Chemistry
University of British Columbia
Vancouver, Canada

F. A. Hopf
Optical Sciences Center
University of Arizona
Tucson, AZ 85721

David L. Hull
Department of Philosophy
Northwestern University
Evanston, IL 60201

Lionel Johnson
Department of Fisheries and Oceans
Freshwater Institute
Winnipeg, Canada

Dilip Kondepudi
Center for Studies in Statistical
  Mechanics
The University of Texas
Austin, TX 78712

David Layzer
Department of Astronomy
Harvard University
Cambridge, MA 02138

Paul H. LeBlond
Departments of Oceanography and
  Physics
University of British Columbia
Vancouver, Canada

Richard T. O'Grady
Department of Invertebrate
  Zoology
National Museum of Natural
  History
Smithsonian Institution
Washington, DC 20560

John Olmsted III
Department of Chemistry and
  Biochemistry
California State University
Fullerton, CA 92634

Eric D. Schneider
Chesapeake Biological Laboratory
University of Maryland
Solomons, MD 20688

Bruce H. Weber
Department of Chemistry and
  Biochemistry
California State University
Fullerton, CA 92634

Jeffrey S. Wicken
Behrend College
Penn State University
Erie, PA 16509

E. O. Wiley
Museum of Natural History
University of Kansas
Lawrence, KS 66045

Preface

The chapters in this volume have their origin in a Conference on 'Evolution, Entropy, and Information' held at California State University, Fullerton, in May 1985. None has been published previously. The conference was sponsored by the university's School of Natural Science and Mathematics. It brought together a wide range of recognized, indeed eminent, scholars from a variety of fields, including cosmology, chemistry, biochemistry, ecology, phylogenetics, and philosophy. All of the participants were intensely aware of the current crisis in evolutionary theory and were interested in exploring further the suggestion that recent developments in thermodynamics and information theory offer a way out of current difficulties.

Within this framework of agreement, intense disagreements arose about the proper way in which this new approach should be pursued, with some voices expressing doubts that it could be pursued at all, at least at present. These debates were gracefully moderated by David Hull, who has contributed an introduction to the volume. Out of this intensive interaction came revised versions of all the papers presented at the conference, as well as a variety of responses to these papers submitted by other participants. These responses have been included in the last part of the volume.

It is our belief that these essays, taken together, provide as accurate and as comprehensive an account of the current state of this developing research program as can be had at this time. It is our hope that they will be helpful in guiding further work.

We wish to thank Jewel Plummer Cobb, President of California State University, Fullerton, and James Diefenderfer, Dean of the School of Natural Science and Mathematics, for providing generous support for the conference. We are grateful to the participants for prompt and collegial cooperation in the editing process, as well as to Betty Stanton and her staff at The MIT Press/Bradford Books for their usual skill in making editors' lives pleasant.

We also wish to thank our computer/word processor consultant Kevin Weber, age 11, for his help, and we are also grateful for our wives' understanding throughout.

Entropy, Information, and Evolution

Introduction
David L. Hull

One of the goals in science from the beginning has been unification—explaining a lot by means of a little. One form of unification is the merging of two theories into one. The synthetic theory of evolution is a recent example of such a merger. We now look back with a mixture of amusement and irritation at the early Mendelians and biometricians who were so sure that their respective theories of inheritance and the evolutionary process were totally incompatible. Each side knew it was right and members of the opposition were ignorant, close-minded, and irresponsible. The Mendelians were sure that they were real scientists. They ran experiments in the laboratory and presented straightforward quantitative findings. Evolutionary biologists were idle speculators and mushy thinkers, hardly scientists at all. On their side, evolutionary biologists found the Mendelians abysmally ignorant about organisms in nature and painfully simplistic in their understanding of the evolutionary process. Eventually the disciplinary biases of the opposing camps were bridged and the two theories merged into one. This merger, however, necessitated modifications on both sides.

A second form of unification in science is reduction. Not all branches of science deal with phenomena that are equally fundamental. In the usual hierarchy, physicists and chemists deal with properties that all entities possess. A very few entities, tucked away in various corners of the universe, also have what it takes to replicate, grow, and evolve. These rare creatures are the subject matter of biologists. A few organisms are also capable of behaving and some even "think." Psychology and the behavioral sciences deal with them. A few of these organisms in turn form social groups. Yet another subdivision of scientists limits its attention to social organisms. When unification takes place across hierarchical levels, it is termed "reduction." A theory at one level is reduced to a theory at a lower level. In general, scientists do not mind when they reduce an upper-level theory to one of their own but become a bit testy when one of their theories is reduced to the theories at a lower level. As in the case of merger, reduction is extremely complicated and cannot be accomplished without modifying all theories concerned. For example, Mendelian genetics has been reduced to molecular biology—sort of. After all, genes are nothing but molecules of DNA and RNA. But spelling out the details of such a reduction turns out to be a good deal more complicated than one might suppose, and the results rarely worth the effort.

Pluralism is as characteristic of science as is unification. Unification is a goal of science; pluralism characterizes the ongoing process of science. Differences of opinion always exist among scientists, especially during periods of fundamental change. Although pluralism is always with us, scientists cannot rest content with it if science is to progress. Alternative views are constantly being tested and certain ones found wanting. Without pruning science would become the repository of a mountain of mistaken views. In order for science to progress, scientists must be simultaneously open-minded and hard-nosed. They must be willing to toy with new ideas, modify old usage, expand their conceptions. They must also take new ideas seriously, insisting that they be expressed clearly and exposed to rigorous testing. The balancing of these conflicting goals can get a bit trying at times, especially when disciplinary arrogance and career interests come into play. Scientists care about their work, and they can get somewhat short of temper when their territory is being invaded by other scientists who do not seem to understand even the rudiments of the field that they propose to revolutionize or cannibalize. The most enthusiastic Mendelians knew very little about evolutionary biology, and many of the leading evolutionary biologists found the new science of genetics a mystery.

This familiar story is replayed in the pages of this volume. This time the two sciences are thermodynamics and evolutionary biology. From the inception of these two disciplines in the work of Lord Kelvin and Charles Darwin, they have largely been at odds with each other. According to Kelvin and his coworkers, the earth could not possibly be as old as evolutionists and geologists claimed. Darwin, for instance, estimated that it took longer to denude a single geological stratum than physicists allotted for the entire existence of the earth. The physicists were imperious in the disdain with which they dismissed the casual, inexact speculations of their scientific inferiors. Evolutionary biologists and geologists were almost apologetic in insisting that something must be wrong. The earth could not possibly be as young as physicists insisted. As it turns out, disciplinary arrogance to one side, the physicists were wrong. Once the principles of thermodynamics were modified to allow for fission and fusion, the two areas of science were shown to be compatible. But compatibility is a weak relation. As the years have gone by, scientists on both sides of the great divide have thought that a more productive interchange might be possible. With the advent of nonequilibrium thermodynamics, the time seemed ripe to explore the interrelations between thermodynamics and evolutionary biology.

From the outside, any area of science seems monolithic. With the exception of a few mavericks, all serious scientists seem to be in fundamental agreement on the essentials of their area of science. There is *the* theory of evolution with its species concept and *the* theory of thermodynamics with its concept of entropy. Scientists on the inside know better. They are aware of the diversity of opinion among even the most sober scientists in their discipline even on the most fundamental principles of their science. From the outside, Ernst Mayr and G. G. Simpson might appear to hold the same species concept, but they do not. When the views of other evolutionary biologists from Niles Eldredge and Verne Grant to Steven Stanley and Michael White are included, the multiplicity only increases. In a recent thermodynamics text, Truesdell (1984) identifies several different "Second Laws," and the physicist-philosopher Mario Bunge (1986, p. 306) compiled a list of "twenty or so ostensibly inequivalent but equally vague formulations of 'the' Second Law." The appearance of consensus, which so impresses outsiders, is enhanced by the insistence of those on the inside that one true view does exist—theirs. Scientists working in a particular area must periodically opt one way or the other on controversial issues. They cannot sit on the fence forever. And they opt for the combination of alternatives that they take to be best. Hence, those scientists seeking to trace the interrelations between thermodynamics and evolutionary biology must settle on one reasonably well-formulated version of each. The danger is that scientists will reason from their failure to connect a particular pair to the impossibility of the program in general. Other alternative combinations are also possible. Perhaps certain features of thermodynamic processes might lead evolutionary biologists to modify evolutionary theory, and just as importantly vice versa.

If the chapters in this volume have one unifying theme, it is that biological phenomena are more law governed than anyone has previously supposed, and several of the relevant laws are purely physical. Biological phenomena are not just consistent with physical laws; some of their most fundamental characteristics follow directly from such laws. For example, biological evolution has always appeared to be an orderly process proceeding from the simple to the complex. For example, in this volume, John Olmsted takes for granted that, once life appeared, "its forms embarked on what seems to have been a consistent movement toward ever-increasing complexity." To be sure, in the early years, living creatures did become more "complex," no matter how one might define this elusive concept. However, numerous authorities have argued that after the Cambrian, life on earth has been a matter of ups and downs, mass extinctions followed by increases in everything until the carrying capacity of the earth was reached, followed by another mass extinction, and so on. One side or the other has to be wrong on this issue.

All natural phenomena are explained by reference to a combination of purported laws of nature and empirical contingencies. Laws spell out which phenomena can and cannot occur. Within these limits, initial conditions determine what in point of fact does happen. For example, the amino acids incorporated into living creatures here on earth are all levo. Until recently, everyone assumed that this regularity was merely an effect of how the first replicating molecules here on earth happened to develop.They could just as well have been dextro. However, recent advances in physics have shown that certain strictly physical interactions are themselves inherently asymmetrical. In this volume, Dilip Kondepudi argues that the asymmetry of certain weak interactions might well have biased the formation of early molecular precursors to life toward one asymmetry rather than another. As a result, we have some reason to expect a predominance of the same asymmetries throughout the universe. But one thing is reasonably clear: life evolved on earth very rapidly when compared to such phenomena as meiosis. Within a billion years life appeared. It took another two billion years for sexual reproduction to evolve.

The relevance of basic physical considerations in the emergence of pre-biological structures and their conversion into those that count as proto-biological has long been recognized. In such matters, the connections between physics and biology are at their clearest. No one claims that bringing thermodynamic considerations to bear on such phenomena is illicit. One of the salient features of many of the chapters in this volume is that their authors insist that the basic principles of thermodynamics under-lie and imply several important features of the evolutionary process itself. The key words in this connection are "entropy," "structure," and "infor-mation." In science as elsewhere clarity of expression is a virtue, while vagueness and ambiguity are corresponding vices. Because the reduction of vagueness and ambiguity enhances communication, the temptation is to conclude that our goal should be perfect expression. If only language were made perfectly precise, everything worth saying could be said with total clarity. Formalistically inclined philosophers pursued this program for several generations. If this research program has anything to teach, it is that this expectation is mistaken. Instead of being able to say everything worth saying with total clarity in such a perfect language, one ends up not being able to say anything at all. For finite beings, vagueness and ambiguity are necessary not only in the genesis of knowledge but also in its communica-tion. As a result, communication is always only partial. Confusion can be reduced in intellectual exchanges but never totally eliminated.

When highly innovative scientists first formulate their views, they are rarely crystal clear. Frequently, in retrospect, these scientists are sure that their initial utterances were totally unambiguous. Their critics were the ones who were confused. However, from a third-party perspective, one can frequently see that clarity emerged only in the give and take of scientific exchanges. Scientists rarely come to understand what they intended to say until they discover what their readers thought they said. For example, Louis Agassiz objected to the use of the term "evolution" by the Darwinians. "Evolution" at the time had a perfectly good meaning— embryological development. Only confusion could possibly result from appropriating the term and applying it to an entirely different phenomenon. When molecular biologists borrowed the term "gene," from Mendelian geneticists, they were greeted with howls of indignation. When evolutionary biologists insisted on making "gene" a theoretical term in population biology, it was the turn of molecular biologists to play the terminological conservative. The recent literature on the "proper" definition of "monophyly" in the dispute between evolutionary taxonomists and cladists is yet another case in point.

In his contribution to this volume, Jeffrey Wicken states that it is "not science's habit to affix the same name to different concepts, since common names suggest shared meanings." Common names do suggest shared meanings. Even so, scientists habitually affix the same name to different concepts. Using old terms in new senses is sure to be met with consternation. "Evolution, indeed." But neologisms are just as likely to be greeted with protests. "The heterobathmy of synapomorphy, indeed." But there is no third alternative. New views require either new terms or new uses of old terms. Scientists cannot tell in advance whether a neologism will turn out to be equivalent to some well-entrenched term or whether using the same term for two or more apparently similar phenomena will turn out to introduce confusing ambiguity. In Darwin's day artificial selection and natural selection were viewed as at best analogous phenomena. Friends and enemies alike insisted that the ambiguous use of the same term in both was sure to lead to pernicious confusion. Today artificial selection is viewed by biologists as a special case of natural selection.

Once a particular area of science enters a "normal" stage, terminology tends to settle down. Redundancies and ambiguities are gradually eliminated. But in interesting times, when an area of science is undergoing conceptual change, no one can distinguish redundancy from ambiguity. For Darwin evolution and embryological development were two quite distinct phenomena. To use present-day terms, embryological development is programmed, while evolution is not. Hence, two different terms were called for. Using the same term for such diverse phenomena would only blur the relevant differences. Herbert Spencer disagreed. He used the same term for both sorts of change because he thought that they are essentially the same. Both are directed. Today the clear distinction between ontogeny and phylogeny is once again being brought into question.

Wicken insists that in strictly physical contexts a single, precise and unambiguous sense of "entropy" has emerged during the development of thermodynamics. Essential to this meaning is the microstate-macrostate distinction. The reason that one cannot know the microstate of a thermo-dynamic system is that it fluctuates stochastically among an ensemble of microstates. All of these microstates are not equally probable, but they are equally consistent with one and the same macrostate. Given a particular macrostate, there is no way of knowing which microstate is producing it. This relation is quite different from the one that obtains between an organized structure and its constituent elements. According to Wicken, thermodynamics can contribute to our understanding of the emergence of prebiological organization, its conversion into more complex proto-biological structures, and even the speciation process, but not the interlevel relations that obtain in organizational hierarchies. As Wicken sees it, no clear connections exist between increased complexity and decreased entropy. In complex structures, the elements are arranged the way that they are, and that is that. Perhaps a variety of elements can produce the same higher-level structure, but in each instance one and only one arrange-ment of elements is involved, and it can be known. Thus, it would seem that even in strictly physical situations, "entropy" can be used ambig-uously. The relationship between the pressure, volume, etc., of a gas and the molecules of that gas is properly characterized in terms of entropy, but once that gas has condensed into a liquid and then a solid, "entropy" in this same sense is inappropriate. The claim that entropy decreases (or increases) as water vapor is condensed into a liquid and then that liquid frozen is sheer nonsense.

If this is so, then the ambiguity of "entropy" as applied to the special sort of organization that can be characterized as "information" follows a fortiori. Structure is necessary but not sufficient for information. An ice cube exhibits structure, but it does not contain information in the sense that a molecule of DNA does. All information presupposes structure, but not all structures embody information in the relevant sense. Much more is required before structure can count as information. For example, the se-quences of bases in DNA are equally likely from a physical point of view. The same can be said for the basic elements in languages in the literal sense, i.e., human languages. With a few minor exceptions, any letter can follow any letter in English. The general characteristics of the genetic code and natural languages are a function of sequences of historical contingencies. However, there are differences between the genetic code and human lan-guages. Intentionality has played a much more significant role in the development and functioning of human languages than it has in biological evolution. Within the loose confines of the language being spoken, the order of words in a sentence is determined by the intentions of the speaker. On this line of reasoning, thermodynamic entropy and information in languages are at least twice removed from each other. According to such authors as Shannon (1978), "information" is being used ambiguously when it is applied to both human languages and the genetic code. The genetic code is not actually a "code." According to such authors as Wicken and Hopf, a second dimension of ambiguity is introduced when terms such as "information" are used to apply to both the genetic code and entropic phenomena. Thermodynamics concerns statistical disorder, not organizational complexity. Some day we might have a physical theory that concerns organizational complexity, but present-day thermodynamics is not that theory. Wicken maintains that in information theory " ... uncertainty is a strictly before-the-fact matter. It reflects the fact that a particular sequence or network of structural relationships is but one of many that might have been generated from a given group of elements. Once those arrangements are specified, the uncertainty vanishes. One has a *structure*, and for structures macrostate-microstate relationships fail to apply."

John Collier disagrees with the preceding lines of argument. He insists that "entropy" and "information" can apply univocally to all dissipative systems, including those that are highly structured. The microstate-macrostate distinction can be made with respect to structured entities. Johnson proposes to extend similar conceptions to ecological systems and Dyke to cities as well. Although John Olmsted agrees with Wicken that the identification of the genetic code with information and information with negentropy is pernicious, he differs with Wicken with respect to the character of information in the context of languages.

What is an outsider to make of such controversies? Future developments in science are unpredictable. I have no idea who will turn out to be right—the hard-headed purists, the cautious extentionalists, or their more daring counterparts. All such positions in science are strategies, and no strategy can guarantee success. Theoretical science is not an automatic process. Nearly all epistemologists and many scientists as well view science as being in principle a process by which we go from no knowledge to total knowledge. To the contrary, science is a much more modest activity. It never starts from scratch. It presupposes that we already have beliefs about the world, regardless of whether these views are well founded. Science is a process by which we go from some knowledge, much of it no doubt faulty, to more and better knowledge. Infallibility, absolute certainty, and total knowledge have no place whatsoever in science. Any attempt to make knowledge acquisition too orderly, too safe from error, or too precise too quickly is liable to result in science grinding to a halt. If anything, theoretical science is the art of judicious finagling.

Nowhere is this characterization of science more appropriate than in the dispute under discussion. In the past, physicists and biologists have not communicated with each other very often or to any great effect. The contributors to this volume are at least trying. It is poetic justice of sorts that one of the issues that makes communication difficult is the one that divides them—ambiguity. Beneath a mural in the Zoological Laboratories at the University of Pennsylvania, a motto appears—Hypotheses That Blur and Grow. Clarity of expression is one of the permanent goals of science. However, it follows from science as an ongoing process that this goal constantly recedes in the distance. It is rarely attained, and such attainment always turns out to be temporary. Like it or not, terminology continues to evolve. As frustrating as such terminological change might be at times, attempts to stop it are likely to be as effective as the prayers of little old ladies dressed all in black kneeling before the encroachment of a wall of molten lava on their village. They pray a while, move back, pray some more, and the lava keeps coming. In science at least the results of conceptual evolution are not always destructive. The only way for hypotheses to grow is by blurring, and once blurred, the sharp differences needed for ambiguity disappear. One of the ambiguities that might well disappear as both evolutionary theory and thermodynamics are reformulated is the sharp distinction between statistical disorder and organizational complexity. One theory might well emerge capable of handling both.

Acknowledgments

I wish to thank John Collier, Jeff Wicken, Ed Wiley, and the editors of this volume for reading and commenting on an earlier draft of this manuscript.

References

Bunge, M., 1986. Review of C. Truesdell, *Rational Thermodynamics* (1984). *Philosophy of Science* 53:305–306.

Shanon, B., 1978. The genetic code and human language. *Synthese* 39:401–416.

Truesdell, C., 1984. *Rational Thermodynamics*, 2nd ed. New York-Berlin: Springer-Verlag.

I
Thermodynamics and Cosmological Evolution

1

Entropy in an Expanding Universe

Steven Frautschi

Ordinary matter in a small closed box approaches equilibrium—the state of maximum entropy.

In the nineteenth century some people applied this description to the cosmos, arriving at a gloomy picture called the "heat death of the universe" in which the entire universe tends toward a state of maximum entropy—that is, uniform temperature and maximum disorder—after which nothing further of interest happens.

Our present picture of the evolution of the universe, based on the Big Bang, suggests a remarkably different and more interesting situation. In the beginning there is a hot gas, nearly homogeneous and in thermal equilibrium (the 3K, or the 3° Kelvin, blackbody radiation, reaching us isotropically from all directions, is a relic of, and evidence for, this early state). As the hot gas expands it breaks into clumps of matter—galaxies, stars, planets, rocks, dust, gas, ...—that are out of equilibrium, exhibiting a wide range of temperatures. Some of these objects develop highly organized structures, nonequilibrium weather patterns, etc., and on at least one planet self-replicating structures called "life" develop. Finally, a form of life emerges with the capacity to ask questions about these systems.

This picture of cosmic evolution, seemingly paradoxical in the light of the second law of thermodynamics, motivates the questions we shall consider:

> 1. How can disequilibrium, order, and in particular the free energy supplies that enable life to maintain its organization emerge from an apparently chaotic early universe in thermal and chemical equilibrium?
> 2. What, if anything, has the abstract and remote physics of the Big Bang to do with the proposals of Wiley and Brooks (1982) and Brooks et al. (1984) concerning entropy in biological systems?

The evolution of free energy and entropy in the universe could not possibly have been treated accurately on the basis of physics known in the nineteenth century. However, various twentieth-century discoveries and ideas make informed discussion of such issues possible, even though definitive answers are not yet in hand. As we shall see, some of the ideas are quite recent, and this subject is currently undergoing rapid development.

As our topic is highly speculative, it has been treated in relatively few research works. Some interesting and accessible general references are Davies (1974) and Dyson (1979). Layzer (1975) has been a pioneer in this field. The present report is based on my recent contribution (Frautschi, 1982). Similar ideas have been advanced independently by Sugimoto et al. (1981).

1.1 Tracing Our Sources of Free Energy Back to Their Origins

To refresh our memory of what entropy means at the everyday level, let us consider the story of The Physicist's Daughter. She comes home and says "Daddy, the school teacher told us we must conserve energy. But you told me energy is *always* conserved, no matter what you do."

Needless to say, the physicist's daughter is not alone in her confusion. We can help understand what the concepts mean by considering water behind a high dam. Initially the water has potential energy. As it runs over the spillway, it exchanges potential for kinetic energy. And when the water reaches the pond below, the energy is converted into heat and random turbulence. Energy is conserved throughout. But by the end it has changed to a more disordered form: the random motions of individual molecules. In its initial potential or kinetic forms, the energy was available to do work (on a paddle wheel or turbine, for example), but in its final disordered form it is hard to convert into work. That is the nature of our "energy crisis": energy is conserved, but it tends to more disorganized forms that are harder to extract work from, so we need to manage it carefully. A technical measure of energy available to do work, which decreases with time, is *free energy*, and the technical measure of disorder, which increases with time, is *entropy*.

Once the water has run down to sea level, how can we get it up into the reservoir behind the dam again to extract more work? We all learned the answer in grade school: the sun does it for us. Sunlight provides energy, some of which evaporates water and raises it up to the clouds, whence it finds its way into the reservoir ready to do more work. And of course sunlight also supplies green plants and ultimately us with usable energy. The sunlight comes in an organized form, and weather systems and plants and animals all tap some of this organized energy to maintain and develop their own organizations, thereby avoiding the tendency toward equilibrium that would be their fate in a closed box that did not have a supply of organized energy from outside.

What is the sun's source of free energy? The answer is to be found in the nuclear binding curve (figure 1.1), which is in the form of a valley with the

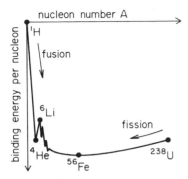

Figure 1.1
The binding energy per nucleon of atomic nuclei.

deepest binding at iron and weaker binding at both high and low nucleon number A. Nuclei can convert energy from Mc^2 to radiation and heat by rolling down the sides of this valley toward iron, either combining lower A elements (fusion) or splitting higher A elements (fission). The sun is mainly hydrogen (H), so its nuclei undergo fusion. Instead of proceeding all the way to the absolute minimum at iron, however, the nuclei normally get stuck in the "crevasse" on the side of the valley at helium (He), so the dominant process is

$$4H \rightarrow {}^4He + (7\,MeV\ per\ H).\qquad(1)$$

This process occurs at the center of the sun, where temperature and density are highest, in a series of steps, for example, the proton—deuteron reaction

$$^1H + {}^2H \rightarrow {}^3He + \gamma\ (5.4\,MeV).\qquad(2)$$

The γ is immediately absorbed, and its energy rapidly equilibrates at the high temperature (about 1.5×10^7K) of the center of the sun. Subsequently this energy flows out to the cooler outer layers, and is finally radiated from the surface at about 6,000K.

In thermodynamic terms, the thermonuclear reaction releases energy in a highly organized form at the center of the sun, and that energy gets degraded—spread randomly among more and more particles—as it equilibrates and works its way out from the center of the sun. Some key stages in the process are listed in table 1.1.

Let us use this important example, the dominant source of organized energy for life on earth, to see how physicists quantify entropy. In the thermodynamic form you may have encountered in freshman physics, heat ΔQ flows from a body at higher temperature T_1 to a body at lower temperature T_2. The entropy change is

$$\Delta S = \frac{\Delta Q}{T_1} + \frac{\Delta Q}{T_2} > 0. \tag{3}$$

As heat makes its way from the center of the sun to the surface, for example, T drops by a factor of 2,500 (table 1.1), so the entropy increases by a factor of 2,500:

$$\Delta S = -\frac{\Delta Q}{T_{center}} + \frac{\Delta Q}{T_{surface}} \simeq 2,500 \frac{\Delta Q}{T_{center}}. \tag{4}$$

Thermodynamic reasoning also tells us that a further entropy increase occurred as the original 5.4 MeV moved through a series of nonequilibrium states toward equilibrium at the center of the sun, but does not provide a numerical value in this case.

In the more general statistical formulation of entropy developed later in the nineteenth century, the entropy of an N-particle system is

$$S = k \ln(\text{numbers of } N\text{-particle states})^N. \tag{5}$$

For a gas of N free particles

$$S \simeq k \ln(\text{number of 1-particle states})^N. \tag{6}$$

Evaluating the one-particle phase space for nonrelativistic particles of mass m with temperature T in volume V, one finds (Huang, 1963)

$$S = kN \ln \left[\frac{V}{N} \left[\frac{2\pi mkT}{h^2} \right]^{3/2} e^{5/2} \right], \tag{7}$$

where k is the Boltzmann constant and h is Planck's constant. There is a similar formula for massless particles. We shall use the simple approximation

$$S \simeq kN, \tag{8}$$

which is normally accurate within two orders of magnitude because the logarithm seldom exceeds 100 whereas N is commonly 10^{23} or more. This crude estimate remains approximately valid for nonfree particles except at low temperatures where N must be replaced by the (smaller) number of degrees of freedom that have not "frozen out."

Table 1.1
Stages of energy flow in the sun

Stage	E/particle (eV)	N = number of particles sharing original E
5.4 MeV γ	5,400,000	1
Equilibrium at $T_{center} = 1.5 \times 10^7$K	1,500	4,000
Equilibrium at $T_{surface} = 6,000$K	0.6	10^7

Let us apply (8) to the entropy increase as the energy from a single thermonuclear 5.4 MeV γ particle is shared among progressively more particles in the sun. With the aid of table 1.1 we find

$$\frac{S(\text{surface})}{S(\text{center})} \simeq \frac{N(\text{surface})}{N(\text{center})} = 2{,}500 \tag{9}$$

for the gain during outward heat flow, in agreement with the thermodynamic result of (4). The statistical approach also allows us to go beyond thermodynamics and calculate

$$\frac{S(\text{surface})}{S(\text{original } \gamma)} \simeq \frac{N(\text{surface})}{1} = 10^7 \tag{10}$$

for the total entropy gain including equilibration of the original γ's energy at the center. For each thermonuclear γ photon, about 10^7 visible photons are emitted from the sun's surface.

The entropy increase on earth can be estimated in a similar way. The main energy source is solar radiation. Photons arriving from the sun have energies in the visible range corresponding to T (solar surface) $\simeq$ 6,000K, whereas photons reradiated by the earth have energies in the infrared corresponding to T (earth surface) $\simeq$ 300K. Since arriving and departing radiation is in approximate energy balance, about $6{,}000/300 \simeq 20$ photons leave the earth per arriving photon for an entropy gain of $20k$ per arriving solar photon.

To put these figures in perspective, we note that the largest well-established stock of entropy in the universe is the 3K blackbody photons, some 10^9 of them per cosmic nucleon. That is somewhat more than the 10^7 photons per nucleon produced in a typical star such as the sun during its lifetime, and far more than entropy production on the earth, which (taking into account that only about one in 10^9 solar photons is absorbed by the earth) amounts to less than one photon per solar nucleon over its lifetime. And yet this latter increase, so minor on the cosmic scale, is crucial for life on earth.

Thus far we have encountered no mystery. The sun is a large, long-lasting, but finite source of free energy. As thermonuclear reactions proceed, entropy is generated, free energy is depleted, and nuclei move toward equilibrium. But why were the solar nuclei out of equilibrium in the first place? We want to trace our free energy supply back to its ultimate roots.

1.2 Nuclear Disequilibrium

Before one second in the Big Bang, nuclei *were* in equilibrium. Most of them were free protons and neutrons, however, for the very high temperature kept most complex nuclei dissociated at that time. Then, as kT fell well below E (nuclear binding) at about one second, helium formation began in earnest. If equilibrium had been maintained, nucleosynthesis would have proceeded all the way to iron as the temperature fell. Stars that formed later would not have had a source of nuclear fuel.

But in fact, to climb out of the He "crevasse" in the nuclear binding curve (figure 1.1) and make heavier nuclei was a slow process. Nuclear reactions among protons and helium nuclei were rare because the Coulomb repulsion kept most of them apart. Neutrons could penetrate other nuclei without Coulomb repulsion, but free neutrons are unstable; they decayed away after 10^3 seconds, leaving only the neutrons that were already bound in He. By that time the continuing expansion of the universe had thinned out the nucleons so their collision rate was much slower. As the thinning continued, the reactions stopped, leaving a mixture of hydrogen and helium nuclei out of equilibrium.

During the period when nuclei had begun to fall out of equilibrium but were still reacting, their reactions generated entropy increases (mainly by creating new photons and neutrinos, as in the center of the sun). But these increases were not enough to restore equilibrium, and in fact the nuclei fell further and further short of the evolving equilibrium conditions as space expanded and the matter cooled. Consequently, even though entropy was increasing, the gap between the actual entropy and the maximum possible entropy that would have been achieved if equilibrium had been restored increased even more. In other words, nuclear free energy was built up, to be released much later when matter reconcentrated in stars and nucleosynthesis resumed.

At this point you may be suspecting that we have gotten a free lunch. Somehow nuclei, initially in equilibrium, got themselves hung up far from equilibrium in the H-He corner of the periodic table, enabling them to supply copious free energy to stars and eventually to us. This free energy must have come from somewhere.

It is believed that the source of the free energy was the uniform expansion of the universe itself. This is obviously nonrandom; though it could have proceeded at different rates in different places, an expansion here and a contraction there, it is in fact highly uniform on large scales. This coherent motion succeeds in sharing a small part of its organization with nuclei when they go out of equilibrium.

1.3 Gravitational Disequilibrium

In addition to the overall expansion, another aspect of the early universe was also highly ordered: the energy distribution. The isotropy of the 3K blackbody radiation shows that the energy distribution was remarkably homogeneous in the early universe. But a homogeneous energy distribution, surprisingly, is far from equilibrium when the mass is sufficiently large that self-gravitation must be taken into account. We can see this by considering a large region of galactic gas, uniformly distributed in thermal and chemical equilibrium. One might suppose that it cannot evolve. But we know the gas eventually clumps into stars. The system reduces its gravitational potential energy by clumping. The energy thus released goes into radiation, local heating, etc., and this generation of new particles increases the entropy. An even larger increase in entropy is possible if the gravitational clumping goes to the extreme limit of forming a black hole, as we shall discuss later. When stars form the temperature, pressure, density, and other intensive quantities take on a nonuniform distribution and the system evolves out of thermal and chemical equilibrium.

Thus the homogeneous, isotropic distribution of matter in the early Big Bang, though high in "thermal" and "chemical" entropy, was in gravitational disequilibrium, i.e., in some sense low in "gravitational" entropy (Penrose, 1979). This gravitational disequilibrium was potentially capable of further evolution—increases in "gravitational" entropy—and was partially convertible into thermal and chemical disequilibrium. To some extent that has happened as galaxies, stars, and planets formed. In particular, the stars have reconcentrated nuclear matter, enabling nucleosynthesis to resume and release more free energy as we have seen. So gravitational disequilibrium has been the second prime mover, along with nuclear disequilibrium, in shaping the world as we know it.

What was the source of the gravitational disequilibrium, i.e., of the extreme homogeneity of the early universe? Here for the first time we pass completely outside the realm of firm experimental information, to purely speculative theory concerning energy densities far above what can be reached in the laboratory. The currently fashionable speculation, called *inflation* (Guth and Steinhardt, 1984), is that early in the first second of the Big Bang, as the universe was expanding and cooling but still enormously hot, it underwent a phase change. But instead of sliding into the new phase immediately, the universe *supercooled*, clinging to the old phase when it no longer minimized the free energy. In other words, it went out of equilibrium because the relaxation time for completing the phase transition exceeded the expansion time (for, say, doubling the distance to the light horizon). Throughout the duration of the supercooled state the energy density remained stuck at a fixed value, rather than falling steadily as it usually does during expansion. This temporarily constant energy density provided an effective cosmological constant similar to the one originally employed by Einstein to prevent his cosmological model from expanding (and later characterized by him, after the discovery that the universe does expand, as the greatest mistake of his life). The effective cosmological constant arising during supercooling, however, had the opposite sign, speeding up the expansion rather than retarding it. In fact the expansion proceeded exponentially—the so-called *inflation*—during the supercooled episode. As a result whatever particles, inhomogeneities, etc., were initially present got spread very far apart—mostly out of sight of one another. Space temporarily became a smooth *tabula rasa*, waiting to receive new content. After the supercooling ended, release of latent heat produced a copious supply of new particles everywhere, while acting in such a smooth manner (at least in carefully arranged versions of the theory) that inhomogeneities remained very small. The particle production restored thermal and chemical equilibrium but left gravity far out of equilibrium, thus providing a form of free energy ready for future evolutionary developments (Davies, 1983).

The ultimate source of this free energy, once again, is believed to be the highly organized uniform expansion that drove the system out of equilibrium.

1.4 Continuous Generation of Disequilibrium

We have now described two crucial episodes of falling out of equilibrium —the incomplete nucleosynthesis between 1 and 10^3 seconds, and the inflationary expansion early during the first second—that have allegedly laid the background for our world. In both of these episodes the entropy S increases (as in any nonequilibrium reaction), but the entropy that would be achieved by attaining equilibrium, S_{max}, increases more (the system lags further behind the evolving conditions for equilibrium). This surprising state of affairs is depicted in figure 1.2. The growing gap between equilibrium and actuality, S_{max} and S, implies the development of free energy sources.

Are incomplete nucleosynthesis and inflation isolated episodes, or is the growth of $S_{max} - S$ (which, as a measure of departure from randomness, we may label as "order") continuous and pervasive in an expanding universe? I shall argue next that it is continuous and pervasive, though the two

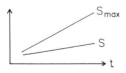

Figure 1.2
Schematic time dependence of entropy S and maximum (equilibrium) energy S_{max} in the expanding universe.

episodes cited thus far may be singled out as the events that generated free energy in the form most available to us.

In the first place, the general mechanism for driving a system out of equilibrium is to change it on a time scale shorter than its natural adjustment time. In our case, this requires

$$\tau(\text{expansion}) < \tau(\text{relaxation}).$$

A convenient measure of $\tau(\text{expansion})$ is the *doubling time* within which the distance to the light horizon expands by a factor of 2. The doubling time grows as the time elapsed since the beginning of the Big Bang, t. By contrast, $\tau(\text{relaxation})$ tends to grow as a higher power of t because it typically depends on a reaction rate involving the product of two or more densities, each of which is thinning as the universe expands. Thus as the expansion proceeds, more and more elements of the universe fall out of equilibrium. This happens not just twice, but many times.

Second, during normal epochs when the universe is not expanding exponentially, space has ordinarily expanded at a slower rate than the distance to the light horizon, the edge of the visible universe, was growing. As a result more and more remote regions of space, and the matter and radiation they contain, have come within the light horizon where they could influence one another and possibly equilibriate. Thus, every time the age of the universe doubles, regions not previously in thermal, diffusive, or other contact are brought into contact. As in ordinary thermodynamics, when two previously separated systems are brought into contact there is a possibility for increasing the entropy:

$$S_{\max}(1 + 2) > S(1) + S(2).$$

Because the universe is so homogeneous, it appears that the blackbody radiation in any two regions satisfies $T_1 \simeq T_2$ and there is not much entropy to be gained by equilibriating temperatures. But precisely because the densities are so homogeneous, there is always a great deal of entropy to be gained by forming larger self-gravitating clumps of matter.

The extreme limit of gravitational clumping, the formation of black holes, provides an especially large entropy gain. Physicists have recently learned how to calculate this gain and thus, to some extent, to quantify "gravitational" entropy. I shall write down the formulas because in many cases black hole formation seems to provide the upper bound for entropy, i.e., $S_{\max}$. Black holes may be the dominant source of entropy in our universe, and even if they are not, the formula for black hole entropy makes possible a rational discussion of how far the observed entropy is from $S_{\max}$.

There are several arguments (Bekenstein, 1973; Hawking, 1976) indicating that a black hole of mass M_{BH} has a huge entropy of order

$$S_{BH} \approx \left[\frac{kG}{hc} \right] M_{BH}^2. \tag{11}$$

In one argument, for example, we note that there is no way to detect the state of the matter inside a black hole and report it back to an observer outside. When a black hole forms, we lose all information on the state inside. We must assign equal probability to all initial states that could have coalesced to form the black hole. So the loss of information implies an increase in entropy (Bekenstein, 1973):

$S_{BH} = k \ln$(number of possible states that could have made black hole)

$\gg k \ln$(number of actual states that made black hole).

Detailed calculation by this method (Zurek and Thorne, 1985) yields (11) for the black hole entropy.

Another argument indicates that the large entropy of a black hole eventually materializes in a directly measurable form. According to the remarkable work of Stephen Hawking (1974, 1975), the black hole radiates quanta by quantum tunneling, and (if not augmented by the infall of fresh new material) will eventually radiate away all its energy. The radiated quanta can be counted to obtain the final entropy. Specifically, the Hawking radiation from a black hole of radius R_{BH} typically has wavelength of order

$$\lambda \approx R_{BH}. \tag{12}$$

This corresponds, in the case of the massless quanta such as photons and gravitons, which predominate, to an average energy per particle

$$\bar{E}_{rad} = h\upsilon = hc/\lambda \approx hc/R_{BH}. \tag{13}$$

By the time the black hole radiates away all its energy, the radiated entropy amounts to

$$S_{BH\ rad} \approx kN_{rad} = k(E_{BH}/\bar{E}_{rad}) \approx k(M_{BH}c^2)/(hc/R_{BH}). \tag{14}$$

But for a black hole, we also know that $M_{BH}c^2$ is of the order of its gravitational self-energy:

$$M_{BH}c^2 \approx GM_{BH}^2/R_{BH}, \tag{15}$$

implying that the radius of a black hole is proportional to its mass:

$$R_{BH} \approx GM_{BH}/c^2. \tag{16}$$

Thus we can eliminate R_{BH} from (14) and write the radiated entropy as

$$S_{BH\ rad} \approx \left[\frac{kG}{hc} \right] M_{BH}^2, \tag{17}$$

which is of the same order as the entropy of the parent black hole, [see (11)].

Table 1.2
Entropy generation per nucleon in various processes

Process	S/kN (nucleon)
Nucleosynthesis in star	10^7
Formation of stellar black hole (10^{57} protons)	10^{19}
Formation of galactic core black hole (10^{66} protons)	10^{28}

A key feature in the formula for black hole entropy is the nonlinear dependence on the mass: if the mass of the black hole is doubled, the entropy increases by four. The nonlinear dependence of S_{BH} on mass ensures that when two regions of space come into causal contact, the entropy potentially obtained by clumping the matter in the combined region into a black hole greatly exceeds the sum of the original entropies.

Numerical entropy gains for several important processes are listed in table 1.2. A useful standard of comparison is the known entropy of the 3K blackbody radiation, S/kN(nucleon) $\approx 10^9$. At present it is not known with absolute certainty whether any star-sized object or galactic core is a black hole, though promising candidates have been identified. Therefore the entropy of the presently observable part of the universe is uncertain by at least 10^{19}.

The huge entropy generations listed in table 1.2 for black hole formation show that

1. At present, with large amounts of matter outside of black holes, the entropy is enormously far from maximal.

2. As the observable part of the universe keeps expanding, ever larger regions are brought into causal contact and could theoretically amalgamate to form larger black holes. Since the real development of black holes lags far behind, the growth of S_{max} outpaces the growth of S (figure 1.2), normally, not just during special episodes. Maintenance and increase of the gap ($S_{max} - S$) in figure 1.2 means that growth in entropy does not preclude increase in order or free energy.

1.5 Generation of Order in Physics and Biology

We now turn to our final topic, the relation of our work to that of Brooks and Wiley. Referring to the genetic material of life, they have presented (Wiley and Brooks, 1982; Brooks et al., 1984) the same plot as figure 1.2 with ($S_{max} - S$) identified as information.

From one point of view, there is no necessary connection between the physicist's and the biologist's interpretation of figure 1.2. The physical laws of entropy refer to the total system; the entropy of a *subsystem* is even permitted to decrease. When one puts ice in a drink, for example, the entropy of the drink temporarily decreases even though total entropy increases. So the laws of the subsystem that is genetic matter, with all their particularities and constraints, do not necessarily have to mimic the physical laws of the cosmos.

Nevertheless, there is a parallelism between the evolution of life on earth and the evolution of the expanding universe. Life on earth has a steady free energy source, so it need not come to equilibrium and may even evolve away from it. The expanding universe has not come to equilibrium and may even evolve away from it, apparently due to free energy transfers from the steady expansion of space. Thus it does not appear incredible that the same entropy plot might capture important aspects of both these evolving open systems, life and the universe.

References

Bekenstein, J. D., 1973. Black holes and entropy. *Phys. Rev.* D7:2333–2346.

Brooks, D. R., P. H. Leblond, and D. D. Cumming, 1984. Information and entropy in a simple evolution model. *J. Theor. Biol.* 109:77–93.

Davies, P. C. W., 1974. *The Physics of Time Asymmetry*. Berkeley: University of California Press, chapters 4 and 7.

Davies, P. C. W., 1983. Inflation and time asymmetry in the universe. *Nature* 301:398–400.

Dyson, F. J., 1979. Time without end: physics and biology in an open universe. *Rev. Mod. Phys.* 51:447–460.

Frautschi, S. 1982. Entropy in an expanding universe. *Science* 217:593–599.

Guth, A. H., and P. J. Steinhardt, 1984. The inflationary universe. *Sci. Am.* 250(5):116–128.

Hawking, S. W., 1974. Black hole explosions? *Nature* 248:30–31.

Hawking, S. W., 1975. Particle creation by black holes. *Commun. Math. Phys.* 43:199–220.

Hawking, S. W., 1976. Black holes and thermodynamics. *Phys. Rev.* D13:191–197.

Huang, K., 1963. *Statistical Mechanics*. New York: Wiley, p. 154.

Layzer, D., 1975. The arrow of time. *Sci. Am.* 233(6):56–69.

Penrose, R., 1979. In *General Relativity: An Einstein Centenary*, S. W. Hawking and W. Israel, eds., Cambridge: Cambridge University Press, chapter 12.

Sugimoto, D., Y. Eriguchi, and I. Hachisu, 1981. Gravothermal aspects in evolution of the stars and the universe. *Prog. Theor. Phys. Suppl.* 70:154–180.

Wiley, E. O., and D. R. Brooks, 1982. Victims of history: a nonequilibrium approach to evolution. *Syst. Zool.* 31:1–24.

Zurek, W. H., and K. S. Thorne, 1985. Statistical mechanical origin of the entropy of a rotating, charged black hole. *Phys. Rev. Lett.* 54:2171–2175.

2

Growth of Order in the Universe

David Layzer

2.1 History

In 1834 a French engineer, Sadi Carnot, laid the foundation for the science of thermodynamics by proving that every ideal reversible heat engine operating between two heat reservoirs at given temperatures has the same efficiency. Carnot believed that heat is an indestructible substance. Under this assumption, he showed that if two ideal reversible heat engines operating between a given pair of heat reservoirs had different efficiencies, they could be hooked together to form a machine that would generate mechanical energy. By 1840 rigorous experiments by James Joule in England and Robert Mayer in Germany had established that, contrary to Carnot's assumption, heat is not an indestructible substance. Rather, heat and mechanical energy are interconvertible at a fixed rate of exchange. This is the First Law of thermodynamics. Around 1850 Rudolf Clausius in Germany and William Thomson in England independently revised Carnot's theory in the light of the First Law. They proved that his theorem—that all reversible heat engines operating between reservoirs at given temperatures have the same efficiency—remains valid if one introduces a new postulate. This postulate, the Second Law of thermodynamics, has two equivalent forms: (1) It is impossible to construct a device whose only effect is to convert heat from a single reservoir at uniform temperature entirely into work. (2) It is impossible to construct a device whose only effect is to transfer heat from a colder to a hotter reservoir.

In the 1850s and 1860s Clausius and Thomson developed the implications of this postulate. Thomson showed that ideal reversible heat engines can be used to define temperature in a manner that does not rely on the properties of any physical substance such as an ideal gas. Using this new definition of temperature, Clausius showed that the Second Law implies the existence of a new physical property, which he called *entropy*. This quantity remains constant in reversible changes of an isolated thermodynamic system but increases in every nonreversible change. Thus the Second Law implies that *all natural processes generate entropy*.

During the 1850s and 1860s Clausius, James Clerk Maxwell, Ludwig

Boltzmann, and others sought to relate the thermodynamic properties of macroscopic bodies, especially gases, to the dynamical behavior of their constituent molecules. At that time, molecules were still hypothetical objects, and some physicists—notably Ernst Mach—objected on methodological grounds to basing explanations of observable phenomena on a theoretical description of unobserved objects. However, the dynamical theory of gases, as it was then called, proved to have a lot of explanatory power. For a modest investment in assumptions about the properties of molecules, it yielded large returns in predictions about the macroscopic behavior of gases. Entropy, however, and with it the Second Law, remained outside the scope of the theory until Boltzmann introduced his famous statistical definition of entropy in the 1870s. Boltzmann also succeeded in deriving a special case of the Second Law from plausible statistical assumptions. Boltzmann's definition makes entropy a measure of disorder at the molecular level. The Second Law implies, therefore, that the molecular disorder of an isolated gas tends to increase until it is as large as possible. The state of maximum molecular disorder corresponds to thermodynamic equilibrium.

In 1946 Claude Shannon, following up work by Leo Szilard and others in the 1920s, explicitly freed Boltzmann's definition of entropy from its thermodynamic context and used it to construct a mathematical theory of communication. Shannon's work inspired several people to apply information theory to biological problems. These efforts were not very productive, however. Some biologists argued that the approach was wrong in principle—that neither information (as it is defined in communication theory) nor negative entropy has much to do with biological order. One of the things I hope to do in this talk is to clarify the connection between information and biological order.

2.2 What Is Entropy?

Consider a gas. Its macroscopic states are defined by variables such as temperature, density, and chemical composition, all of which represent average properties of the gas. Many different molecular configurations, or *microstates*, have the same average properties and hence represent the same macroscopic state, or *macrostate*. We may think of a macrostate as the set of all microstates that have a given set of average properties. Boltzmann defined the entropy of a macrostate as the logarithm of the number of its microstates. If H denotes the entropy of a given macrostate and W the number of microstates that belong to it—the number of ways in which the macrostate can be realized—then Boltzmann's definition reads

$$H = \log W. \tag{1}$$

If the microstates have unequal weights w_i (where the w_i are positive numbers that add up to 1), the entropy is given by

$$H = \sum w_i \log(1/w_i), \tag{2}$$

which reduces to the preceding formula when $w_i = 1/W$.

To apply Boltzmann's definition to communication theory, we identify microstates with strings of characters, and macrostates with sets of strings that share specified properties. Consider, for example, strings of English letters that have a certain length. The entropy of this set of strings is the logarithm of the number of its members. If the letters are weighted according to their frequency in some sample of English prose, we may use formula (2) to calculate the entropy. For a string of given length, this will yield a smaller value of the entropy. If we require our strings to consist of English words, we obtain a still smaller value of the entropy. And if we require the strings to be meaningful English sentences, the entropy is again smaller.

In the last example it is probably impossible to assign a precise value to the entropy, because competent judges are likely to disagree about whether certain strings of words are meaningful. But if doubtful cases constitute a small fraction of the total number of candidates the definition is still useful.

Let us now consider a biological example: the entropy of a set of variants of some biomolecule—hemoglobin, say. We may define a variant of hemoglobin as a molecule that performs the biological function of hemoglobin well enough to enable an individual that synthesizes this molecule to survive and reproduce. This definition, like the definition of a meaningful English sentence in our earlier example, is not absolutely precise. It depends on the population and the range of environments one chooses to consider. Even when these are specified it will probably be impossible to draw a line separating functional from nonfunctional molecules, just as it is impossible to draw a line separating meaningful from nonmeaningful English sentences. Here again, however, the borderline cases constitute a negligible fraction of the whole.

2.3 What Is Information?

The class of meaningful English sentences containing 100 or fewer characters is much smaller than the class of word-strings with 100 or fewer characters, and its members are more orderly. Reducing the entropy of a class increases the orderliness of its members. But we have to be careful. The entropy of the class of character-strings of length 5 is much smaller than the entropy of the class of English sentences of length 100 or less, but its members are less orderly. In the scientific contexts I wish to consider it is useful to define information not as negative entropy but as *the difference between* **potential** *entropy and* **actual** *entropy.*

By *potential entropy* I mean the largest possible value that the entropy can assume under specified conditions. In thermodynamics one usually specifies the values of conserved quantities such as the total energy and the number of molecules or molecular building blocks. In communication theory we may choose the specified conditions in various ways, each of which yields a different value for the potential entropy and hence a different value for the information. For example, we may choose to consider strings of English characters or strings of English words. The value we assign to meaningful English sentences of a given length will obviously depend on this choice. Analogously, in calculating the potential entropy of a gene, we may consider strings of DNA bases or strings of codons.

Potential entropy is also potential information, because the largest value that the entropy can assume under specified conditions is also the largest value that the information can assume. We can express this symmetry by writing the relation between entropy and information in the form

$$H + I = H_{max} = I_{max} \equiv J. \tag{3}$$

2.4 Information and Order

The relation between biological organization and thermodynamic order has been warmly debated for at least half a century. In the late 1930s and early 1940s Erwin Schroedinger (1944) popularized the thesis that biological organization is created and maintained at the expense of thermodynamic order, while Joseph Needham (1941) argued that "the two concepts are quite different and incommensurable. We should distinguish [Needham said] between *Order* and *Organization*." Needham's view has been endorsed and elaborated by many biologists, including Peter Medawar (1969) and André Lwoff (1968).

The conflict between the two points of view involves several distinct issues that have not always been clearly separated.

1. *Are order and organization "different and incommensurable" at the level of physics and chemistry?* Needham and Medawar argued that they are, because when hydrogen and oxygen combine to form liquid water or when a supercooled liquid crystallizes, the thermodynamic order of the system of molecules decreases while its degree of organization increases.

This argument overlooks the fact that the thermodynamic order of a collection of molecules refers to their distribution (or, more precisely, the distribution of their representative points) in six-dimensional phase space. When a supercooled liquid crystallizes, the increase in its *spatial* order is more than offset by a decrease in the order associated with the distribution of its representative points in velocity space. Crystallization releases energy and allows the distribution to spread in velocity space. Analogously, the increase in organization that accompanies the folding of a protein or the spontaneous self-assembly of a ribosome is more than offset by the decrease in the order of the surrounding water molecules.

In short, spatial organization represents one aspect of thermodynamic order, but there are other aspects as well. The relation between spatial organization and thermodynamic order is analogous to the relation between kinetic energy and total energy.

2. *Does biological order transcend spatial organization?* For a biologist, the order of a protein is intimately bound up with its structure. A single change in the amino-acid sequence of a protein may destroy its function and hence its biological order, but from a purely chemical standpoint the protein and its nonfunctional mutant are equally orderly. Does it follow that Boltzmann's definition of order does not apply to biological order? I think not.

Consider a gas composed of oxygen-16 and oxygen-18 molecules. Is the thermodynamic order of the gas larger when the two isotopes are spatially separated than when they are mixed? The answer depends on the context. In purely chemical contexts the degree of mixing of the isotopes does not affect the entropy, because both isotopes have the same chemical properties. The order associated with the degree of mixing of the two isotopes is a separate additive component of the total thermodynamic order of the gas. Symbolically,

$$I = I_{chem} + I_{mixing}, \tag{4}$$

where the first term on the right is the part of the information that depends only on properties of the gas that do not discriminate between the two isotopes.

Analogously, we may express the information content of a functional hemoglobin molecule as the sum of a chemical contribution, which does not depend on the sequence of amino-acid residues, and a biological contribution, which does:

$$I = I_{chem} + I_{bio}. \tag{5}$$

According to our earlier discussion, the biological contribution to the information is given by the formula

$$
\begin{aligned}
I_{bio} &= J - H_{bio} \\
&= \log W - \log W_{bio} \\
&= \log(W/W_{bio}),
\end{aligned}
\tag{6}
$$

where W is the number of distinct polypeptides of the same length as a functional hemoglobin molecule and W_{bio} is the number of functional variants.

We can define biological order more precisely and more generally in terms of *fitness*. Population geneticists assume that every variant of a trait can be assigned a definite (multiplicative) fitness—a measure of how effectively that trait contributes to its possessor's expectation of reproductive success under given conditions. In the preceding formula we now set W_{bio} equal to the number of variants that are at least as fit as the variant under consideration. Natural selection always increases the proportion of relatively fit variants in a population and decreases the proportion of relatively unfit variants. Hence, as I shall discuss in more detail presently, natural selection always generates biological order.

3. Some writers have argued that thermodynamic order and biological order must be fundamentally different because thermodynamic order is continually decreasing while biological order is continually increasing. Others have argued that the growth of biological order is driven by the growth of thermodynamic entropy, much as the regular oscillations of the pendulum in a grandfather clock are driven by a falling weight. Both arguments are based on a false premise: that the thermodynamic order of the universe is continually decaying. But the growth of entropy does not imply the decay of order. Remember that information, the measure of thermodynamic order, is the difference between potential and actual entropy:

$$H + I = J.$$

In thermodynamic contexts J, the potential information or entropy, is constant, but in astronomical and biological contexts it may increase with time. If J increases faster than H, information will be generated.

This point is worth emphasizing. When Eddington wrote about the "running down" of the universe, he assumed that because all natural processes generate entropy, a measure of disorder, the universe must have been more orderly in the past than it is today. Many later writers have drawn the same fallacious conclusion. The reason it is fallacious is that information, the measure of order, is not simply negative entropy. It is the difference between potential entropy or potential information (the quantity denoted above by J) and entropy (H). All natural processes generate entropy; but some processes—astronomical and biological processes in particular—also generate potential entropy. As I shall discuss presently, the universe could well have begun to expand from a state of zero entropy *and* zero information.

Let us now take a closer look at the processes that create and destroy order.

2.5 Growth of Entropy

Entropy is a measure of the spread of a discrete frequency distribution. In a gas of classical particles, the distribution is over blocks of equal size in phase space. In evolutionary contexts the distribution is over a genotype space. In a genotype space every point represents a genotype or a segment of a genotype. For example, the variants of a single gene are represented by points in a space whose dimension is equal to the number of codons.

Molecular interactions in a gas or liquid normally generate entropy. That is, they tend to distribute molecules (or rather, their representative points) as broadly as possible over phase space, if they are not so distributed to begin with. The Second Law of thermodynamics asserts that this is so. Kinetic theories, the first of which was invented by Boltzmann, seek to explain why and under what circumstances molecular interactions generate entropy.

One might suppose that any very large collection of interacting molecules would evolve toward its state of maximum entropy, but numerical simulations have shown that this is not the case. A classic example is the work of Fermi, Pasta, and Ulam, who used a computer to simulate the behavior of a long chain of coupled anharmonic oscillators. They found that the system did not relax into its state of maximum entropy but oscillated irregularly between states of high and low entropy. Thus size and complexity do not guarantee entropic behavior. On the other hand, it is easy to prove that a system of *randomly* interacting molecules evolves irreversibly toward its state of maximum entropy, provided the individual interactions are time reversible. Randomness or quasi-randomness of the underlying microscopic processes seems to be a necessary condition for entropic macroscopic behavior. The technical difficulties of kinetic theories, which need not concern us here, center on elucidating the notion of quasi-randomness in systems that are in fact completely deterministic.

Mutation and genetic recombination play a role in biological evolution analogous to the role of molecular interactions in the evolution of a gas. The central dogma of molecular biology, that information flows uni-directionally from the genotype to the phenotype, guarantees that genetic variation is blind to its phenotypic consequences. In this sense genetic variation is random. Accordingly we may expect that *genetic variation always generates entropy*. Although I believe this to be true, it is only part of the truth. As I will discuss presently, genetic variation may also generate *potential entropy/information*.

Let me try to be more concrete. Consider the genotype space corresponding to a particular trait or group of closely related traits in a given population. Genetic variation always tends to increase the spread of genotypes in this genotype space. It does this in two ways: (a) It makes the distribution of genotypes flatter, more uniform. (b) In addition, it may allow the population to colonize previously uninhabited regions of the genotype space. The first process generates entropy but not potential entropy. Hence it necessarily destroys information. The second process generates potential entropy as well. It does not *necessarily* generate entropy. More important, it is an essential preliminary to the generation of information by differential reproduction, as I shall discuss shortly.

2.6 Growth of Potential Entropy/Information in Astronomical Contexts

In thermodynamic systems the potential entropy has a fixed value that depends on the values of appropriate conserved quantities such as the total energy. Hence the growth of entropy leads to a decline of order. In other contexts, however, the potential entropy is not fixed but may increase. If it increases faster than the entropy itself, information is generated.

Astronomy offers many examples. Let us look at a few.

1. In a star composed initially of pure hydrogen, thermonuclear reactions gradually convert hydrogen to helium in the core. The potential mixing entropy of the star thereby increases. A star of the sun's mass is stable against convection, so mixing occurs very slowly. Helium accumulates in the core, so order and information are generated.

2. In self-gravitating systems, contraction releases energy that appears partly as kinetic energy of random motions. For example, a self-gravitating gas cloud contracts and gets hotter as it radiates away energy. Thus a self-gravitating gas cloud has negative specific heat. This is a sign that it does not have a stable state of maximum entropy. (The specific heat of a system in a stable state of maximum entropy is necessarily positive.) As the gas cloud contracts, its molecules colonize new regions of velocity space. This example also illustrates how entropy growth can result in increased spatial order. As the cloud contracts, its spatial order increases, but it occupies an increasing volume of velocity space.

3. Cosmology offers the most important astronomical examples of the growth of potential entropy. In the early universe, thermodynamic equilibrium prevails locally. As the universe expands, the rates of equilibrium-maintaining reactions fall below the expansion rate and nonequilibrium conditions are frozen in. To quote from an earlier paper (1970):

> *Expansion or contraction from an initial state of thermodynamic equilibrium generates both specific entropy and specific information.* This conclusion obviously applies under much more general assumptions about the state and composition of the cosmic medium. The essential elements of the argument are (a) that the 'initial' state is one of maximum specific entropy (zero information), and (b) that the rate of cosmic

expansion or contraction ... may be comparable to or greater than the rates of processes that tend to produce the state of local thermodynamic equilibrium. Because the cosmic expansion or contraction is not quasi-static, it generates departures from local thermodynamic equilibrium and hence generates information. At the same time, irreversible processes generate entropy.

Consider, for example, a uniform mixture of blackbody radiation and gas in an expanding universe. So long as the radiation and the gas exchange energy sufficiently rapidly, they remain at the same temperature, which decreases as the universe expands. Eventually, the rate of energy exchange becomes too small to keep the gas and the radiation at the same temperature. (In an initially hot universe filled with hydrogen, this happens when the hydrogen recombines, at a temperature of a few thousand degrees Kelvin. Neutral hydrogen interacts very weakly with blackbody radiation at this temperature.) Thereafter, the gas cools faster than the radiation. If there is no interaction at all between the two components, the specific entropy of each one remains constant. But because the gas and the radiation are at different temperatures, their combined entropy is smaller than it could be, given their combined energy density. In other words, the potential entropy of the cosmic medium exceeds the actual entropy, and the difference increases as the universe expands. Thus the cosmic expansion generates information.

What is going on in this example? Linear scales are increasing like a. Momentum is decreasing like $1/a$. For energy there are three possibilities: for relativistic particles $E \propto p$. For nonrelativistic particles $E \propto p^2$. For internal energy, E is constant. Hence the rate at which energy per unit mass decreases depends on the degree of equilibration between the gas and the radiation.

Consider a relativistic and a nonrelativistic gas initially in equilibrium at the same temperature. If they remain in equilibrium as the universe expands (or contracts), their common temperature varies as $(a_1/a)^q$, where a is the cosmic scale factor, a_1 is its initial value, and q is between 1 and 2. If equilibration does *not* occur, a temperature difference between the two gases develops. Thus the expansion (or contraction) generates thermodynamic order.

What happens to the entropy? If equilibration is instantaneous, the entropy per unit mass stays constant. If the two gases do not interact at all, the entropy also remains constant! If equilibration occurs subsequently, the resulting common temperature is higher than it would have been if equilibration had been instantaneous. (This is true in a contracting as well as in an expanding universe.) Thus the energy is higher than it would be if equilibration were instantaneous, and the *potential* entropy is also higher.

The rate of entropy generation is actually greatest at some intermediate (finite, nonzero) rate of equilibration.

A simple example will illustrate this conclusion. Consider two disks spinning at different rates on a common axis, as in a clutch assembly. If the disks are not in contact or if they are in contact but there is no slippage, there is no frictional dissipation. The dissipation is greatest when the disks are in contact but there is some slippage.

Because the energy per unit volume in our expanding mixture of gas and radiation is greater than it would be if equilibration were instantaneous, the cosmic expansion increases the accessible volume of phase space. If equilibration were instantaneous, the accessible volume would remain constant, the accessible region of momentum space contracting at a rate that just compensates for the expansion of physical space.

Does the growth of potential entropy distinguish between cosmic expansion and cosmic contraction? No. The preceding discussion applies equally well to a contracting universe.

Note that what *drives* the growth of chemical and structural order is the cosmic expansion (or contraction), not the tendency toward randomization. The Second Law has nothing to do with the growth of *potential* entropy. This illustrates an important general proposition:

Processes that generate order are in no sense driven by the growth of entropy.

In particular, biological evolution is not driven by the growth of entropy.

4. In the preceding example, the cosmic expansion generates a temperature difference between two homogeneous components of the cosmic medium. This temperature difference could in principle be used to run a heat engine. Thus it is a potential source of free energy. By far the most important *practical* source of free energy on earth is sunlight. Sunlight is a by-product of the burning of hydrogen into helium in the deep interior of the sun. Hydrogen, in turn, was produced by chemical (more specifically, nuclear) reactions in the early universe. Let us look more closely at this process.

The rate of a two-body reaction is inversely proportional to the density and increases with increasing temperature. The cosmic expansion rate is proportional to the square root of the mass density and is independent of temperature (except insofar as thermal energy contributes to the mass density). Hence two-body reaction rates increase relative to the expansion rate as we look back in time. At sufficiently early times, the rate of any given two-body reaction will exceed the cosmic expansion rate. Conversely, the rate of any given two-body reaction eventually falls below the cosmic expansion rate.

Now consider a specific chemical equilibrium—for example, the equilibrium between neutrons, protons, electrons, positrons, neutrinos, and antineutrinos. Sufficiently early in the history of the universe, the equilibrium-maintaining reactions (e.g., the capture of an electron by a proton to give a neutron and a neutrino, and the reverse reaction) will proceed rapidly enough to keep the ratio of neutrons to protons at its equilibrium value. Eventually, however, the relevant reaction rates fall below the expansion rate. The relative abundances of the reactants are then frozen in. They retain the values appropriate to earlier values of the cosmic density and temperature.

As the cosmic density and temperature diminish, chemical equilibrium favors the formation of compound particles with progressively larger binding energies. If the expansion took place slowly enough, and if the cosmic medium remained uniform, nearly all of the matter in the universe would eventually be in the form of iron, the element with the largest binding energy per nucleon and thus the ultimate product of nuclear reactions at low temperatures and densities. In fact, chemical equilibrium is frozen in at an epoch when most of the matter is in the form of protons. That is why hydrogen is still available to produce starlight—and to support life on earth.

5. The cosmic expansion generates two important kinds of order: chemical order, which we have just discussed, and structural order. Structural order manifests itself in the *clumpiness* of the cosmic mass distribution—in the fact that matter is not uniformly distributed in space but is concentrated in a hierarchy of self-gravitating systems. Most cosmologists believe that a satisfactory cosmological theory must explain how this complicated kind of clumpiness has evolved from an initially uniform distribution of mass. Most cosmologists assume that the cosmic microwave background, a blackbody radiation field whose present temperature is 3K, is the remnant of a primeval fireball. This assumption has not so far led to a satisfactory theory for the evolution of clumpiness. The alternative cosmological assumption, that the universe began to expand from a uniform state at zero temperature, forms the starting point for a theory that predicts the gradual emergence of structure in the course of the cosmic expansion. Whether or not this theory proves to be correct, it serves to illustrate how structural order can evolve in an initially structureless universe.

2.7 Growth of Organization in Biological Evolution

Evolutionary change results from the interplay of two elementary processes: genetic variation and differential reproduction (natural selection). Molecular biology has strongly confirmed the neo-Darwinian postulate that there is no feedback of *specific* information from the living organism's life experience to variations in the genes it passes on to its descendants.

Thus genetic variation and differential reproduction are independent processes.

In the 1940s and 1950s I. I. Schmalhausen, using evidence from comparative embryology, elaborated the important thesis that evolution is a process of *hierarchic construction*. This process has two complementary aspects: *differentiation*, the increasing specialization and diversification of parts; and *integration*, the formation of new aggregates in which the structure and function of the parts are subordinated to and regulated by the structure and function of the aggregate as a whole, in the manner of cells in a tissue, tissues in an organ, or organs in an organ system. (Individual development, including psychological development, is also largely a process of hierarchic construction. This is the central idea in the work of Heinz Werner and of Jean Piaget.)

Hierarchic construction has given rise to what Stebbins, in *The Basis of Progressive Evolution*, calls a "hierarchy of complexity." Stebbins distinguishes eight major levels of overall organization in this hierarchy, represented by "free-living viroids," procaryotes, eucaryotes, sponges and fungi, flatworms and higher plants, arthropods and vertebrates, mammals and birds, and man. Each level in this hierarchy is distinguished from the preceding level by a major evolutionary innovation, and organisms on each level retain the innovations that distinguish earlier levels. Thus flatworms and higher plants are not only multicellular organisms; they also have differentiated tissues and organs. Arthropods and vertebrates have, in addition, a central nervous system and sense organs. Mammals and birds are warm-blooded, and man has the capacity for language and culture.

The "strategy" of hierarchic construction must itself be a consequence of the more elementary processes of genetic variation and differential reproduction. I have discussed the implications of this requirement elsewhere (1980). The chief implication (I have argued) is that genetic variation cannot be a completely random process, though of course it must be blind to its phenotypic consequences. For hierarchic construction to evolve as an evolutionary strategy, genetic regulation must be regulated by a genetic system that has evolved along with the genetic system that specifies an organism's development. When this idea was put forward, in 1977, several examples of genetically regulated mutation and recombination rates were known. Since then, movable genetic elements (transposons) that regulate mutation and recombination rates have been found to be ubiquitous in both procaryotes and eucaryotes.

2.8 Hierarchic Construction and the Growth of Information

To understand how evolution generates biological information, let us consider some elementary evolutionary processes.

1. *Mutation.* Consider a population whose members all carry the same variant of a gene that codes for a certain protein. Now suppose that a mutation causes a new variant of this gene to appear in some fraction of the population. The biological information associated with the new variant may be greater or less than that associated with the original one. There are two cases: (a) If the original variant is as fit as possible—if its representative point in genotype space is at a fitness peak—then any mutation decreases fitness and destroys biological information. (b) If the original variant is not as fit as possible, a mutation may increase or decrease fitness, or leave it unchanged. But the average effect of the mutation in a large population will ordinarily be to decrease fitness or to leave it nearly unchanged. Conclusion: *Mutations either diminish the average biological information associated with a given trait or leave it unchanged.*

2. *Differential reproduction* always increases the relative abundance of the fitter variants in a population and decreases the relative abundance of the less fit variants. Hence *differential reproduction always increases the average biological information associated with a given trait in a given population.*

3. *Gene duplication.* Because the duplicated genetic material is redundant, this process by *itself* alters neither the potential information nor the actual information associated with the template. But it is a necessary preliminary to the two following processes.

4. *Differentiation.* Mutations may alter copies of a duplicated segment of genetic material. Thus if A denotes a segment of genetic material, duplication may replace A by the sequence AA, and mutations may then alter this sequence to AA'. If A' were nonfunctional, this process would leave the information unchanged but would increase the potential information and the entropy (by the same factor). In reality, however, differentiation is always accompanied by

5. *Integration.* Suppose that the segment A and A' jointly take over the function of A. Among the segments AA' there may be some that are fitter than A. Natural selection now has an enlarged region of genotype space in which to act. As the frequency of the fitter variants increases, the average biological information associated with the segment AA' and its variants also increases. Gene duplication and differentiation jointly open up new regions of genotype space for colonization by an evolving population. In so doing, they create potential information. Natural selection converts this potential information into actual information.

2.9 What Drives Evolution?

It seems clear that evolution must be driven by something. Nonliving matter does not organize itself, except under very special circumstances. Even then the degree of organization attained is quite modest compared with even the simplest examples of biological organization. What is so special about living matter?

Before the advent of molecular biology, many people, including some outstanding biologists, answered this question by positing a "life force." Molecular biology and biochemistry have convincingly demonstrated that no such postulate is necessary. What distinguishes living matter from nonliving matter is "just" its organization. A virus synthesized in the laboratory would be indistinguishable from its natural template. But that does not answer the question.

A common modern answer is the growth of entropy. Evolution, on this view, is driven by the tendency of order to decay into chaos. To explain how order can result from a general tendency toward the dissolution of order, people often use the example of two unequal weights hanging on opposite sides of a pulley. As the center of mass of the two weights descends, the lighter weight rises. Analogously, protein molecules that have been denatured and then returned to their normal cellular environment spontaneously refold; the diminished entropy of the protein molecules is more than compensated by the increased entropy of the surrounding water molecules.

But we are still in the realm of analogy. To see what drives evolution we need to analyze a true evolutionary process. Consider, for example, the evolution of self-replicating strands of RNA in the well-known experiments of Sol Spiegelman. The "driving force" here is just the "Malthusian instability," the tendency of any population of self-replicators to grow exponentially so long as the supplies of building blocks and fuel molecules hold out. If two populations competing for the same building blocks and the same source of free energy have different exponential growth rates, the population with the larger growth rate will eventually take over completely. Of course, free energy and building blocks must be constantly supplied. But it would be misleading to regard the flow of free energy or of molecular building blocks as driving the evolutionary process. On the contrary, the ability of living organisms to mobilize free energy and organize matter is an evolutionary adaptation—a consequence of the reproductive instability of genetic material.

The notion that evolution is driven by the "Malthusian instability" was, of course, Darwin's key idea. If we need to be reminded of it, it is partly because generations of population geneticists have focused their studies not on instability but on statistical equilibrium. Yet, as Ernst Mayr has persuasively argued, significant evolutionary changes probably occur only, or at least primarily, in populations far from equilibrium—small, peripheral "founder" populations, where the tendency toward exponential growth is not held in check by a limited food supply, by competition, or by predation.

There is another reason why many people have been tempted to identify the driving force in evolution with the growth of entropy. We have all encountered the following argument. "Evolution, like all natural processes, rests ultimately on physical laws. All physical laws, with one exception, fail to distinguish between the two directions of time. The one exception is the Second Law of thermodynamics, which states that all physical processes generate entropy. Hence evolution, which more than any other natural phenomenon distinguishes between the direction of the past and the direction of the future, must ultimately derive its 'arrow' from the Second Law."

This argument is flawed because the Second Law is not the same kind of law as the time-reversible laws that govern elementary particles and their interactions. Those laws are independent of initial and boundary conditions. By contrast, the Second Law depends in an essential way on initial and boundary conditions. This was explicitly recognized by Maxwell, who invented a famous thought experiment to demonstrate it. Maxwell had a demon opening and shutting a trap door in a partition down the middle of a box of gas. The demon let fast molecules pass from right to left, slow molecules from left to right. Thus the temperature of the left half of the box gradually increased, while the temperature of the right half decreased, in violation of the Second Law. Half a century later, Leo Szilard pointed out that information has its price in entropy. In order to gain information about individual molecules, the demon must interact with them, and each interaction generates entropy. Szilard showed that the entropy of the system (gas molecules + demon) would increase with time, as the Second Law predicts.

It is not difficult, however, to construct a version of Maxwell's thought experiment that illustrates his original point, namely, that the Second Law presupposes certain initial (and boundary) conditions. Replace the demon by a tiny robot programmed to open and close the trap door according to the results of a calculation carried out before the start of the experiment. The calculation predicts the positions and velocities of all the molecules in the gas at any moment after the initial moment, and the robot's program allows it to use this information to do the demon's job. Of course, such a calculation would need to be based on an immense quantity of data about a still earlier state of the gas and its container, but that is all right in a thought experiment. In *this* experiment, the entropy of the system (gas molecules + robot) does decrease with time. Thus the Second Law fails if certain kinds of microscopic information about the initial state are present. This is just the sort of constraint on the Second Law that Maxwell had in mind.

Thus the Second Law presupposes the absence of certain kinds of microscopic order in the initial states of natural systems. Why these kinds of order are absent is a question that lies beyond the scope of this lecture (Layzer, 1970, 1976). The point I wish to make now is that biological

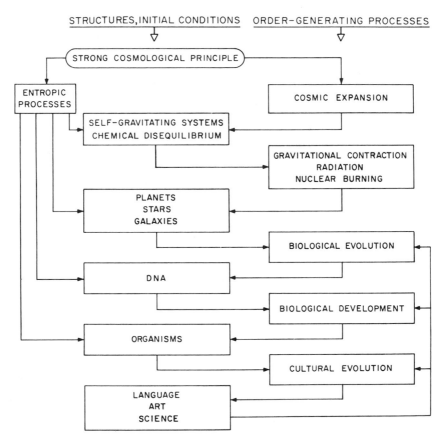

Figure 2.1
[Reproduced by permission of The MIT Press from D. Layzer, "Quantum Mechanics, Thermodynamics, and the Strong Cosmological Principle," in A. Shimony and H. Feshbach, eds., *Physics as Natural Philosophy*, Cambridge, MA: MIT Press, 1982]

evolution obviously has nothing to do with the absence of microscopic order in natural systems. Indeed, none of the order-generating processes I have discussed in this lecture depends directly on the Second Law. There is a single universal law governing processes that dissipate order, but order is generated by several hierarchically linked processes. Figure 2.1, taken from an earlier publication (Layzer, 1982), illustrates how these processes are related to each other, to the processes that generate entropy, and to a cosmic symmetry condition that I call the Strong Cosmological Principle, which supplies the initial conditions needed to derive the Second Law from the time-reversible laws of microscopic physics (Layzer, 1976).

References

Layzer, D., 1970. *Pure and Applied Chemistry* 22:457.

Layzer, D., 1976. The arrow of time. *Scientific American* December; *Astrophysical Journal* 206:559.

Layzer, D., 1980. *American Naturalist* 115:809.

Layzer, D., 1982. Quantum mechanics, thermodynamics, and the strong cosmological principle. In *Physics as Natural Philosophy*, A. Shimony and H. Feshbach, eds., Cambridge, MA: MIT Press.

Layzer, D., 1984. *Constructing the Universe*. Scientific American Illustrated Library, chapter 8.

Lwoff, A., 1968. *Biological Order*. Cambridge, MA: MIT Press.

Medawar, P. B., 1969. *The Art of the Soluble*. London: Methuen, pp. 99–100.

Needham, J., 1941. Evolution and thermodynamics. In *Moulds of Understanding*, New York: St. Martin's Press.

Schroedinger, E., 1967. *What Is Life?* Cambridge: Cambridge University Press.

3

Parity Violation and the Origin of Biomolecular Chirality

Dilip Kondepudi

In recent times we have become more and more aware that the whole universe is far from thermodynamic equilibrium and that it is in a process of evolution (Frautschi, 1982 and this volume). Biological evolution is a consequence of this nonequilibrium process, in which irreversibility plays a fundamental role. On a biomolecular level the thermodynamic aspects can be more easily and clearly analyzed than on a level of living individuals or species; nevertheless, it is quite interesting to see if thermodynamic principles can lead to some general and nontrivial conclusions for the evolution of individuals and species.

I wish to focus attention on a particular and fundamental aspect of life on earth. This is the remarkable discovery of Louis Pasteur that living systems are comprised of molecules that have a particular handedness or chirality. Today we know that all proteins are made of L-amino acids and that the genetic material is made of D-sugars. Biochemical structure and function are very crucially dependent on this chiral purity. In fact, Pasteur in his day considered this molecular asymmetry "the only sharply defined difference which can be drawn ... between the chemistry of the living and of dead matter" (Dubos, 1960).

From a thermodynamic point of view, life is in a state of 'broken symmetry,' a state that can only be realized under nonequilibrium conditions. The notion of a 'broken symmetry' is analyzed as follows: The *state* of a chemical system is specified by the concentrations of the reactants (which may be functions of position and time). This state is the result of chemical and other thermodynamic *processes* taking place in the system. Let us consider a system in which none of the processes has an intrinsic sense of handedness or chirality. When such a system is in thermodynamic equilibrium, the state of the system will have no chirality; for example, the concentrations of L and D enantiomers will be equal. The same system, when far from thermodynamic equilibrium, can evolve into a state in which the L and D concentrations are not equal. Here the state does not reflect the chiral symmetry, or nonchiral nature, of the processes. Thus, if the *state* of a system does not have the symmetry of the *processes* that give rise to it, we have a notion of a state of broken symmetry. In the above example, when the chiral symmetry is broken, either L or D enantiomer concentration can be the larger. In a particular instance, which one of these possibilities is realized is left to chance. Also, as such a system is forced away from thermal equilibrium it will reach a well-defined critical point beyond which the symmetry breaking states will begin to appear.

The great advantage of thinking in terms of symmetries, or broken symmetries, is that one can then see that the dynamics of such a process is described by equations whose mathematical form derives from the symmetry properties of the system and not from the particular type of chemical reactions involved. So we can develop a general theory that describes chiral-symmetry breaking in chemical systems.

Until the 1950s it was generally believed that all the fundamental interactions in nature had no intrinsic sense of handedness. Physicists refer to this as 'conservation of parity.' It was then found that in certain interactions, called the 'weak interactions,' there is an intrinsic handedness, and so it is said that parity is not conserved, or "parity is violated," in these interactions. I wish to present the interesting possibility that the parity violation in weak interactions, which is very small, can have a strong influence on symmetry breaking chemical systems in that it could determine which enantiomer, L or D, will dominate. Then, with the help of a model, I shall present the implications of such a process in the context of biomolecular evolution.

3.1 Theories on the Origin of Biomolecular Chirality

Ever since Pasteur's discovery, there have been various theories for the origin of biomolecular chirality (Thiemann, 1981; Mason, 1984). One theory is that the origin of life was a "single event," and so the particular chirality of life on earth is simply one of the many aspects of this singular event. Another theory is that even if two kinds of life (one with L-amino acids and the other with D-amino acids) evolved, they competed with one another, and one eliminated the other—such is the nature of evolution and living things (Wald, 1956; Noyes, 1984). There are other, more involved theories that are essentially extensions of these basic ideas, but all of them share the common view that L-amino-acid life on earth is a consequence of chance; life on earth could equally well have developed with D-amino acids. Pasteur, however, advocated the opposite view and tried very hard to substantiate it experimentally. He believed that "l'univers est dissymetrique" and held the view, "Life as manifested to us, is a function of the asymmetry of the universe and of the consequence of this fact" (quoted in Dubos, 1960). In his own time, Pasteur could not find that fundamental asymmetry of the universe.

The conviction of Pasteur that the universe is asymmetric found support in the realm of nuclear forces. In the 1950s, it was discovered that nature exhibited an intrinsic sense of handedness in beta decay. The interactions that are responsible for beta decay are the weak interactions. When we take the spin of the electron into consideration, we see that, as it is emitted from the nucleus as a beta particle, it can be moving in the sense of a right- or left-handed screw. Electrons that move forward like a right-handed screw are said to have positive helicity and those that move like a left-handed screw are said to have negative helicity. Now it was found that in beta decay nature produced negative-helicity electrons more plentifully. We do not have a deeper understanding of this handedness: Nature is that way "dissymetrique."

During the last two decades a new unified theory of electromagnetism and weak interactions was developed principally by S. Weinberg and A. Salaam. This theory predicted that there is an interaction between the electron and the nucleons (the neutrons and the protons) that depends on the helicity of the electron. This interaction is mediated by a neutral particle called the Z_0 and is called the weak-neutral-current interaction. These theoretical predictions were confirmed by the discovery of the Z_0 in 1977. This meant that nature's handedness was not confined to nuclear processes but existed on the level of atoms and molecules. For example, it implied that even atoms can give rise to optical rotation, just as chiral molecules do. This optical rotation, which is extremely small, was recently measured (Forston and Lewis, 1984; Bouchiat and Pottier, 1984) in a set of remarkable experiments with metal vapors. (The effect is larger for atoms with large atomic number.) The existence of weak-neutral-current interaction also implies that the energies of L and D enantiomers of a chiral molecule will be unequal.

All this new understanding of nature's asymmetry has led to new considerations of Pasteur's hypothesis that biomolecular chirality is a consequence of some fundamental asymmetry. One suggestion, called the Vester-Ulbricht process, relates the helicity of the beta particles directly or indirectly to chirally selective decomposition of biomolecules. There is no experimental verification of this process yet, but closely related experiments are underway (Van House et al., 1984). It is not yet known if such an effect indeed favors the L-amino acid life. On another front, a most interesting consequence of weak-neutral-current interactions was reported recently by Mason and Tranter (1984 and 1985). In all five amino acids that were studied it was found that it is the L enantiomer that has the lesser energy. Also, based on the average configuration in aqueous solution of 2,500 amino acid residues in 13 proteins, Mason and Tranter found that the L-alpha-helix and L-beta-sheet are more stable, i.e., have lesser energy, than the corresponding D structures.

These results imply two things. One is that, if we consider a system of amino acids in thermal equilibrium, according to the fundamental principle of statistical mechanics, the number of molecules with lesser energy will be larger, so the number of L enantiomers will be larger than the number of D enantiomers. If NL and ND are the number of L and D molecules, respectively, then $(NL - ND)/(NL + ND) = \Delta E/kT$, where ΔE is the energy difference, k the Boltzmann constant, and T the temperature in degrees Kelvin (K). The results of Mason and Tranter show that $\Delta E/kT \simeq 10^{-17}$, when $T \simeq 25°C$, which is extremely small. The second implication is that, in the chemical reactions that produce these amino acids or polypeptides, there will be a small difference in the reaction rates so that $KL = KD(1 \pm (\Delta E/kT))$, where KL and KD are the L and D reactions, respectively and E the difference in the reaction energy barrier. If we take the results of Mason and Tranter to be an indication—there is no firm evidence at this point— that the L-amino acid rates are larger, we may expect it to be about one part in 10^{17}.

Similar estimates for the Vester-Ulbricht processes lead to population and reaction-rate differences that are very small, but that in certain circumstances could be as large as one part in 10^{11} (Hegstrom, 1985). All this, of course, leads to the question, Can such small differences have an influence on the selection of molecular chirality when we take into consideration the thermal and other inevitable fluctuations? It is generally thought (Morozov et al., 1984) that the random fluctuations are too large compared to the systematic chiral effects of the above type, and that parity violation in weak interaction could not have had an influence in the selection of biomolecular chirality. This, however, is not quite true. When we consider nonequilibrium chiral-symmetry breaking, which I shall describe in some detail below, the system can become extremely sensitive to very small systematic chiral effects if it evolves very *slowly* through the critical point. The price paid to realize a high degree of sensitivity is the slow passage through the critical point. In the context of biomolecular evolution, with reasonable assumptions that will be specified below, it turns out that a reaction rate difference of one part in 10^{17} can decide the outcome of chirality with 98% certainty if the system evolves through the critical point in a time span of about 15,000 years. So it seems we cannot reject Pasteur's hypothesis so easily—it deserves further careful investigation.

3.2 Nonequilibrium Selection of Molecular Chirality

Chiral-symmetry breaking in chemical systems has been studied in great detail in model reactions (Decker, 1974), but there is not yet a real system that can be studied in the laboratory. Consider the following model:

$$S + T \underset{K_{-1}}{\overset{K_1}{\rightleftharpoons}} X_{L(D)},$$ (1)

$$S + T + X_{L(D)} \underset{K_{-2}}{\overset{K_2}{\rightleftharpoons}} 2X_{L(D)},$$ (2)

$$K_L + X_D \overset{K_3}{\rightarrow} P.$$ (3)

Here S and T are achiral substrate molecules that react to produce the chiral molecule X in the L and D forms. The notation $X_{L(D)}$ means the reaction is identical for X_L and X_D. The second reaction is autocatalytic, while the third, in which X_L and X_D combine to form P irreversibly, amounts to mutual destruction. Because of these two reactions one of the enantiomers can dominate the system—it can autocatalytically produce its own kind while destroying the other. This tendency of growth of one of the enantiomers is counteracted by the reverse reactions, which tend to equalize the populations of the two enantiomers. When such a system is close to thermodynamic equilibrium the concentrations of X_L and X_D will be equal. Now let us consider an open system into which S and T are supplied, so as to keep their concentrations at a fixed level, and from which P is removed. Let us consider a volume V in which the concentrations of all the reactants are maintained homogeneous by some processes such as diffusion and other mixing. In this volume V, the concentrations of X_L and X_D will be described by the kinetic equations

$$\frac{dX_L}{dt} = K_1 ST - K_{-1} X_L + K_2 STX_L - K_{-2} X_L^2 - K_3 X_L X_D,$$ (4)

$$\frac{dX_D}{dt} = K_1 ST - K_{-1} X_D + K_2 STX_D - K_{-2} X_D^2 - K_3 X_L X_D.$$ (5)

Here X_L, X_D, S, and T are concentrations. The steady-state concentrations X_L and X_D can easily be found by setting $dX_L/dt = dX_D/dt = 0$. (A detailed study of this system can be found in Kondepudi and Nelson, 1984.) One can then see the following: When the product (ST) is less than a critical value, $(ST)_c$, the steady state is symmetric, i.e., $X_L - X_D$. When (ST) is greater than $(ST)_c$, however, this symmetric solution becomes unstable and the system evolves into a state in which the symmetry is broken, i.e., $X_L = X_D$, although the reaction kinetics are identical for X_L and X_D.

It is convenient to study this model in the variables $\alpha = (X_L - X_D)/2$ and $\beta = (X_L + X_D)/2$. In the vicinity of the critical point $(ST)_c$, it can be shown that (Kondepudi and Nelson, 1984) α obeys an equation of the form

$$\frac{d\alpha}{dt} = -A\alpha^3 + \alpha B(\lambda - \lambda_c).$$ (6)

Here A and B are constants that can be calculated from the reaction rates, and $\lambda = ST$ with $\lambda_c = (ST)_c$. It then follows that, if we look at the steady states by setting $d\alpha/dt = 0$, we see that for $\lambda < \lambda_c$, $\alpha = 0$ is the only real solution, but if $\lambda > \lambda_c$ there are two new steady states, $\alpha_{\pm} = \pm\sqrt{(B/A)(\lambda - \lambda_c)}$. The important point to note is that the form of equation (6) derives from the symmetries of the system. (Here it is the symmetry under the interchange of X_L and X_D.) If we started with any other chemical system that shows chiral-symmetry breaking, then we can always find an α, λ, etc., that obey an equation of the form (6), and α will be a measure of the difference between the L and the D concentrations.

Suppose now that due to parity violation in weak interaction, or any other systematic chiral influence (like something we can produce in a lab), the reaction rates K of the L and D enantiomers are unequal. Let us say

$$K_L \simeq K_D(1 + g), \tag{7}$$

where g is the factor of asymmetry. For the case of weak-neutral-currents, as mentioned above $g = (\Delta E/kT) \simeq 10^{-17}$. Then, once again, using symmetry arguments, one can deduce that the general form of the equation that describes the system near the critical point is of the form

$$\frac{d\alpha}{dt} = -A\alpha^3 + B(\lambda - \lambda_c)\alpha + Cg. \tag{8}$$

The steady states of α for equations (6) and (8) are shown in figure 3.1. The

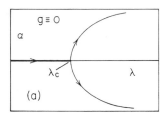

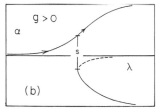

Figure 3.1
Steady states of obeying equation (9), as a function of the critical parameter λ: (a) the appearance of symmetry-breaking states at $\lambda = \lambda_c$ when $g = 0$; (b) the effect of a systematic influence g is to separate the two branches. The minimum separation S between the two symmetry-breaking branches is proportional to $g^{1/3}$.

chiral influence g splits the two branches. In the regions well below or well above λ_c the shift of the steady states due to g is proportional to g. In the vicinity of the critical point, however, the influence of g is comparatively large; the separation between the branches is proportional to $g^{1/3}$. If g is a very small number, like 10^{-17}, we see that its effect near the critical point is relatively much larger. We should keep this in mind when we consider the effect of a given chiral influence.

When we consider the evolution of a nonequilibrium chemical system, which of the states, L or D dominant, will be realized depends on the internal and external fluctuations. This means, with reference to figure 3.1, that whether the system will reach the "upper branch" (where $\alpha > 0$), or the "lower branch" (where $\alpha < 0$), can be discussed only in probabilistic terms. To obtain the probabilities of such branch selection, one must consider a modified form of equation (8) in which the fluctuations are included:

$$\frac{d\alpha}{dt} = -A\alpha^3 + B(\lambda - \lambda_c)\alpha + Cg + \varepsilon^{1/2}F(t). \tag{9}$$

The term $\varepsilon^{1/2}F(t)$ represents fluctuations whose rms value is $\varepsilon^{1/2}$. We may assume $F(t)$ is a Gaussian white noise; i.e., at any time t, the value of $F(t)$ has a Gaussian distribution, and its values at two times t and t' are completely uncorrelated. When we consider all kinds of fluctuations we must expect the parameters A and B also to be fluctuating. A detailed study (Kondepudi et al., 1985) shows that such fluctuations have only an insignificant effect on the branch selection probabilities. So we shall ignore them in our discussion, and focus on the essentials.

Now we can ask the central question: For a given value of $\varepsilon^{1/2}$ how big a g is necessary for the system to evolve to the branch favored by it with high probability? To our knowledge, all the previous studies came up with the answer that only when $Cg > \varepsilon^{1/2}$ can we have significant g-influenced branch selection (Thiemann, 1981; Morozov et al., 1984). Indeed, if one looks at equation (9) this seems a reasonable conclusion: We have the fluctuations with an rms value $\varepsilon^{1/2}$ and the term Cg added to it, and so if $\varepsilon^{1/2} \gg Cg$ the fluctuations will dominate and wash out the effect of Cg on the evolution of α.

This conclusion, while true in certain situations, turns out to be quite wrong in other situations. Most of the earlier studies considered the evolution of the system when λ is well above the critical value λ_c, and α initially at 0. In this case one does find—barring some technicalities—that in general Cg must be greater than $\varepsilon^{1/2}$ to have an observable influence on the system. However, the situation is entirely different if we consider another case that is in fact quite appropriate for biomolecular evolution. We start with the system initially well below the critical point λ_c, and let λ slowly evolve through λ_c to a value well above the critical point—say, $\lambda = \lambda_0 + \gamma t$, where $\lambda_0 < \lambda_c$ and γ is the average rate at which λ increases. In the model considered above, this corresponds to a slow increase of the concentrations of S and T. In this case, due to the concurrence of several features, such as the large separation of the branches mentioned above, the slowness of the processes near λ_c (often called "critical slowing"), even a small Cg, $Cg \ll \varepsilon^{1/2}$, can have a profound influence on the system. The probability P_+ of the system evolving to the $\alpha > 0$ branch is given by

$$P_+ = \frac{1}{\sqrt{2\pi}} \int_{-\infty}^{N} e^{-x^2/2} \, dx, \tag{10}$$

where

$$N = \frac{Cq}{(\varepsilon/2)^{1/2}} \left(\frac{\pi}{B\gamma} \right)^{1/4}.$$

The whole process of passage through the critical point due to which the influence of g is enhanced is discussed in detail in Kondepudi and Nelson (1985). The above result shows that if γ is small—meaning slow passage of λ through the critical point—P can be very large. (This phenomenon of enhanced sensitivity due to slow passage through the critical point is quite general and has been demonstrated well on a simple electronic system [Kondepudi et al., 1986].)

To understand more precisely the implication of this result in the context of biomolecular evolution, we considered the above-mentioned model, so that we can obtain numerical values for the coefficients, A, B, etc., of equation (9) with reasonable values for concentrations and reaction rates. For any other chemical model with the rate constants and concentrations of the same order of magnitude, we can expect a similar equation for the appropriate α; the results are somewhat model independent. We assumed that the concentrations of X, S, and $T \sim 10^{-3}$M. The reaction rate for the production of X was taken to be such that X was produced at a rate of 1 mole per liter, per 100 years. These values can be reduced by several orders of magnitude without affecting the conclusion. To estimate the size of $\varepsilon^{1/2}$ we considered intrinsic fluctuations in the chemical reactions and assumed that in a period of about 1,000 years diffusion and other mixing processes, as in an ocean, can keep the system homogenous (i.e., disperse any excess concentration) at least over a volume of 10^9 liters $= 1$ km $\times$ 1 km $\times$ 4 m. In addition, we also included external fluctuating chiral influences such as circularly polarized light. One must note here that most other chiral influences on chemical kinetics, such as the earth's magnetic field combined with other fields, are even in the most extraordinary cases orders of magnitude less than one part in 10^{17}. With these assumptions for the "prebiotic soup," our theory shows that in a period of 15,000 years a $g \simeq 10^{-17}$ can select the $\alpha > 0$ state with 98% probability. Thus, even weak-neutral-current interactions are quite capable of determining the biomolecular chirality. If there are any other systematic effects, such as beta radiation, then *they* could determine the chirality of biomolecules. Whatever the sources, even a very small systematic influence can have a big effect on the selection of chirality if the system evolves slowly through the critical point. Pasteur's hypothesis cannot be ruled out.

An experimental study of this type of sensitivity, not at the level of $g \simeq 10^{-17}$, but at the level of, say, $g \simeq 10^{-11}$, seems not too demanding. First, we must find a chemical system with suitable kinetics to produce spontaneous symmetry breaking. Then, one can create a small difference in the reaction rates of the L and D enantiomers by some means, such as circularly polarized light. In order to see the effects of a difference in the rates of one part in 10^{-11}, a simple estimate shows that we require a one-liter reactor that goes through its critical point on a time scale of minutes or less. Also, it is clear that there are systems other than chemical systems in which such sensitivity can be studied.

Acknowledgments

Most of the results reported here were obtained in collaboration with G. W. Nelson. I am very grateful to Serge Pahaut for help in typing this paper. This work is supported by the U.S. Department of Energy, Basic Energy Sciences, grant No. DE-AS05-81ER 10947.

References

Bouchiat, M. A., and L. Pottier, 1984. An atomic preference between left and right. *Sci. Am.* June:76.

Decker, P., 1974. The origin of molecular asymmetry through the amplification of 'stochastic information' (noise) in bioids, open systems which can exist in several steady states. *J. Mol. Evol.* 4:49–65.

Dubos, R., 1960. *Pasteur and Modern Science*. New York: Anchor Books, Doubleday & Co.

Forston, E. N., and L. L. Lewis, 1984. Atomic parity nonconservation experiments. *Phys. Reports* 113:289–344.

Frautschi, S., 1982. Entropy in an expanding universe. *Science* 217:593–599.

Hegstrom, R. A., 1985. Weak currents and radiolysis effects on the origin of biomolecular chirality. *Nature* 315:749–750.

Kondepudi, D. K., and G. W. Nelson, 1984. Chiral symmetry breaking states and their sensitivity in nonequilibrium chemical systems. *Physica* A125:465–496.

Kondepudi, D. K., and G. W. Nelson, 1985. Weak neutral currents and the origin of biomolecular chirality. *Nature* 314:438–441.

Kondepudi, D. K., I. Prigogine, and G. W. Nelson, 1985. Sensitivity of branch selection in nonequilibrium systems. *Phys. Lett.* A111:29–32.

Kondepudi, D. K., et al., 1986. Observation of symmetry breaking, state selection and sensitivity in a noise electronic system. *Physica D* (in press).

Mason, S. F., 1984. Origins of biomolecular handedness. *Nature* 311:19–23.

Mason, S. F., and G. E. Tranter, 1984. The parity-violating energy differences between enantiomeric molecules. *Mol. Phys.* 53:1091–1111; The electroweak origin of biomolecular handedness. *Proc. R. Soc. Lond.* A397:45–65 (1985).

Morozov, L. L., V. V. Kuzmin, and V. I. Goldanskii, 1984. Mathematical grounds and general aspects of mirror symmetry breaking in prebiological evolution. *Sov. Sci. Rev. D., Physico-Chem. Biol.* 5:357–405 (and references therein).

Noyes, R. M., 1984. Commentary: on selection of chirality. In *Aspects of Chemical Evolution, Adv. in Chem. Phys.*, vol. LV. G. Nicolis, ed., p. 111.

Thiemann, W., ed., 1981. *Origins of Life* 11:1–194. (Almost all the current ideas can be found in this volume devoted to the origins of biomolecular chirality.)

Tranter, G., 1985. The parity-violating energy differences between the enantiomers of α-amino acids. *Chem. Phys. Lett.* 120:93–96.

Van House, J., A. Rich, and P. W. Zitzewitz, 1984. Beta decay and the origins of biological chirality: new experimental results. *Origins of Life* 14:413–420.

Wald, G., 1956. The origin of optical activity. *Ann. NY Acad. Sci.* 69:255.

II
Thermodynamics of Ecology and Evolution

4

Kinetic Theory of Living Pattern and Form and Its Possible Relationship to Evolution

Lionel G. Harrison

Thirteen years ago, I was a classical physical chemist concerned only with processes in simple inorganic solids and not at all with biological systems. By a curiously stochastic series of causative events, I made a random flight into developmental biology. But to write this paper I am asked homeotically to sprout a second pair of wings to fly over the field of evolution.

I was therefore encouraged to read, in Douglas Futuyma's (1985) review of the recent book *Beyond Neo-Darwinism* (Ho and Saunders, 1984), his opinion that "the most interesting chapters are by developmental biologists." There is an excellent reason for developmental and evolutionary biologists to feel, in this late part of the twentieth century, a strong kinship. Each of us senses the presence of a Great Unknown, which is very close yet remarkably difficult to approach. This is not so for most workers in chemistry, physics, or the structural aspects of biology. For them, the first few decades of this century produced revolutionary advances in theory: the quantum mechanics of small particles, and in terms of that, the explanation of the chemical bond and of molecular structure, and in terms of molecular structure, the nature of the gene. All these have achieved general acceptance. For those who are ferreting out the details, they form a secure philosophic basis as well as reliable signposts to experimental pathways for further investigation.

But both in evolution and development, there are no such secure bases. Indeed, it is quite difficult to devise for oneself or find in the literature a satisfactory definition of evolution. One may read books up to a century old and find basic questions that, today, remain unsolved and can be restated in the same words. Here is a paragraph: "If the gradualistic view is true, such evolutionary innovations as the bird's feather or the angiosperm's carpel must have antecedents in other structures and must have evolved through many intermediate states. Some evolutionists have held that such features arose by saltations, mutations that transform the phenotype drastically in a single step. The preliminary question, then, of the degree of continuity with which the process of evolution occurs, has never been decided."

That was not a paragraph written by one person. The first two sentences are from Douglas Futuyma (1979); the third is from William Bateson (1894). "Preliminary question" indeed; a century later, it is unsettled. Again, in the developmental field: "The *things* which we see in the cell are less important than the *actions* which we recognize in the cell; events are ordered rather than structures." The first statement is from D'Arcy Thompson's *On Growth and Form* (1917); the second, from Thurston Lacalli's Ph.D. thesis (1973). Neither represents a view yet generally accepted. The bit from Thompson comes from a chapter "on the internal form and structure of the cell" that John Tyler Bonner thought wholly out-of-date and omitted entirely from his 1961 abridgment of the book. But to practitioners, like myself, of kinetic explanations of development, that quotation is the text to which we still evangelically preach in the 1980s.

In that spirit, I intend to explore three topics: spontaneous optical resolution, biological morphogenesis, and biological evolution. I shall discuss dynamics rather than thermodynamics; but properly done, chemical kinetics and irreversible thermodynamics should be about as equivalent as the same book well translated into two very different languages.

If I may continue my random saltations about the twentieth century, in 1932 W. H. Mills gave an address to a regional meeting of the British Association on the topic of *Inorganic Stereochemistry*. In the course of this, he speculated upon the origin of optical activity as follows:

> It may be profitable to enquire whether the property of growth which is characteristic of living matter may necessarily lead to its dissymmetry. Let us consider the growth of a tissue in which the d- and l-systems are not present in equal quantities. Let us suppose, for example, that there is twice as much of the d-system as of the l-system. In the process of growth, the complex dissymmetric components will be built up by chains of synthetic reactions, and the rates of formation of the end-products will be controlled by the velocity of the slowest link in the chains. If, as must frequently happen, this is an interaction involving two dissymmetric molecules, and the reaction velocity is proportional to the second power of the concentration, then the rate of formation of the d-component will be four times that of its enantiomorph. Then, whereas there was twice as much of the d- as of the l-system in the old tissue, there would be four times as much of the d- as of the l-system in the new growth.
>
> Though the reactions of living matter may be less completely stereospecific than I have assumed, and though the velocities may increase more slowly with the concentration than according to the second power, yet as long as they increase more rapidly than according to the first power, any excess of one system over the other in the old tissue will become greater in the new growth. From this point of

view the optical activity of living matter is an inevitable consequence of its property of growth.

Mills went on from there to discuss the original bias and to show that the statistically expected uncertainties in numbers of molecules would be adequate to start the asymmetrization in something about the usual size of a cell, say 30 micrometers diameter.

This proposal is a concrete example of how dynamic actions, or chemical kinetics, may acquire ascendancy over things, or structures. And it shows, further, that a simple kinetic idealization, in this case a stereospecific second-order reaction, may express quite faithfully an essential property of a structurally and dynamically very complex system. The model is of a system with uncontrolled self-enhancement, or positive feedback, or auto-catalysis, to use three synonymous terms. It contains, as I shall try to show, the rudiments of dynamic theory of both development and evolution. But to do the job properly for either of those needs at least a little more in the model. Specifically, some control is needed, and that seems to require putting into one's model at least two dynamic systems interacting with each other. To state my thesis in advance: *First*, an uncontrolled self-enhancement will produce optical resolution. *Second*, a self-enhancing system interacting with a self-inhibiting system will produce controlled pattern, that is, development. *Third*, a self-enhancing system interacting with another self-enhancing system will produce evolution.

I want now to illustrate each of these statements in turn. At a meeting four years ago (Harrison, 1982) I showed a film of a simple analogue computation, which I had done with paper and pencil only, to illustrate Mills' mechanism for optical resolution. A solid catalyst is (figure 4.1) in a fixed position, shown by the row of boxes, each of which is a possible

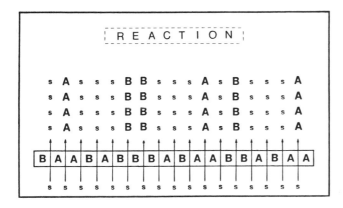

Figure 4.1

adsorption site for a molecule. A substrate S in solution flows continually upward through the catalyst. Arrows represent flow paths over catalytic sites. The substrate can react to the two enantiomers, A and B, of a product. A site is activated for production of A if there is an A adsorbed on both sides of the arrow. Likewise for B. An A on one side and a B on the other gives an inactive site. For the initial arrangement of figure 4.1, which is as random-looking as you can get with only 18 objects in a row, 6 of the 17 channels are active. In the solution, A and B can spread sideways by diffusion (figure 4.2a), and they can exchange back into the adsorbed layer on the catalyst (figure 4.2b). The immediate result is the beginning of a sorting-out of A and B into patches on the catalyst—some suggestion, in other words, of pattern formation—with consequent increase in the number of active channels. One may continue the dynamics of the model in the same way. In my manual calculation, with the required random choices made by guesswork, the model produced a two-part pattern (figure 4.3). I

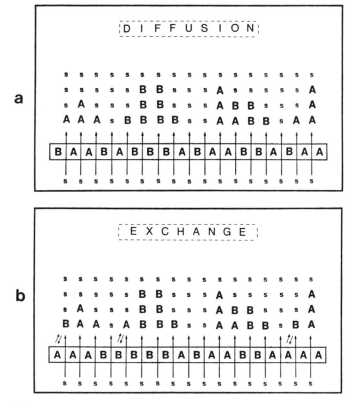

Figure 4.2

expect I managed to bias the model toward this outcome. If you program a microcomputer to do this simulation, and try it repeatedly, you do not by any means always get the symmetrical two-part pattern, though there is usually a conspicuous wandering patch of Bs on the left.

This pattern is not going to stay there. If we follow the operation of the model through quite a lot more stages, the essence of what happens is that the boundary between the A and B regions executes a random walk. In each full cycle through the operations, it either stays put, jumps one place to the left, or jumps one place to the right. Occasionally the pattern can regress slightly, and the boundary become fuzzy, but it then usually sharpens up again in the next stage. The movement of the boundary is an example of one of the best-known and most fundamental of all statistical problems, called The Gambler's Ruin. Two gamblers start, each with a certain number of dollars, and go on repeatedly flipping a coin. One dollar changes hands as the result of each flip. In the end, one gambler must lose everything. One cannot predict which, neither can one predict how long any one game will take. But statistically, for two gamblers starting with N dollars each, the average length of a game until one is ruined is N^2 coin flips. Thus for the starting configuration of figure 4.3, which corresponds to $9 in the hands of each gambler, an average of 81 jumps of the boundary is needed before either A or B wins the game with the total destruction of the other. I have seen this simulation carried out repeatedly to the final stage of optical resolution by a program written for a microcomputer by B. R. Green, and it works quite in accordance with statistical expectation. Now is this a model for development or for evolution? One can look at it various ways, according as one regards the whole model as one organism or as an ecosystem in which each separate A and B is an organism and the bimolecular autocatalysis is a primitive kind of isogamous sexual reproduc-

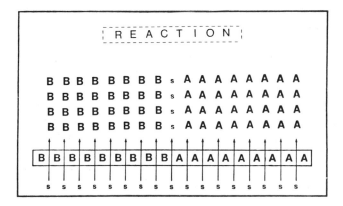

Figure 4.3

tion. If we look at it in the latter sense, with A and B as two species, it is interesting to note that, when two exactly equally matched adversaries compete, with the environment providing no selective advantage whatever to either, one of them must inevitably be annihilated completely. The message of The Gambler's Ruin is that, for at least some evolutionary events—and remember, optical resolution is one that actually occurred at some early time—natural selection of the form better adapted to the environment is not necessary as a driving force. There is a good piece of ammunition for those who like to shoot at neo-Darwinians; but it does not mean that I have yet joined their forces. Good ammunition manufacturers operate from neutral countries while the war is on; that way, *they* maximize their survival chances.

Now in this model I have added something to Mills' 1932 suggestion: that is, the spreading by diffusion and, in consequence of it, the transient formation of pattern as an intermediate stage on the way to resolution. For a moment, I would like to take diffusion out of it and consider optical resolution in a well-stirred system. If we look at rate equations for the growth of A and B and then enquire how rapidly the optical asymmetry $(A - B)$ grows, we find that it grows at a rate proportional to its current value:

$$\partial A/\partial t = k_f SA^2/(A + B)^2 \quad \text{and} \quad \partial B/\partial t = k_f SB^2/(A + B)^2, \tag{1}$$

so that

$$\partial(A - B)/\partial t = k_f S(A - B)/(A + B). \tag{2}$$

Here, A and B are concentrations in solution, $A^2/(A + B)^2$ is the fraction of the catalyst sites having two As attached, and similarly for B, and k_f is the rate constant for autocatalytic formation of A or B out of S. Now there are many conditions in which, while the asymmetry is growing rapidly, the reactant concentration S is constant and the total product $(A + B)$ is approximately constant. In that case, the asymmetry $X = (A - B)$ will grow roughly exponentially. This sort of behavior, in which a rate of departure from equilibrium is proportional to the measure of that departure, is quite typical of the things that turn up in morphogenetic reaction-diffusion models. These, if they are set up as chemical reaction equations, usually have a biomolecular autocatalysis somewhere in the mechanism, leading to squared concentrations in the rates. But if they are set up as rate equations, they contain mysterious-looking measures of departure from equilibrium called X and Y, which look like concentrations except that they can be positive or negative, and catalyze their own increase in either sense. I hope the illustration of optical resolution may have helped to clarify what sort of things these variables are.

To talk about pattern formation, I need to use a distribution that is not

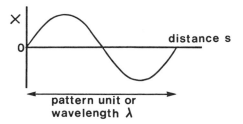

Figure 4.4

just all the A stacked up one one side and all the B on the other, but that has continuous variation of concentration with position. The simplest pattern of this kind is a sine wave displacement in both directions from equilibrium (figure 4.4). Suppose you had this as initial distribution in a solution, e.g., a solvent in a rectangular dish, and some colored solution distributed across it in stripes, looking fuzzy-edged because of the sinusoidal distribution. If there were no chemical reactions, but the substance diffused, you would see that the pattern would not change in shape or spacing of stripes (wavelength) but would just fade away in intensity according to an exponential decay law. This is the Cheshire Cat of patterns, fading with all features intact until only the grin is left.

Now suppose you put reaction and diffusion together—the exponential departure from equilibrium of my optical resolution model, and the Cheshire Cat decay of diffusion—and try a sine wave pattern of some arbitrary wavelength as initial disturbance. The two opposing effects combine to give either an overall decay or overall growth, exponential in either case. Which happens depends on the wavelength. The growth constant k_g increases monotonically with wavelength. That is the essence of the optical resolution model (figure 4.5):

Initial disturbance:

$$X = A \sin(2\pi s/\lambda) \tag{3a}$$

so that

$$\partial^2 X/\partial s^2 = -(4\pi^2/\lambda^2)X. \tag{3b}$$

Diffusion only:

$$\partial X/\partial t = D(\partial^2 X/\partial s^2) = -D(4\pi^2/\lambda^2)X. \tag{4}$$

With autocatalysis:

$$\partial X/\partial t = k_f X + D(\partial^2 X/\partial s^2), \tag{5a}$$

$$\partial X/\partial t = (k_f - 4\pi^2 D/\lambda^2)X. \tag{5b}$$

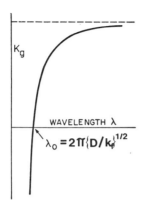

Figure 4.5

Exponential growth or decay constant (according to wavelength):

$$k_g = k_f - 4\pi^2 D/\lambda^2. \tag{6}$$

For a chaotic, random initial disturbance, containing a mixture of all sorts of wavelengths, the dynamics of the system suppress all short-wave components, shorter than λ_0, by exponential decay, and amplify all long waves with the longest being amplified most rapidly. Hence, though pattern of intermediate wavelengths may arise transiently, in the end the biggest patch grows fastest and takes over the whole system. In fact, my simulation with the As and Bs started from a random-looking arrangement in which there was a rudiment of long-range order concealed, as you may see by comparing it with a strict short-range alternation (figure 4.6).

This is not good enough for a model of pattern formation in development. To stabilize pattern, some finite wavelength must grow faster than anything longer or shorter. The model devised by Turing (1952) accomplishes this. He proposed a set of rate equations involving two morphogen concentration variables X and Y, both of which are like the X I have discussed so far. They are displacements from equilibrium, or from a spatially uniform steady state, and all catalytic or inhibitory effects that they have on themselves or on each other are two-way, changing sign with the sign of the displacement. The essence of the model is

X catalyzes itself: X diffuses slowly,
X catalyzes Y: Y diffuses quickly,
Y inhibits X,
Y may or may not catalyze or inhibit itself.

Maynard Smith (1968) gave an enlightening illustration of how the Turing model works, by considering a system initially in the spatially

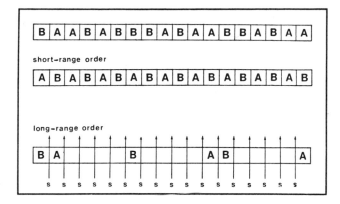

Figure 4.6

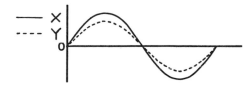

Figure 4.7

uniform steady state and introducing a local X disturbance. He showed that X and Y disturbances spread out and appear to be settling down into standing waves in phase with each other. Suppose, instead, that we use that kind of delocalized disturbance as the initial state (figure 4.7), and enquire what will happen to it as time goes on. Mathematically, we could do this by taking Turing's equations, as follows (X and Y are displacements from equilibrium),

$$\partial X/\partial t = k_1 X + k_2 Y + D_x \partial^2 X/\partial s^2, \tag{7a}$$

$$\partial Y/\partial t = k_3 X + k_4 Y + D_y \partial^2 Y/\partial s^2, \tag{7b}$$

and putting into them a guess at what will happen, namely, that X and Y will stay sine waves in phase at the same wavelength, but that their amplitudes will change with time:

$$X = A(t) \sin(2\pi s/\lambda), \tag{8}$$

$$Y = \theta(t)X. \tag{9}$$

This approach was used by Lacalli and Harrison (1978), who showed that X and Y would settle down to a constant ratio θ. Then, the X and Y

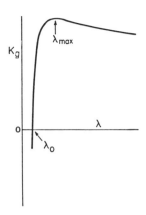

Figure 4.8

waves would grow or decay exponentially with a growth rate constant k_g. But, unlike the case of optical resolution (figure 4.5), k_g passes through a maximum at some finite wavelength (figure 4.8). That fastest-growing pattern will eventually dominate the system.

I would like to try to give you a nonmathematical picture of why the introduction of the second substance Y makes k_g pass through a maximum and then decrease as the wavelength is stretched. We have seen that X alone decays as a result of diffusion and grows as a result of autocatalytic formation, both changes being exponential in time without distortion of the sine wave shape. Now Y inhibits X [that is, k_2 in equation (7a) is negative]; so Y tends to make the X wave decay. Because the Y wave is the same shape, it brings X down everywhere in proportion to its concentration: another exponential decay. How big this effect is, and whether it can change overall growth of X into decay, depends on the amplitude of the Y wave in relation to that of the X wave. Suppose they have settled down to a constant ratio, and that we then stretch the whole pattern to a longer wavelength. Both X and Y diffuse, but Y diffuses faster. The stretching reduces the effect of diffusion, by reducing concentration gradients. Since Y diffuses faster, the benefit is greater to Y. Its ratio to X increases, and so it can more effectively slow down the growth of X, and perhaps even turn it into decay.

Figure 4.9 shows the same curve of growth rate against wavelength as figure 4.8; but, as you can see from the label on the axis, it is not plotted against wavelength here but against the length of the system. And there are three different versions of the same curve plotted, stretched out to different extents along the horizontal axis. These are curves for patterns of different *complexity*. That, of course, is an important word in evolution.

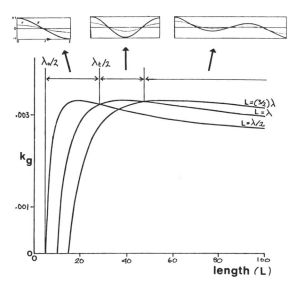

Figure 4.9

(This article does eventually get back to the topic of evolution.) This diagram was devised for a paper in which Lacalli and I (1978) were discussing the differentiation of a slime mold slug into two types of cell and the regulation of this pattern upon chopping up the slug into pieces. The question was, If reaction-diffusion has anything to do with this, over what size range might you expect to find a simple two-part pattern formed? The first curve refers to this pattern, which is the two-part one, in which the length of the system is half a wavelength. For a three-part pattern, the system would be one wavelength long, so the second curve has to be stretched out a factor of two relative to the first; and for a four-part pattern, system length is one-and-a-half wavelengths; and so on. This diagram shows that a two-part pattern could start to form when the system reached this length, and would be fastest growing until the system was about five times longer, when the three-part pattern should begin to grow faster.

Lacalli later pointed out (Lacalli and Harrison, 1979) that there are some instances in which a succession of patterns, each more complicated than the preceding one, arises. One of these sequences, for instance, is the set of clone compartment boundaries on a *Drosophila* wing disc, which Stuart Kauffman had been trying to interpret as reaction-diffusion patterns, all from the same mechanism, and becoming more complex as the system became larger. For this case, a rather clear separation of each pattern from the preceding one was needed. Lacalli found some values for the Turing parameters that made the growth rate curves, instead of what we have just

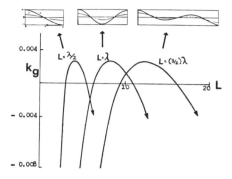

Figure 4.10

been looking at, look like figure 4.10. The patterns are almost separated so that, as the system gets bigger, each starts to decay before the next starts to grow.

There is quite a contrast in the degree of pattern control between the last two figures. The trick in choosing parameters to get one kind of behavior or the other is really quite complicated. Pattern formation is not the only thing that a Turing mechanism can do. It can, for instance, go into oscillations that never die away but grow in amplitude faster than any stable pattern that it is simultaneously trying to produce. It can produce no pattern at all that grows; every disturbance decays back to equilibrium. Which kind of behavior occurs depends on the values of the rate constants k_1, k_2, k_3, and k_4. The details are rather complicated; but for the present purpose, the essential point is that the very precise control of pattern represented by figure 4.10 requires negative k_4 (that is, Y is self-inhibiting) while the sloppier control represented by figure 4.9 arises when k_4 is zero or positive, that is, Y is either not self-interacting at all or self-enhancing. The curves in figure 4.9 were actually calculated for $k_4 = 0$, but ones for self-enhancing Y are very similar indeed.

What would happen in a system behaving like this if we went out to a very large system size? The overall pattern would look rather complex and irregular, because so many different patterns are growing at very similar rates. What we have is, in fact: the simultaneous growth of patterns of diverse complexity, with the more complex somewhat favored over the less complex, and with the highest level of complexity increasing as the overall system becomes larger.

Why did I have difficulty defining evolution? If the system is not one organism but a whole ecosystem of organisms, is not that it? I am suggesting, in other words, that the driving force for evolution is to be sought in dynamical principles; and that the essence of the matter is that, when one

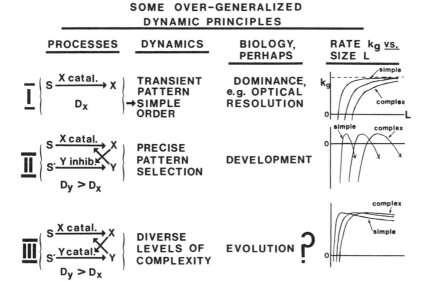

Figure 4.11

self-enhancing system interacts with another, or with a self-neutral system, the result is identifiable as the characteristic product of evolution. In making this suggestion, I am trying to do for evolution what Mills did for optical resolution. That is, taking a simple mechanism, apparently concerned with just one or two molecular species, and maintaining that what the mathematical analysis of its behavior shows will still be present in systems operating on a much grander scale. Very much grander: X is the whole complex of developmental processes; and Y is the genome.

Figure 4.11 is a summary of the dynamical argument. Three mechanistic situations are contrasted. Each of them has some kind of passive long-range communication. It is envisaged as diffusion, but could be all sorts of other kinds of communication. The difference between the situations lies in the kinetic interactions. One simple autocatalysis leads to an uncontrolled competition, leading to a simple dominance. An autocatalysis and a self-inhibition, with the two systems also speaking to each other, gives the precision needed in development. Two self-enhancing systems, or one self-enhancing and one self-neutral, give less precision but enduring diversity. The instructive thing, in these curves of growth rate against system size, is the relative positions of complex and simple patterns: in the second case, nicely separated; in the other two, stacked, but in reverse order in the first and third cases.

By this time, the reader will have noticed the implication that Y, which I

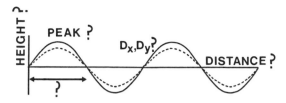

Figure 4.12

identified with the genome, is not necessarily self-replicating. If I maintain that, you may think I am an even more dubious character than some of the developmental biologists who, in the book *Beyond Neo-Darwinism*, apparently argued that only the passing on of cytoplasmic substances mattered. But I am going to maintain that maybe the genome is not self-replicating; and herein lies the contrast between structural and kinetic approaches. I am not at all denying all the beautiful structure of DNA, and its replication, transcription, and translation. I am just taking all that as irrelevant to the immediate purpose. The point is, What determines the *rate* of its replication? What, for instance, keeps a cell in the cell cycle, or gets it to kick out and stop dividing? We do not yet know a lot about that, but I think it will be generally recognized that a lot of that control may lie in the extranuclear developmental processes, that is, in my terminology, in the effect of X on Y, not the effect of Y on itself.

Now if I am looking at an enormously complex system, which is related to the dynamics of a Turing model only in a metaphorically transferred sense, the big question is, What are the labels on the axes (figure 4.12)? When I introduced complexity into this discussion, I was using the number of peaks in a pattern, or, if you like, the shortness of its wavelength, as an analogue for the count of developmental processes in a so-called "higher" organism. So a peak has to be, in some sense, a developmental event. What is the width of a developmental event? My variables are not just simple spatial dimensions, because my system is the whole of life, or at least the self-interacting part of it called a species. Nor is this precisely an ecological model, in which the spatial variable would be a measure of the ground occupied by an ecosystem.

At the beginning of his textbook of biochemistry, Lehninger (1975) gives an estimate that there are about 5,000 different chemical compounds in *E. coli* including 3,000 proteins and 1,000 nucleic acids. He contrasts this with an estimate of 100,000 proteins in a human being. Even if the latter estimate is seriously low, I think it is evident that *E. coli* has a vast number of compounds to do almost nothing in the way of pattern-forming events, and that the human being is biochemically "higher" in the sense of much more efficient use of chemical substances and chemical processes to gen-

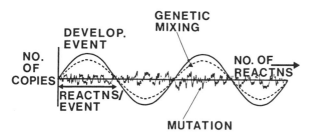

Figure 4.13

erate complexity. I suggest that the width, or wavelength, of a developmental event is the number of substances, or, probably more precisely, the number of chemical reactions used to bring it about; and that what we are plotting along the horizontal axis is, therefore, a measure of the available chemical substances or reactions (figure 4.13).

What then is diffusion in this model? Evidently, it must be the exchange of chemical substances between different developmental events. This may comprise a variety of processes; but surely the main one is the well-known and widely accepted source of variation, genetic recombination in sexual reproduction. The vertical axis is easier: it must represent the number of organisms, or number of occurrences in organisms of reactions associated with a particular developmental event.

There is some noise here. It is the initial input that starts the pattern growing. Of course, it is the creation of new chemical processes; and that is identifiable with mutation. All sorts of mutations could be in here: ones that determine a trivial attribute of some complex sequence, such as, in the production of an eye, whether it is blue or brown; ones that, by modifying an enzyme, change some kinetic constant and hence a developmental wavelength, and hence the fraction of an organism occupied by some structure; homeotic ones that switch a developmental sequence from producing one organ to producing the likeness of a different one; and ones involving, say, an essential step in chondrogenesis that makes possible or impossible all the developmental events of the shaping of the vertebrate skeleton; all these could share the characteristic of being a change by a count of one in the set of elementary chemical processes governing development.

I hear the critic red in tooth and claw, rustling through the undergrowth again saying that I cannot solve all the disputes between evolutionary schools by lumping all these diverse things together under the heading "chemical processes." On the one hand, I do want to suggest that a path to the resolution of disputes in evolutionary theory may lie in that direction, that is, in the analysis of development as chemical reaction mechanism. On the other hand, yes, I do recognize the diversity of the categories I just listed; and I want to hark back to something I called a moment ago the "width" or "wavelength" of a developmental event, as measured by the number of chemical processes intimately involved in setting up the event. What, in my analogy of simple reaction-diffusion theory, determines the wavelength of a pattern?

Physicists who believe that everything significant should be done on the back of an envelope really love dimensional analysis. In those terms, if you have a diffusivity in cm^2 per second, and a kinetic constant in sec^{-1}, the way you get a measure of distance out of them is $(D/k)^{1/2}$. All wavelengths in reaction-diffusion theory are more or less complicated variations on that theme. If we think of the simplest case, the optical resolution mechanism in which this formula gives the threshold wavelength above which pattern will grow rather than decay, then diffusion represents mixing of A and B, and reaction is coupling of A with itself or B with itself. In these terms, I could write the wavelength expression as $2\pi(\text{SCRAMBLING/COUPLING})^{1/2}$. In a complex set of reactions one should be able to find some measure of the kinetic coupling of a few reactions to each other. The stronger this is, the fewer reactions it takes to make a developmental event, that is, the shorter the wavelength of that event in the tally of chemical processes. The broad distinction between different kinds of mutations is the strength of coupling to other reactions of the new chemical process provided by the mutation.

If I ended this article here, I would have managed to write ostensibly on evolutionary theory without once mentioning the following four words: information, entropy, speciation, and environment. Perhaps I should mention them. *First, speciation*: My analogy for evolution is the dynamic behavior of a simple chemical system that forms a number of patterns simultaneously in the same space. These would all be superimposed in a polychromatic waveform that one might call "white pattern." To resolve it into its separate sinusoidal components would need a Fourier analysis, that is, a kind of spectroscopy.

The "white pattern," however, can arise only if there is "white input." What we are thinking about is a rather indiscriminate amplifier for spatial waveform. It is hi-fi: it amplifies input without distortion. If the only input is a pattern of one particular complexity, the output is going to be the same pattern, with higher peaks; just as an amplifier in a good stereo system takes a pure note off a record and gives you the same pure note, louder.

We might normally expect a simple chemical system, which uses all the random disturbances within it as input, to recognize their overall whiteness and produce a disorderly mixture of patterns. But the evolutionary analogue is very different. Its input is the current composition of the genome, representing a frozen history of the disturbances we call mutations. They would all mix to white input if it were not that some of them lead to reproductive barriers that prevent the mixing of all this input throughout the system. This is of course speciation, and it acts as the spectroscopy of the system. One species has only the long-wave components for its developmental amplifiers to respond to, and remains a simple organism. Another has only short-wave components, and is a higher organism, like our own bodies, a symphony for massed flutes and piccolos, a far uv spectrum.

Second, environment: I gather that a large part of the contention between neo-Darwinians and other groups concerns the matter of whether evolution is largely internally generated in the evolving systems or externally driven by natural selection; and that a neo-Darwinian is someone who thinks that the latter effect is totally dominant. In the kind of dynamic model I am describing, there is no contest. Both initial conditions and boundary conditions can significantly affect the evolution of the system, and I identify them respectively with the internal and environmental interactions. The same principle would apply to any mechanism for evolution that was expressible as partial differential equations, with one reservation. The relative importance of initial and boundary conditions can be different in different cases. Turing, in his original proposal of the reaction-diffusion mechanism, exhorted people not to worry about the initiation of pattern formation, indicating that there are always enough disturbances around to get things going. He called attention to the fact that, if one has an electrical oscillator, one expects it to produce the same hum in a loudspeaker every time it is switched on. One knows that the characteristics of the circuit—resistance, inductance, and capacitance—give it a particular resonant frequency, and one does not ask where the initial kick came from.

That kind of behavior is what one expects from the "developmental" regime of the model, which has the capacity of precise pattern selection. As I have already said, it is characteristic of the evolutionary regime that it is less discriminating and hence sensitive to input, like the stable non-oscillating hi-fi amplifier, not the self-oscillating circuit.

Now back to the environmental effect. Figure 4.14 shows two possible patterns of the same wavelength in systems of the same size. In a simple reaction-diffusion model, the first (A) arises with no-flux boundary conditions; that is, the ends of the system are passive barriers. The other (B) involves delivery of material by diffusion from within the system to both ends; this pattern can be sustained only if there is considerable activity outside the system to remove or destroy that material as it arrives. Thus the extent of interaction with the environment can select between different patterns of similar complexity.

Third, entropy: About the beginning of the nineteenth century, a thing was developed, called the steam engine. It had the unusual property for dynamical systems of a rather neat separation of material flow and energy

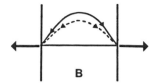

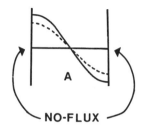

Figure 4.14

flow. Because of this, there was an extraordinary reversal of the common progression in science from pure to applied. The practical engineering led directly to the development of the fundamental science of thermodynamics. This paper is about material flow, dynamics, not energy flow, thermodynamics; and that is because living things, though certainly engines obeying the laws of thermodynamics, are not steam engines. In living things, with the exception of certain aspects of the green plants, energy is generally conveyed along with matter, as part of its baggage, and it is to my mind usually more straightforward to deal with the flows and changes in living machinery primarily as flows and changes of matter, that is, as chemical dynamics, reaction and diffusion. Never think of those terms together as specifying a couple of highly specialized equations invented by Turing and possibly relevant to a few examples of development. They embody, if they are of any use at all, huge general principles; but stated in the dynamic form, not the thermodynamic, as appropriate to things that eat and breathe and sweat and excrete, not ones that get stoked and chug and puff.

In my 1974 paper on spontaneous resolution, I tackled something that Mills did not put into his suggestion; that is, if one has an autocatalytic reaction going on, there must be a finite chance of the reverse reaction occurring. Otherwise, you have a thermodynamic monster, a reaction with an infinite driving force. This reaction, because it is subject to the same A^2 or B^2 catalytic term as the forward reaction, multiplied by A or B for the thing that is being destroyed, is of higher order (cubic) than the forward reaction. What I discovered with a few simple kinetic equations is that this reverse reaction (rate constant k_r) in fact destroys Mills' suggestion: spontaneous resolution will not occur. Mills was wrong, for any thermodynamically realistic reaction with a finite equilibrium constant. Unless, that is, there is another process removing A and B, of lower order; and that can happen if you have nonstereospecific external interference. I represent that by a rate constant k_{ext}; in a flow system, it is just proportional to the flow rate carting the products away. There is, as I showed, a very simple threshold criterion: if k_{ext} exceeds one quarter of k_r, Mills was right: optical resolution will occur. I look at this dynamically, in terms of rates of reaction; but, done properly with reverse reactions put in, it must be precisely equivalent to the thermodynamic treatment, which is much more difficult to set up and find one's way around. Thus, my threshold criterion is simply the condition needed for the entropy of the universe to increase. If the products removed are externally reprocessed into reactant, the whole thing may be formulated as an irreversible cycle. If the cycle is driven slowly, development via pattern to optical resolution does not occur. If it is driven quickly, the entropy of the universe is doing just fine and pattern formation occurs. Satisfaction of the second law in this sort of way is the norm throughout biological development. I do not see anything in evolution that is thermodynamically any more mysterious or anomalous.

It must be clear that I have no sympathy whatever with the view that living material somehow manages to violate the second law. I am always surprised when I hear that such views are still around. So long as there is a nonliving environment around for the living things to interact with, the second law is easily satisfied in all that is going on. There would only be a thermodynamic problem if, as I believe Fred Hoyle has recently been suggesting, the whole universe is in some sense alive.

But there is a sense in which the complex reaction sequences of living matter are unique and, without actually violating any established physical principles, give an impression of doing something different. In the matter of optical resolution, we are thinking of a remote epoch in biochemical evolution, in which we are not really quite clear whether A or B means a large molecule formed by bimolecular autocatalysis or a small organism with a primitive kind of sexual reproduction. When reaction systems become more complex, the two are distinguished. For a simple chemical reaction, we must always, for thermodynamic reality, put in the reverse process in our schemes. But a reverse reaction for sexual reproduction is, if you will excuse the term, inconceivable. In other words, complex systems of interdependent reactions have, effectively, the property that $k_r = 0$. In that case, any rate of flow around the cycle, any rate whatever, satisfies the thermodynamic criterion. This is the property of complex assemblages of chemical reactions, which is in practice seen only in living material, and which makes it seem different.

The last of my four words: *information*, specifically, genetically coded information. The details of it are clearly very important; but, from a developmentalist's point of view, the quantitative use of "information entropy" in relation to the driving force for evolution is rather worrying me; I tend to feel that extensive use of this concept just now would be mistimed in the philosophical development, or evolution of the subject. What bothers me is that, in the current state of our knowledge, there is somewhere a breakdown in the functional relationship between genetic information and the developmental events, and their results in morphological structure from which we try to ferret out phylogenies. It is a breakdown in our knowledge of the relationship of the macroscopic to the microscopic.

In dynamic terms, in which one regards development, the expression of genetic information, as something to be described by differential equations, the problem is that the genome effectively provides the equations, not their solutions. The parameter values for the dynamics are there: rate constants determined by an enzyme activity, determined by its structure, determined by the genome. But to the dynamics of the system, the very diverse solutions that one differential equation can have, and hence the development, is a big jump. That is where we know that functional relations exist, but do not have a good handle on them.

I suggested earlier that what we need is a good count of chemical processes involved in developmental events; and I hope my overview of dynamics has shown that, if we had that, we would have something functionally relatable both back to the genome and forward to the developmental progressions. But that is where, currently, we know the least; and until we know much more, the relation of genetic information to development and hence to evolution cannot be quantitated. One new reaction, or one existing reaction removed, can have a tiny effect on one developmental process, or an enormous effect on several: a step on the gradualist's interminable stairway to heaven, or a seven-league saltation.

Evolution was first perceived in terms of the structures and functions of organisms showing great diversity and enormous changes over long enough periods of time. The first great attempt to explain it mechanistically was, as everyone knows, Darwin's theory of natural selection. I think we recognize today that evolution has not yet been fully explained, and still poses very big problems for the scientific endeavor. To my mind, the resolution of these problems cannot be reached in the Darwinian sense, by trying to relate macroscopic structure and function directly to mechanism. This is in no way to say that natural selection should disappear from the scene. It is, I believe, a valid theory, which is destined to remain a permanent and prominent part of evolutionary theory.

But evolution also involves that intrinsic property of living material, which is manifested in the development of the organism: the power of self-organization. If the relation of evolution to that property is to be pursued, it is going to be necessary to envisage an organism in an abstract way, not as a remarkable geometry of assembled molecules, but as an even more astonishing assembly of mutually interacting chemical processes. To ferret out the nature of these interactions is the work of the developmental biologist. Little is yet known about them. I expect that major advances in this kind of developmental biology will lead almost automatically to advances in the understanding of evolution.

If I have indicated anything in this paper that could be regarded as a new philosophical direction for evolutionary theory, it must lie in this dynamic view of an organism as a set of interacting reactions, in which rates are more important realities than substances. This view was expressed above particularly in relation to the labeling of the horizontal axis of figure 4.13 as "reactions/event"; that is, that organization has become "higher," or "more evolved" when it discovers kinetic economy, the use of fewer processes in more efficiently interactive ways to bring about the formation of complex geometrical structures.

References

Bateson, W., 1894. *Materials for the Study of Variation*. London: Macmillan.

Bonner, J. T., 1961. Abridged edition of *On Growth and Form*, by D'Arcy W. Thompson. Cambridge: Cambridge University Press.

Futuyma, D. J., 1979. *Evolutionary Biology*. Sunderland, MA: Sinauer.

Futuyma, D. J., 1985. Neo-Darwinism in disfavor; review of *Beyond Neo-Darwinism* (M.-W. Ho, and P. T. Saunders, eds.). *Science* 226:532–533.

Harrison, L. G., 1974. The possibility of spontaneous resolution of enantiomers on a catalyst surface. *J. Mol. Evol.* 4:99–111.

Harrison, L. G., 1982. An overview of kinetic theory in developmental modelling. In *Developmental Order: Its Origin and Regulation* (40th Symp. Soc. Develop. Biol., 1981), S. Subtelny, and P. B. Green, eds., New York: Alan R. Liss, pp. 3–33.

Ho, M.-W., and P. T. Saunders, eds., 1984. *Beyond Neo-Darwinism*. Orlando, FL: Academic Press.

Lacalli, T. C., 1973. Morphogenesis in Micrasterias. Ph.D. thesis, The University of British Columbia, Canada.

Lacalli, T. C., and L. G. Harrison, 1978. The regulatory capacity of Turing's model for morphogenesis, with application to slime moulds. *J. Theor. Biol.* 70:273–295.

Lacalli, T. C., and L. G. Harrison, 1979. Turing's conditions and the analysis of morphogenetic models. *J. Theor. Biol.* 76:419–436.

Lehninger, A. L., 1975. *Biochemistry*, 2nd ed. New York: Worth Publishers.

Maynard Smith, J., 1968. *Mathematical Ideas in Biology*. Cambridge: Cambridge University Press.

Mills, W. H., 1932. *Chem. and Industry*, 750–759.

Thompson, D'Arcy W., 1917. *On Growth and Form*. Cambridge: Cambridge University Press.

Turing, A. M., 1952. The chemical basis of morphogenesis. *Phil. Trans. Roy. Soc. London* B237:37–72.

5

The Thermodynamic Origin of Ecosystems: A Tale of Broken Symmetry

Lionel Johnson

5.1 Introduction

This paper attempts the further development of a thermodynamic framework for biological processes. It is an extension of the premise that the emergent properties of biological systems reflect a response both to the physical environment in which the systems are currently existing and to the changing environments in which they have existed over the course of evolutionary time (Johnson, 1981). Although it is believed that biological phenomena are interpretable in thermodynamic terms, the concepts presented have been developed from ecological observations and principles and not from a starting point in the physical sciences. This perspective stems from the notion that the biological sciences express the integration of physical and chemical principles at a higher hierarchical level than is expressed in either science alone. Such a view is consistent with that of Mayr (1982), who insists that in biology all physical and chemical principles are evident, whereas the separate disciplines examine only certain aspects of the full range of possibilities. This means that thermodynamics must accommodate biology. Only through full exposition of the biological properties of systems can this higher level of integration be examined since biological systems possess properties not derivable from the more basic physical and chemical premises. From this starting position, observation and deduction have led to extremely interesting conclusions, without, so far as I am able to judge, doing violence either to biology or to thermodynamics.

The most significant necessary modification to thermodynamic considerations is the transposition of conventional, rather static thermodynamic concepts into ones that are truly dynamic, even if this relegates the foundation of thermodynamics, thermodynamic equilibrium, to a subsidiary role and infringes on the prerogatives of the second law.

5.2 Emergent Properties of the Biosystem

1. *The number of species (species richness) existing in the world during any one time period has increased over evolutionary time.* It is now generally accepted that this increase in the number of species is a true 'evolutionary signal' identifiable above the background 'noise' (Hutchinson, 1959; Simpson, 1949, 1969; Sepkoski et al., 1981; Raup and Sepkoski, 1982) (figure 5.1). There is however, some reluctance to accept the generality of the principle; Boucot (1983), for example, considers that it may be an artifact resulting from the methods necessarily employed by paleontologists. Species richness combined with equitability, the relative representation of the various species, is represented by species diversity. Diversity reflects complexity and is an expression of the number of interconnections or the number of interactions between species. Species richness is correlated with diversity (Tramer, 1967). Hence, it may be concluded, diversity has increased over evolutionary time.

2. *Diversity increases from the poles to the equator*—a generalization first established by Wallace (1878). This, and comparable geographical trends, have subsequently been examined, and the reasons for their existence discussed in an extensive literature (Fischer, 1960; Connell and Orias, 1964; Stehli, 1968; Stehli et al., 1969; Schall and Pianka, 1978).

3. *There is a trend toward increasing structural complexity in many evolu-*

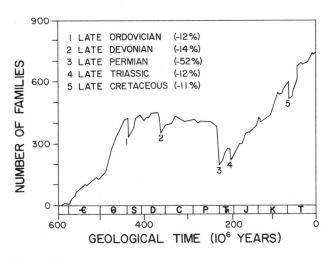

Figure 5.1
Changes in species diversity over geological time. The negative percentages in parentheses indicate the relative loss of species over the five major periods of decline. [Redrawn from Raup and Sepkoski, 1982]

tionary lines, and a general increase in the average complexity of all evolutionary lines (Simpson, 1949, 1953, 1969; Thorpe, 1974).

4. *During the course of succession diversity increases in the initial stages, reaches a maximum in the penultimate phase, then declines as the steady state or climax is approached.* This generalization has received considerable attention from various authors (Clements, 1905; Margalef, 1963, 1968; Odum, 1969; Whittaker, 1969); it can be accepted as a principle more apparent in relatively autonomous systems than in those exposed to a high level of material exchange in which a steady state is less well-developed.

5. *During the course of succession there is a decline in the Production/Biomass ratio.* The concept of the Production/Biomass ratio is central to the main argument. The P/B ratio is, in effect, a measure of the rate of energy flow through an ecosystem, or a species, relative to the energy accumulated in the biomass. Dimensionally the P/B ratio at the steady state is equivalent to the reciprocal of the mean age ($P/B = 1/$mean age) (MacArthur in Leigh, 1965), hence an inverse measure of the 'turnover time.' It is a measure of the rate at which new material must be produced to replace that lost through natural death, grazing, or predation in the maintenance of a steady state. The P/B ratio is therefore a relative measure of the rate of energy dissipation, or rate of entropy production. A more accurate representation of the energy flow is the Respiration/Biomass ratio, but inclusion of the factor for basic metabolism obscures certain aspects of the process rather than clarifies them.

It has frequently been stated that a decline in the value of the Production/Biomass ratio over the course of succession is a general property of ecosystems (Margalef, 1963, 1968; Odum, 1969). This is true in its overall aspect but the situation is somewhat more complex when examined at a deeper level. As a result of studies on the relatively simple ecosystems in Arctic lakes, I concluded (Johnson, 1976, 1983) that it is the species, individually, that proceed to a 'least value' of the P/B ratio while interaction between species tends to *increase* the value of the P/B ratio. This trend to increased energy flow, however, is masked by the sum of the individual effects of the various species present. The dominant species (and this is particularly noticeable in heterotrophs) while itself tending to proceed to a 'least attainable' value of the P/B ratio actually stimulates energy flow and production at lower hierarchical levels (cf. McNaughton, 1984). The greater the number of heterotrophic interactions, therefore, the greater will be the rate of energy flow. This can perhaps be most clearly seen in *Homo sapiens* himself. As biomass of the human species has increased through increasing numbers and increased longevity, energy flow at supporting levels has been canalized and stimulated through agriculture.

There are thus two processes operating simultaneously. Individual species proceed toward a state of least dissipation, within the constraints to which they are subjected, but interaction between species tends to stimulate an increase in the rate of dissipation. However, if the system is to remain in existence the *trend to reduced dissipation must exceed that toward increasing energy flow. If this were not the case the system would dissipate completely*. Within this constraint, the ecosystem tends toward increasing energy flow, until a stationary state is reached when the rates of energy input and output equalize. This may be expressed

$$\sum \text{Autecology} \geqslant \text{Synecology}. \tag{1}$$

This inequality reflects the energy relationships over the course of succession, accounting for the observed overall trend of ecosystems toward a least value of the P/B. This least attainable value is reached at the steady state, or climax, where the two trends assume equality.

Over evolutionary time, species diversity increases with a concomitant increase in energy flow, hence

$$\text{Synecology} > \sum \text{Autecology}. \tag{2}$$

This inequality is 'open-ended' [as opposed to (1)], allowing diversification over evolutionary time to proceed virtually without limit.

Given the above energy relationships, the dominant species (the one least constrained by interactions with other species) will be the one to express most clearly the trend toward least dissipation. The attainment of a 'least value' of the P/B ratio by the dominant fish species in Arctic lakes is quite evident in the length- and age-frequency distribution of the stocks. This is characterized by the Arctic charr (*Salvelinus alpinus*) population in a small Arctic lake (figure 5.2). The 'least value' of the P/B ratio is evident by the large size of individuals, uniformity in size, great mean age, a low level of juvenile stock, and an indeterminate age at death. Uniformity in size can clearly be seen to be largely independent of age. However, length and age can not be completely decoupled since size is a monotonic function of time [Medawar's first law of growth (Medawar, 1945)]. It is also apparent that the greater the mean age, the lower the value of the P/B ratio, and the larger the size, the smaller the specific metabolic rate (Kleiber, 1932). Large uniform size, an indeterminate life span, and greatest attainable age are thus prerequisites for a small P/B ratio. The fundamental biological prerequisites of growth and limited life span prevent the attainment of a completely uniform state. This basic configuration is repeated almost indefinitely in lakes across the Canadian Northwest Territories (Johnson, 1976, 1983). These northern lakes appear to come close to realization of the Clementsian concept of the climax, where the system is in equilibrium with the prevailing climatic conditions.

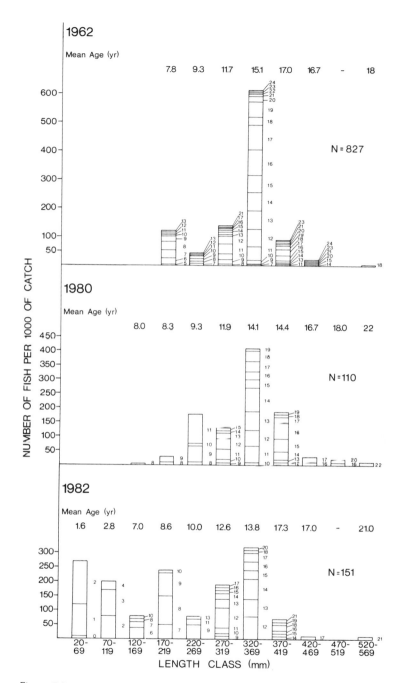

Figure 5.2
Arctic charr, *Salvelinus alpinus*, from Nelson Lake, Cornwallis Island, N.W.T. (Northwest Territories), showing a population in a state of 'least dissipation.' In the initial sampling (1962) there is a high degree of uniformity with a great spread of age within the modal size group. The outlines of this structure remain in 1980 and 1982 following heavy exploitation; this indicates a high degree of cohesion within the stock even under considerable change in density. [From Johnson, 1983]

6. *Homeokinesis.* The partial decoupling of age and size in the attainment of size uniformity is a group property that could not have been predicted from knowledge of individual behavior. It seems most probable that the observed length-uniformity of these populations has been attained through operation of the interactive energy-sharing mechanism described by Soodak and Iberall (1978) under the doctrine of homeokinesis. Homeokinesis provides the physical basis for the equipartitioning of the available energy between complex atomisms, or thermodynamic engines, freely interacting in a fluid medium. Homeokinesis leads to the symmetrical distribution of energy among the components and the attainment of a state of 'least change.' Homeokinesis thus expresses antagonism to the second law of thermodynamics in that it creates uniformity rather than the adoption of the 'maximum number of complexions.'

If individuals of the same species interacting *symmetrically* reach a state of relative uniformity and a least value of their P/B ratio through homeokinesis, then it must be concluded that *asymmetrical* interaction between different species will tend to increase the value of the P/B ratio of the system. Thus, each species, individually, assumes a least value of its P/B ratio through symmetrical interaction, while the ecosystem as a whole (tending as it does to increase in diversity indefinitely) proceeds toward increasing values of the P/B ratio through an increase in the number of asymmetrical interactions. The two processes are thus set in opposition, with the individual tendency (most clearly expressed by the dominant species) exceeding, at least over ecological time, the opposing tendency of the system toward increasing diversity.

7. *Homogeneity and Heterogeneity.* Symmetrical interaction in nonequilibrium systems may be regarded as giving rise to a state of homogeneity, whereas asymmetrical interaction results in heterogeneity. Thus an ecosystem is formed through antagonistic processes, leading on the one hand to homogeneity and a reduced rate of dissipation, and on the other hand to heterogeneity and reduced dissipation (figure 5.3). This interaction can be most readily observed during the course of succession where two simultaneous processes can be isolated in the initial stages: (1) Relatively short-lived pioneer species are gradually replaced by longer-lived ones ensuring that the rate of energy flow is reduced as biomass accumulates. (2) The number of species increases, tending to increase the energy flow relative to the biomass accumulated (figure 5.4). Flow rates are thus simultaneously being decelerated and accelerated, with deceleration always maintaining ascendancy over acceleration. Acceleration increases up to the point of maximum diversity and then declines in the terminal stages with the emergence of the dominant species and an increase in homogeneity.

Over the long timeframe of evolution, this steady state is ephemeral. The advantage is with the trend to increasing diversity and increased

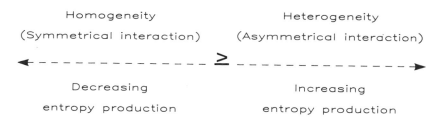

Figure 5.3
Diagram indicating the interaction taking place between homogeneity and heterogeneity. Homogeneity results in symmetrical interaction and least dissipation or least entropy production. Heterogeneity results in increased entropy production.

dissipation. Thus periods of relative stability may be interspersed with periods of increasing diversity. This process is not monotonic: occasional disjunctive environmental events, or the emergence of a superior acquisitor and accumulator, may reset the system to a lower level of diversity (figure 5.1). *Evolution is the outcome of the ultimate ascendancy of the trend toward increasing diversity and acceleration of the energy flow, counteracted and retarded by the individual species attempting to proceed in the direction of greater homogeneity and deceleration of the energy flow.* Succession represents the temporary triumph of homogeneity; evolution results in the long-term erosion of this homogeneity. Succession terminates in a steady state where the dominant species imposes the maximum attainable degree of homogeneity on the system. Increasing diversity is open-ended; hence evolution can continue indefinitely.

A geographical analogy is provided by a region of mountain building in a wet climate where the erosional processes hasten river development. As the mountains rise, the rivers draining them continually cut down toward their baselines, eliminating falls and developing the smoothest and most rapid flow possible. But, as the mountains continue to rise, new falls and irregularities are introduced. Similarly with ecosystems, the energy accumulations as represented by the various species (the falls created by impediments to flow) tend to fragment with a smoothing of the flow path. A thousand minor pools and riffles in the mature system replace the more dramatic cascades of the younger stages. Physical analogies, although indicative of comparable trends, must not be pressed too far as they are representative of a fundamentally different type of system. There is, for example, no terminal stage in the development of a river system, in which energy accumulates; development ceases at the point equivalent to that of maximum diversity in the successional process.

8. *The Dissipative System.* Dissipative structures form as patterns in the energy flow (Prigogine, 1978; Prigogine and Stengers, 1984). Individual

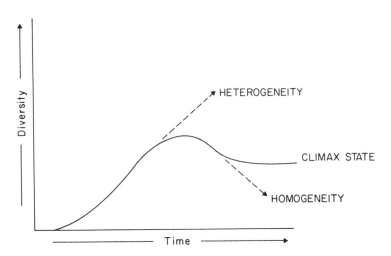

Figure 5.4
Successional changes in species diversity. Heterogeneity increases during the earlier stages, then declines as the climax state is approached. This is interpreted as indicating the antagonism between the forces inducing heterogeneity and those inducing homogeneity. The ascendancy of the forces inducing homogeneity is shown by the increase in homogeneity in the terminal stages. The shape of the curve is taken from Odum (1969).

organisms function as dissipative structures (Prigogine and Wiame, 1946) assuming a state of least dissipation at maturity. This is demonstrated by the decline in the specific metabolic rate observed over the course of individual development. Through homeokinesis, like-individuals are constrained to function in concert because all are driven to equal energy potential. *Together* they form a coherent dissipative structure. As goes the individual so must go the coherent group.

It is evident from observation that biological species interacting within the boundaries of an ecosystem express the tendency to assume a state of least entropy production. Such functional groups are manifestly far from thermodynamic equilibrium. However, Prigogine contends that dissipative structures only exhibit the characteristic of least dissipation when they are close to equilibrium "... Far from equilibrium the thermodynamic behaviour could be quite different, in fact, even opposite that indicated by the theorem of minimum S production" (Prigogine, 1978). This apparent conflict, I believe, can be resolved by the fact that the biological dissipative system is built on the antagonism between the parts and the whole. The system as a whole tends to increase the rate of dissipation, while the individual structures tend to a state of least dissipation. Thus a dissipative system, as represented by an ecosystem, can be viewed from two perspectives —that of the individual components, which attain a state of least dissipation, and that of the system that attains the greatest rate possible. Thus a constant configuration, in which dissipation simultaneously attains both greatest and least values, can only be attained in the vicinity of the quasi-equilibrium established when the two factors achieve equality.

Dissipative structures have the capacity for self-organization in the face of environmental fluctuations. Self-organization involves an increase in complexity, and an increase in complexity, demanding greater work be done, demands an increase in the rate of energy expenditure. Self-organization is a reordering of old elements and the addition of new and possibly accidental components to provide a smoother and more ordered energy flow. Organization implies the existence of a goal (Pittendrigh, 1958; Mayr, 1976). The "goal" of the individual species is homogeneity and reduced energy flow, the "goal" of the system is heterogeneity and increased energy flow. Self-organization emerges from the antagonism between these two conflicting goals, stimulated by the slightly superior trend to ever-increasing dissipation.

Self-organization may also include an initial shift in the opposite direction, whereby simplification, through a reordering of the energy pathways, may allow a subsequent increase in complexity. An appropriate physical analogy is the replacement of the thermionic valve with the transistor.

9. *Diversity*. Given these basic relationships *diversity can be measured in terms of the distribution of energy within the system in a form similar to the Shannon-Weaver equation for information* (MacArthur, 1965), *or the Maxwell-Boltzmann equation for the statistical entropy of a system*:

$$S = -k \sum_{i=1}^{i=n} p_i \log p_i,$$

where $\sum p_i = 1$ and p_i is the probability of an idealized physical system being in the state i of n possible equivalent states, and k is the Boltzmann constant. The interpretation of this equation will emerge later. Diversity is not synonymous with either "information" in the sense of the number of 'yes/no' bits, or with Boltzmann's statistical entropy. Nevertheless, there does seem to be a close correspondence between all three concepts.

In addition to the above, the following thermodynamic precepts are important in ecosystem formation:

10. *The world exists as a closed system, exchanging energy and entropy, but not matter, with the external universe.* In such a system radiant energy in the form of light crosses the boundaries of the system, and having been converted to long-wave radiation, is ultimately dissipated to the universe in the form of heat. At the steady state, or quasi-equilibrium, energy input and output are equal.

84   Lionel Johnson

11. *An energy flow from source to sink necessitates the existence of at least one cycle* (Morowitz, 1968).

12. *For energy flows to be sustained, continuous asymmetry must exist between source and sink.* This implies that a biological system must be maintained in a continuing state of nonequilibrium.

13. *The rate of dissipation of energy following a rectilinear path is greater than the rate of dissipation of energy following a circular or cyclic pathway.* That is, the existence of a cycle in the flow of energy from source to sink involves a reduction in the rate of dissipation.

14. Onsager's reciprocal relationships (Onsager, 1931) indicate that *when two energy transport processes, such as diffusion or conduction, interfere with each other in the vicinity of equilibrium, then the variational principle of Lord Rayleigh comes into play and the system proceeds to a state of least dissipation.*

5.3   A Physical Interpretation of Biological Phenomena

The earth, because of its rotational patterns, functions as a commutator, interrupting the energy flow from the sun. The interruptions in energy flow prevent reactions from going to completion, allowing work to be done on a continuously sustained basis.[1] Such regularly repeated energy input pulses induce resonance. Resonance results in the formation of cyclic patterns of temporary energy storage.

In a fluid system close to thermodynamic equilibrium, cyclic, or reversible processes may exist. The rate at which these reversible reactions proceed in one direction is equal to the rate at which they proceed in the reverse direction (figure 5.5). These changes occur without alteration in the

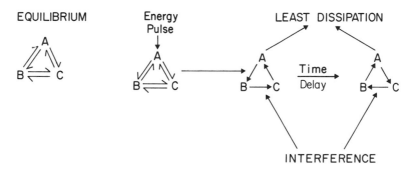

Figure 5.5
Reversible reactions at thermodynamic equilibrium may be caused to resonate by a suitable periodic input of energy. Interference between the forward and reverse energy transfer processes induces a state of least dissipation.

entropy of the system. If such a system in equilibrium is subjected to a low intensity energy pulse of appropriate frequency, the reaction may be stimulated to proceed in one direction, inducing a time-delay before the ground state is regained. A degree of synchronization will be imposed on what was formerly a uniform, but statistically random process.

Close to equilibrium, where energy potentials are extremely low, the forward and reverse transport processes induced by resonance interfere with each other. The components of the system thus assume a state of least dissipation, with the formation of dissipative structures in the flow pattern. Dissipative structures arising in nonequilibrium conditions have the capacity for self-organization, implying a movement away from thermodynamic equilibrium. It is postulated that dissipative structures can move away from thermodynamic equilibrium and continue to obey the theorem of least dissipation, *provided they stay in the vicinity of the quasi-equilibrium state in which energy input and output are equal.* All activity in this stable state must follow a circular or cyclic pattern. Such a quasi-stable state can be attained only within the boundaries of a closed system.

Rectilineally propagating light-energy is thus converted to energy having a circular pathway in the protoorganism. The antagonism between the high rate of dissipation in the rectilineal energy flow, and the lower rate of dissipation in the cyclic flow, results in interference leading to a state of least dissipation. Rectilineal propagation is asymmetrical, or 'irreversible'; cyclic activity is 'reversible,' in the sense of being symmetrical with respect to time. Dissipative structures arise at the point of interference between the two processes.

1. *The Initiating Cycle.* The activity that, through resonance, initiates the development of the protoorganism is evident at the molecular level. If one electron of an electron pair, in a sensitive molecule, is elevated to a higher energy state, it remains in this excited condition for 10^{-7} to 10^{-8} sec before falling back to the ground state with the emission of a photon (Szent-Gyorgi, 1961; Morowitz, 1968). This activity is cyclic and symmetrical with respect to time. The energy input has the effect of inducing a time delay in the dissipative process. In the excited state the molecule is more reactive. This allows complex molecules to be formed, prolonging the time-delay before the system returns to the ground state. If the stimulus is repeated before the ground state is reached there will be interference between the forward and reverse processes, leading to a state of least dissipation. A state of least dissipation thus results from the amplification of the initial time-delay, a time-delay contingent on the fact that the rate at which the ground state is regained is governed by the laws of probability. The energy pulse thus establishes a resonance effect leading to the temporary accumulation of energy and the assumption of a less probable state.

Energy accumulation promotes order in thermostatic conditions; it promotes order and organization in nonequilibrium conditions. There is thus established an antagonism between the tendency to return to the ground state as rapidly as possible with the emission of photons, and the tendency toward increased time-delay in energy flow through increasingly complex, cyclic flow patterns stimulated by periodic energy input.

In living organisms light energy raises the energy state of excitable molecules. The captured energy, formerly dissipated in the flash of a photon, is now dissipated slowly in the cyclic processes maintaining life.

2. *The Analogy of the Steam Traction Engine.* The antagonism between rectilinear and circular energy dissipation may be likened to the functioning of an old-fashioned steam traction engine (figure 5.6). A flow of steam from water constantly boiling within a confined space is fed to a cylinder having a movable piston. The flow of steam is periodically interrupted through suitable valving, but synchronized with the movement of the piston so as to deliver steam only when the piston is moving in one direction. A

Figure 5.6
The old-fashioned steam traction engine, showing the massive flywheel. Interaction between the rectilinear motion of the piston and the circular motion of the flywheel ensure system homeostasis. [Photo: J. Townsend]

continuous energy stream is thus converted to an oscillating movement capable of doing useful work.

Work results from differences in energy configuration. In any heat engine the power developed (the rate at which work is done) is dependent on the difference in temperature between the input and the output ports. By increasing the temperature difference, increased power can be obtained without increasing energy input. In other words the faster the energy flow through the system the greater the potential for doing work and the greater the power that can be developed.

In rudimentary form the steam engine will be very sensitive to changes in boundary conditions, such as differing load factors. To overcome this, a massive flywheel is added that has the capacity to store energy when the load is relatively light, relinquishing it as the load increases. The high inertia of the flywheel has the effect of damping, or time-delaying, responses to fluctuations in load. Regulation of the system is further improved by the addition of a governor, which increases or decreases the steam supply in response to changes in the speed of rotation of the flywheel, as brought about by changes in load. If the load is relatively constant, the system will settle down to a quasi-stable state in which the rates of energy input and output are constant. The system now functions as a homeostatic unit, returning to the original steady state if temporarily displaced by changes in load. Homeostasis is ensured because, at all speeds up to the quasi-equilibrium steady state, the rate of dissipation of energy by the circular motion of the flywheel is less than the rate of dissipation by the rectilinear movement of the piston. In the start-up phase energy input exceeds output; this condition is maintained until equality is attained at the steady state. Given these conditions the system can assume a steady state over an almost infinite range of values for the energy input, provided the work load does not increase to the point where the machine stalls. The engine can thus function effectively only between certain limits: the input must exceed zero and the load must be proportional to the input.

The biological system, damping fluctuations in energy flow, may be likened to the flywheel. However, in the biological context, the energy available is more or less consistent over considerable time periods, so that an increase in power cannot be obtained by increasing the energy input; it must come from increasing the energy throughput by internal redesign. Internal reordering of the ecosystem results from essentially random changes in configuration, with those that allow an increase in energy flow being retained, the rest being discarded.

3. *The Signal System.* At any point on the earth's surface the energy available as sunlight forms a regular pattern based on the earth's rotational characteristics. However, this regularity is clothed with a degree of variabil-

ity resulting from apparently random changes in oceanic and atmospheric circulation patterns. The regularity in the pattern of energy availability forms a time-series of signals but the variability introduces 'noise' inhibiting signal identification. Each point on the earth's surface is exposed to a unique time-series of signals since the annual energy input decreases continuously from the equator to the poles and, similarly, the variability of the signals increases with latitude. Further differences are created by local geographic factors. Over time, variability changes and over long time periods there may be changes in the mean values of individual signals. The biosystem apparently originated as a resonant response to these signals.

The availability of energy for the support of biological processes depends not only on the pattern and intensity of sunlight, but the pattern of moisture and nutrient availability and the changes in ambient temperature. These factors combined, determine the amount of energy assimilated and the pattern of its assimilation. Together they determine the local signal medley.

The characteristics of the time-series of signals at any one locality are reflected in the structure of the ecosystem at that point. In Southwood's (1977) terminology, the environment forms a 'templet' around which the ecosystem is structured from the species available.

The trend to increasing energy flow rates causes organisms to explore the 'signal hyperspace' of the system. Heterogeneity and maximum attainable energy flow is achieved by the identification of the greatest number of signal sets possible. This tendency is opposed by the individual species. Within the symmetrically interacting group, or ecodeme, organisms function coherently, expanding in the direction of an increase in the bandwidth of the signal set identified. Homogeneity is the identification and assimilation of all signals by a single species. Heterogeneity is the identification of the greatest number of signals by individual species.

4. *Information and Symmetry Breaking.* In the 'primeval ooze' resonant energy storage processes may be presumed to have occurred simultaneously over a finite area. Within this confined area the charged molecules (atomisms or thermodynamic engines) interacted symmetrically, distributing the energy uniformly among individuals. In a uniform environment this results in uniform spatial distribution and a state of no change. Such homogeneity, it is postulated, was the initial condition of life. The system was well-damped, resonating to a wide range of signals. The potential between the charged components (in contradistinction to gas molecules in a closed container) was close to zero (Polanyi, 1968). These conditions, in fact, provided a *tabula rasa* available for the coding of information. *Species were formed by the breaking of the initial symmetry* (Anderson, 1972). Thus the *tabula rasa* was able to respond to the various identifiable signal sets

within the signal medley. Information of a qualitative as well as a quantitive nature was encoded. Species may be regarded as the 'hard copy' of this information extraction process.

However, *information can be extracted only at the cost of work done* (Mercer, 1981). *Hence, if the input remains constant, an increase in information can be obtained only through an increase in power.* Such an increase in power is contingent upon an increase in the rate of energy flow through the system. *An increase in information thus demands an increase in the work done and an increase in the rate of entropy production.*

5. *Hierarchy Formation.* Once the initial symmetry was broken a hierarchy formed. A hierarchy can be represented as a state of tension between uniformity and sequence. Out of this tension arises order. From the initial uniform state sequence arises by the emergence of differences. As differences develop each species will achieve a different level of integration of energy acquisition and conservation; hence a sequence is imposed on the demand for the energy available. Such a hierarchy can exist and maintain its integrity only where asymmetry is limited, that is, where the trend to uniformity slightly exceeds the trend to sequence. If this were not the case the system would enter a runaway condition and come to rest at a new position, or, in the limit, dissipate entirely. Thus, as Iberall et al. (1981) maintain, a hierarchy must attain a state of equipollence (= equal power) if it is to maintain a constant configuration. Equipollence is the state in which the power of the few at the upper level is counteracted by the power of the relatively many at the lower level. Complete symmetry can never be attained, however, since there is always a residual asymmetry inherent in the conditions essential for the maintenance of the energy flow.

A stable hierarchy thus exists in a state of tension between the two 'attractors' of homogeneity and heterogeneity. The 'treads' of the hierarchical stairway, or 'holons' (Koestler, 1967), must maintain internal uniformity and a degree of cohesion. The 'risers' (the intervals between the holons) must be finite if the holons are to remain discrete entities—continuous variation would eliminate redundancy and the capacity to store information. In the formation of an ecosystem, species must, therefore, exist as discrete entities. As complexity increases, hierarchy develops within hierarchy. Each new level adds to the information on environmental conditions and provides the means to explore new environments and overcome environmental variability. Only those species that *can* exist together in a state of equipollence *do* exist together. As McIntosh (1980) succinctly states, "All things are not possible, only some." Over a wide geographical region, ecosystems thus develop as areas of relative uniformity in spite of a continuously variable environment.

At the head of the hierarchy is the dominant species. This is the species exhibiting the 'best' integration of energy acquisition and conservation. It is the species that most closely approaches a state of homogeneity in space and time. Therefore it is the species with the smallest P/B ratio and the species exhibiting least dissipation. It is, as McNaughton and Wolf (1970) maintain, also the species with the broadest bandwidth of resource utilization. Species lower in the hierarchy are 'forced' into more specialized niches (finer tuning) and faster turnover rates.

Changes in energy availability, as the earth's environment evolves due to biological and geomorphological change, necessitates intermittent re-ordering of the hierarchical system as individual species gradually move further away from thermodynamic equilibrium, and in turn, bring about further environmental change. To continue in existence, the whole system must remain in the vicinity of dynamic quasi-equilibrium. This is possible so long as the trend to reduced dissipation exceeds the trend to increasing dissipation. To remain in quasi-equilibrium, however, may necessitate considerable changes in the system configuration. Thus organisms and ecosystems come into existence in a dynamic world of quasi-equilibrium in a region 'beyond equilibrium.' Through self-organization they improve their homeostatic capability in the face of environmental fluctuations of increasing magnitude (figure 5.7), simultaneously moving further and further away from thermodynamic equilibrium.

6. *The Ratchet Effect.* The trend to increasing diversity implies that the rate of energy flow through an ecosystem tends to increase. This may be interpreted as the inherent tendency to return to near-instantaneous dissipation of energy with the emission of photons. This property of flowing energy is reflected in a generalization of Fermat's 'Principle of Least Time.' Originally developed for light rays passing through various media of differing refractive indices, it was found that the light path could be described by the trajectory taking the least time to traverse the system, not by the least distance traveled.

Opposing this trend to least time, individual species tend to increase the time-delay in energy flow. This is achieved by mechanisms such as an increase in mean life span or an increase in size. It is furthered by an improvement in methods of energy acquisition, and the prevention of energy loss through improvement in defense mechanisms. Increased parental investment in offspring will reduce the need for juvenile replacement stock. These methods generally involve an increase in complexity; therefore they demand an increase in energy expenditure. In these circumstances, such methods will only be appropriate if they improve the integrated position of the species with respect to energy acquisition and conservation. Improved energy acquisition and accumulation in one species will reduce the total energy available to the remainder. Increased time-

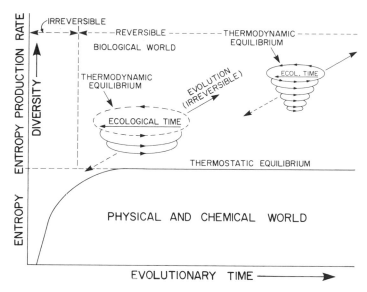

Figure 5.7
The world of quasi-equilibrium "beyond" thermodynamic equilibrium. A homeostatic system develops as a result of the reduction in the rate of dissipation of rectilineally propagating light energy due to the formation of cyclic energy pathways formed on the earth's surface. Homeostsatic dissipative structures form and evolve, provided the system remains in the vicinity of the quasi-equilibrium, where energy input equals output. Evolution is stimulated by acceleration of the rate of energy flow through the system.

delay will also tie up vital nutrients, making them unavailable to other species. To survive, the other species must also move in the direction of an improved position with respect to acquisition and conservation. However, the trend to diversity is ultimately supreme. This creates an inflationary spiral, driven by the trend toward increasing energy flow rates, in which an increasing number of species chases a finite energy supply (figure 5.8). The upward spiral is maintained by the irreversible nature of the evolutionary process—the pawl in the evolutionary ratchet.

Any significant improvement in homeostatic control attained by a particular species eventually tends to be offset by an increase in diversity at the new level (adaptive radiation) and an increase in dependent species (predators, parasites, etc.). The interaction between homogeneity and heterogeneity, with the 'edge' always in favor of heterogeneity and irreversibility, 'winches-up' the system toward greater complexity, greater diversity, and an increased rate of energy flow.

7. *Directionality and Cyclic Activity.* Asymmetricality imposes directionality on the cyclic component. The asymmetrical, irreversible component of

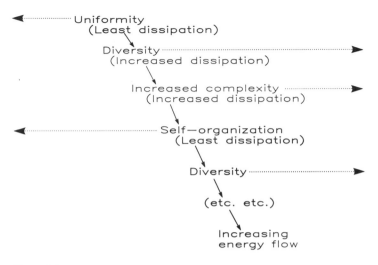

Figure 5.8
The ratchet effect. The *Pull-devil-pull-baker* effect of the interaction between uniformity and diversity. These two nearly equal forces struggle for ascendancy. Over ecological time the trend to homogeneity prevails but over evolutionary times the system is gradually 'winched-up' to increased diversity and an increase in average complexity through the slight ascendancy of the forces leading to increased energy flow rate.

increasing dissipation is recognizable in the evolutionary continuum. Cyclic (time-symmetrical), energy accumulating processes form the 'ecological' component. The individual organism is the cyclic, reversible component, eventually returning to water, carbon dioxide, and nutrients at the termination of its life span; the species or ecodeme through the genetic mechanism provides continuity through ecological time. Ecosystems characteristically exhibit natural cyclic processes in the vicinity of the climax, as Watt (1947) discusses in his classic examination of ecosystem 'pattern and process.' Similarly Wright (1974) concluded that long-term cyclic effects result from intermittent fires in northern woodlands of the United States. A mosaic of cells, each at a different stage within the cycle, is thus formed allowing the whole to remain in a dynamic steady state. The formation of cells is, in itself, a damping mechanism since complete synchronization of oscillations would lead to violent and possibly lethal fluctuations. By analogy, inadequately damped mechanical structures may resonate to small vibrations at their natural frequency, resulting in a buildup of self-destructive energy levels. Interestingly, this characteristic of strong oscillations in energy level is inherent in certain species, such as the Pacific salmon (*Oncorhynchus spp.*); it is apparently induced by the adoption of a set life span. Presumably, fluctuations are under some degree of internal control and are an adaptation to the environmental setting in which the species finds itself. On the other hand, extreme fluctuations in abundance, stimulated by environmental disturbance, preceded the total demise of the blue pike, *Stizostedion vitreum glaucum*, in Lake Erie (Parsons, 1967; Regier et al., 1969).

8. *The Biosystem as an Information Processor.* As diversity increases energy flow rates increase, reducing the internal resistance, hence reducing internal damping. Reduced damping necessitates finer-tuning to the signal set identified. Since fine-tuning represents specialization, the trend to specialization, imposed by interspecific interactional processes, is offset by the trend of the individual species toward a broader bandwidth of resource utilization. Broad resource utilization spectra and high damping capacity are characteristic of species in the upper part of the hierarchy (*K*-selected); species at lower levels have faster turnover rates and shorter response times (*r*-selected). A fast response time enables a species to track energy fluctuations quite closely, making for efficient energy acquisition in a fluctuating energy stream. The whole biosystem thus functions as an information extraction and storage device, in which units of information function as a series of coupled shock-absorbers imposing increased damping (and less precise information) at each successive hierarchical level. A great array of small shock-absorbers develops, and more work is done relative to the biomass, where environmental fluctuations are small and where energy input is high and uniform. Where environmental variability is high and/or total energy availability is low a few, 'heavy-duty' shock-absorbers develop. This 'heavy-duty' equipment utilizes a high degree of redundancy and a long turnover time to ensure adequate transmission of the rather poorly defined information. Consequently, with increasing latitude and increasing environmental variability, diversity declines and the number of individuals in each species increases.

The view that emerges is that the whole biosystem functions as a communications network, extracting, storing, and transmitting information. Support for this position is provided by the work of J. W. MacArthur. MacArthur (1975) showed that there is an inverse relationship between environmental fluctuation and species diversity, similar in its characteristics to that relating changes in the transmission of information to increasing noise in an information channel. This relationship he found to hold good over a wide range of species and environments.

9. *The Nonequilibrium World.* Asymmetries cause change. The second law of thermodynamics is a reflection of the inherent tendency of energy and matter to eliminate inequalities and approach a steady state of uniform energy distribution. This state of no change is reached by a route diametrically opposed to that taken in the process of homeokinesis. Asymmetries

are, however, essential for energy flow, and flows initiate change; continuous changes in energy flow initiate continuous change. Since energy flow must be maintained, a state of maximum entropy is a static, nonallowable state. It is therefore largely irrelevant in the biological world and only becomes of major significance when the energy flow ceases. Uniformity, attained through homeokinesis and energy equipartitioning, allows charged atomisms temporarily to evade the rule of the second law. This demands that the system be continuously recharged through a suitable energy input.

In the dynamic context of the nonequilibrium biological world the appropriate equivalent law is that the system tends toward *an increase in the rate of entropy production*. The result is an inversion, in the 'looking-glass' world of quasi-equilibrium, of many of the characteristics prevailing in the world of thermodynamic equilibrium. An increase in the number of complexions is equivalent to an increase in diversity and an increase in the number of asymmetrical interactions. This demands an increase in work done and an increase in entropy production; hence increased diversity emerges as increased 'information,' not as increased 'disorder.' The increase in power is obtained from the inherent trend of the energy flow to least residence time. The increase in information is qualitative as well as quantitative. The qualitative information is expressed in the innumerable characteristics of organisms that are generally recognized in the term 'adaptation.'

5.4 *Testing the Hypothesis*

If a hypothesis is to gain scientific credibility it must be testable. The basic proposition to be tested in the present context is the clash between the fundamental realities that are represented by various concepts. This clash of underlying realities is reflected in the antagonism between symmetrical and asymmetrical interaction, between reversibility and irreversibility, between rectilinear and circular energy flows, between total redundancy and zero redundancy, between acceleration and deceleration of the rate of dissipation, and between increasing specialization and reduced damping, and broader resource use spectra with increased damping. It seems most likely that these concepts represent manifestations of the same basic phenomenon, since the significant feature, in each case, is that life exists at the point of intersection of each antagonistic pair. Life thus emerges as a compromise between two extreme positions that can be attained only in the vicinity of quasi-equilibrium.

Direct testing of such concepts is extremely difficult for reasons similar to those that have made direct testing of evolutionary theory a long and tedious process, namely, the relative shortness of one investigator's life span and the lack of adequate controls, since ultimately a single system is under consideration. Testing must therefore be carried out for the most part indirectly through inductive processes. This cannot be done in detail at present for it involves the greater part of ecology and paleontology. Only the general outlines of the testing procedure can be sketched. Four main avenues have been selected. The first, following Einstein, is the thought experiment, used to determine how a theory stands up in hypothetical circumstances. The second is how the theory accords with accepted generalities and its capacity to develop new general conclusions. Third is the light the theory can throw on specific cases or apparent anomalies, and finally there is the intriguing question of communication.

1. *The Thought Experiment.* The first approach, through 'thought experiments,' is most revealing. If we consider an ecosystem in a quasi-equilibrium state, poised between the two attractors of homogeneity and heterogeneity, we can examine the limiting conditions by eliminating the effect of each attractor in turn. If heterogeneity is allowed to proceed to the limit of infinite diversity, then dissipation will be instantaneous. Photons will be emitted and the system will cease to exist as the light passes on its rectilinear way. Discontinuous variation within an ecosystem is thus mandatory for existence since infinite diversity presupposes continuous variation.[2] Species must therefore function as discrete entities. It is also relevant that instantaneous dissipation of energy occurs, with the emission of photons, when organic matter 'burns.' Burning is the instantaneous completion of the 'reversible' cycle to carbon dioxide, water, and mineral nutrients with the liberation of heat.

Proceeding toward the limit of homogeneity, the rate of dissipation falls to zero. Such a state of symmetry and zero dissipation is found in crystals, formed from symmetrically arranged molecules. Crystals, like organisms, can exist only within certain well-defined environmental conditions, and they can form only in the vicinity of equilibrium under the effect of very delicate forces. The greatest crystal growth is achieved when the energy exchanges associated with crystal formation proceed extremely slowly. It is also significant that many of the most important biological compounds, such as proteins, have a crystal-like structure. As Anderson (1972) comments, "This type of 'information-bearing crystallinity' seems to be essential to life." The essential difference between a 'regular' crystal and an organism is that the organism must remain in a dynamic state of 'incipient crystallization.' The reaction must never proceed to completion.

Paradoxically, both 'attractor states' of homogeneity and heterogeneity are lethal. To remain in existence organisms must remain in the vicinity of the null-point in the field established between them; this is effected through assimilation of the appropriate energy flows. Only in the vicinity of the null-point can a quasi-equilibrium state be attained. This state, as in the quasi-equilibrium of the steam engine, can only exist within the homeo-static capability of the system.

2. *The Vertical and Horizontal Components of Evolution.* One of the major generalities in evolutionary theory is the recognition of 'vertical' and 'horizontal' components to evolution (Mayr, 1976, 1982). The vertical component is represented by the gradual increase in complexity in certain evolutionary lines. This directional component has given rise to the general notion of 'progress.' At the leading edge of this 'progressive' trend is, of course, man himself. This trend is certainly real. Progress can be regarded as increasing homeostatic ability, or the capacity to withstand increasing levels of environmental fluctuation and the ability to utilize a wider range of resources. Man himself lives in a wider range of environmental con-ditions and utilizes a wider range of resources than any other species now existing. This trend has given rise to innumerable disputes about teleology and directionality in evolution. According to the present thesis, the vert-ical, 'progressive' element in evolution arises from the directionality im-parted by the continual acceleration of the energy flow rate through in-creased diversity, stimulating increasing complexity. The 'telos' or goal of a species is homogeneity, to be attained through the acquisition and equi-partitioning of the total energy available (a goal man himself appears to be approaching rapidly). The 'goal' of the system is diversity and instanta-neous dissipation.

The horizontal component of evolution is 'speciation,' the adaptive radiation of species at equivalent levels of organization. In the present context, this is the exploration of the various melodies in the total signal medley. At any point in evolutionary time there is the possibility of change in either one of two directions. Each advance in a vertical direction through self-organization, temporarily providing a closer approach to homogeneity, is subsequently 'undercut' at the new level by thorough exploration of the new signal hyperspace.

3. *Interspecific Organization at High Diversity.* The third approach to test-ing the hypothesis is with respect to specific cases. Can the hypothesis be used to explain apparent anomalies? One of the most interesting aspects of high diversity is the development of what appears to be interspecific organization, or the development of true communities within an eco-system. A true community is defined as a group of species exhibiting a common goal. This concerted activity is clearly seen in the 'Mbuna fish communities of Lake Malawi (Fryer, 1959; Fryer and Iles, 1972; McKaye and Marsh, 1983), the bird communities of the Peruvian rain forests in the Amazon Basin (Munn, 1984), and in the grazing sequence of ungulates in the Serengeti National Park in East Africa (Bell, 1971; McNaughton, 1984). This interspecific organization can be interpreted in terms of 'near-

symmetry,' although these cases appear to have arisen through 'restored symmetry' rather than 'broken symmetry.'

With increasing diversity, interactional differentials between species necessarily decline, provided energy input remains constant. Thus, at extremely high diversity, a state of near-symmetry is reached with respect to species at an equivalent trophic level. At a certain point these near-symmetrically interacting species enter the 'domain of attraction' created by the state of incipient homogeneity. This state of near-symmetry allows interspecific organization to develop, the common goal being the elimination of potentially lethal fluctuations that would otherwise occur if diversity were less. Where differences in potential are very low (approaching zero) stability depends on complex relationships and multiple interactions. At the microscopic level, Monod (1971) recognizes this multiplicity of interactions as essential to the stability of those complex organic molecules that are dependent on noncovalent bonds.

Symmetrical interaction between species appears to be essential for coevolution, the attainment of mutually beneficial goals. The extreme example of coevolution would be exhibited, if fully substantiated, in the highly probable proposition that the eucaryote cell originated from the integration of several quite different life-forms (Margulis, 1970, 1971). Only through symmetrical interaction between the partners could such a composite organism have originated.

4. *Communication.* The final matter for present consideration is the field of communication. Communication is defined in this context as an exchange of signals that has the effect of restricting the behavior of the ensemble (Mercer, 1981). Prigogine and Stengers (1984) recognize that the existence and functioning of dissipative structures is dependent upon communication between the components. Communication between component atomisms is also implicit in the doctrine of homeokinesis propounded by Soodak and Iberall (1978). If atomisms interact and equipartition the energy available to them, they must communicate. As Soodak and Iberall state, "Such complex atomisms do not equipartition interaction energy per collisional cycle, but instead internally time-delay, process and transform collisional inputs, generally using many fluidlike dissipative mobile steps." This is communication at its most basic level, but only through communication at this level can cohesion and uniformity within a group be maintained. Additionally, the atomisms must exist in a state of near-symmetry if communication is to be established.

Perhaps the most significant communications network established in the biological field is that of the genetic system. Through the genetic mechanism information is stored and passed from generation to generation down the long halls of time. By means of the process of natural selection, environmental information is coded only when it has been established that the signal is true, in the sense of being repeated indefinitely. The genetic system thus functions as an information control mechanism, extracting and maintaining the essential signal and damping the effect of environmental noise through a delayed response to change.

By contrast, the transmission of acquired characteristics is inherently unstable since it eliminates the damping factor, promoting immediate and possibly lethal fluctuation in response to short-term change. There is thus imminent danger in the situation in which man now finds himself; having adopted the inheritance of acquired characteristics through cultural development and, in recent times, even throwing off the damping mechanisms inherent in tradition and natural conservatism, he is on a wave of rapidly increasing biomass. Perhaps the inheritance of acquired characteristics has evolved in other species in times past, only to be eliminated with great rapidity.

In more immediate circumstances, any group acting coherently is dependent on instantaneous, or undamped, communication. This clearly exists in many groups, as demonstrated by the activities of communal insects, fish schools, and ungulate herds, no less than in the societies of man. The evolutionary cause of coherent group action, which may be described in general terms as 'herding,' has been sought in a specific advantage as, for example, in defense against predators. But, as McNaughton (1984) points out, the causes of herding are multiple and its occurrence widely distributed throughout many phyla. If it is recognized that there is a fundamental need in all organisms to communicate to maintain coherence, it is not necessary to regard herding, or any other group activity, as an original evolutionary direction each time its existence is recognized. The existence of a basic communication faculty allows any advantage gained by communal activity to be magnified rapidly, irrespective of specific circumstances.

Less well accepted is the effect of group activity on the population dynamics of organisms—the field of self-regulation (Wynne-Edwards, 1978). Nevertheless, its significance is emerging. Responses to disturbance demanding cohesion between individuals are clearly apparent in the population dynamics of Arctic charr, *Salvelinus alpinus*, and other northern fish species (Johnson, 1976, 1983). The major features indicating coherence of the fish stocks are (1) the capacity to maintain a constant size-frequency distribution following perturbation, and (2) the return to a former size and density configuration, without oscillation, following displacement (Johnson, 1976, 1983). It is also apparent, since only a single fish species is involved, that these responses are internally mediated, and are not the result of interspecific interaction. Populations as widely separated as the tawny owl, *Strix aluco* (Southern, 1970a,b), the blind cave fish, *Amblyopsis*

(Poulson, 1963), and the giant tortoise of Aldabra, *Geochelone gigantaeus* (Gaymer, 1968; Grubb, 1971; Gibson and Hamilton, 1983) have all been shown to exhibit similar population characteristics.

If communication is a general attribute of living organisms, then it is also necessary to postulate its existence in plants. This is a subject that has been relatively little explored, yet there is considerable evidence to indicate that it does exist. For example, in European virgin forests, Jones (1945) found a high degree of uniformity in the size structure of the dominant tree species, despite great differences in age between individuals. This situation is identical to that found in the fish stocks of Arctic lakes. Perhaps even more intriguing are the results of Harper's (1967) reanalysis of Tamm's (1948, 1956) data on Scandinavian meadows. Harper showed that species with high individual turnover rates maintained constant density; in addition he found that species disappeared from an ecosystem experiencing environmental change, *not abruptly, but in a slow, orderly manner*. Werner and Caswell (1977) also showed in their study of the teazel, *Dipsacus sylvestris*, that there were population effects that would not have emerged from a study of the properties of individuals. Interesting studies are at present in progress on ethylene as a gaseous plant hormone (Sisler and Yang, 1984) and on the chemical stimulation of protective compounds in trees adjacent to individuals of the same species subject to insect attack (Schultz, 1983; Schultz and Baldwin, 1982).

5.5 *Conclusions*

The origin and evolution of organisms, it is hypothesized, is dependent on the existence of very delicate forces inducing energy equipartitioning and symmetry, only evident in the physical world close to equilibrium. Organisms appear to represent a macroscopic amplification of these processes. As Orians (1980) suggests, "Meaningful aggregate variables must be based upon—and be a reasonable extension of—known or suspected processes at lower levels." In the biological world the processes occurring in the vicinity of equilibrium have been amplified by resonance. This has resulted in self-organization through a 'ratchet effect,' induced by continual interaction between symmetry and asymmetry in a fundamentally asymmetrical environment. In this state of near-symmetry, resonance allows the forces inducing homogeneity to attain short-term ascendancy through magnification of the time-delay exhibited by the excited molecule before it returns to the ground state. The resulting energy-charged atomisms have the capacity for self-organization, but only if the whole system is maintained close to a quasi-equilibrium state. Only in conditions of quasi-equilibrium can the symmetry be broken and information coded and yet overall symmetry at the same time be maintained.

Many of the foregoing aspects of the living world are most clearly illuminated by man's present condition and his relationship with the rest of the biological world, for we are a species in transition, imposing changes of great magnitude on the biosystem. Ever since the Newtonian-Cartesian paradigm ordained science to be objective and free from value judgments, we have been peering out from our near-symmetrical, cyclic world, originally close to thermodynamic equilibrium, onto a world where the more interesting and most studied events and activities have been caused by asymmetrical interaction. In the name of science this led to the application of value-free precepts to the biological world. Action based on simple, asymmetrical notions of causality has led to much undesirable ecological change.

If we wish to maintain the world in a near-steady state then we must think in terms of symmetrical interaction and cyclic processes. Only in this way will it be possible to regain the fragile quasi-equilibrium on which all existence ultimately depends. Asymmetrical interaction has stimulated a great increase in the rate of energy flow that will be difficult to maintain over future generations. We have been further misled, through the great development of robust homeostatic mechanisms in living organisms, into believing that systems could survive irrespective of their treatment. In reality we have been living on borrowed stability that has taken 3.5 billion years to evolve.

If we are to reestablish a near-symmetrical biological world it will be essential to reconnect ethics with the sciences (Toulmin, 1981). Ethics depend on judgment and judgment and the biological sciences become intimately associated for there are no fixed points of reference in the nonequilibrium world; life is a compromise. Ethics may be defined as the maintenance of near-symmetry through the conscious limitation of the degree of asymmetry that we impose on the rest of the world, both with respect to our conspecifics and with respect to all other species. "Social interaction is the thread from which the fabric of moral character is woven" (Thomas, 1985). The paradox is that we live in a slightly asymmetrical world, and this we cannot alter, nor perhaps would we want to, since it would preclude all further development of thought or action. Highly asymmetrical interaction may bring immense immediate reward, but it also induces potentially lethal fluctuations. Only if the level of asymmetry is such as to induce change very slowly, allowing the system to accommodate continuously, will a satisfactory *modus vivendi* be attained. This state can be achieved only through the application of value-judgments.

The forgoing of immediate self-interest with the aim of future general good is thus an essential ingredient of near-symmetry maintenance at all levels of organization. If this is not recognized then the system will itself eliminate the inequalities, without regard to ethical or 'humanitarian' precept.

Acknowledgments

I greatly appreciate the support and encouragement of Eric Schneider, Gordon Koshinsky, and an organizer of the symposium at California State University, Fullerton, James Smith, during the preparation of this manuscript. I also thank Gordon Koshinsky, Mary Layton, and Bonnie Burns for their editorial assistance and Laurie Tate, who drew the figures. I am indebted to J. Townsend of the Department of Agriculture, University of Manitoba, for supplying the photograph of the old-style traction engine.

I thank the editors of *Science* for permission to reproduce figure 5.1, and the editors of the *Canadian Journal of Fisheries and Aquatic Science* for allowing me to reproduce figure 5.2.

Notes

1. Anderson (1972, p. 14) states, "... most methods of extracting energy from the environment in order to set up a continuing, quasi-stable state process involve time-periodic machines, such as oscillators and generators, and the processes of life work the same way." If I understand Anderson correctly, however, he is suggesting that organisms have the inherent capacity to oscillate, thus extracting energy from the environment, rather than the present thesis that the driving oscillations are the alternating periods of darkness and daylight and periodic seasonal shifts. Organisms are, in fact, resonators, not just adapted to oscillations.

2. I believe that it is most relevant that Gribbin (1984, p. 31), describing how Planck, searching for a satisfactory mathematical interpretation of blackbody radiation, derived his famous constant using Boltzmann's equation, albeit, it appears, somewhat reluctantly. This demanded "cutting energy up into chunks, mathematically and treating the chunks as real quantities that could be handled by the probability equations." Gribbin continues, "Instead of dividing the available amount of energy up in an infinite number of ways, it could only be divided into a finite number of pieces among the resonators, and the energy of such a piece of radiation (E) must be related to the frequency (denoted by the Greek letter nu, v) according to the new formula,

$$E = hv,$$

where h is the new constant, now called Planck's constant."

References

Anderson, P. W., 1972. More is different: broken symmetry and the hierarchical structure of science. *Science* 177:393–396.

Bell, R. H. V., 1971. A grazing system in the Serengeti. *Sci. Amer.* 225:86–93.

Boucot, A. J., 1983. Does evolution take place in an ecological vacuum? *J. Paleontology* 57:1–30.

102   Lionel Johnson

Clements, F. E., 1905. *Research Methods in Ecology*. Lincoln, NE: Univ. Publ. Co.

Connell, J. H., and E. Orias, 1964. The ecological regulation of species diversity. *Am. Nat.* 98:399–414.

Fischer, A. G., 1960. Latitudinal variations in organic diversity. *Evolution* 14:64–81.

Fryer, G., 1959. The trophic interrelationships and ecology of some littoral communities of Lake Nyasa, with especial reference to the fishes and a discussion of the rock-frequenting Cichlidae. *Proc. Zool. Soc. Lond.* 132:153–181.

Fryer, G., and T. D. Iles, 1972. *The Cichlid Fishes of the Great Lakes of Africa*. Edinburgh: Oliver and Boyd.

Gaymer, R., 1968. The Indian Ocean giant tortoise, *Testudo gigantea*, on Aldabra. *J. Zool. Lond.* 154:341–363.

Gibson, C. W. D., and J. Hamilton, 1983. Feeding ecology and seasonal movements of the giant tortoises on Aldabra Atoll. *Oecologia* 56:4–92.

Gribbin, J., 1984. *In Search of Schrodinger's Cat; Quantum Physics and Reality*. Toronto: Bantam Books.

Grubb, P., 1971. The growth, ecology, and population structure of the giant tortoises on Aldabra. *Phil. Trans. Roy. Soc. Lond. (B)* 260:327–372.

Harper, J. L., 1967. A Darwinian approach to plant ecology. *J. Ecol.* 55:274–280.

Hutchinson, G. E., 1959. Homage to Santa Rosalia: or why are there so many different kinds of animals? *Am. Nat.* 93:145–157.

Iberall, A. H., H. Soodak, and C. Arensburg, 1981. Homeokinetic physics of societies—a new discipline: autonomous groups, cultures, polities. In *Perspectives in Biomechanics*, H. Real, D. Ghista, and G. Rau, eds., vol. 1. Part I. New York: Harwood Academic Press.

Johnson, L., 1976. The ecology of Arctic populations of lake trout, *Salvelinus namaycush*, lake whitefish, *Coregonus clupeaformis*, arctic char, *S. alpinus*, and associated species in unexploited lakes of the Canadian Northwest Territories. *J. Fish. Res. Board Can.* 33:2459–2488.

Johnson, L., 1981. The thermodynamic origin of ecosystems. *Can. J. Fish. Aquat. Sci.* 38:571–590.

Johnson, L., 1983. Homeostatic mechanisms in single species fish stocks in Arctic lakes. *Can. J. Fish. Aquat. Sci.* 40:987–1024.

Jones, E. W., 1945. The structure and reproduction of the virgin forest of the north temperate zone. *New. Phytol.* 44:130–148.

Kleiber, M., 1932. Body size and metabolism. *Hilgardia* 6:315–318.

Koestler, A., 1967. *The Ghost in the Machine*. London: Picador.

Leigh, E. G., 1965. On the relation between productivity, biomass, diversity, and stability of a community. *Proc. Natl. Acad. Sci. U.S.A.* 53:777–783.

MacArthur, J. W., 1975. Environmental fluctuations and species diversity. In *The Ecology and Evolution of Communities*, M. L. Cody and J. M. Diamond, eds., Cambridge, MA: Bellknap Press.

MacArthur, R. H., 1965. Patterns in species diversity. *Biol. Rev.* 40:510–533.

Margalef, R., 1963. On certain unifying principles in ecology. *Am. Nat.* 47:357–374.

Margalef, R., 1968. *Perspectives in Ecological Theory.* Chicago: University of Chicago Press.

Margulis, L., 1970. *Origin of Eukaryotic Cells. Evidence and Research Implications for a Theory of Origin and Evolution of Microbial, Plant, and Animal Cells on Precambrian Earth.* New Haven: Yale University Press.

Margulis, L., 1971. Symbiosis and evolution. *Sci. Amer.* 225:48–57.

Mayr. E., 1976. *Evolution and the Diversity of Life.* Cambridge, MA: Bellknap Press.

Mayr, E., 1982. *The Growth of Biological Thought.* Cambridge, MA: Bellknap Press.

McIntosh, R. P., 1980. The relationship between succession and the recovery process in ecosystems. In *The Recovery Process in Ecosystems,* J. Cairns, ed., Ann Arbor: Ann Arbor Science.

McKaye, K. R., and A. Marsh. 1983. Food switching in two specialized Cichlid fishes in Lake Malawi, Africa. *Oecologia* 56:245–284.

McNaughton, S. J., 1984. Grazing lawns: animals in herds, plant form and coevolution. *Am. Nat.* 124:863–886.

McNaughton, S. J., and L. L. Wolf, 1970. Dominance and the niche in ecological systems. *Science* 167:131–139.

Medawar, P. B., 1945. Size, Shape and Age. In *Essays on Growth and Form,* Le Gros Clark and P. B. Medawar, eds., London: Oxford University Press.

Mercer, E., 1981. *Biological Theory.* New York: Wiley Interscience.

Monod, J., 1971. *Chance and Necessity.* New York: Alfred Knopf.

Morowitz, H. J., 1968. *Energy Flow in Biology.* New York: Academic Press.

Munn, C. A., 1984. Birds of a different feather also flock together. *Nat. Hist.* 93:34–42.

Odum, E. P., 1969. The strategy of ecosystem development. *Science* 164:262–270.

Onsager, L., 1931. Reciprocal relations in irreversible processes. *Phys. Rev.* 37:405–426.

Orians, G. H., 1980. Micro and macro in ecological theory. *Bioscience* 30:1

Parsons, J. W., 1967. Contributions to the year classes of blue pike to the commercial fishery of Lake Erie, 1943–1959. *J. Fish. Res. Board Can.* 24:1035–1059.

Pittendrigh, C. S., 1958. Adaptation, natural selection and behaviour. In *Behavior and Evolution,* A. Rowe and G. G. Simpson, eds., New Haven: Yale University Press.

Polanyi, M., 1968. Life's irreducible structure. *Science* 160:1308–1312.

Poulson, T. L., 1963. Cave adaptation in Amblyopsid fishes. *Am. Mid. Nat.* 70:257–290.

Prigogine, I., 1978. Time, structure, and fluctuations. *Science* 201:775–785.

Prigogine, I., and I. Stengers, 1984. *Order out of Chaos.* New York: Bantam.

Prigogine, I., and J. M. Wiame, 1946. Biologie et thermodynamique des phenomenes irreversibles. *Experientia* 2:451–453.

Raup, D. M., and J. J. Sepkoski, 1982. Mass extinctions in the marine fossil record. *Science* 215:1501–1503.

Regier, H. A., V. C. Applegate, and R. A. Ryder, 1969. The ecology and management of walleye in western Lake Erie. Great Lakes Fishery Commission, Tech. Rep. 15.

Schall, J. J., and E. R. Pianka, 1978. Geographical trends in the number of species. *Science* 201:679–686.

Schultz, J. C., 1983. Tree tactics. *Nat. Hist.* May.

Schultz, J. C., and I. T. Baldwin, 1982. Oak leaf quality declines in response to defoliation by gypsy moth larvae. *Science* 217:149–150.

Sepkoski, J. J., R. K. Bambach, D. M. Raup, and J. W. Valentine, 1981. Phanerozoic marine diversity and the fossil record. *Nature* 293:435–437.

Simpson, G. G., 1949. *The Meaning of Evolution: A Study of the History of Life and of Its Significance for Man.* New Haven: Yale University Press.

Simpson, G. G., 1953. *The Major Features of Evolution.* New York: Columbia University Press.

Simpson, G. G., 1969. The first three billion years of community evolution. In *Diversity and Stability in Ecological Systems*, G. M. Woodwell and H. H. Smith, eds., Brookhaven Symp. Biol. 22.

Sisler, E. C., and S. F. Yang, 1984. Ethylene, the gaseous plant hormone. *BioScience* 34:234–238.

Soodak, H., and A. Iberall, 1978. Homeokinesis: a physical science for complex systems. *Science* 201:579–582.

Southern, H. N., 1970a. Ecology at the crossroads. *J. Ecol.* 58:1–11.

Southern, H. N., 1970b. The natural control of a population of tawny owls, *Strix aluco. J. Zool. Lond.* 162:197–285.

Southwood, T. R. E., 1977. Habitat, the templet for ecological strategies? *J. Animal Ecol.* 46:337–365.

Stehli, F. G., 1968. Taxonomic diversity gradients in pole location: the recent model. In *Evolution and Environment*, Ellen T. Drake, ed., New Haven: Yale University Press.

Stehli, F. G., R. G. Douglas, and N. D. Newell, 1969. Generation and maintenance of gradients in taxonomic diversity. *Science* 164:947–949.

Szent-Gyorgi, A., 1961. Introductory comments in *A Symposium on Light and Life*, W. D. McElroy and B. Glass, eds., Baltimore: Johns Hopkins Press, pp. 7–10.

Tamm, C. O., 1948. Observation and survival of some perennial herbs. *Bot. Not.* 3:305–321.

Tamm, C. O., 1956. Further observations on survival and flowering of some perennial herbs. *Oikos* 7:273–292.

Thomas, L., 1985. Love and morality: the possibility of altruism. In *Sociobiology and Epistemology*, J. H. Fetzer, ed., Boston: D. Reidel.

Thorpe, W. H., 1974. *Animal Nature and Human Nature.* New York: Doubleday.

Toulmin, S., 1981. How can we reconnect the sciences with the foundations of ethics? In *The Roots of Ethics: Science, Religion and Values*, D. Callahan and H. I. Englehart, eds., New York: Plenum Press.

Tramer, E. J., 1967. Bird species diversity: components of Shannon's formula. *Ecology* 50: 927–929.

Wallace, A. R., 1978. *Tropical Nature and Other Essays*. London: MacMillan.

Watt, A. S., 1947. Pattern and process in the plant community. *J. Ecol.* 35:1–44.

Werner, P. A., and H. Caswell, 1977. Population growth rates and age versus stage-distribution for Teazel (*Dipsacus sylvestris* Huds.). *Ecology* 58:1103–1111.

Whittaker, R. H., 1969. Evolution of diversity in plant communities. In *Diversity and Stability in Ecological Systems*, G. M. Woodwell and H. H. Smith, eds., Brookhaven Symp. Biol. 22.

Wright, H. E., 1974. Landscape development, forest fires, and wilderness management. *Science* 186:487–495.

Wynne-Edwards, V. C., 1978. Intrinsic population control. In *Population Control by Social Behavior*, F. J. Ebling and D. M. Stoddart, eds., Symp. 23, Inst. Biol. London.

6

Thermodynamics, Ecological Succession, and Natural Selection: A Common Thread

Eric D. Schneider

Darwin's proposal that biological variation, replication, and selection were the essential aspects of the evolution of species has provided a century-long research program. Even though Darwin and the neo-Darwinian researchers have developed powerful descriptions of "how" certain aspects of evolution have occurred, present evolutionary theory does not answer the question "why" evolution has proceeded to develop into the patterns observed in nature. Present day Darwinism is also limited because it fails to uphold some of the basic tenets required of other scientific disciplines, that of predictability and scientific hypothesis testing (Popper, 1972; Wicken, 1980). Evolutionary theory has remained aloof from basic physical principles and never seems to have broken away from tautological arguments such as, "Survival of the fittest. Fit for what? Fit for survival." Natural selection cannot predict future states or functions and never really answers the question, What does natural selection select? However, today there are a group of evolutionary theorists who are attempting to develop a theoretical foundation for Darwinian evolution within the confines of modern thermodynamics. Wicken (1980, 1984, and this volume), Allen (1985), Ulanowicz (1980, 1986), Conrad (1983), Wiley (1983 and this volume), Wiley and Brooks (1982), Peacocke (1983), Saunders and Ho (1981), Kay (1984), Johnson (1981 and this volume), and others are building on the work of Clausius, Boltzmann, Schrödinger, Onsager, Prigogine, Morowitz, and Lotka, and an exciting and an important dialogue has developed that may permit this bold synthesis to define research programs for evolution and thermodynamics as well.

This paper enters this discussion from the field of ecology and explores the universal process of ecological succession in a thermodynamic context. Specifically, I shall examine the suggestion that early in the successional process, growth, or the maximization of structure, information and free energy dominates and later in succession the development of complexity and efficiency prevails (Lotka, 1925; Odum and Pinkerton, 1955; Margalef, 1968; and Wicken, 1980). These thermodynamic selection principles have been tested mathematically and experimentally, and produce recognizable phenomenological manifestations in natural ecosystems. The principles ap-

pear applicable to all other living systems from cells, organisms, populations, and ecosystems to phylogenetic evolution itself.

I shall begin with a synthesis of modern thermodynamics, integrating
these principles into ecology and developing a thermodynamically based
selection principle that can provide evolutionary theory with a much
needed linkage to mathematics and physics.

6.1 A Review of Thermodynamics

The initial principles of thermodynamics first were developed by Carnot in
1824 and later refined by Clausius in 1865. Carnot's principles, known as
the first and second laws of thermodynamics, were developed during his
study of the mechanical power developed by steam engines. The first law,
refined by Rumford and Joulee, may be best stated, "Energy cannot be
created or destroyed." This simply means that, despite the transformation
that energy is constantly undergoing in nature (i.e., mechanical work,
electrical energy, or chemical transformation), the total energy within that
closed or isolated system remains unchanged. Einstein added another form
of energy to science with his equivalence of mass and energy. Mass
represents a potential energy. Brillouin (1962) noted accordingly that the
old principle of conservation of mass is enlarged and integrated into a
newer energy conservation principle including energy and mass.

Simply stated, the second law provides that no process in nature involving physical, chemical, biological, or informational energy transformations
will occur spontaneously without some energetic cost (entropy). Clausius
borrowed the word "entropy" from the Greek word for transformation,
and mathematically defined entropy S with the equation

$$dS = \frac{dQ}{T},\tag{1}$$

and according to Clausius

$$dS = \frac{dQ}{T} \geqslant 0,\tag{2}$$

or the entropy change (dS) is related to the reversible heat addition (dQ) to
the system divided by the absolute temperature (T).

Entropy constrains the direction that natural processes take. Its increasing production results from irreversible transformations in nature. This
universal increase in entropy has been called the "arrow of time" (Eddington, 1958), resulting in an increase in randomness within our presumably
bounded universe.

Entropy is a macroscopic or an extensive property of systems, and like volume and size, is presumed to be an integrative aspect of some assumed sets of microstates. Boltzmann developed the statistical representation of the macrostate-microstate relationship and defined entropy as

$$S = -K \sum_{i=1}^{n} p_i \log p_i, \tag{3}$$

where p_i is the probability of an individual element of the system being in any one of the n cells constituting a phase space and K is Boltzmann's constant. Thus entropy can be thought of as the statistical constraints on the filling of a microstate in a thermodynamic system.

The first and second laws are subject to one important condition that is generally not true of all nature: that all these energy exchanges take place in a closed and isolated system. Natural chemical or physical systems rarely are closed, as energy or material fluxes through most regions of the universe. The earth is not a closed and isolated system, as solar energy bombards the earth, from outside the system, at prodigious levels. This observation does not preclude the application of these laws, but it does restrict them either empirically to isolated microscopic subsystems or to seemingly unbounded and theoretically isolated cosmic systems.

Most of nature belongs to another class of thermodynamic behavior. These are systems that do not live within the isothermal adiabatic assumptions of equilibrium thermodynamics and represent systems subject to energy or material fluxes. These systems not only have internal sources of entropy production S_i but also an external source of entropy production associated with the energy or mass transformations to or from its surrounding environment. Prigogine (1955) noted that in nonequilibrium systems

$$dS = dS_e + dS_i; \tag{4}$$

dS_i is > 0. Thus with open systems it is possible to increase or decrease the entropy of the system. If $-dS_e > dS_i$, then $dS \leqslant 0$.

Such systems, termed "dissipative structures" by Prigogine, maintain their form or structure by continuous dissipation or consumption of energy. Nonliving systems (like clouds) and living systems (from organisms to ecosystems) are dependent on outside energy fluxes to maintain their organization. Nonequilibrium systems exchange matter or energy with the outside world and maintain themselves for a period of time in a state away from thermodynamic equilibrium and at a locally reduced entropy state. The larger "global" system accepts the increased entropy cost for maintaining such systems. Prigogine and his colleagues have studied the mathematical, physical, and chemical behavior of dissipative structures. They appear to self-organize through fluctuations, and small instabilities lead to irreversible bifurcations and new system states. An important property of these processes is that future states of this system are not completely deterministic.

Dissipative structures are stable over a finite range of conditions and are very sensitive to fluxes and flows from outside the system. Glansdorff and Prigogine (1971) have shown that these thermodynamic relationships are best represented by nonlinear differential equations, many of which lead to macroscopic coherent behavior away from the equilibrium state. The production of coherent structure in the development of Benard Cells, hurricanes, and living cells are examples of far-from-equilibrium coherent behavior.

Morowitz (1968) has shown that the flow of energy through a system will lead to cycling in that system. The Morowitz Theorem, probably a "fourth law of thermodynamics," is very general and applies from quantum states through complex living systems. The cyclic nature of dissipative systems can be seen in periodic attractors or limit cycle solutions to differential equations (Glansdorff and Prigogine, 1971). It appears that the cyclic nature of these structures not only allows them to develop stability but to develop structure and hierarchy within themselves. Wicken (1984) notes that "a cycle ... becomes autocatalytic by virtue of the positive feedback as some of its reaction products become incorporated into one of the kinetic steps and its generation becomes a competitive entity in nature by expressing the emergent ability to *pull* resources into its own production."

Morowitz (1968) details this process of developing order, where the flux of energy is the organizing factor in the dissipative system. With flow from a higher kinetic temperature, the upper energy levels of the dissipative system become occupied, and these take a finite time to decay into thermal modes. It is this time delay that allows for the development of structure within the system. During this period energy is stored at a higher Helmholtz free energy than at the equilibrium state. A system comprised of a monatomic perfect gas cannot develop much order, as potential energy can be stored only in rapidly decaying excited electron states. Systems of complex structures, e.g., chemical elements and compounds, which can develop further structural order through stable chemical binding, can, however, store large amounts of energy and achieve a high amount of internal structural order. The development of order in a dissipative system results in structure with a stored free energy that is stable, has a lower internal entropy, and resides some distance from thermostatic equilibrium.

Morowitz (1968) extends this concept in suggesting a thermodynamic principle of maximum order: A dissipative system selects stable states with the largest possible stored energy. Lotka (1925) suggested an energetic law for all living systems. His maximum energy law proposed that what is most important for the survival of an organism is a large energetic output in the form of size, growth, reproduction, and maintenance (Odum and Pinkerton, 1955). This maximum energy principle is materially identical to the Morowitz maximum order principle. It also corresponds to an increase in the thermal mode, in accord with Wicken's (1980) analysis of evolving thermodynamic information. Similarly Kay (1984), using Jaynes' maximum entropy principle, concludes that natural systems will maximize their exergy during development. This growth principle with its requisite *increase* in total system entropy production is a basic law for living systems.

Glansdorff and Prigogine (1971), in their development of a thermodynamic theory of structure, stability, and fluctuations, developed an evolutionary criterion for steady near-equilibrium dissipative processes. Building upon the reciprocity relationships of Onsager (1931) they found that as a system approaches a steady near-equilibrium state, the entropy production per unit volume and time is minimized. A compact form of their evolutionary criteria for dissipative systems is

$$\frac{dP}{dt} \leqslant 0, \tag{5}$$

where

$$P = \frac{dS_i}{dt}. \tag{6}$$

dS_i is the change in irreversible entropy production; P is the entropy production per unit volume and time.

James Kay and I are presently reexamining Prigogine's "minimum entropy principle" to determine whether systems are actually minimizing their *specific* entropy production rather than total entropy production in stable regimes. During the growth phase of living systems the *total* entropy production of the system rises. As the system approaches stability, specific entropy production decreases, specific entropy production being entropy production per unit of energy flow, structure, or information. Ulanowicz (personal communications) has suggested normalizing entropy production to the flow of energy or material through the system.

In dealing with general stability problems of nonequilibrium, Glansdorff and Prigogine (1971) found that changes in the forces always proceed in the direction that lowers the value of "specific" entropy production with time. This criterion is independent of any assumption about the phenomenological relationships between rates and forces. The existence of an evolutionary criterion is a direct consequence of local equilibrium stability conditions and is an important expansion of the laws of thermodynamics. This principle manifests itself in Fourier and Ficks laws, which are heat and diffusion laws where flow is proportional to a gradient in potential.

Prigogine was also able to prove that steady states corresponding to a minimum of "specific" entropy production are automatically stable and "if that system is perturbed, entropy production will increase, but the system reacts by returning to the state at which its 'specific' entropy production is lowest" (Prigogine, 1980).

Although these proofs pertain to linear, near-equilibrium conditions, far-from-equilibrium dynamically stable structures are also apparent in nature. The question then arises: Do these far-from-equilibrium systems also minimize their specific entropy production in stable regimes? As we shall see, phenomenological observations of biological dissipative systems appear to suggest this process, but as yet no macroscopic-microscopic proofs have been developed for this condition. Prigogine recognized this problem and "for many years great efforts were made to extend this theorem further from equilibrium" (Prigogine, 1980). The Benard instability is one where increased structure is the result of convection in a fluid due to a strong temperature gradient. When "organization" occurs as a result of convection, entropy production is increased. Here then, is a far-from-equilibrium situation where order is produced and yet entropy production increases. However, because of the structure or order developed in this reaction, the specific entropy production would decrease. During development the overall entropy production of the system will increase, although the specific entropy production of the system will decrease over time.

Trichner (1965), building on the work of Prigogine, has suggested that dissipative states evolve according to their boundary conditions. When energy or material are not the limiting aspects of the growth of the structure

$$dS/dt \geqslant 0. \tag{7}$$

However, where the growth of the system is bounded by intrinsic or external factors, its structure assumes a minimum specific entropy production rate

$$dP/dt \leqslant 0. \tag{5}$$

This evolutionary aspect of entropy production rates appears applicable to biological dissipative systems as well (Zotin, 1985; Trichner, 1965; Wicken, 1980; Proops, 1983).

Kirkaldy (1965) extends the minimum entropy principle to stable states beyond the near-equilibrium region. He suggests that a stable steady state of an open system can be represented by a saddle point in the configuration of the surface of entropy production rate. This potential surface is developed from the tension between the system's observed tendency toward chemical imperialism (high dissipation) and at the same time its accommodation to the development of dynamic efficiency (low specific dissipation).

This theoretical discussion is far from over. Its outcome is an exciting research program for new workers. The issue may be resolved by developing a quantitative description of near-equilibrium and far-from-equilibrium stable regimes, the analysis of entropy production in evolving systems with variable boundary conditions, and investigations of specific entropy production measures.

6.2   Information and Entropy

In 1949 thermodynamics was dealt a confusing hand when Shannon developed a mathematical representation of information and called it "entropy" (Shannon and Weaver, 1949). Shannon suggested that possible knowledge about a particular question can be represented by a probability. Information is anything that causes a change in that given probability assignment (Tribus and McIrvine, 1971). His name for the statistical state of knowledge about a question was "entropy":

$$S(A/X) = -K \sum_{i=1}^{n} p_i \ln p_i. \tag{8}$$

The entropy S of a well defined question A, and knowledge X about A, are related to the probability p_i assigned to the answer to the question being asked. Information (I) is the difference between two uncertainties or entropies:

$$I = S(A/X) - S(A/X_i). \tag{9}$$

Shannon's information measure is a quantitative tool for measuring the knowledge or complexity of a system, but it carries no qualitative content. The Shannon entropy is symbolically isomorphic with the Boltzmann equations, and Brillouin (1962) has mathematically linked this concept with that of Clausius' classical entropy measure.

A major epistemological debate has been raging over the fusion of information theory into the framework of thermodynamics. Schrödinger (1945), Brillouin (1962), and Tribus and McIrvine (1971) closely link thermodynamic entropy and information, order, and structure. In "exorcising" Maxwell's demon Brillouin was able to show that the minimum entropy cost for obtaining one bit of information is 10^{-23} joules per degree K (Tribus and McIrvine, 1971). Thus, information is an energetically small but important factor in our universe.

Wicken (1987) and Stuart (1985) strongly question the thermodynamic-information theory relationship. These workers and others have recognized the nonobjective nature of microstate partitioning. They suggest that probabilistically defined concepts are flawed because the properties of the system and those of the observer can become confused. Wicken (1987) then separates these two entropies, as he suggests Shannon's measure does not conform to the macro-microstate relationship of the Gibbs-Boltzmann formulations. Moreover, one 'entropy' measures the sequential generation of averages from statistical options (Shannon), while the other measures the movement of a system of elements in a probability space (Boltzmann and Gibbs). Denbigh (1975) and Wicken (1987) consider that Shannon's entropy is just a measure of the "spread-outness" or the complexity of a sequence.

Denbigh (1975) and Rutledge et al. (1976) have suggested more useful information measures for the complexity and the organizational relationship of the components of a system. Denbigh's integrality is

$$\phi = cnf(x), \tag{10}$$

where c = the number of connections that facilitate the functioning of the whole, n = the number of the different kind of parts, and $f(x)$ is a weighting factor taking account of the relative importance of various corrections to the actual existence of the organized system. Thus the measure is a system parameter of the relationship of elements in a system, not just its complexity. Integrality can increase in a closed system, is not conserved, is not identical with information, and is not directly related to entropy (Peacocke, 1983). Rutledge et al. (1976) and Ulanowicz (1980) have developed a similar measure that quantifies the articulation of a dynamic network by measuring the average mutual information of the system. This measure describes the coherence in a flow network or the average degree of unambiguity with which a compartment communicates with any other compartment within the system. This dynamic measure of system coherence is a much more useful tool in understanding the nature of complex interacting systems than the simple measure complexity proposed by Shannon.

This paper is not the place to resolve the conflicts and relationships between complexity, order, structure organization, information, and entropy. These are probably nested concepts whose exact meaning should be debated in the process of developing a common mathematical language. The recent dialog among Wiley and Brooks (1982), Wiley (1983), Løvtrup (1983), and Wicken (1983), as well as papers in this volume, shows the confusion apparent in the use of these terms. Clarification of these issues is important, for formalization of a common language is required before this important arena of science can be utilized further by biology and other related sciences.

6.3   Thermodynamics and Living Systems

Physicists, e.g., Schrödinger (1944), chemists, e.g., Prigogine and Nicolis (1971) and Morowitz (1968), and biologists, e.g., Margalef (1968) and Wicken (1980), have already made significant progress in fusing thermodynamics to biology and especially to evolutionary theory.

Schrödinger (1944) extended thermodynamics into biology more than any other theorist, and no discussion of this subject can dismiss the fundamental thoughts presented in his interdisciplinary multiscience synthesis *What Is Life?* In this essay he noted that life displayed two fundamental processes. One process he called "order from order," and the other "order from disorder." Schrödinger forecast the existence of DNA with his order from order premise and he integrated the laws of thermodynamics with biology in his observations about order from disorder. He observed that some chemical functions in the cell (the gene with its DNA) produce genetic order from themselves. The progeny has the same order as the parent, or order from order. He predicted that the hereditary chemical was an aperiodic, coded crystal and even suggested the size and informational packing density of the molecule. This farsighted prediction was demonstrated later in Watson and Crick's analyses of ribonucleic acids, and has led to some of the most exciting findings in biology over the past several decades.

Perhaps Schrödinger's most important and least studied observation, however, was his order from disorder premise, which links all biological systems (from living cells to ecosystems) to the expanded fundamental theorems of thermodynamics. Schrödinger (1945) noted that, at first glance, living systems seem to defy the second law of thermodynamics. The law stipulates that, within isolated systems, entropy should be maximized and disorder should reign at equilibrium. However, living systems are the antithesis of disorder, as they display marvelous levels of order made from disorder. Highly organized plants and animals grow from disordered atoms of carbon, nitrogen, oxygen, etc., via metabolic changes; order from disorder. Schrödinger solved this dilemma by turning to "non-equilibrium thermodynamics," recognizing that living systems live in a world of energy flux that does not conform to the basic assumptions of classical thermodynamics. Schrödinger suggested that an organism stays alive in its highly organized state by taking energy from outside itself, or from a larger encompassing system, and processing it to produce a lower entropy state within itself.

Morowitz (1968) and more recently Prigogine (1980) have extended thermodynamics into the realm depicted by Schrödinger. New and rapid advances are being made in biology that are firmly rooted in this new thermodynamic paradigm. Living systems, from cells to ecosystems, are best described as nonequilibrium dissipative complex structures. Life is maintained through energy fluxes and represents lower entropy states whose structure develops from free energy time delays through dissipation. These living systems seem to have all the attributes of other dissipative systems, e.g., nonlinear reactions, autocatalysis, evolution via bifurcation and multifar-from-equilibrium steady states.

It is interesting that even though Schrödinger titled his monograph on living systems *What Is Life?* he never seemed able to put his finger precisely on the definition that he desired. Perhaps a better insight can be provided by asking "What is death?" When an organism dies, it no longer has the ability to produce order from disorder. The flow of material energy ceases and the organism decays into less ordered elements and molecules. Thus, when energy flow stops within a living system, it decays away from its far-from-equilibrium state and enters a realm of equilibrium thermodynamics or death.

6.4 Thermodynamics and Ecology

The remainder of this paper will examine the application of thermo-dynamics and especially the dissipative paradigm to ecosystems, an inter-mediate scale phenomenon between cells and macroevolution and a natural laboratory for the study of dissipative complex systems.

Ecosystems are the results of the biotic, physical, and chemical compo-nents of nature acting together in a structurally and functionally organized system. Ecology is the science of how these living and nonliving compo-nents function together in nature. Ecology is a young, data-rich science with a weak theoretical base. Except for well defined concepts in biology, such as biological limits (e.g., Liebig's Law of the Minimum), and popu-lation dynamics (Hutchinson, 1978), ecology offers little theory to allow one to predict future system functions or states. Thermodynamics, and in particular nonequilibrium thermodynamics, appears to offer ecology a framework for the development of such a theory.

Biology and ecology are replete with evidence of compliance with the expanded principles of thermodynamics. The living cell is an expression of lower entropy and higher order than the nonliving components of nature. From organisms to ecosystems we find dissipative structures that use energy from outside systems to subsidize their highly ordered states of life (Schrödinger, 1944; Morowitz, 1968).

It is the flux of energy from the sun or from chemical reactions that sets the process of life in motion and maintains it. One need only to look at primary production data to realize the massive entropy production that is required to sustain life. Eugene Odum (1971) notes that the most efficient natural system converts only about 3.5% of the incoming solar radiation into biomass. The biosphere extracts a high energy-entropy cost for the organization of living things. This cost increases even more when one includes the transfer inefficiences among hierarchical levels within an ecosystem. Howard T. Odum's (1971) classic rainforest study showed that 1,500,000 calories/meter^2/year were converted up the food chain to yield only 0.4 calories/meter^2/year for a man living within that system. Energy and material transmission up food chains and trophic levels, and their accompanying entropy losses at each step, give rise to the pyramidal trophic structure commonly seen in nature. The energy or mass transfer efficiencies between trophic levels range between 0.01% and approximately 20%, and the most inefficient step in this energy transformation is the initial photosynthetic reaction. Once nature organizes metabolites, the next level of the food chain need not resynthesize the most basic biochemicals of life again.

Hannon (1979) and Ulanowicz (1984) have formalized energy network flow analysis to include import-export, internal flow, and entropy dissipations. This analysis allows for the quantification of trophic structure, cycle analysis, and total energy flows through the system. Their methods formalize energy network analysis and provide a powerful tool for analysis of ecosystem energy or material flows.

Cybernetic control mechanisms abound in biology and in ecology. Homeostatic control is a well studied concept in physiology and ecologists have documented biochemical and energy cycles in ecosystems for decades (E. Odum, 1971). The simple regulation of predator and prey populations is an easily recognizable cybernetic feedback control mechanism (Hutchinson, 1978). Ecosystems are not hardwired informational networks, but do have informational attributes: feedback, amplification, and stability all abound in nature (Margalef, 1968; Patten and Odum, 1981). These processes not only control the biotic components of an ecosystem but affect the nonbiotic components as well. Life in a small pond controls not only inorganic and organic chemical cycles but also physical parameters such as light penetration in the pond. Lovelock (1979) has proposed that living systems drive, and their requisite cybernetic controls affect, the major geochemical cycles of the earth. He proposed that the global atmospheric composition was not only developed by living systems but also is buffered and controlled by the global ecosystem. Thus, the expanded laws of thermodynamics fit comfortably into biology and ecology, and their applications help explain many of the observations that rule the so-called "balance of nature." The interdependence and interrelationships seen in ecology are examples of basic thermodynamic principles in action.

Perhaps no other ecologists have advanced the principles of thermodynamics in ecology farther than the brothers Eugene and Howard Odum. They have provided ecology with valuable conceptual paradigms on energy flows in nature, but even more important they are active experimental ecologists who synthesize data and write well and often. In his more recent writings, H. T. Odum (1971) attempts to apply these energy flow/thermodynamic concepts to economics, theories of history, and energy flow analysis of fossil fuels. He suggests that energy utilization shapes the structure and function of ecosystems and he attempts to explain why energetic principles control how an ecosystem will succeed or evolve. H. T. Odum and Pinkerton (1955) repostulated Lotka's energy law, which states that living systems that maximize power will be the most likely to succeed, with success being defined in the broad Darwinian sense of abundance and distribution. Odum and Pinkerton (1955) paraphrased Lotka by saying that, those systems that survive in competition among alternative choices are those that develop more power inflow and use it best to meet the needs of survival.

If power is defined as the rate of flow of useful energy, then the Lotka-Odum maximum power principle would suggest that the organism with the highest energy flow would be the most successful in nature. The Lotka-Odum energy law is the same maximum energy principle of Morowitz (1968) and Kay (1984); maximum exergy and corresponds to the increase in thermal modes of thermodynamic information spoken of by Wicken (1980). These principles hold in unlimiting conditions or until the structuring of the system equals its rate of breakdown. The Lotka-Odum postulate appears to be a property of all dissipative living systems and is a selection principle in ecology and in biological evolution. It must be stressed that this principle assumes unbounded energy and resources. However, most living systems are, for a portion of their lives, limited in their growth and size by intrinsic (genetic) and external (resources) factors.

Eugene Odum (1971) has gone on to ask another question: "Does nature maximize the ratio of structure to maintenance metabolism, or is it energy flow itself that is maximized?" Morowitz (1968) was also hunting for an underlying thermodynamic principle that would guide ecosystem development: "The principle we appear to be missing is the guide as to which of all possible systems will in fact arise and evolve in a given energy flow situation. In ecology we would like some principle to indicate the path of the development of a climax community."

One of the first ecological biologists to become a serious student of the laws of thermodynamics and information theory is Ramon Margalef (1968). In *Perspectives in Ecological Theory* he extended thermodynamic thought deeper into ecology than any previous author. He considered an ecosystem to be a cybernetic system living within and controlled by the second law of thermodynamics. Margalef, a plankton ecologist, had studied the changes in algal species following perturbation of their ecosystem state. These species changes, which occur as an ecosystem ages or matures, are known as the process of succession. If an ecosystem is allowed to mature without reperturbation, it follows a repeatable sequence with species. Margalef's linkage between succession and the principles of thermodynamics are nowhere more evident than in the succession of plants and animals recovering from natural or man-made perturbations.

One of the first in-depth discussions of succession in natural systems was presented by Henry Thoreau in a lecture "The Succession of Forest Trees" given in 1860 at the Middlesex Agricultural Society Annual Cattle Show in

Concord, Massachusetts. Thoreau, known more for his naturalist observations and musings than for his contributions to ecology, recorded the deforestation and reforestation of land parcels in eastern Massachusetts. By the time of his death he had written about 400 pages on the subject (Worster, 1979). He observed that nature displayed an orderly process of plant development that results in a sequential change of species that is both observable and predictable. If the ecosystem is left undisturbed, the progression from bare field to grassland to grass-shrub to pine forest and finally to an oak-hickory forest is a predictable, 150 year process (figure 6.1).

Almost at the same time as Thoreau's observations Darwin published his *Origin of Species* and formulated a formal theory proposing that organisms evolve through variation and selection. Darwin (1859/1968) observed that natural selection is the result of the struggle of the one organism against others for limited physical, chemical, and biotic resources. As we shall see later, an effect of this constant competition is that plants and animals progress toward a greater overall efficiency. The competition in natural systems is so fierce that, as Darwin (1859/1968) wrote, "The merest trifle would often give the victory to one organic being over another." Darwin saw progressive changes by organisms resulting from competition as results of adaptation to fit optimally into niche space, and evolution as a long-range protraction of this process. One may argue whether the process is slow and gradual or occurs in small to large spasmodic steps (Gould and Eldredge, 1977), but the enduring aspect of Darwin's thought is the direction of the process in both the short-term successional scale and the long-term evolutionary process.

Margalef suggested that succession is a cybernetic self-organizing process that develops a biological "assemblage in which the production of entropy per unit of preserved and transmitted information is at minimum" (Margalef, 1968). Where intrinsic or external factors limit development of the system, the ones that endure are those that can optimize the physical, chemical, and biological niche components with the least entropy production per unit of biomass, information, or structure, i.e., those minimizing the specific entropy production. Thus, the more entropy/energy efficient systems are those that survive and prosper in the limiting conditions found within nature. Succession in the final analysis is a self-organizing process that involves a substitution of one piece in the system for some other piece so as to preserve more information or structure at the same or less energetic cost (Margalef, 1968).

Margalef was particularly intrigued with the efficiency of ecological systems and suggested that the measure of the energy flow per unit of biomass (the primary production of the system divided by the total permanent biomass) was an appropriate measure for ecological or evolutionary

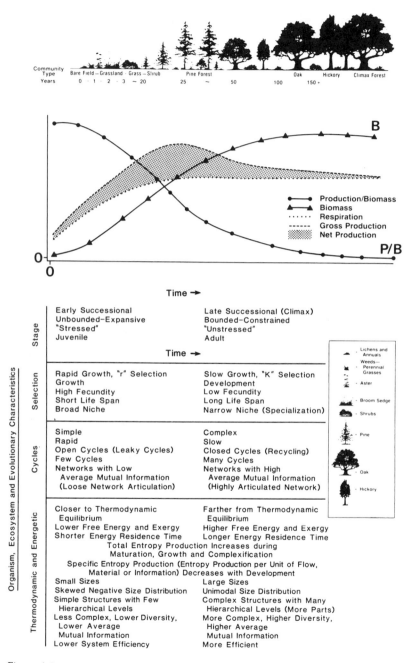

Figure 6.1
Changes in ecosystem characteristics over time and during the selection success and process. Adapted, synthesized, and updated from Odum (1969).

efficiency. Production (*P*) in biological systems is conventionally measured in grams of carbon fixed per unit area of time, and biomass (*B*) is measured in total grams of carbon. Margalef chose *P/B* ratios as a measure of the energy flow per unit of biomass produced. For instance, bacteria have high *P/B* ratios, as they fix large amounts of carbon per unit of time and are large consumers of energy in comparison to their biomass. Margalef was searching for a measure of entropy production used in sustaining a unit of biomass or structure in ecosystems. Although Margalef's *P/B* ratios were proposed as a measure of ecosystem efficiency, he did not go on to support that apparently intuitive hypothesis with rigorous application of thermodynamic theory or ecological data.

Eugene Odum (1969) synthesized predictive descriptors of ecological successions in his important paper "Strategy of Ecosystem Development." He not only described the expected development patterns in successional ecosystems but highlighted thermodynamic characteristics exhibited in ecosystem succession. High on Odum's list are measures of community energetics, production/respiration ratios, production/biomass ratios, and production/energy flow ratios. Odum called these measures "Schrödinger ratios," thus implying, like Margalef, their firm footing in thermodynamics. He noted that "entropy production" was low in mature ecosystems and that information and structure also are maximized in mature systems. Odum (1969) suggested thermodynamic measures other than production/biomass ratios. He proposed production/respiration ratios and biomass/energy flow ratios. A better measure of entropy production per unit of biomass, structure, or information would be respiration/biomass ratios. Respiration results in lower grade energy compounds and low grade thermal heat. Margalef's use of production/biomass ratios is not objectionable, as production and respiration are closely linked, and these measures quantify similar aspects of an underlying process. If, as Zotina and Zotin (1982) suggest, respiration approximates entropy production, then production or respiration/biomass ratios would represent a specific entropy production rate.

Cybernetically, mature ecosystems exhibit long, complex life cycles and closed mineral cycles while the opposite is apparent in developing ecosystems. Odum, in support of Margalef, noted that early in a successional sequence, biomass is low, as there is little competition for potentially limiting resources, and the productivity per unit of biomass is high. Later in the successional sequence (assuming no changes in outside environmental parameters) resources become limited and more efficient species have a competitive advantage in the community. Since this conceptual leap is so important to ecological theory, we should look at the concept of limits or boundaries in the living process, then at entropy production in limited systems, and finally examine the Margalef proposal in light of relevant ecological data.

6.5 Quantitative Boundaries in Living Systems

Life itself is a product of the thermodynamic histories of the global eco-system as it evolved from chemical elements and, through energy flux transformations, developed useful genetic materials that reproduce and me-tabolize into highly organized systems through stepwise energy trans-formations. Morowitz (1968), describing common attributes of life, has noted that a few processes, i.e., DNA replication, ATP energy storage, and flow, and a limited number of molecular compounds, control the living process. Scientists are not required to discover new chemical or physical processes to explain the biological processes known today.

Every living organism's success is dependent not only on its genetic heritage and its life-producing chemical reactions (intrinsic factors) but also on its ability to succeed in a sea of ever-changing environmental variables. This fact depends on Liebig's Law of the Minimum Tolerance. According to E. Odum (1971), Liebig's Law, first expressed in 1840, states that "The growth of a plant is dependent on the amount of foodstuff which is presented to it in a minumum quantity." The concept recognizes that there are variable limiting requirements, e.g., nutrients or micronutrients, upon which life is dependent, and that any one of these variables governs the potential for success and well-being of the organism or population in ques-tion. In 1913 Shelford expanded Liebig's Law to include the concept of max-imum as well as minimum limits of life. These limits and tolerances define the physical, chemical, and biological boundaries of the living system.

We have now defined one of the fundamental concepts in ecology, the niche. Hutchinson (1978) describes a niche as an N-dimensional hyper-volume within which environmental conditions at every point permit an organism to live. This definition seems adequate, has theoretical usefulness in describing conditions under which a species can survive, and can be derived from Liebig's Law. Hutchinson (1978) also noted that within the niche volume there will be optimal survival regions and suboptimal con-ditions near the boundary. Finally, the niche volume is soft and not rigid. A shift in one vector may affect the shape of the rest of the volume. For example, a shift in organism temperature causes changes in nutrient up-take, metabolism, and competition (Sastry and Vargo, 1967). Patten (per-sonal communication) noted that the niche is an even more complex space in nature, as its shape is controlled by a host of indirect variables that may affect the niche domain as much as, or even more than, direct forcing functions. Perhaps a niche might be best thought of as the totality of thermodynamic boundaries of a living system.

Ecologists would like to have the theoretical and mathematical tools to predict future ecosystem states (both function and structure) resulting from changes in both direct or indirect state variables. The idea of such a mathematical formulation is appealing, but the feasibility of such a representation is slim. This is not only because ecology lacks the theoretical base for such predictions, but also because of the large number of state variables in the equation, and the interactive relationships that are generally nonlinear and have time lags. In addition, random events affect the ecosystem state and ecosystems themselves exhibit high order interactions. Even the most sophisticated computer program would struggle to keep up with the fate of a single phytoplankton cell as it tumbles through variable light fields, temperatures, salinities, trace metal concentrations, and predatory pressures in a local estuary.

The concepts of limits in biological systems is never more evident than in the studies of population dynamics. Where an organism or population has unlimited niche space and resources to draw upon, the rate of increase through reproduction appears limited only by the number of individuals reproducing, their reproduction strategy, and their death rate. However, when an organism or population starts to be limited by any one of the niche variables, whether it be living space, food, predation, etc., this rate of growth slows and reaches the limits of the niche at hand. These limits on a growing population are dependent on the number of individuals in the growing population N, the upper limit of the population K, and r, the unrestricted rate of increase of the population at hand (birth rate — death rate). Mathematically this is shown by

$$\frac{dN}{dt} = rN\left(\frac{K - N}{k}\right). \tag{11}$$

The above equation, known as the Lotka-Voltera or logistic equation, is nonlinear in nature. The term $(K - N)/K$ is negative feedback as the population reaches its asymptotic level of stability. The rate of increase of the population rises until N reaches $K/2$ and then falls to 0 as the asymptote is reached. The unrestricted growth rate (r) assumes that the growing population is restricted only by birth and death rates, and that changes in these rates can be caused by any density-dependent or density-independent factors. K, on the other hand, [or $(K - N)/K$] is the environmental resistance generated by the population itself bringing about the reduction in the population size as it approaches the limits of its environmental carrying capacity. Glansdorff and Prigogine (1971) analyzed the general Lotka-Voltera model and showed that it represents a limit cycle with variable steady states.

Population dynamics has been reviewed by E. G. Hutchinson (1978). His mathematical derivations permit nonlinear analysis of populations with time lag, stochastic interactions, and predator/prey variations. His equations have become so widely used that the "r" and "K" have become part of the standard vocabulary of ecologists, with "r selection" characterizing species that have adapted to unlimited resource growth and "K selection" denoting species that are specialized to live in limited niche boundary conditions. Prigogine and Stengers (1984) and Gould (1977) extended the logistic equation far beyond its original uses in population dynamics and suggest that "K" species are more "valuable" as they store memories and represent a greater biological investment. "K" organisms develop complex traits such as family and social behavior to adapt to the limits of their niche.

So far this section has stressed the exogenous limits or boundaries of living systems. However, hereditary or endogenous factors also provide limits or boundaries to cells and organisms. The genetic boundaries are coded in the genome and represent a hyperspace confining the structure and function of the phenotype. These genotypic boundaries must represent stable states and intrinsic limits to the system at hand.

6.6 Entropy Production in Limited and Stable Ecosystems

As mentioned above, Prigogine developed an evolutionary criterion for dissipative processes. Prigogine (1955) expanded Onsager reciprocity equations and showed that stable near-equilibrium dissipative systems minimize their rate of entropy production. He proposed that

$$dP/dt \leq 0. \tag{5}$$

Although these proofs appear to apply only to linear near-equilibrium regions, living far-from-equilibrium stable living systems appear also to follow minimum entropy principles.

Prigogine and Wiame (1946) were the first to suggest the use of a minimum entropy principle to describe aspects of living systems. They suggested that the observed decrease in the rate of metabolism per unit volume compared to increase in organism size was a manifestation of the minimum entropy principle. Zotin (1985) related the decrease in heat production rate during later stages in the development of chicken embryos to decreases in the specific rate of entropy production. Zotina and Zotin (1982) have shown that the intensity of heat production or respiration can be equated to the specific rate of entropy production. Their data show that respiration intensity or the specific rate of entropy production decreases with development in fish, embryogenesis in chickens, and oogenesis in frogs. These proposals and the theoretical developments of Kirkaldy (1965) and Wicken (1980) suggest that a form of minimum entropy production is manifested in all living systems. As we shall see, ecosystems boldly display similar traits.

These results agree with Matsuno's (1978) mathematical inquiry into Margalef's suggestion that succession in a photosynthetic ecosystem will proceed so that the ratio of biomass production to total biomass per unit of time, in a unit area, will decrease with time.

Matsuno assumed that in a dissipative biological system biomass is the only measure of substance or order in the ecosystem, that the system is homogeneous, and that the biomass production and degradation rates are Markovian stochastic variables. He concluded that the lasting structure of the dissipative system minimizes its irreversible decay rate. He further concluded that the long-term succession of an ecosystem will proceed in a direction along which the irreversible decay rate will decrease with time, which supports the deduction that the ratio of production of biomass per unit of time to the total biomass present in the same area will decrease. Matsuno was mathematically searching for the most stable structure in a dissipative system, which in this case is an ecosystem exhibiting metabolic interaction with its external environment (Matsuno, 1978).

His equation 34 states

$$W = \lim_{T \to \infty} \frac{1}{T} \int_0^T \frac{\dot{Z}_t(u)\, dt}{B}, \tag{12}$$

where W is the irreversible decay of the dissipative system, $Z_t(u)\, dt$ is the irreversible outflow of material from the system, T is time, and B is the un-decomposable unit of material, i.e., permanent biomass. In this equation the material flow from outside the system into the ecosystem is due to photosynthetic biomass production, and the outflow of biomass from the system is due to its degradation via processes like herbivorous grazing. The rate of photosynthetic biomass production in the ecosystem will equal the degradation rate if the metabolic interaction rate between the ecosystem and its supporting larger outside system are equal. Matsuno (1978) shows the most stable and the most likely structure appearing in the course of evolution will be a system that tends to minimize the irreversible decay rate W of the system.

A more complete picture of the development of a dissipative system is seen when it is viewed as an evolutionary process whose boundary conditions constrain its entropy production. When one combines Trichner's (1965) prebounded stage of system development,

$$dP/dt \geqslant 0, \tag{7}$$

with Prigogine's (1980) bounded stable stage of development, where

$$dP/dt \leqslant 0, \tag{5}$$

one can obtain a complete view of the changes in entropy production rates with the development of complex living systems. The specific high entropy production stage represents the Lotka-Odum maximum power principle and the later stage is marked by lower specific entropy production rates. The *total* entropy production increases over the entire development of the system, whereas the rate of *specific* entropy production initially increases and later decreases with the evolution of the system. This relationship is also represented by the Lotka-Voltera model. When a system's unbounded growth is exponential, specific entropy production rates are high. In bounded situations when the systems reach stable regimes, specific entropy production rates decrease.

6.7 Ecological Succession

Ecological data also support this theoretical model. E. Odum (1969), Margalef (1968), and Johnson (1981 and this volume) all contend that P/B ratios or Schrödinger ratios decrease as a system reaches maturity. All three are field ecologists and have observed that early successional stages of ecosystems are dominated by organisms with high production rates, e.g., bacteria, weeds, "r" species, and organisms having little permanent biomass. It is, however, difficult to measure quantitative changes of many important total ecosystem parameters because of the spatial and temporal variations of these variables in natural systems. Measurement of total system biomass and total system production in a natural ecosystem requires a prodigious, ingenuous sampling and measurement program. If one were to attempt to measure the production:biomass ratio following a succession from a plowed field to a forest, it would take years, and the practical measurement of production in such a large system would be difficult at best.

In the past few years, however, ecologists have developed experimental mesocosms that allow the experimenter to capture and sustain most of the structural and functional attributes of whole natural ecosystems in large enclosed bags or tanks (Oviatt et al., 1980). Within these systems one can carefully control experimental variables and can measure quantitatively whole-system attributes such as production. The Marine Ecosystem Research Laboratory (MERL) at the University of Rhode Island has developed a sophisticated marine mesocosm facility and has documented that control ecosystems closely replicate the local natural ecosystem of Narragansett Bay. The facility maintains 14 large (13,000 liters) marine ecosystem mesocosms. The land based systems have a large pelagic volume of water overlying a captured benthic substrate and community of 2.5 m². These chambers are the cyclotrons of experimental ecology, for in these experiments, ecologists can control many of the boundary conditions and

manipulate individual portions of subsystems. Not only do the experimenters have replicate control systems, and the ability to control and manipulate niche vectors, but these chambers allow one to watch in detail the
system's response to induced stress in experiments that may last for over
two years. Fortunately, successional indicators (P/B ratio changes) have
response times similar to the lengths of the experiments in these systems.
During the past eight years, MERL experimenters have perturbed these
controlled systems by changing nutrient concentrations and sediment substrates, and by stressing them with toxic concentrations of oil.

The experiment most germane to this paper was a study of the response
of a natural estuarine ecosystem to stress caused by chronic toxic levels of
No. 2 fuel oil hydrocarbons (Oviatt et al., 1980). The test chambers were
initiated by transferring a 30-cm-thick benthic substrate from Narragansett
Bay into the bottom of each tank, filling the tanks with local bay water, and
leaving it undisturbed for several months. After a stabilization period the
systems were dosed continually for 160 days with toxic concentrations of
No. 2 fuel oil hydrocarbons, until the tanks contained 190 parts per billion
(ppb) of water-accommodated hydrocarbons. The ecosystems within the
tanks were allowed to recover from this controlled stress for 64 days
following cessation of oil dosing. During the entire experiment the ecosystem phytoplankton community (^{14}C production) and the community
macrobenthos biomass, a good measure for permanent biomass, were
determined. Data sets synthesized by Oviatt and the author show that
production/biomass (P/B) ratios remained near unity prior to the oil stress
(figure 6.2). The stressed system retreated to a high P/B condition, and
returned to the previous steady state (lower P/B) only when the stress was
removed. When this experiment was repeated at lower concentrations of
oil (90 ppb), similar but damped P/B ratio responses were observed. This
experiment supports the proposal that P/B ratios are raised during ecosystem stress, and succession results in higher permanent order and structure
per unit of energy metabolism. Specific entropy production rates were
reduced and information or structure was enhanced in the recovery or the
successional process.

An important result of this experiment was that the stress (oil) acted to
perturb the system and drove it down the successional sequence. When
the stress was removed the successional process started again. Some ecosystems can be, or are, maintained in a low state of maturity by constant
stress. The constantly mowed field, the estuarine phytoplankton, and the
high energy beach are all stable, less mature ecosystems. Margalef (1968)
recorded successional changes in species composition, size, and color
pigment of phytoplankton following perturbation. These observations
corroborate his theoretical conclusions on entropy production rates in evolving living systems. Kilham and Kilham (unpublished) have compared phyto-

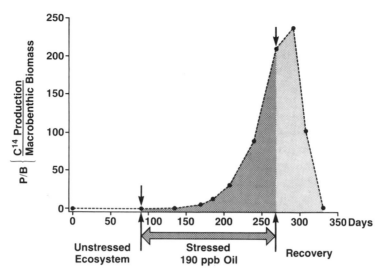

Figure 6.2
Changes in the ratio of ecosystem production (P) and microfauna biomass (B) in an experiment run in macrocosms at the Marine Ecosystem Research Laboratory, University of Rhode Island. The microcosms were initialized, allowed to stablize, and then were dosed with toxic concentrations of pertroleum oil from 14 February 1977 to 1 August 1977 (190 parts per billion of water accommodated oil). The ecosystems were then allowed to recover until October 1977 with no more additional oil added to the systems. P/B ratios rose when the ecosystem was stressed and returned during the succession that accompanied the recovery period. (Control values have been subtracted from oil treatment values.)

plankton communities in high variable estuarine environments (stressed) with less variable environments in the open ocean. The estuarine community had the same attributes of Odum "r" selection and the open ocean community "K" attributes. Similar community attributes have been recorded in plant succession in forest systems (Bormann and Likens, 1979), and in bird communities (MacMahon, 1979).

Ulanowicz (1986) has recently analyzed an excellent data set for carbon flows in two tidal marsh ecosystems adjacent to a large power generating facility on the Crystal River in Florida. One marsh was perturbed (elevated 6°C by the effluent of the facility), while the other adjacent marsh was the unstressed control. Flows were compartmentalized and quantified using the methods of Hannon (1979) and then analyzed for a variety of measures, including total throughput, respiration, trophic aggregation, and cycling. The stressed ecosystem had a lower material throughput and a higher respiration per unit of flow, and a larger percentage of the total flow was involved in cycling. These findings fit comfortably into the successional framework developed by Odum (1969) and in this paper. Of particular interest was the increase in cycling in the stressed system. Similar observations were made in the Hubbard-Brook Ecosystem, (Bormann and Likens, 1979), corroborating the data of Seki (1982), who noted increasing rates of amino acid cycling in stressed plankton communities. This increase in energy or material cycling in stressed systems is a fundamental property of living systems and is probably a general rule for other dissipative systems. This phenomenon should be tested in general autocatalytic models like the Busselator (Prigogine and Stengers, 1984), and in mesocosm experiments using different ecosystem characteristics.

Woodwell (1965) performed a critical experiment that showed a relationship between ecosystem state and succession. The purpose of his experiment was to determine the effect of gamma radiation on a forest ecosystem. He imposed a strong gamma radiation source on a mature northeastern oak-pine forest: "Exposure of the intact forest to radiation first destroyed pine trees and other trees, leaving sprouts, shrubs and ground cover. Longer exposure to radiation kills shrubs and finally the sedge, grasses, and herbs of the ground cover" (Woodwell, 1965). Although he did not measure system production, it was apparent that close to this lethal source only grasses and high P/B organisms survived. Farther away shrubs, and even farther the mature forest, survived. What developed was a successional series of plants dependent on the level of stress applied to the system. The more stress, the less mature the ecosystem.

These experiments and other data suggest another fundamental ecological/thermodynamic process. When a complex interacting system is stressed it will revert back to a lower and less efficient state; after the stress is released it will, if possible, return to a more efficient state. Ecosystems thus act like Prigogine's far-from-equilibrium systems as they maintain order, reaching different steady states through fluctuations or perturbations: "Indeed we see that the entropy production rate in the perturbed state is always larger than in the reference state" (Glansdorff and Prigogine, 1971, p. 86).

Johnson's (1981) analysis of fish stocks in isolated Canadian lakes show that if the lakes were all unperturbed they developed a structure similar to dominant tree species in a climax forest. These data, combined with a thorough knowledge of nonequilibrium thermodynamics, led Johnson to conclude that the climax steady state is a null or saddle point between two attractors, the first being the tendency toward increasing entropy production, information, and complexity over evolutionary time and the second the tendency of dissipative systems to minimize their entropy productions and maximize their structure and information over a shorter time frame.

Larger natural ecosystems respond to stress very much like their miniaturized counterparts, the laboratory microcosm or isolated lakes. In 1978 the oil tanker *Amoco Cadiz* ran aground in the English Channel. The result-

ing spill oiled over 200 kilometers of beaches, estuaries, and rocky inter-
tidal ecosystems along the Brittany coast of France. The recovery from the
impact of the oil resulted in similar energetic successional responses in
the different ecosystems. Opportunistic, fast breeding and high P/B ratio
organisms filled gaps left by the more established resident "K" community
(CNEXO, 1981). An ecosystem's recovery response was variable depending on characteristics of the ecosystem involved. Heavily impacted, long-
lived, slow-reproducing "K" strategists, like an oak forest, may require
decades to reestablish via succession (figure 6.1). It is obvious, then, that
succession is a ubiquitous telenomic process in ecosystems and, as Odum
and Margalef have suggested, is to be understood by reference to the
principles of dissipative thermodynamics.

6.8 Succession and Evolution

I have documented the phenomenological and thermodynamic aspects of
ecological succession. I now wish to extend these observations to the
process of natural selection in evolution. Margalef (1968), Odum (1969),
Wicken (1980), and others have proposed that the successional process
observed in ecosystems is the framework of Darwinian selection. Margalef
(1968) is fond of the title of G. E. Hutchinson's book *The Ecological Theater
and the Evolutionary Play*. He notes that "evolution cannot be understood
except in the frame of ecosystems. By the natural process of succession,
which is inherent in every ecosystem, the evolution of species is pushed
or sucked into the direction taken by succession. Succession is in progress
everywhere and evolution follows encased in succession's frame."

Odum (1969) proposed that the "strategy" of succession, a short-term
process, is basically the same as the "strategy" of the long-term evolutionary development of the biosphere. Life probably originated in the
ecosystem framework and evolved in an ecosystem context (Wicken,
this volume). Ecosystem succession is an orderly predictable process of
natural selection, and evolutionary selection operates under the same
principles.

Successional attributes can be seen in the major features of evolution.
Cope's Law or the tendency for organisms to become larger as their
lineages evolve is discernible in the successional process, as well as in the
maximization of energy structure or information over time (Odum and
Pinkerton, 1955; Margalef, 1968; Wicken, 1980). The development of
phylogenetic trees or hierarchical complexity is a fundamental process in
evolution. It too is mirrored in the development of ecosystems. A great
deal has been written on the emergence of complexity in biological systems. Much of the discussion is confused because of the ambiguous use of
terms (Wiley and Brooks, 1982; Wicken, 1983; Saunders and Ho, 1981).

The development of complexity is influenced not only by thermodynamic factors. MacArthur and Wilson (1967) found that species diversity, a measure of complexity, increased with the size of the habitat. Sanders (1969) showed that constancy of the physical environment and stable system boundaries resulted in higher diversity in benthic coastal ecosystems. Stehli et al. (1969) and Johnson (unpublished) have noted that an increase in energy flux and general climatic stability leads to the higher diversity at the equator than at the poles. But generally an increase in complexity, whether measured in informational, structural, energetic, or flow component terms, is a characteristic of both succession and evolution (Denbigh, 1975; Margalef, 1968; Ulanowicz, 1980). The decrease in production or respiration biomass ratios seen in ecosystem succession is also observed in the evolution of species. Early life, i.e, bacteria and algae, has high P/B and R/B ratios. Later evolutionary stages of invertebrafes and vertebrates reduce these ratios (Banse and Mosher, 1980). Zotin (1984) explicitly proposed this phenomenon, noting the decrease in specific respiration with organism development over evolution.

The process of evolution, like succession, can be perturbed. The punctuated evolutionary paradigm of Gould and Eldredge (1977), and specifically the extraterrestrial event of the late Cretaceous (Alverez et al., 1980), are examples of perturbations that reset the evolutionary clock. The development of a new evolutionary/equilibrium via fluctuation is highly reminiscent of Prigogine's equilibrium via fluctuation. It should not be surprising to find exceptions to the above general rules. That the late Cretaceous large dinosaurs gave way to smaller organisms was to be expected with perturbation-causing events.

6.9 Discussion

This chapter has discussed the principles of modern thermodynamics and showed that the science of ecology nests comfortably within its extended laws. Specifically, we have studied the process of ecological succession and showed it to be an evolutionary process, with its initial stages involved in growth and maximization of free energy and structure: Lotka's Power Law. Succession's later stages are represented by the development of complexity and efficiency, and minimizations of specific entropy productions. These processes can be extended to selection principles in Darwinian selection. It should be stated that these two thermodynamic aspects of selection are *not* the only processes by which natural selection takes place. MacArthur and Wilson (1967) showed that there were fewer species of birds on small islands than on large islands, indicating a spatial relationship with selection. Spatial coherence is required for the strategy of sexual reproduction. Denbigh (1975) has suggested that his measure of "integrality" or the degree of interconnection in systems is itself a selection process. Ulanowicz (1980) has developed a phenomenological measure, "ascendency," which is a product of size or system throughput and of a measure of the system's dynamic interrelatedness, its mutual average information. The Ulanowicz ascendency combines the Lotka Power Principle with the system's increase in internal structure seen in ecosystem and evolutionary development. Ascendency is a thermodynamically derived measure increasing with ecological succession and decreasing in stressed ecosystems. The cycling dynamics in ecosystems must be rooted in the autocatalytic process, and the increases in cycling observed in stressed and early stage ecosystems must be explained in terms of the thermodynamic paradigm. Finally, the adaptability of the organism or the genome to its environment plays a major role in its success. The interrelations between constraints of the genotype and external constraints of its environment result in specific adaptations that are not predictable in this general theory.

It appears that the principles of thermodynamics may have a role in the variational aspects of evolution as well. Wicken (1980 and this volume), Wiley and Brooks (1982), Wiley (this volume), and Saunders and Ho (1981) have proposed that the generation of biological variation is due to the overall randomization process of the Second Law. Genetic variation, while unpredictable, is mandated by the randomization and probabilistic nature of the Second Law. Wicken (1980) notes that error-free genetic replication is forbidden by the Second Law, in the same way that it is impossible to generate flawless crystals. Thus, Second Law randomization produces new genetic material for ecosystems to test (Schneider, H. W., personal communication). Selection is a rugged sorting process that also operates within the framework of thermodynamics.

Monod (1972) is partially correct in recognizing that random events shape future evolutionary structure and function. However, this randomness is overwhelmed by the structure and order of nature, much of which can be ascribed to the principles of nonequilibrium thermodynamics. This dilemma was best described by Blum (1968), a student of this problem for over 35 years:

> I like to compare evolution to the weaving of a great tapestry. The strong unyielding warp of this tapestry is formed by the essential nature of elementary non-living matter, and the way in which this matter has been brought together in the evolution of out planet. In building this warp the second law of thermodynamics has played a predominant role. The multi-colored woof which forms the detail of the tapestry I like to think of as having been woven onto the warp principally by mutation and natural selection. While the warp establishes the dimensions and supports the whole, it is the woof that

most intrigues the aesthetic sense of the student of organic evolution, showing as it does the beauty and variety of fitness of organisms to their environment. But why should we pay so little attention to the warp, which is after all a basic part of the whole structure? Perhaps the analogy would be more complete if something were introduced that is occasionally seen in textiles—the active participation of the warp in the pattern itself. Only then, I think, does one grasp the full significance of the analogy.

Even though thermodynamics itself is a probabilistically derived set of formulations, and is combined with the random events of nature, the ideas presented here corroborate Blum's views: The warp of thermodynamics is highly apparent in ecosystem development and in evolution itself.

In the past few years several theorists have suggested that random aspects of nature can best be quantified by a "simple set of game theories and strategy laws" that elucidate some of the major features of the evolutionary process (Eigen and Winkler, 1983; Smith and Morowitz, 1981). These genetic strategy rules help describe how new alleles or genetic characteristics are selected or rejected in populations. The most complete set of these strategy laws was developed by Smith and Morowitz (1982), who suggested that the game of life may be governed by the following rules:

(1) No allele which is not currently advantageous at least, or compatible at worst, can be selected or initially saved just in case it might later prove useful.
(2) The probability of the addition or the deletion of any allele being compatible with past selected alleles is an inverse of the hierarchical depth at which the effects are manifest.
(3) Each player is allowed a limited number of resources. Thus the finite sizes of population, and the limited available energy and space, force each player continually to discard allelic alternatives through selective rejection and fluctuations induced by the statistical nature of population dynamics.
(4) Each player must play his best hand no matter how poor the hand and no matter who the challenger.

Since it takes time to select or reject these random events, many moves are in progress at any one time. Long-term prediction of ecosystem or evolutionary state is made impossible by random events in the system. However, it is obvious that certain outcomes or states have much lower probability than others. Perhaps ecological succession is a dimension of the game of life played like five-card stud poker, where no new genes are allowed in the game, and where each player must play his hand with the given cards or the genetic makeup, at the time. Evolution is a dimension of life more like draw poker, which allows the system to draw new cards or new alleles and to reject or accept them according to the rules of the game.

The synthesis and development of a firmer theoretical basis for describing the ecological process of succession and evolution can be fostered in several ways. First, a common theory and language needs to be developed that merges thermodynamics, information theory, and cybernetics. Further analysis is needed of entropy production rates in far-from-equilibrium dissipative systems. The relationship between the distance from equilibrium, boundary conditions, dissipation rate, complexity, and entropy production needs further clarification. Mathematical manipulation of Busselator type models may allow better understanding of processes such as cycling and entropy production. These models should be run with different boundary conditions and in perturbed and unperturbed states. Common theoretical attributes of dissipative systems should be determined and quantified in natural systems.

Natural and mesocosm scaled ecosystems should be studied to quantify further ecosystems at various stages of development. Energy and material flow data need to be carefully collected so as to allow calculations of system input-output matrices, cycles, respiration, production, and biomass. At present, little data exist about whole ecosystems to allow good analysis of these measures.

If the thoughts presented in this paper withstand the test of scientific scrutiny and hypothesis testing, these concepts could be applied toward understanding other complex systems. Jantsch (1972), in a book written ahead of its time, attempted to apply many of these principles to human systems, especially social systems and human behavior. Proops (1983) suggests that economic systems may have several properties common to other complex dissipative systems.

Acknowledgments

H. Morowicz, R. Ulanowicz, L. Johnson, J. Wicken, and C. Oviatt have offered me invaluable guidance and help in this study. I completed much of this research at the Center for Ocean Management Studies, the University of Rhode Island, while being funded by the U.S. Environmental Protection Agency.

References

Allen, P. M., 1985. Ecology, thermodynamics and self-organization: towards a new understanding of complexity. In *Ecosystem Theory for Biological Oceanography*, R. E. Ulanowicz and T. Platt, eds., Canadian Bull. of Fish and Aquatic Sci. 213, Dept. of Fisheries and Oceans, Ottawa, pp. 3–37.

Alverez, W., W. Alverez, F. Assaro, and H. V. Michel, 1980. Extraterrestrial cause for the Cretaceous-Tertiary extinction. *Science* 208:1095—1108.

Banse, K., and S. Mosher, 1980. Adult body mass and annual production/biomass relationships of field populations. *Ecological Monographs* 50:355—379.

Blum, H. F., 1968. *Time's Arrow and Evolution*, 3rd ed. Princeton: Princeton University Press.

Bormann, F. H., and G. E. Likens, 1979. *Pattern and Process in a Forested Ecosystem*. New York: Springer-Verlag.

Brillouin, L., 1962. *Science and Information Theory*, 2nd ed. New York: Academic Press.

CNEXO, 1981. *Amoco Cadiz: Fates and Effects of the Oil Spill*. Paris: Center for National Exploration of the Oceans (CNEXO).

Conrad, M., 1983. *Adaptability: The Significance of Variability from Molecule to Ecosystem*. New York: Plenum Press.

Darwin, C., 1859/1968. *The Origin of Species by Means of Natural Selection*. Middlesex: Penguin Books. First published by John Murray, 1859.

Denbigh, K. G., 1975. *An Inventive Universe*. London: Hutchinson.

Eddington, A., 1958. *The Nature of the Physical World*. Ann Arbor: University of Michigan Press.

Eigen, M., and R. Winkler, 1983. *Laws of the Game, How the Principles of Nature Govern Change*. New York: Harper and Row.

Glansdorff, P., and I. Prigogine, 1971. *The Thermodynamic Theory of Structure, Stability and Fluctuations*. New York: Wiley-Interscience.

Gould, S. J., 1977. *Ontogeny and Phylogeny*. Cambridge, MA: Harvard University Press.

Gould, S. J., and N. Eldredge, 1977. Punctuated equilibria: the tempo and mode of evolution reconsidered. *Paleobiology* 3:115—151.

Hannon, B., 1979. Total energy costs in ecosystems. *J. Theoret. Biol.* 80:271—293.

Hutchinson, G. E., 1978. *An Introduction to Population Ecology*. New Haven: Yale University Press.

Jantsch, E., 1972. *The Self Organizing Universe*. New York: Pergamon Press.

Johnson, L., 1981. The thermodynamic origin of ecosystems. *Can. J. Fish Aquat. Sci.* 38:571—590.

Kay, J., 1984. Self organization in living systems. University of Waterloo, Canada. Ph.D. Thesis, Systems Design Engineering, 458 pp.

Kirkaldy, J. S., 1965. Thermodynamics of terrestrial evolution. *Biophysical J.* 5:965—979.

Lotka, A. J., 1925. *Elements of Mathematical Biology*. New York: Dover.

Lovelock, J. E., 1979. *Gaia; A New Look at Life on Earth*. Oxford: Oxford University Press.

Løvtrup, S., 1983. Victims of ambition: comments on the Wiley and Brooks approach to evolution. *Syst. Zool.* 32:90—96.

MacArthur, R. H., and E. O. Wilson, 1967. *The Theory of Island Biogeography*. Princeton: Princeton University Press.

MacMahon, J. A., 1979. Ecosystems over time: successions and other types of change. In *Forests: Fresh Perspectives from Ecosystem Analysis*, H. Waring, ed., Corvallis, Oregon: Oregon State University Press, pp. 27–58.

Margalef, R., 1968. *Perspectives in Ecological Theory*. Chicago: University of Chicago Press.

Matsuno, K., 1978. Evolution of dissipative systems: a theoretical basis of Margalef's principle on ecosystem. *J. Theoret. Biol.* 70:23–31.

Monod, J., 1972. *Chance and Necessity*. New York: Vintage Books.

Morowitz, H., 1968. *Energy Flow in Biology*. New York: Academic Press.

Odum, E. P., 1969. The strategy of ecosystem development. *Science* 164:262–270.

Odum, E. P., 1971. *Fundamentals of Ecology*. Philadelphia: W. B. Saunders.

Odum, H. T., 1971. *Environmental Power and Society*. New York: Wiley-Interscience.

Odum, H. T., and E. P. Odum, 1976. *Energy Basis for Man and Nature*. New York: McGraw-Hill.

Odum, H. T., and R. Pigeon, 1970. *A Tropical Rain Forest. A Study of Eradication and Ecology at El Verde, Puerto Rico*. Springfield, VA: Nat. Tech. Inform. Service.

Odum, H. T., and R. C. Pinkerton, 1955. Times speed regulation, the optimum efficiency for maximum output in physical and biological systems. *Amer. Sci.* 43:331–343.

Onsager, L. 1931. Reciprocal relations in irreversible processes. *Phys. Rev.* 37:405–426.

Oviatt, C. A., H. Walker, and M. E. Q. Pilson, 1980. An exploratory analysis of microcosm and ecosystem behavior using multivariate techniques. *Mar. Ecol. Progress Series* 2:179–191.

Patten, B. C., and E. P. Odum, 1981. The cybernetic nature of ecosystems. *Am. Nat.* 118:886–895.

Peacocke, A. R., 1983. *The Physical Chemistry of Biological Organization*. Oxford: Clarendon Press.

Popper, K., 1972. *Objective Knowledge*. Cambridge: Cambridge University Press.

Prigogine, I., 1955. *Introduction to Thermodynamics of Irreversible Processes*. New York: Wiley.

Prigogine, 1980. *From Being into Becoming*. San Francisco: W. H. Freeman.

Prigogine, I., and G. Nicolis, 1971. Biological order, structure and instabilities. *Quart. Rev. of Biophysics* 4:107–148.

Prigogine, I., and I. Stengers, 1984. *Order out of Chaos; Man's New Dialogue with Nature*. New York: Bantam Books.

Prigogine, I., and J. M. Wiame, 1946. Biologie et thermodynamique des phenomenes irreversibles. *Experientia* 2:451–453.

Proops, J. L. R., 1983. Organization and dissipation in economic systems. *J. Soc. Biol. Structure* 6:353–366.

Rutledge, R. W., B. L. Basone, and R. J. Mulholland, 1976. Ecological stability: an information theory viewpoint. *J. Theoret. Biol.* 57:355–370.

Sanders, H., 1969. Benthic marine diversity and the stability time hypothesis. In *Diversity and Stability in Ecology Systems*, Brookhaven National Laboratory 22, pp. 71–81.

Sastry, A. N., and S. L. Vargo, 1967. Variation in physiological responses of crustacean larvae to temperature. In *Physiological Responses of Marine Biota to Pollutants*, F. J. Vernberg, A. Calabrese, and W. B. Vernberg, eds., New York: Academic Press, pp. 122–138.

Saunders, P. T., and M. W. Ho, 1981. On the increase in complexity in evolution II. The relativity of complexity and the principle of minimum increase. *J. Theoret. Biol.* 90:515–530.

Schrödinger, E., 1944. *What Is Life?* Cambridge: Cambridge University Press.

Seki, H., 1982. Monitoring of eutrophication by microbial uptake kinetics of dissolved organic matter in waters. *Environ. Mont. and Assessment* 2:387–391.

Shannon, C. E., and W. Weaver, 1949. *The Mathematical Theory of Information*. Urbana: Illinois Press.

Smith, T., and H. J. Morowitz, 1982. Between history and physics. *J. Mol. Evol.* 18:265–282.

Stehli, F. G., R. G. Douglas, and M. D. Newell, 1969. Generations and maintenance of gradients in taxonomic diversity. *Science* 164:947–949.

Stuart, C. I. J. M., 1985. Bio-informational equivolence. *J. Theoret. Biol.* 113:611–636.

Tribus, M., and E. C. McIrvine, 1971. Energy and information. *Sci. Amer.* 225:179–187.

Trichner, K. S., 1965. *Biology and Information: Elements of Biological Thermodynamics*. Trans. from Russian by E. S. Spiegelthal, New York: Consultants Bureau.

Ulanowicz, R. E., 1980. An hypothesis on the development of natural communities. *J. Theoret. Biol.* 85:223–245.

Ulanowicz, R. E., 1984. Community measures of marine food networks and their possible applications. In *Flows of Energy and Materials in Marine Ecosystems*, M. Fasham, ed., New York: Plenum, pp. 23–47.

Ulanowicz, R. E., 1986. *Growth and Development: Ecosystems Phenomenology*. New York: Springer-Verlag. (Ulanowicz has provided an excellent sounding board for this analysis. His suggestion for normalizing entropy production rates to energy or material flow is an important suggestion.)

Wicken, J. S., 1980. A thermodynamic theory of evolution. *J. Theoret. Biol.* 87:9–23.

Wicken, J. S., 1983. Entropy, information and nonequilibrium evolution. *Syst. Zool.* 32:438–443.

Wicken, J. S., 1984. On the increase in complexity in evolution. In *Beyond Neo-Darwinism*, P. T. Saunders and M. W. Ho, eds., London: Academic Press, pp. 89–112.

Wicken, J. S. 1987. Entropy and information. *Philosophy of Science*, in press.

Wiley, E. O., 1983. Nonequilibrium thermodynamics and evolution: a response to Løtrup. *Syst. Zool.* 33:209–219.

Wiley, E. O., and D. R. Brooks, 1982. Victims of history—a nonequilibrium approach to evolution. *Syst. Zool.* 31:1–24.

Woodwell, G. M., 1965. Effects of ionizing radiation on ecological systems. In *Ecological Effects of Nuclear War*, G. M. Woodwell, ed., Brookhaven National Laboratory, Publication No. 917, pp. 20–38.

Worster, D., 1979. *Nature's Economy: The Roots of Ecology*. New York: Doubleday.

Zotin, A. I., 1984. Bioenergetic trends of evolutionary progress of organisms. In *Thermodynamics and Regulations of Biological Processes*, I. Lamprecht and A. I. Zotin, eds., Berlin: Walter de Gruyter, pp. 451–458.

Zotin, A. I., 1985. Thermodynamics and the growth of organisms in ecosystems. In *Ecosystems Theory for Biological Oceanography*, R. E. Ulanowicz and T. Platt, eds., Canadian Bull. of Fisheries and Aquatic Sci. 213, Dept. of Fisheries and Oceans, Ottawa, pp. 27–37.

Zotina, R. S., and A. I. Zotin, 1982. Kinetics of constitutive processes during development and growth of organisms. In *Thermodynamics and Kinetics of Biological Processes*, I. Lamprecht and A. I. Zotin, eds., Berlin: Walter de Gruyter, pp. 424–435.

7

Thermodynamics, Evolution, and Emergence: Ingredients for a New Synthesis

Jeffrey S. Wicken

7.1 Introduction

Ludwig Boltzmann was a man gloriously, and in ways tragically, ahead of his time. He echoes the sentiments of many in referring to his century as "the century of Darwin" (Prigogine and Stengers, 1984). What makes Boltzmann's comment particularly memorable is that the nineteenth century was also the century of thermodynamics, in whose development he figured so importantly. Each science contributed fundamentally to the nineteenth century's special identity as the century of *time*. Yet for Boltzmann, the Darwinian revolution was the singular accomplishment of the age.

Unlike most of his contemporaries, Boltzmann was no positivist. The fact that entropy always increased in natural processes had to be brought into the orbit of mechanistic science, and that required the same general motif of populational thinking that was so central to Darwin's theory. As natural selection required populations of organisms, so did the law of entropic increase require populations of corpuscles in which energy could be partitioned in alternative ways.

More than a century after Boltzmann's sense of the conceptual affinity between evolution and thermodynamics, scientists are still enormously divided on the relationship between these two sciences of time. One difficulty has been a prevailing misunderstanding that evolution and thermodynamics follow altogether different arrows. One has generated organizational complexity; the other generates statistical disorder. This issue may not have troubled Boltzmann. But it certainly troubled others— to a degree that led to the expression of a spectrum of vitalistic doctrines, and to distinctions between "integrative tendencies" and "dissipative tendencies" in nature (e.g., Koestler, 1967). The early steps to resolving this conundrum taken by Schroedinger (1944) have given birth to a research program (e.g., Nicolis and Prigogine, 1977; Wicken, 1979) that ties the dissipative arrow to the arrow of complexification and organization.

Darwin may have engaged Boltzmann's imagination, but Darwin's theory truncated a tradition to which Boltzmann belonged. Ever since

Empedocles, the evolutionary vision had always involved a belief in coherence—that living things were connected in some fundamental way with nature's dynamics, however poorly conceived. Darwin knew he could not do this—that he had to begin with a preexisting kernel of *organization*—which could vary and be selected according to how well it did in the ecological arena. This move was the basis for establishing evolution as a *science* as opposed to a perspective on change or creation.

It also has had the misfortune of closing evolutionary discourse to input from the physical sciences generally, leading to an autonomy-of-biology posture on evolution that is now badly out of date (Wicken, 1985a). The exclusion of thermodynamics from evolutionary discourse is a special irony of history. Thermodynamics provides a lawlike basis for the temporalization of nature, and evolution has been the most singular expression of that temporalization. Yet evolutionary theory has looked with alarm at thermodynamics ever since Lord Kelvin instructed Darwin (incorrectly) on the possible age of the universe. This adversarial relationship rages on in the contemporary paradigm, with some of its leading spokesmen militantly opposed to seeking contact with physical dynamics to the point of defending what amounts to a two-epistemologies culture (e.g., Mayr, 1982).

In spite of our obvious differences and disagreements, most of the contributors to this volume believe that this gap should be closed. Bringing this view to a higher level of articulation and consensus is not only the next stage in a dialectic, but also a necessary move toward a new, more open, evolutionary synthesis. Attacking the autonomy-of-biology citadel is therefore an implicit theme of this volume. We are far from united in our *approach* to this project. Since many of the conspicuous disagreements among contributors concern basic vocabulary, these must be aired. If thermodynamics is to be united with evolution, such terms as "entropy" and "information" must be used with a precision sufficient to permit dialogue.

Now that it is finally becoming an invited guest in evolutionary discourse, thermodynamics should be on its best behavior. That it presently suffers from a kind of identity crisis does not help this cause. Are there different *kinds* of "entropy," all sharing the property of increasing in irreversible processes? Are there dissipative processes that are not "thermodynamic" in the traditional sense at all? What are the ground rules by which the entropy-evolution game must be played?

These remarks set the thematic structure of what follows, which I shall develop in three general movements. The first focuses on specific semantic issues that presently obstruct communication between physical and biological scientists working to understand the role of thermodynamics in evolution. The second discusses ways in which thermodynamics can contribute to enriching evolutionary theory and epistemology by providing an expanded conceptual framework for understanding macroscopic processes.

The final section aims to make the Darwin-Boltzmann connection explicit, by showing that those thermodynamic "forces" (we have no better word at this point) that underlie the principles of variation and selection begin their operation in prebiotic evolution, lead through the emergence of life and then into the biotic and socioeconomic spheres (Adams, 1982; Wicken, 1986b).

This is an ambitious agenda, and I shall make no pretense of offering definitive solutions. For this Socratic admission, I make no apology. Evolution is the most complex of sciences, requiring great breadth of disciplinary input to keep open and vital. History has shown science motivated by a search for "simple," "elegant" unifying principles that bring conceptual order to empirical complexity. Kepler and Newton did this magnificently with astronomy. But there is no clean road from thermodynamics and cosmology to biology and evolution, and to assume otherwise will serve only to undermine the long-term project of connecting life with physical nature.

7.2 Entropy and Information

Entropy: The Question of Generalization

Like most physical concepts, that of entropy has evolved in the direction of increasing abstraction. Its roots lay with empirical observations of irreversibility. The first statements of the second law came with Carnot's down-to-earth computations on the possible efficiencies of heat engines. The entropy function was first formulated explicitly by Clausius, as that state parameter that had the property of changing directionally in any irreversible process.

Then came its statistical interpretation—first in the hands of Boltzmann, who introduced a primitive version of the microstate-macrostate distinction to explain irreversibility, then its more refined treatment by Gibbs, and finally the justification of the microstate-macrostate relationships by quantum mechanics. This is not an appropriate forum to debate whether thermodynamics has been *reduced* to statistical mechanics. The point simply is that statistical equations explain *why* the classical entropy function should have the property of increasing in irreversible processes, and also expand the *terrain* of the second law to probabilistic processes generally: Sevens show up more often than snake-eyes at gambling tables for reasons identical to the mixing of two liquids; similarly, if one rolled 2×10^{23} dice thousands of times, one would get a narrow band of results centering around 7×10^{23}.

In these accomplishments, statistical thermodynamics has paved a *psychological* road for an overextension of the entropy conception. Claude

Shannon's arrival at a Boltzmann-like function from the field of communications theory (Shannon and Weaver, 1949) has seemed to many a true *generalization* of the entropy conception, its freeing from the disciplinary framework of thermodynamics for application to probability distributions generally (Gatlin, 1972; Yockey, 1977). This mistaken belief is the source of much confusion when brought into the realm of biology and evolution, sciences that deal with systems that are *both* informational and thermodynamic.

The point of classical thermodynamics was to identify those minimal sets of parameters that could uniquely describe a system macroscopically, such as temperature, pressure, composition, and to establish relationships among them in systemic changes. Entropy was specifically defined as that state parameter that possessed the property of increasing during any irreversible process. Any concept claiming to be a generalization of classical entropy would have to share this essential property.

Boltzmann gave thermodynamics its first, rough statistical interpretation by introducing the microstate-macrostate distinction. Irreversibility in statistical thermodynamics hangs on this distinction. Beginning with the assumption that the energy of a system could be partitioned discretely in W alternative arrangements, Boltzmann defined his entropy function by the equation

$$H = k \ln W, \tag{1a}$$

or

$$H = -k \ln P, \tag{1b}$$

where k is Boltzmann's constant and $P = 1/W$. These insights were vindicated by the development of quantum mechanics, which indicated that a thermodynamic system did in fact have only a finite number of microscopic complexions through which its total matter-energy could be spread or randomized. Only a fraction of a system's possible complexions is available to any given macroscopic state. A nonequilibrium system can therefore be regarded as *compressed in probability space*. Irreversible processes are expansions in probability space, from macrostates having relatively few microscopic complexions to macrostates having relatively many such complexions.

Microstates are only equiprobable if they have the same energy. For systems that are open to energy exchanges with their environments, this is not usually the case. A more general formula for statistical entropy is

$$H = -k \sum P_i \ln P_i, \tag{2}$$

where the P_i refer to the energy-dependent probabilities of the various i microstates. Under isolated conditions, or under conditions where kinetic barriers to reaction keep the system in a single, nonequilibrium macrostate, this reduces to Boltzmann's equation.

The Shannon equation is $H = -\sum P_i \log_2 P_i$. Since proportionality constants and logarithm bases are more matters of convenience and scaling than of substance, the relationships among the variables in the two equations are identical. The question is whether this constitutes a sufficient condition for generalization.

First of all, concepts are not reducible to equations. What is special about $E = mc^2$ is not that it is a parabola, but that the *terms* in it depict essential matter-energy relationships. In the Boltzmann and Shannon equations the terms involve probabilities and uncertainties. These are calculated in particular ways and convey particular meanings.

For thermodynamics, "uncertainty" reflects something *fundamental* about the system: One cannot know the microstate of a thermodynamic system because it fluctuates stochastically among an ensemble of microstates all consistent with its macroscopic description.

In information theory, on the other hand, uncertainty is a strictly before-the-fact matter. It reflects the fact that a particular *sequence* or network of structural relationships is but one of many that might have been generated from a given group of elements. Once those arrangements are specified, the uncertainty vanishes. One has a *structure*, and for structures macrostate-microstate relationships fail to apply. This is a crucial difference: *Irreversibility, and the claim of the Boltzmann-Gibbs equations to represent entropy analogues, depends on the microstate-macrostate relationship.*

Shannon Entropies and the Second Law

As a result of its independent lines of development in thermodynamics and information theory, there are in science today two "entropies." This is one too many (see also Denbigh, 1982). It is not science's habit to affix the same name to different concepts, since common names suggest shared meanings. Given the inevitable tendency for connotations to flow from the established to the new, the Shannon entropy began from the beginning to take on colorations of thermodynamic entropy. In his introductory chapter to Shannon's paper, Weaver revealingly quotes Eddington as follows: "The law that entropy always increases—the second law of thermodynamics—holds, I think, supreme position among the laws of Nature" (Shannon and Weaver, 1949). Shannon goes on to rhapsodize that "thus when one meets the concept of entropy in communication theory, he has a right to be excited—a right to expect that one has hold of something that may turn out to be basic and important" (Shannon and Weaver, 1949).

To appreciate the importance of restricting "entropy" to thermodynamic applications—or, at most, to other probabilistic applications where microstate-macrostate relationships provide a condition of irreversibility—

one need only reflect on these remarks. While an indisputably important contribution to science, the Shannon formulation does not make contact with the second law. Shannon himself made no claims that it did. But as long as the term "entropy" buttresses the Shannon formula, the second law remains a steady source of justification for ideas that must find their own grounds of support. If it were possible to treat "entropy" simply as an equation, with properties dependent on area of application, calling Shannon's function by that name would be relatively unproblematic. In point of fact, most who use the term "entropy" feel something of Weaver's conviction about contacting a universal principle that provides sweeping laws of directional change.

In inventing special, Shannon-like entropies of cohesion and cladogram information and claiming for them the property of increasing under the second law, Wiley and Brooks (1982, 1983) succumb to the Weaver syndrome. The initial paper by Wiley and Brooks (1982) on "nonequilibrium evolution" was an invitation to the biological and physical community to talk about the *sense* in which thermodynamics applies to evolutionary processes. There is much of suggestive value in that paper. That species can be regarded as nonequilibrium systems, and that speciation is driven by the randomizing directives of the second law, is in my estimation an insight that will ultimately prove fruitful. But the subsequent development of that theme (Wiley and Brooks, 1983; Brooks and Wiley, 1985) plays very loose and easy with the concept of entropy and the second law generally. In this, it threatens the expanded conceptual structure for a thermodynamically informed evolutionary theory presently struggling for articulation, and clouds the waters of dialogue between physical and biological scientists.

Brooks and Wiley (1985) correctly point out that the Boltzmann equation did not originate with Boltzmann or with thermodynamic relationships, but with the eighteenth-century mathematician DeMoivre's analysis of games of chance. This is just more evidence that equations are not equivalent to concepts. Everything that bears the stamp

$$H = -k \sum P_i \log P_i$$

does not have the property of increasing in time. Irreversibility must be independently demonstrated. If one has a nonequilibrium system governed by stochastic dynamics and negotiable energy barriers, then entropy will increase.

Precision in the use of terms is an important mechanism for keeping such Spencerian ambitions in check. Entropy is that which increases in irreversible processes. If a function does not have this property, it is not an entropy. [I admit to having contributed to these confusions in ascribing Shannon "sequence entropies" to biopolymers (Wicken, 1979, 1983). This is infelicitous terminology whose usage I recant.]

There is a more appropriate alternative to "entropy" in information theory (Chaitin, 1966, 1975). This is *complexity*. What the Shannon formula measures, simply, is complexity of structural relationships—the extent to which those relationships are not predictable just from the properties of their elements. It is in complex systems that *information* can be stored. Replacing "entropy" by "complexity" in dealing with structured relationships eliminates the connotative field of the second law from arenas of discourse where it does not belong.

However, doing computations with the DeMoivre equation does not guarantee that the results will be *either* entropies or complexities. What one gets depends on the meanings of the probabilities fed into the equation. Consider Wiley and Brooks' (1983) application of it to their concept of "cohesion entropy." Figure 7.1 schematically depicts a species consisting of four populations in two different states of reproductive interaction. Figure 7.1A represents a state of maximal panmixus; in 7.1B reproductive linkages have dropped to two per population.

The P_i values for these diagrams are obtained by dividing the number of reproductive linkages issuing from each population by the total number of linkages. So in the above case, the P_i values are all $1/4$, and the H value computed from each is 2.00. The interested reader can show that when one linkage is removed the H value is 1.96 (units are omitted intentionally). Evidently, there *are* no systematic correlations between linkages and H values. What then do these functions mean? To qualify as "entropies," they must have the property of increasing in time. Elementary calculations show the reverse to be true (Wicken, 1983). To qualify as "complexities," they must portray the amount of information required for a structural specification. Surely, more than two binary identifications are required to specify

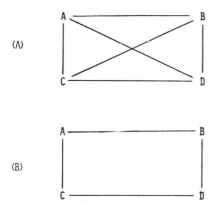

(A)

(B)

Figure 7.1
Cohesion diagrams for 4-population species.

the constituent populations of a species and their reproductive interactions. Nothing that I can perceive is measured by "cohesion entropy." Yet, the *intuition* is correct: *Breakdowns in reproductive cohesion due to entropy genera-tion are essential to speciation.* I shall return to this point later.

Problems with Information

"Information" is an elusive term. Its meaning seems obvious, yet flees under denotative pressure. The reason for this informational slipperiness has to do with the communications problems the Shannon formula was designed to treat, i.e., the information required to put a message together knowing the absolute and conditional probabilities of all the symbols involved. But "information required for specification" has little to do with "information content." To have "information content" is to *convey* some-thing. This requires rules of interpretation (grammar) and a receiver capable of using those rules to decode or utilize the transmission in its intended way.

These kinds of quantification difficulties have encouraged some informa-tion theorists (notably Brillouin, 1962) to disconnect information from its functional setting, and to treat random sequences as informationally equiv-alent to organized treatises. It has encouraged others, concerned with retaining the sense of *function* in information content (notably Gatlin, 1972) to fuse "information content" with those orderings and redundancies re-quired for message intelligibility that *subtract* from its complexity. This reasoning leads Gatlin to the remarkable conclusion that the more *redun-dant* the message, the greater its information content. Obviously, there is far more semantic work to be done in making the concept of "information content" less slippery than can possibly be dealt with in this chapter. So I shall talk only about information in its formal sense, i.e., information re-quired to specify a structure uniquely.

Information depends on *alternatives*. This has given it a certain con-ceptual and historical affinity with entropy, for the most part a misleading one. It is a common misapprehension that entropy measures "disorder" in all its manifestations—that a random arrangement of coins, scrabble pieces, or whatever, has a higher entropy than an ordered arrangement. But in fact, no "arrangement" of anything has an entropy in the sense understood by statistical thermodynamics. The basis for assigning a thermodynamic sys-tem an entropy comes from the fundamental indeterminability of its micro-states. A thermodynamic macrostate *cannot be tied down* in an arrangement. Entropy is a measure of this lack of "tied-downability." It is a property of the *macrostate*, of the ensemble of possibilities, rather than of any micro-state. An inert arrangement of scrabble pieces does not possess an entropy. It does, however, have the capacity to convey *information*.

Dice examples are heuristic here. If one rolls a die repeatedly, a unique sequence is generated that, being unpredictable from the properties of the die, is informational. A thousand dice rolling randomly present a very different situation. Now there are no individual casts that can be recorded in an informational sequence. A register attuned to die surface visibility from some arbitrary direction would record a sequence of "macrostates" deviating for the most part very slightly from the expectation value of 3,500. Now we have converted to a "thermodynamic" system, with "macrostates" centering around 3,500 commanding most of the microscopic arrangements. This is the condition for irreversibility, for expansions in probability space. But the criteria for *information*, in the sense of specifiable structural relationships, have disappeared.

Again, information depends on alternatives. No information is conveyed by a series of flips of a two-headed coin, however long, that registers only heads. Similarly, if an inorganic crystal has only one allowable lattice structure, its arrangement of elements has no capacity to convey information. Each is an example of "order" of "algorithmic compressibility" (Chaitin, 1975). In each case, the structure or sequence could be generated by an algorithm much briefer than the number of elements or interconnections involved. To have the *capacity* to convey information, a sequence or structure cannot be compressible in this way. It must be generated from an alphabet, or from a set of elements, whose affinities for interconnection are not sufficient to determine that structure. Such systems are *complex*. *Structural* information is carved from complexity-space rather than from entropy-space. There is another context, however, in which the term "information" is sometimes applied. This involves thermodynamic state specifications.

Thermodynamic information is indeed carved from entropy-space. If information is a measure of *a priori* improbability, one can assign a thermodynamic system a macroscopic information $I_M = -k \ln P_i$, where P_i measures the probability of its particular macrostate occurring (its proximity to equilibrium). We shall discuss this below with special emphasis on *modes* of thermodynamic dissipation and their evolutionary relevance. The point here is that *the more remote a system is from equilibrium, the higher its thermodynamic information*. In an expanding universe, where potential microstates are generated in excess of their equilibrative filling, thermodynamic information can grow even while total entropy increases (Layzer, 1975; Brooks and Wiley, 1985). Again, semantic problems obstruct these general grounds of agreement.

Layzer (1975) has referred to thermodynamic information as "macroscopic," to distinguish it from the "microscopic" information that would be available if one actually had access to fine-structure in phase space. This "microscopic" information is strictly a heuristic abstraction, since quantum mechanics forbids Laplacian divine calculators and Maxwellian demons. If the snapshot cannot in principle be taken, then the term "information" is misapplied. So whereas I have been semantically comfortable with applying the expression "macroscopic information" in Layzer's sense (Wicken, 1979), I have used "microscopic information" very differently, to refer to the *structural information* coded in biopolymers.

In this semantic wilderness, there is much confusion over "who said what." Brooks and Wiley (1985) assert that only *macroscopic* information counts in evolution, and defend their theory against my (Wicken, 1983) criticisms by asserting that "Wicken used a measure of microscopic information derived from the theory of dilute gases as a basis for his assertions." The precise passage in which I introduce microscopic information is as follows:

> It is to ... structured systems that the concepts of "complexity" and "organization" can be applied. The information provided by a sequence or structure-specification is *microscopic* information [original italics]; in evolution we are interested primarily in the accumulation of microscopic information in the primary structures of macromolecules. (Wicken, 1979)

That usage of microscopic information is clearly not from the theory of dilute gases. Among its many vices, semantic imprecisions can be enlisted in the cause of paradigm struggles. The fundamental distinction is between *structural* information and *thermodynamic* information. Each is crucial to the evolution and operation of living systems. *As remote-from-equilibrium systems, organisms have thermodynamic information content; maintaining their nonequilibrium states requires structurally-informed autocatalytic processes. In evolution, the dissipation of thermodynamic information drives the generation of molecular complexity from which structural information can be selectively honed* (Wicken, 1979; 1987).

7.3 Philosophical Issues

The Arena of Discourse

Fine theories have grown from bizarre metaphysical soil, and all kinds of strange bedfellows have conspired to do most constructive scientific business. It would therefore be fatuous to suggest that a theory can be no stronger than the weakest of its philosphical suppositions.

Still, there is no questioning the importance of epistemology to science. In this section, I shall suggest ways in which thermodynamics can contribute to the epistemology of evolution. As fruitful as the Darwinian program has been, evolutionary theory remains relatively immature. It is therefore presumptuous to assume (as certain advocates of the synthetic theory continue to do) that everything that transpires in evolution over the next 50 years will come comfortably to rest within some immutable conceptual framework. My general theme is that advancing the Darwinian program requires an epistemology of evolution that maximizes contact with the physical sciences, and a view of life's emergence that maximizes contact with the realities of biological organization.

Most critics of neo-Darwinism are united in believing that a mature evolutionary theory requires a revivified concept of "organism" (e.g., Gould, 1980). Treating organisms as mediators between genes and environments is an act of misplaced concreteness if ever there was one. The aspect of organism that has been most strongly emphasized in this critique is "internal constraint": Phylogenetic history limits the hand of variation on which selection can act. Less emphasized, however, is an equally important dimension of the organism conception: All organisms are *ecological* entities.

The tenor of this play-off is that since Darwinism developed as an ecological theory of evolution, it was the internal-constraint side of things that most needed emphasizing in bringing the theory into closer mesh with biological reality. Ecological selection has been treated by some biologists as a theory of "external force," which effectively molds organisms to environments. This is far from the truth. Ecology is the science of relationship, and organisms are networks of internal relationships sustained by external networks of relationship, rather than the products of imposed forces.

Here is where natural organizations distinguish themselves from machines. Machines are not ecological entities, but the product of design. Natural organizations exist, and evolve, by the interdigitation of internal and ecological relationship. Understanding the physicochemical sources of this relationality joins the "historical constraint" theme with the ecological theme, and will prove to be the key to the next synthesis.

Reinforcing evolutionary theory with thermodynamic concepts is in all ways a project whose time has come. Alfred Lotka (1922) pioneered the treatment of ecosystems as networks of energy flow long ago. Many ecologists (e.g., Odum, 1971) have advanced this theme still further, in proposing general thermodynamic rules for ecosystem development. Many physicists and chemists have applied thermodynamics to making sense of prebiotic evolution. In the biological realm, the randomizing forces of the second law underlie the Darwinian principle of variation, from point mutations to chromosome rearrangements to sexual recombination. For its part, *the principle of natural selection is inextricably connected with the competition for and effective utilization of energy resources.*

Yet in spite of this growing evidence of its deep relevance to evolution, thermodynamics remains an uninvited discipline in most contemporary evolutionary discourse. The field of protobiology shares equal blame with neo-Darwinism for this deplorable state of affairs. Later, I shall consider the sense in which thermodynamics brings protobiology into the Darwinian program. In this section, I shall consider the autonomy-of-biology stance that closes the doors of interdisciplinary dialogue.

Hows and Whys

The seventeenth century was one of great conceptual change, where enduring philosophical foundations for the natural sciences were enunciated by the likes of Galileo, Descartes, Bacon, and Newton. All recognized that the universe was ordered in a way that suggested design; and all could look back on the inability of Scholastic teleology to account for *either* the existence or the operation of that order (Wicken, 1985a). The emergence of modern science came, in no small measure, with the bracketing of the problem of *why* nature's order was as it was. What could be known with certainty were motions and their proximate causes. Galileo's admonition to pronouce the words "I know it not" in the face of ultimate causes exemplified the positivistic spirit of the age.

This mentality had profound implications for biology. The essential difference between physical and biological systems was discussed at length by Immanuel Kant in his *Critique of Judgment*: An organism was a "natural purpose" (natural organization), whose parts and processes were so organized as to be their own ends and means. In contrast to machines (artificial organizations), whose existences are entirely separable from their operations, in organisms existence is inseparable from operation. But if demonstrable knowledge of nature was indeed restricted to mechanical relationship, as Kant believed, to proximate but never ultimate causes, biology was confronted with a grave epistemological limitation: We might come in time to understand how an organism operated, but we could never hope to understand the causes of that organization. Biology would never enjoy its Newton, able to explain the existence of "a single blade of grass" (Kant, 1952). His enormous contributions to biology notwithstanding, Darwin was not that Newton. For he could not explain the genesis of organization.

The evolutionary vision prior to Darwin had always involved a belief in the *coherence* of life with the rest of nature. Darwin established evolution as a *science* by breaking this tradition, understanding that he could not address the Kantian problem, but had to *begin* with organization. This recognition set the stage for the autonomy-of-biology mentality that has hardened over the past 30 years in the hands of some of our most prominent theorists.

The heart of this problem is the status of the "why" question in science. Any organized system confronts us with three kinds of questions: What is the system we are describing, how does it work, and by what causes and reasons does it exist? For machines, the latter question has always included a "why" component—the purpose in the mind of its inventor who imposes principles of design that determine the "hows" of its construction and operation. The same why-how complementarity applies to natural organizations, but without benefit of a designer.

Why-questions have been the traditional domain of *teleology*. Since biology cannot avoid asking them (e.g., what is a structure or process *for*?), it has had to legitimize them in some way. This process of legitimization has led to the development of a special epistemology of evolution, and to perennial accusations (e.g., Grene, 1974; O'Grady, 1984) that Darwinism deals in adaptational teleology, but not in mechanisms.

"Mechanism" is an overused term, and that it has become such a ubiquitous buzzword in neo-Darwinian rhetoric points to still more grounds for semantic housecleaning. "Mechanism" is not coextensive with causation. Yet it does have a certain *nonnegotiable* meaning. In every other branch of learning that claims the status of science, "mechanism" means a description of *how*, not why, a phenomenon occurs.

On this subject the evolutionary literature becomes so embarrasingly muddled, with whys blurring into hows and teleology blurring into mechanism, that it is a wonder creationists have not gleefully translated it into poster material. It is a problem that needs to be frankly faced in expanding evolutionary epistemology. Insisting on the mechanistic purity of evolutionary science while holding to a rigid autonomy-of-biology posture serves only to elevate adaptation to the status of final cause and to reduce mechanism to a slogan.

Opening up evolutionary discourse to the physical sciences is bedeviled by this autonomy-of-biology fortress. Ernst Mayr in particular has taken pains to stress the epistemological differences between the physical and biological sciences. Mayr has made enormous contributions to the maturation of evolutionary theory, and my remarks here are made in great respect of these contributions. But solutions are never final, and Mayr's Whiggish view of the history of biological thought does not sufficiently engage the dialectic nature of progress.

In his efforts to establish a special evolutionary epistemology, Mayr paints himself into the proverbial corner. He goes so far as to assert that evolution is strictly the science of *ultimate* explanations: "Instead of concentrating on what? and how? as does the biology of proximate causes, it asks why?" (Mayr, 1982, p. 72). Does not evolution also have its *proximate* causes? If adaptation is the why of evolution, must not variation and natural selection provide its hows? This *has*, after all, been the Darwinian theme from the beginning. Mayr is far from the only culprit. Ayala (1970) brings this confusion to a head by referring to natural selection as a "teleological mechanism." Heuristic metaphor perhaps, but most certainly a conflict in concepts.

Biology, and evolution, need *philosophic* as well as hard-fact input from the physical sciences. From a methodological point of view, in which integrating life with the rest of nature is a desirable goal, Mayr's triumphant remark that "the last 25 years have seen the final liberation of biology from the physical sciences" (Mayr, 1982, p. 131) is very much a step in the wrong direction (toward vitalism). We evidently need a richer explanatory structure, where hows and whys can coexist in a complementary, rather than in a mutually muddling adversarial, relationship. Bringing evolution expressly into nature by understanding the thermodynamic bases of *variation, constraint, and selection* provides such a structure. And it does so not by eliminating the why-question, but by giving it physical legitimization.

Thermodynamics has much to contribute to evolutionary epistemology, such that it need not run forever from the Kantian challenge. First, it allows for the physical legitimization of the why-question in macroscopic processes generally, by expanding the single-tiered causal framework derived from classical physics wherein mechanism and teleology can only have adversarial relationships to each other to a two-tiered hierarchy (Wicken, 1984a, 1985a). Second, it establishes principles of continuity that bring prebiotic evolution and life's emergence into the broad Darwinian scheme.

The Teleomatic Perspective

Ever since Aristotle, teleology has implied both an ontological world view in which processes were seen as occurring for an end or goal of some sort, and a mode of explanation that appealed to the consequences of a process as a reason for its occurrence. In the tight Aristotelian system inherited by the Scholastics the two were inseparable. But mode of explanation and ontology are not mutually implicative, and thermodynamics provides the needed blade for severing their Gordian knot (Wicken, 1981a).

Thermodynamic processes are "teleomatic." This excellent term was coined rather casually by Mayr (1974) to cover all inorganic phenomena perceived as end-directed, from those governed by gravity to those of thermodynamics. My recommendation that it be confined to thermo-dynamic-statistical phenomena (Wicken, 1981b) is based on the following considerations. First, end-direction has physical significance only in connection with the concept of irreversibility. Second, by limiting "teleomatic" to irreversible processes, a materialistic basis is achieved for reserving an essential place in science for the teleological *form* of explanation, while eliminating its ontological implications. Teleomatic and mechanistic explanations are complements. *Thermodynamics concerns itself with the whys of irreversible processes, and mechanisms with their "hows."*

In the interest of communication between biological and physical scientists, it should be pointed out that Mayr (1974, 1982) has developed his autonomy-of-biology posture against a *mythological* physical science, where no one asks *why* processes occur. This central plank of the autonomy-of-biology platform is made of straw and should be burned in full view of the scientific community. When we explain the occurrence of a thermodynamic process, we do so with respect to its *consequence* of producing entropy. If we want to explain *how* it occurs, we leave thermodynamics for the microscopic realm of kinetics.

The discipline of chemistry, which has taken an unfortunately distant second place to physics as a source of philosophical principles for explanation, is full of these why-explanations, because they concern irreversibility. When we explain the formation of molecular bonds to students, we do not primarily talk about mechanisms of electron movement. And the fact that these are poorly understood has little to do with it. Mechanisms for bond-breaking are, according to microscopic reversibility, the same as those for bond-formation. Chemical bonds form in statistical populations of molecules because, *as a consequence*, potential energy is converted to entropy. Kinetic mechanisms are means for teleomatic expansions in probability space.

So the two-tiered hierarchy of causal principle that operates in all macroscopic change involves mechanistic or quantum-mechanistic laws at the lower level and thermodynamic or statistical laws at the higher. For any natural process, a complete explanation requires a specification of both the teleomatic why and the mechanistic how.

Applications to evolution immediately follow. *Variation in all its aspects, from point mutations to chromosome rearrangements to sexual recombinations, occurs by virtue of the teleomatic drive toward configurational disorder.* With regard to mutation: Although individually they are errors in replication, as a class of events they are mandated by the entropy principle, which forbids error-free replication in *populations* of biopolymers. But the second law makes no prescriptions about *how* mutations occur or about which portions of the genome are affected. The kinetic mechanisms of replication operate in potential energy wells whose depths vary both systematically as a function of position in the DNA superstructure and randomly as a function of quantum uncertainties in vibrational energies. The extension of the how-why complementarity into the causes of variation exemplifies both the hierarchical character of evolutionary explanations and the generality of principle that operates through each level. (For its part, *selection* occurs via competitions among thermodynamic flow patterns for resources.)

Thermodynamics thus allows discussion of evolutionary whys apart from mechanistic particulars, and provides general rules or guidelines for *kinds* of mechanisms. It cannot comment, however, on their specifics. In the next section, I shall use this complementarity in suggesting a framework for understanding life's emergence. Here, let us consider its application to the problem of *speciation*.

Speciation follows from breakdowns in reproductive cohesion (Wiley and Brooks, 1982) resulting from the entropic drive to genome alteration. This is *why* it occurs. The general *how* of speciation, the accumulation in time of reproductively isolating chromosomal incompatibilities, follows from this entropic why. But the how of any *given* speciation process lies in particularities to which thermodynamics has no access: What kinds of isolating mechanisms, if any, are operating? What kinds of genome alterations are occurring? What are the epigenetic constraints on the expression of these alterations? What are the ecological circumstances in which they occur? Teleomatic explanations are partial ones, addressing only one level of the causal hierarchy. Partial explanations are better than none at all.

Biology is a qualitative science, and many practicing biologists are properly wary about reducing their discipline to some combination of physical sciences. Yet there is a counterprejudice to this protection of subject matter—nurtured perhaps by the solid feel of number—that when one is not actively mathematically modeling, one is not doing theory. The costs to economics of this mentality have been pointed out by many (see Kuttner, 1985). Its costs to biology have been discussed carefully by Saunders (1984). Economic systems and biological systems share the common bond that each evolve, in part, as new ways are discovered to utilize physical resources (Wicken, 1985b). Thermodynamics contributes basic equations of constraint that allow one to talk *qualitatively* about these matters, apart from specific models or scenarios. Adams (1982) has used this approach convincingly in discussing the effects of capital investments on industrial development. Ecologists have applied it to ecosystem development for many years. Dyke, in this volume, applies it to cities. In the next section, I shall consider its application to connecting the prebiotic and biotic phases of evolution.

Natural Selection
Unlike thermodynamics, natural selection is an "uninvited guest" in this volume. Those schooled in the prepotency of selection might wonder about this. One difficulty has been the ambiguous causal status of selection alluded to above: It is appealed to variously as a mechanism, tautology, or teleological perfecting principle. If we do not know what selection is, we can hardly wonder that a significant minority of evolutionists have relegated it to the low rung of the explanatory ladder, to be pulled out like Bergson's "vital impetus" only when all else fails.

Another, related difficulty seems to be a predictable swing of the dialectic pendulum. The antiselectionist mentality is a reaction against the adaptational excesses of neo-Darwinism, which many feel compromise the concept of "organism" as a historical entity. The aspect of organism that has been most strongly emphasized in the criticisms of neo-Darwinism is "internal constraint"—the idea that phylogenetic history limits the hand of variation and developmental possibility.

This emphasis is often played off against the *ecological* dimension of the organism conception, the tenor of which is that selection is a kind of "external force" (e.g., O'Grady, 1984) that effectively molds organisms to environments. This kind of misapprehension must be remedied if a new, more open evolutionary synthesis is to be achieved. Organization *is* organization by virtue of its ecological relationality. Understanding the physicochemical sources of this relationality is essential to the Darwinian program. In the next section, I shall discuss the sense in which the dissipative structure paradigm offers basic conciliatory tissue between the understandings of ecologists and developmental biologists by connecting the themes of historical constraint and ecological relationality.

Thermodynamics has much to contribute to restoring to selection its earlier esteem. First, it invests it with genuine predictivity. Selection is not a mechanism in the sense understood in the physical sciences. Nor is it on that account an empty tautology. Selection is a historical mechanism, an *a posteriori* accumulator of success. Were it *just* an accumulator of success, where no guidelines are imposed on what constitutes success, then tautology-accusations would be inescapable. But in fact, evolution occurs in a real world in which organisms must bring specific strategies to bear on the business of wresting survival-reproductive livelihoods from nature. These strategies are conditioned by both ecological factors and historical constraints.

The *general* characters of these selectionist strategies are predictable according to the constraints of ecosystem operation. E. P. Odum (1969) enumerated twenty-four interdependent indices of ecosystem development, most of which involve strategies for resource utilization at the macroscopic level. The cycling of limiting nutrients, for example, is a strategy common to all ecosystems. It connects with other trends, such as that toward increased biomass/throughput ratios and (hence) toward decreased specific entropy production. Most of these trends can be derived by straightforward thermodynamic analyses (Ulanowicz, 1980).

Second, thermodynamics provides a general solution to the "levels of selection" problem that has beset natural selection throughout its post-Darwinian history. Individual selection seems not enough to explain the order of things, especially of altruistic aspects of social behavior. Group-selection, on the other hand, runs afoul of fundamental Darwinian tenets (Ghiselin, 1974). A thermodynamics of selection implicitly solves this problem, since constraints on ecosystem operation determine the kinds of strategies that *can* be competitively successful.

There are two interactive tendencies in the thermodynamics of selection. One involves Lotka's (1922) flow-expanding principle: Those innovations will tend to be selected that focus resources into themselves, while increasing total ecosystemic throughput. The latter rider is not *necessary* for selection, but it is a powerful *strategy*, based on the identity of an ecosystem as a web of energetic relationships. An innovation that stabilizes or enhances that web stabilizes the innovation as well. The selective premium on this interdigitation of thermodynamic flow patterns is at the heart of the globalizing trend of socioeconomic evolution (Wicken, 1985b).

The other tendency involves effective use of resources within a given energetic economy. Thermodynamic efficiency is one ingredient here, but a relatively minor one. Of major import is energy allocation (Callow, 1977). The greater the proportion of energy input that can be focused into self-production and reproduction, and the smaller the collateral costs of this operation in such activities as biosynthesis and locomotion, the greater the selective payoff under conditions of resource limitation. Hence, the move toward mutualistic relationships and the economies of specialization in ecosystem maturation and evolution. Each tendency figures strongly in giving selection predictivity, and each has figured fundamentally in the overall course of evolution by establishing general constraints on what individual characteristics would be likely to *have* selective value.

Selection is thus essential to keep in the picture as a *creative* influence in evolution, but not through the anthropomorphic "sculptor" metaphors used in previous decades. "Fitness" carries meaning only within specific contexts of resource utilization. *The most general objects of selection are not individuals or genes or populations, but informed patterns of thermodynamic flow.* An organism is such a pattern; so too are ecosystems and socioeconomic systems. The evolutionary process began with the emergence of informed patterns of flow. *Emergence* is thus the central base that must be touched in seeing the Boltzmann vision through toward making contact with the Kantian challenge. In the next section, I shall offer a *perspective* on emergence consistent with the teleomatic principles advanced above—but little in the way of theoretical solutions.

7.4 *Emergence*

There is no shortcut from thermodynamics and cosmology to phylogeny. Connecting life with prelife requires a process of emergence. Here, we shall look at those thermodynamic principles of connectivity that begin with prebiotic evolution and extend, through the process of emergence, into biotic evolution. The expression "driving forces" in this connection is a poor one, since it implies external propulsion. But using it metaphorically underscores the thesis that the teleomatic directives of the second law provide a kind of motor for the variation-selection schema.

Driving Forces
As dated life forms extend further back in the fossil record, it seems likely that the prebiotic phase of evolution may have been relatively rapid. But whether rapid or slow, it depended on thermodynamic gradients able to bring about thermodynamic flows. With the emergence of the biosphere, the gradient of greatest moment to the subsequent evolution of life has been that resulting from solar radiation and the sink of space. At life's dawn, it may have depended more on geothermal sources. Thermodynamic flows proceeding under these source-sink conditions have had two consequences essential to establishing the chemical conditions for emergence. First was the "charging" of the prebiosphere to higher levels of free energy. Second was the generation of molecular complexity though the dissipation of that free energy, according to the principles discussed above.

For any irreversible process, the second law takes the form

$$dS = dS_i + dS_e, \tag{3}$$

where dS represents the infinitesimal entropy change in the system resulting from irreversible processes carried out within the system S_i and that resulting from environmental exchanges S_e.

Any energy flow from a source at temperature T_1 to a sink at temperature T_2 is bound by the Carnot relationship

$$Q_2/T_2 - Q_1/T_1 > 0. \tag{4}$$

This relationship expresses the role of the second law as a constraint on possibility. First, it says that heat cannot flow uphill. Second, it says that for a portion of input Q_1 to be used for mechanical work or increasing the internal energy of the system, it is necessary to have a temperature gradient to drive the process.

If heat flows into the system from a source at T_1 and out to a sink at T_2, the above expression is a negentropic environmental exchange S_e term that, when substituted into equation (3) and integrated over some arbitrary unit of time yields

$$\Delta S = \Delta S_i + (Q_1/T_1 - Q_2/T_2). \tag{5}$$

This equation represents a necessary condition for evolutionary self-organization, but hardly a sufficient one. In itself, it says nothing about whether the buildup of two commodities required for the biosphere's emergence—chemical potential and molecular complexity—will occur. Buildup of chemical potential requires the *penetration* of energy into the system such that, at certain points, Q_1 exceeds Q_2. When this occurs, the consequent gain in internal energy

$$\Delta E = Q_1 - Q_2 \tag{6}$$

represents a "charging" of the prebiosphere. For this, mechanisms for absorbing energy are required. These range from electron excitation by photon absorption to the driving of endothermic reactions by geothermal heat flows.

With respect to the generation of molecular complexity, two other ingredients are required. First is structuring. The flow equation indicates that gradients will have *negentropic* effects on systems, but says nothing about their structural correlates. However, the forces of nature being as they are, structuring reactions provide *means* for thermal dissipation, and putting atoms together to make molecules, putting molecules together to form supramolecular structures such as microspheres, dissipates electronic potential energy to heat.

The second requirement for complexity is heterogeneity or aperiodicity in molecular primary structures. This is also promoted by the second law.

Randomization, Structuring, and Complexification
The biosphere is to a high degree of approximation a closed thermodynamic system, cycling a relatively constant supply of elements under the impress of free energy gradients deriving from solar radiation and the sink of space. Closed systems are governed by the Gibbs canonical ensemble, in which the probability of any macrostate occurring is given by the equation

$$P_i = W_i e^{(A - E_i)/kT}, \tag{7}$$

where E_i is the internal energy of state i, W_i is the number of microstates in which it can be expressed, and A is the ensemble average value of the Helmholz free energy.

The thermodynamic information content $I_M = -k \ln P_i$ of any such macrostate is

$$I_M = -k \ln W_i + (E_i - A)/T. \tag{8}$$

The second term of this equation represents the potential-energetic mode of thermodynamic information I_e. The first term is negative entropy. Under ideal conditions (equal numbers of thermal quantum states for each configuration of entities), the W_i are factorable into configurational and thermal components ($W_i = W_c \cdot W_{th}$). Then we can write

$$I_c = -S_c = -k \ln W_c \tag{9a}$$

and

$$I_{th} = -S_{th} = -k \ln W_{th}, \tag{9b}$$

where W_c and W_{th} are, respectively, the number of configurations available to the system and the number of quantum assignments of energy in any given configuration. Even where factoring is not possible, each represents a mode of dissipation.

To return to equation (3): The positive entropy production ($dS_i > 0$) is equivalent to the dissipation of thermodynamic information ($dI_M < 0$). If we are dealing with dissipation of energy from a closed system acquired by the "charging" represented in equation (6), then $\Delta S_e = Q/T = \Delta E/T = \Delta I_e$. Then replacing ΔS by $-\Delta I_{th} - \Delta I_c$ allows one to write the second law in thermodynamic-information terms as

$$dI_c + dI_{th} + dI_e < 0. \tag{10}$$

Evidently, increases in one of these parameters must be tied to decreases in another. *The flow of thermodynamic information from its energetic and configurational modes to its thermal mode constitutes the tie between the evolutionary and thermodynamic arrows* (Wicken, 1979).

Thermal entropy is a measure of kinetic freedom. It decreases (and I_{th} increases) with associative reactions that increase *structure*, since in those processes thermal energy moves from densely packed translational modes to relatively sparsely packed vibrational modes. It is therefore convenient to represent equation (10) as

$$dI_{th} < -dI_c - dI_e. \tag{11}$$

The prebiotic generation of molecular complexity was preconditional to the emergence of biopolymers carrying structural information. The thermodynamic sources of this complexification come from dissipation of thermodynamic information from energetic and configurational modes.

The former source of structuring is obvious. Since the formation of chemical bonds, and of supramolecular associations as well, is a means for dissipating potential energy, there tends to be a reciprocal relationship between I_{th} and I_e. Since I_e pours steadily into the biosphere in the form of radiant energy, and contributes to its energetic "charging," LeChatelier's principle favors the buildup of I_{th} at the expense of I_e.

While dissipation of I_c is a less important source of structuring, it is *essential* for generating the compositional heterogeneity and aperiodicity required for molecular complexity. Configurational entropy production also underlies the Darwinian principle of *variation*. The reasons for this become clear when we examine the ingredients in configurational entropy.

The number of configurational possibilities available to a system can be calculated from the permutational equation

$$W_c = N!/N_1!N_2! \cdots N_i!, \tag{12}$$

where N is the total number of molecules, or other chemical entities, in the system, and the various N_i represent the number of molecules of each distinct chemical species. Configurational entropy is thus an increasing

function of both number and variety. Variety is the dominant consideration. S_c always increases when new chemical species are introduced, regardless of whether N increases or decreases as a consequence (Wicken,
1978).

*In the context of biological evolution, this means that there is an entropic
pressure for variation, and hence for the breakdowns in reproductive cohesion*
Wiley and Brooks (1982, 1983) *talk about.* What is generated in those processes is not "cohesion entropy," but thermodynamic configurational
entropy.

These dynamics highlight, rather than minimize, the importance of natural selection in evolution. For I_c to dissipate, it must be produced. Since
the biosphere has no exogenous source of I_c, it must be endogenously
generated by replication and selection, processes that focus resources into a
relatively few organizational types and genomes.

The Emergence of Organization

The above dynamics, and the thermodynamic sources of the principles of
variation and selection generally, are relatively unproblematic. But the
move from prebiology to protobiology is so appallingly problematic that it
feeds into the autonomy-of-biology disposition to ignore emergence altogether. Biological organization has the annoying quality of being circular, the existence of each part both cause and effect of the operation of
the whole—the Kantian "natural purpose" motif. This circularity extends
into genesis: Chickens requiring eggs requiring chickens, proteins requiring
nucleic acids requiring proteins. While the Darwinian revolution has tended
to blur the Kantian challenge, this basic problem of circularity remains
unsolved: Where can beginnings be appropriately sought?

Scientists seem to abhor the circle with the same intensity that Aristotle
abhorred the vacuum. A favorite starting point for breaking into these
generative dynamics has been with primal replicators—naked genes replicating in the prebiotic soup and gradually building phenotypic bodies
about themselves. The most rigorously worked-out version of this schema
is Eigen and Schuster's (1979) tremendously influential hypercycle theory.

While mathematically elegant, hypercycle theory abridges all the tenets
of "reasonableness" in evolution (Wicken, 1985b). First, it requires that
RNA strands "cooperate" in coding for replicases with higher specificities
toward other, theretofore competitive strands. Second, it conjures up a
translation mechanism on strictly adaptive grounds. (If there were not one,
translation and cooperation could not occur.) Third, it perceives primordial
catalysis of polymerization to proceed on the backs of short peptides
composed of four amino acid residues (glycine, alanine, valine, aspartic
acid) that are virtually without relevance to this process. Finally, it abridges
the rules of selection themselves: Genetic information is always selected

against, unless there is some context in which it is functionally useful. This has been shown again and again in experiments with both microbial mutants (Pauling and Zuckerkandl, 1972) and viral RNA (e.g., Spiegelman, 1971).

What, then, are the options? A clue can be found in Eigen and Schuster's (1979) reference to Plato's *Timaeus*: "If anyone can name a more beautiful triangle underlying the composition of bodies, we will treat him not as an opponent but a friend in the right." What we need are not better triangles, but—another Platonic fondness—more perfect circles, which allow for understanding the coevolution of parts and wholes in relational networks. Circles begin with cycles, and cycles are driven by thermodynamic flows.

The thermodynamic perspective supports the microsphere scenario advanced by Sidney Fox over the years (e.g., Fox, 1984). Pulses of geo-thermal energy in the prebiotic soup generate thermal proteinoids, dissolution of a single gram of which gives birth to 10 billion microspheres. Since these microspheres have considerable catalytic powers, including activities toward both amino acid and nucleotide polymerization, they would seem reasonable settings for the emergence of functional relationships.

What comes next is template-instructed polymerizations via a translation mechanism. The emergence of these mechanisms and coding relationships remains the central riddle in protobiology. But the hard reality that exceedingly little is known about the particulars of life's emergence does not make all speculation on the subject empty. Nor does it imply that there are no ground rules for emergence essential to enriching evolutionary discourse.

Thermodynamics says much about these ground rules. Suppose we have a photoreceptor X, excited to X(*) by photon absorption. This will of course regenerate X in a reverse reaction through photon emission. But for this process to serve as a dissipative pathway, for it to lead to a flux of energy through the system, there must be other ways to regenerate X, which degrades this incident radiation to higher wavelengths.

We can represent this as follows:

$$nhv + X \overset{\frown}{\underset{\smile}{}} X(*) + n'hv',$$

where h is Planck's constant, v and v' represent frequencies of incident and degraded radiation, respectively, and energy conservation requires that $nhv = n'hv'$. Such processes are kinetic cycles. When there is a fixed supply of material elements available, cycling is the only route to dissipation. Natural selection is based on the competition of cycles, and components of cycles, for resources. The cycle is the precursor of biological organization. Once a cycle becomes autocatalytic, it is able to *exploit* thermodynamic gradients instead of being passively driven by them.

In this case, one dissipative pathway will simply be the gradual slipping of an electron into its potential energy well by giving up thermal energy to the environment. But some of this electronic energy might also be used more constructively—for example, in generating the high-energy phosphates that are critical to enzyme catalyzed polymerizations at ordinary temperatures.

We can therefore envisage the following rough stages in life's emergence: first, the generation of chemical potential and complexity, in the production of thermal proteinoids, microspheres, and high-energy substrates such as nucleotides and phosphorylated amino acids; second, the polymerization of those activated monomers by catalytic microspheres; third, the emergence of coding relationships and a translation machinery to make those polymerizations informed and subject to natural selection.

This is the difficult part. I would offer the following suggestion. Extended RNA strands capable of carrying protein-synthesizing information (as opposed to highly folded tRNA adaptors) are very unstable to hydrolysis and difficult to synthesize abiotically. Yet they do form stable complexes with the more robust proteinoid strands. Because of charge effects, the most important amino acids in fostering these complexes are the basic ones such as lysine (see Fox, 1984, and references therein). These are precisely the amino acids that are most crucial to catalyzing the synthesis of nucleic acids and proteins. Moreover, lysine-rich proteinoid-RNA complexes are very reasonable candidates for the protoribosomes crucial to the emergence of the translation machinery (Waehneldt and Fox, 1968). Because of its stabilizing hydrophobic milieu, ability to concentrate organic materials, and emergent protoorganizational properties, the microsphere would have provided an excellent setting for these processes.

Selective binding and stabilization of RNA strands by microsphere proteinoids provides a potential mechanism where information relevant to instructed polymerization might accrue. I doubt that this informing process was "fast," or that it resulted from some "frozen accident" of RNA-protein interaction. More likely, it evolved in some version of Darwinian gradualism. But thermodynamic selection assuredly presided over this development. Each innovation that enhanced the mutually catalytic relationships between RNA and protein would have been punctuated by a burst of entropy production and a pulling of resources into particular organizational frameworks, the genesis of both microscopic structural information and thermodynamic configurational information. In each step toward the establishment of the translational machinery, templates and enzymes became more reciprocally involved in focusing resources into their own productions. In this spectrum, evolution entered its biotic phase.

Let us consider the "ecology" of events here. The introduction of autocatalysis changed the status quo of near-equilibrium systems forming and dissipating. If the biosphere were an open system, with activated amino acids raining steadily into the prebiotic oceans and deactivated monomers evaporating steadily out, a new, higher-dissipating steady state would eventually be established following the introduction of an autocatalytic innovation. But since resources were limiting, the period of exponential growth following such introductions would have tended to deplete ambient acid and nucleotide resources, the conditions for ecological collapse. Limits to growth are imposed by the need to cycle limiting resources. The strategy of evolution from the beginning has been to discover ways of overcoming resource limitations (Wicken, 1986b). Hence, the very character of life is ecological. One of the first projects for the emergent autocatalytic core of organization was to find ways of "replacing its divots," of regenerating resources.

There have been two general strategies for this. One was the development of a metabolism able to focus resources into the production and utilization of amino acids and nucleotides necessary for informed replication. The second was ecological differentiation, with its attendant economies of specialization. Both have powerfully influenced the course of phylogeny (Wicken, 1987).

Constraints
Evolution involves variation, constraint, and selection. Neglect of the constraint corner of this triangle has fueled much criticism of neo-Darwinism over the years. *Most constraints have some thermodynamic underpinning.* Many come directly from equilibrium thermodynamics. Selectivities in amino acid polymerizations influenced the compositions of the first proteins, and these selectivities bear traces in modern, genetically coded proteins (Steinman, 1971). Morphologies of organic microspheres resemble those of spherical bacteria, down to microstructure revealed by electron microscopy (Fox, 1973). This can hardly be accidental. Life emerged in an aqueous milieu, and microspheres self-assemble as minimum free energy systems under hydrophobic tension with water. Phylogenetic evolution has proceeded from the general (what used to be archetypes) to the differentiated. This same process would seem to have characterized evolution on a cellular level. Structural constraints have limited the hand of variation from the beginning.

A thermodynamic approach to the concept of organism helps reconcile the developmental and ecological approaches to evolution by establishing physical grounds for adjudicating the old form-function controversy. Certain rational morphologists (e.g., Arber, 1950) have always maintained that the form-function distinction is artificial, that form understood in its fullest sense *is* function (cf. Lauder, 1982). The "dissipative structure" paradigm speaks very suggestively to this subject.

A given dissipative form or regime is not indefinitely modifiable by

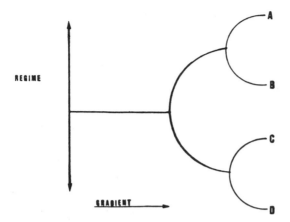

Figure 7.2
Bifurcation tree illustrating transitions between thermodynamic regimes as a function of applied gradient.

environmental forces. It has a range of autonomy with respect to both external perturbations and internal fluctuations. When stability thresholds are exceeded, the system undergoes a discontinuous transition to a new regime, which belongs to a limited set of kinetic transforms available to the system, as schematically represented by the bifurcation tree in figure 7.2. At bifurcation points, the macroscopic laws governing the system are unable to determine its behavior (Nicolis and Prigogine, 1977), and the evolutionary path it takes is determined either by internal fluctuations within the system or by external influences, such as positional effects or hormonal regulations.

The same general principles of discontinuous transformation apply to organisms, and offer support for the kind of structuralist approach to evolution advocated by Webster and Goodwin (1982), as well as grounds for bringing together its ecological and developmental dimensions. A *genuinely* ecological theory of evolution must also be a theory of organizational constraint, because the system of kinetic relationships that constitutes an informed dissipative structure is inseparable from environmental exchanges. The epigenetic landscape is an extremely complex, informed bifurcation landscape (cf. Ho and Saunders, 1979).

All this bears pregnantly on the issue of adaptationalism and the sources of historical constraints in evolution. A nonequilibrium regime carries historical content. Regime A cannot be transformed into regime C by "adaptive pressures" or an ecology of "external force." It would first have to devolve to the original bifurcation point by relaxing those gradients that led to its original evolution, then start again. In addition to providing principles of variation and selection, and for static constraints on composition in life's emergence, thermodynamics provides the basis for a physics of history.

7.5 Conclusions: A New Synthesis?

Contemporary evolutionary theory does not deal adequately with the genesis and transformation of organization, and new disciplines need to be explicitly accommodated within the Darwinian framework to make this possible. Perspective on a new, more open synthesis can be gained by considering what problems led to the original synthesis, what sciences were involved, and which were excluded. The synthetic theory was forged to accommodate the naturalists' understanding of variation and selection with the geneticists' understanding of heredity—and their erroneous belief that genes express themselves atomistically in phenotypic traits. Population genetics emerged from this synthesis, and with it a bias to treat selection as changes in allelic distributions within gene pools. What co-emerged was a diminished conception of "organism" as an expression, and an ephemeral repository, of genetic information. Excluded were the developmental sciences, by which form is generated, and the physical sciences, by which organisms produce and reproduce themselves through environmental transactions. The next synthesis must include these sciences at a fundamental level.

The evolutionary project is to explain the existence and transformation of natural organizations. Darwin's theory was a seminal move in that direction. The research program has been slowed in recent years by a prevailing autonomy-of-biology posture that discourages dialogue with the physical sciences. Thermodynamics has much to contribute to enriching this dialogue, in ways suggested (rather cursorily) in this chapter. A few summary remarks:

All natural organizations (as opposed to machines) are nonequilibrium systems that operate, and autocatalytically produce themselves, by degrading energy resources. This sets the basic currency of the organization-environment interaction, as well as the general terms on which natural selection operates. Natural selection is based on competitive success in autocatalytically converting resources into organization.

"Competitive success" is not, however, reducible to competitions among organismic individuals. One immediate benefit of treating the informed autocatalytic flow pattern as the general object of selection is that it resolves the *grounds* on which the perennial levels-of-selection controversy takes place. Ecosystems, for example, are subject to selection and undergo predictable macroscopic changes that can be expressed thermodynamically in such concepts as "ascendency" (Ulanowicz, 1980). These higher levels of selection establish boundary conditions and functional contexts that define the *terrain* of competition.

Another benefit is that it provides for the natural extension of the terrain of the Darwinian program to include life's emergence at one spectral end and socioeconomic evolution at the other. Adams (1982) in particular has advanced the latter cause, to which I have added a few general integrative principles (Wicken, 1985b).

At the other spectral end, the thermodynamic connection of operation and existence of natural organizations suggests grounds on which the problem of "origins" might at least be approached. Treating the auto-catalytic pattern as the general unit of selection allows life's emergence to be woven into the overall Darwinian framework as an *ecological* phenomenon (Wicken, 1984a,b). The prebiotic phase of evolution involved the build-up of chemical potential and molecular complexity under thermodynamic gradients (solar or geothermal). At threshold levels of these parameters, catalytic activities began to emerge, which, in such protoorganizational contexts as microspheres (Fox, 1984), might have led to the first informed autocatalytic systems.

For its part, understanding the organism as an informed dissipative structure is enormously important to the Kantian project of connecting life with the rest of nature, and in making in-principle restrictions on the hand of variation in evolutionary processes.

These considerations require a radical reevaluation of the organism concept. The "genotype produces phenotype" metaphor has far outlived its fruitfulness. Needed is a more *relational* perspective that updates the Kantian natural purpose (organization) in light of contemporary science. Organisms are autocatalytic patterns of thermodynamic flow in which genes play special informational roles, but are not "things in themselves." They are systems of internal relationships that maintain themselves in the face of both environmental and genetic changes, but that possess certain possibilities for heterorhetic switchings to new regimes (Ho and Saunders, 1979) when those relationships are destabilized.

They also enrich the epistemology of evolution. As the sciences of teleomatic ends and mechanistic means, thermodynamics and kinetics provide a physical ground for replacing the adversarial dichotomy of "whys" and "hows" on which the autonomy-of-biology thesis rests by *complementarity* within a two-tiered causal hierarchy.

References

Adams, R. N., 1982. *Paradoxical Harvest*. Cambridge: Cambridge University Press.

Arber, A., 1950. *The Natural Philosophy of Plant Form*. Cambridge: Cambridge University Press.

Ayala, F. J., 1970. Teleological explanations in evolutionary biology. *Philosophy of Science* 37:1–15.

Bookstein, F., 1983. Comment on a "nonequilibrium" approach to evolution. *Syst. Zool.* 32:291–300.

Brillouin, L., 1962. *Science and Information Theory.* New York: Academic Press.

Brooks, D. R., and E. O. Wiley, 1985. Nonequilibrium thermodynamics and evolution: responses to Bookstein and to Wicken. *Syst. Zool.* 34:89–97.

Burtt, E., 1932. *The Metaphysical Foundations of Modern Science.* Garden City: Doubleday, p. 103.

Callow, P., 1977. Ecology, evolution and energetics: a study in metabolic adaptation. In *Advances in Ecological Research,* vol. 10, A. MacFayden, ed., London: Academic Press, pp. 1–62.

Chaitin, G., 1966. On the length of programs for computing finite binary sequences. *J. Assoc. Comp. Mach.* 13:547–569.

Chaitin, G., 1975. Randomness and mathematical proof. *Sci. Amer.* 232:47–52.

Denbigh, K., 1982. How subjective is entropy? *Chemistry in Britain* 17:168–184.

Eigen, M., and P. Schuster, 1979. *The Hypercycle: A Principle of Natural Self-Organization.* New York: Springer-Verlag.

Fox, S., 1973. Origin of the cell: experiments and premises. *Naturwissenschaften* 60:359–368.

Fox, S., 1984. Proteinoid experiments and evolutionary theory. In *Beyond Neo-Darwinism,* P. T. Saunders and M. W. Ho, eds., pp. 15–60.

Gatlin, L., 1972. *Information Theory and the Living System.* New York: Columbia University Press.

Ghiselin, M., 1974. *The Economy of Nature and the Evolution of Sex.* Berkeley: University of California Press.

Gould, S. J., 1980. Is a new and general theory of evolution emerging? *Paleobiology* 6:119–130.

Grene, M., 1974. *The Knower and the Known.* Berkeley: University of California Press.

Ho, M. W., and P. T. Saunders, 1979. Beyond Neo-Darwinism—an epigenetic approach to evolution. *J. Theor. Biol.* 78:573–591.

Kant, I., 1952. *Critique of Judgment.* R. Hutchins, ed., Chicago: Encyclopedia Britannica, chapter 65.

Koestler, A., 1967. *The Ghost in the Machine.* Chicago: Henry Regnery.

Kuttner, R., 1985. The poverty of economics. *Atlantic* 255:74–84.

Lauder, G., 1982. Introduction to E. S. Russell, *Form and Function.* Chicago: University of Chicago Press.

Layzer, D., 1975. The arrow of time. *Sci. Amer.* 233:56–69.

Lotka, A. J., 1922. Contribution to the energetics of evolution. *Proc. Nat. Acad. Sci.* 8:147–155.

Løvtrup. S., 1983. Victims of ambition: comments on the Wiley and Brooks approach to evolution. *Syst. Zool.* 32:90–96.

Mayr, E., 1974. Teleological and teleonomic: a new analysis. *Bost. Stud. Phil. Sci.* 14: 91–117.

Mayr, E., 1982. *The Growth of Biological Thought*. Cambridge, MA: Harvard University Press.

Nicolis, G., and I. Prigogine, 1977. *Self-organization in Nonequilibrium Systems: From Dissipative Structures to Order through Fluctuations*. New York: Wiley-Interscience.

Odum, E. P., 1969. The strategy of ecosystem development. *Science* 164:262.

Odum, H. T., 1971. *Environment, Power and Society*. New York: Wiley.

O'Grady, R. H., 1984. Evolutionary theory and teleology. *J. theor. Biol.* 107:563–578.

Pauling, L., and E. Zuckerkandl, 1972. Chance in evolution—some philosophical remarks. In *Molecular Evolution: Prebiological and Biological*, D. Rohlfing and A. Oparin, eds., New York: Plenum, pp. 113–126.

Prigogine, I., 1955. *Introduction to the Thermodynamics of Irreversible Processes*. New York: Wiley.

Prigogine, I., 1980. *From Being to Becoming*. San Francisco: Freeman.

Prigogine, I., and I. Stengers, 1984. *Order out of Chaos*. New York: Bantam.

Saunders, P. T., 1984. Mathematics in biology. *Riv. Biol.* 77:325–341.

Schroedinger, E., 1944. *What Is Life?* Cambridge: Cambridge University Press.

Shannon, C., and W. Weaver, 1949. *The Mathematical Theory of Communication*. Urbana: University of Illinois Press.

Spiegelman, S., 1971. An approach to the analysis of precellular evolution. *Quart. Rev. Biophys.* 4:213.

Steinman, G., 1971. Non-enzymic synthesis of biologically pertinent peptides. In *Prebiotic and Biochemical Evolution*, A. Kimball and J. Oro, eds., New York: American Elsevier, pp. 31–38.

Thompson, D'Arcy, 1977. *On Growth and Form*. Cambridge: Cambridge University Press.

Ulanowicz, R., 1980. An hypothesis on the development of natural communities. *J. Theor. Biol.* 85:223–245.

Waehneldt, T., and S. Fox, 1968. The binding of basic proteinoids with organismic or thermally synthesized polynucleotides. *Biochim. Biophys. Acta* 160:239–245.

Webster, G., and B. Goodwin, 1982. The origin of species: a structuralist approach. *J. Soc. Biol. Str.* 5:15–47.

Wicken, J., 1978. Information transformations in molecular evolution. *J. Theor. Biol.* 72:191–204.

Wicken, J., 1979. The generation of complexity in evolution: a thermodynamic and information-theoretical discussion. *J. Theor. Biol.* 77:349–365.

Wicken, J., 1980. A thermodynamic theory of evolution. *J. Theor. Biol.* 87:9–23.

Wicken, J., 1981a. Causal explanations in classical and statistical thermodynamics. *Philosophy of Science* 48:65–77.

Wicken, J., 1981b. Evolutionary self-organization and the entropy principle. *Nature and System* 3:129–141.

Wicken, J., 1983. Entropy, Information, and Nonequilibrium evolution. *Syst. Zool.* 32:438–443.

Wicken, J., 1984a. The cosmic breath: reflections on the thermodynamics of creation. *Zygon* 19:487–505.

Wicken, J., 1984b. Autocatalytic cycling and self-organization in the ecology of evolution. *Nature and System* 6:119–135.

Wicken, J., 1985a. Thermodynamics and the conceptual structure of evolutionary theory. *J. Theor. Biol.* 117:363–383.

Wicken, J., 1985b. An organismic critique of molecular Darwinism. *J. Theor. Biol.* 117:545–561.

Wicken, J., 1986a. Connecting evolution and emergence: a structuralist perspective. *Riv. Biol.* 79:51–74.

Wicken, J., 1986b. Thermodynamics and the evolution of biological and socioeconomic systems. *J. Soc. Biol. Str.*, in press.

Wicken, J., 1987. *Evolution, Information, and Thermodynamics: Extending the Darwinian Program.* Oxford: Oxford University Press, in press.

Wiley, E. O., and D. R. Brooks, 1982. Victims of history—a nonequilibrium approach to evolution. *Syst. Zool.* 31:1–24.

Wiley, E. O., and D. R. Brooks, 1983. Nonequilibrium thermodynamics and evolution: a response to Løvtrup. *Syst. Zool.* 32:209–219.

Yockey, H., 1977. A calculation of the probability of spontaneous biogenesis by information theory. *J. Theor. Biol.* 67:377–398.

III

Thermodynamics and Phylogenetic Order

8
Entropy and Evolution
E. O. Wiley

In *The Structure of Biological Science* Rosenberg (1985) reviews some of the major controversies surrounding the philosophy of biology and how biology might differ philosophically from the "hard sciences." Two views are prevalent. "Autonomists" believe that the biological sciences are sufficiently different from the physical sciences that, in Rosenberg's words, "biological theory and practice must remain permanently insulated from the distinctive methods and theories of physical science." In contrast "provincialists" hold that biological science is a subset of the physical sciences, and that "biological findings and theories must be not merely compatible with those of physics but must actively cohere with its theoretical achievements." Not surprisingly, Rosenberg (1985) finds fault with both extremes. More surprising, however, are the reasons why neither view is satisfactory. Provincialists have the correct logical and philosophical attitude: "What there is in biology that cannot be accommodated in principle to physical sciences should be jettisoned" (Rosenberg, 1985, p. 226). However, provincialists err in not understanding that biological systems are hierarchical and disjunctive and thus may elude satisfactory reduction. For example, there is no smooth reduction between Mendelian and molecular genetics. Autonomists have the wrong philosophical attitude, but they are often correct in asserting the practical (perhaps actual) irreducibility of some kinds of biological phenomena. Why should there be hierarchies and disjunctions between levels of biological organization? Perhaps because biological entities are spatiotemporally restricted entities with singular and distinctive histories. They are not "natural kinds" of the sort usually studied by physicists and chemists but "individuals" (Ghiselin, 1969, 1974; Hull, 1976, 1980; Wiley, 1980, 1981). The unity of science may be best served by attempting reductions whenever possible, while at the same time not jettisoning certain biological theories just because they cannot be reduced to physical theories. Biological systems may show phenomena not accounted for by physical theories, while still being consistent with them. "Active coherence" is not synonymous with smooth reduction.

Dan Brooks and I find ourselves in a rather curious position. We wish to reduce evolutionary theory in such a way that the phenomemon of evolution can be explained as a consequence of a more general physical theory. But we do not wish for this reduction to proceed in the direction of the microscopic laws of physics and chemistry. Rather, we wish to do our reduction in the opposite manner, from a macroscopic law, the second law of thermodynamics. In doing so, we hope to avoid the pitfalls that tend to plague reductionism and to preserve the "modest claims" of the autonomists (Rosenberg, 1985, pp. 226–228). Further, we do not feel that evolution can be deduced from studying the thermodynamics of nonliving physical systems because we embrace the view that there are levels of biological organization and biological phenomena that cannot be fully explained by lower levels of biological (much less physical) organization.

8.1 Dynamics and Thermodynamics

Biological systems, like physical systems, are subject to processes that lend themselves to either dynamic or thermodynamic descriptions. As characterized by Layzer (1981), dynamic descriptions are deterministic, reversible, and require a detailed knowledge of initial data. In contrast, thermodynamic descriptions are stochastic, irreversible, and require selective description of initial data. I would like to illustrate these distinctions by considering two biological cases.

An excellent example of a system that lends itself to a dynamic description is a large population of organisms undergoing selection at a particular locus. Consider a sexual population of 100,000 breeding individuals. We shall set the allelic frequencies of two alleles at a single locus to be equal (i.e., frequency A = frequency A'), and we shall assume that the population begins in Hardy-Weinberg equilibrium. Let us move our population to an environment where allele A has a selective advantage over A'. We can predict, from standard population genetic theory, that A will increase in frequency in the next and subsequent generations. But the specifications of the initial frequencies of the two alleles and the direction of selection will not allow us precisely to predict the dynamic changes of the allelic frequencies. We can be more precise to the extent only that we have more detailed knowledge of the system. Such knowledge involves

1. the selection coefficient,
2. whether there is dominance at the locus,
3. the forward and back mutation rates,
4. the extent of gene flow from other populations and its character,
5. whether there is assortative mating, and
6. whether there is linkage to other loci influenced by selection.

Further, so long as A' is present in the population, there is no reason to think that the system is changing in an irreversible manner. A change in the environment might well give A' a selective advantage. And, even if A' is eliminated in a given generation, there is no reason to think that it will not reoccur in the next generation via mutation given the rather large size of the population. Finally, once the population has evolved for several generations, the fact that we began at equal allele frequencies becomes quite irrelevant to predicting the frequencies of the next generation. These facts point to the power of dynamic descriptions and reflect the power of population genetics.

Now consider species. Species may be ordered according to their genealogical relationships. This ordering may take the form of a phylogenetic tree (a directed graph) or of a hierarchial classification (Hennig, 1966). Each documents the history of common ancestry that exists between the species considered. A few simple axioms (Wiley, 1975) permit us to reconstruct these histories by applying the methods of phylogenetic systematics (Hennig, 1966; Wiley, 1981). We do not need to know the details of dynamics (specific evolutionary mechanisms, particular modes of speciation, etc.) in order to accomplish this task. When we examine available phylogenies we observe that evolution at the level of species is quite irreversible (Dollo's Law) in the following sense: We do not observe the same species evolving, going extinct, and then reappearing again at some later date when environmental conditions are right for it. Species are not analogous to alleles, and speciation is more than natural selection. As Collier (this volume) notes, one consequence of these observations is that the dynamical descriptions of population genetics are not sufficient to explain the irreversible nature of phylogenies, and thus cannot explain this aspect of biological order. Of course, biological order at the level of phylogenies is fully *consistent* with the dynamical descriptions provided by population genetics and we can fruitfully seek explanations about mechanisms of speciation for particular species. Dynamics and thermodynamics are complementry, not antagonistic.

8.2 Thermodynamics and Evolution

There are several levels of biological organization that exhibit irreversible behavior. Three obvious ones are reproduction, ontogeny, and phylogeny. Certain early twentieth-century scientists believed that organic evolution was the biological manifestation of the second law of thermodynamics (see Lotka, 1924, reprint 1956, pp. 26, 357). Later workers were not so sure (cf. Schrödinger, 1945). They sensed a potential conflict because, while the direction of change in the universe as a whole seemed to be toward greater "disorder" and increasing entropy, the direction of evolution seemed to be toward greater "order" and decreasing entropy. Schrödinger (1944) proposed a solution: The existence of living systems depends on increasing the entropy of their surroundings. The second law is not violated. It is only locally circumvented at the expense of a global increase in entropy (see Morowitz, 1968, for discussion).

As the century progressed, it became apparent that classical, equilibrium, thermodynamics could not account for the behavior of biological systems. Obviously, biological systems were nonequilibrium systems. Equilibrium was death. Ilya Prigogine and his colleagues began to exploit the discipline of nonequilibrium thermodynamics (cf. Prigogine and Wiame, 1946; Prigogine, Nicolis, and Babloyantz, 1972; Prigogine, 1980; Prigogine and Stengers, 1984). They have tended to approach organisms using the analogy of physical dissipative structures and have sought the mechanism of irreversibility in the dynamics of microscopic laws. A quite different approach has been developed by Layzer (1975, 1977, 1978, 1980), who suggests that history, manifested in macroscopic information, is at the core of the problem of irreversibility. Organisms are not analogous to physical dissipative structures in a manner interesting to biologists. Rather, evolution is characterized by an ever increasing phase space that is genetic (see Layzer, 1980, and this volume). The analogies between evolution and physical systems lie in considering such systems as the expanding universe, where both entropy and order increase together because the realization of structure lags behind the expansion of phase space. (This particular view of cosmological evolution has been discussed by Frautschi, 1982, and in this volume; Landsberg, 1984a,b; as well as Layzer, loc. cit.)

8.3 Models

A full discussion of the Brooks-Wiley model of nonequilibrium evolution can be found in Brooks and Wiley (1986). Its somewhat ragged development can be traced in various papers (Wiley and Brooks, 1982, 1983; Brooks and Wiley, 1984, 1985; Brooks et al., 1984). A detailed account is not warranted here.

We take as a general thesis that evolution is a special case of the second law of thermodynamics. We submit that it is a special case because the irreversible behavior of certain biological systems has a quite different basis from that exhibited by purely physical dissipative structures. The order and organization of biological systems, such as organisms and species, is based on information that is carried by these systems in the form of genes, cytoplasmic organization, and chromosomal organization. (The latter two are of ultimate genetic origin.) Thus, biological systems exhibit order and organization based on properties that are inherent and heritable. Physical dissipative structures lack these characteristics. Because organisms have these characteristics, we can conceive of their relevant phase space as genetic (Layzer, 1978, 1980, and this volume). Of course, organisms obey the rules of physical dissipative structures at the chemical level. But this is irrelevant to our understanding of the order and organization observed in evolution (see Collier, this volume, for a detailed discussion of this point). Our models are similar to the cosmological models I discussed above, but they differ in the same manner from ours as models of physical dissipative structures in that macroscopic information resides within the system rather than being purely phenomological (i.e., observer dependent). Our concept of "information" has a physical basis. It differs from both Brillouin's (1962) and Shannon's (Shannon and Weaver, 1949). In Brillouin's sense, information does not reside within the system and is thus phenomonological. In Shannon's sense, information resides within the system, but, as Brillouin (1962) has pointed out, this information lacks a physical interpretation. In our sense, information resides within the system and has a physical interpretation (see Brooks and Wiley, 1986; Collier, 1986, and this volume).

Since biological information resides in biological systems and has a physical interpretation, it must be subject to the consequences of the second law. In short, the entropy of biological information must increase in irreversible processes. Biological systems are open information systems because both the size and variety of the genome may increase. The system as a whole (that is, the total phylogeny) is characterized by an increasing genetic phase space. New genes originate, preexisting genes mutate, tandem duplications occur, genetic material is reshuffled. The first living organism had but a fraction of the genetic diversity now observed among organisms (and inferred from extinct organisms). The dynamics of molecular genetics and population genetics, as well as the observations of comparative biology, corroborate these conclusions.

These characteristics of biological systems have consequences. Since biological information resides within organisms, we can calculate meaningful entropy measures for this information. We predict that the irreversible aspects of reproduction, growth, and phylogeny are characterized by increases in these entropy measures. We predict that evolution is constrained in such a manner that realized complexity (measured as entropy of information) lags behind the expansion of genetic phase space for the simple reason that reproduction occurs at a faster rate than mutation. Further, we submit that there are other capacities residing within certain biological systems that are also amenable to physical description. The most important of these capacities is "cohesion," the capacity to transmit information to subsequent generations. This capacity is missing from physical systems (although, perhaps, it has its analogue, gravity, in certain cosmological models). Dissipation in biological systems is not limited to energy and mass. It also takes the form of information dissipation.

In the following sections I shall discuss four aspects of the Brooks-Wiley theory. First, I shall use a simple model to show how complexity and organization can increase together. Second, I shall present a short discussion of genotypic information and the connection between this kind of information and measures of complexity (= entropy). Third, I shall briefly discuss cohesion. Fourth, I shall briefly discuss speciation and entropy measures of phylogenetic trees.

8.4 A Simple Model

I shall use Layzer's (1977) basic formula for macroscopic information to investigate the growth of a very simple (and purely hypothetical) organism. Layzer defines macroscopic information as

$$I = H_{max} - H_{obs},\tag{1}$$

where I is macroscopic information, H_{max} is the maximum entropy of the system if it were in equilibrium, and H_{obs} is the observed entropy of the system. H_{max} is defined as

$$H_{max} = \log A,\tag{2}$$

where A is the number of microstates available to the system. H_{obs} is defined as

$$H_{obs} = -\sum (p_i \log_2 p_i),\tag{3}$$

where p_i is the probability of the ith microstate being realized. (These formulas are similar to the formulas used for thermodynamic measurements of entropy, but differ in using log base 2, thus $k = 1$. The units are arbitrarily termed "bits.") Macroscopic information (I) is a measure of the organization of a system; H_{obs} is a measure of the complexity, or entropy, of a system.

The system I wish to discuss is a cartoon of a developing organism that starts as a single cell and grows to the eight-cell stage. As the organism develops, the cells (represented by circles in figure 8.1) will differentiate into two types. One type will occur at the corners of the organism, the other type will occur "inside." We shall consider these fates to be controlled genetically through clues gained by the topographic position a cell finds itself in before the next cell division. We may consider the phase space ($\log_2 A$) to be defined by the number of cells at any given time period (a reflection of the genetic information expressed), and p_i to be defined as the probability of a particular cell occurring at a particular position within the embryo.

Figure 8.1 shows the growth of the organism through the selected time period. In table 8.1 I have computed I, H_{max}, and H_{obs} for each step. Note that H_{max} does not remain static, but grows through time as cells are added by cell division. The results are graphed in figure 8.2. Note that initially no

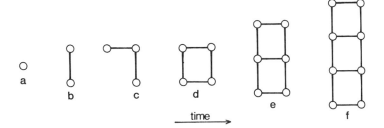

Figure 8.1
The ontogeny of a hypothetical organism over six time periods (a–f). Open circles are cells; lines denote connections between cells.

macroscopic information is generated because there are no constraints on where any particular cell is located. However, once the organism grows to the six-cell stage, we observe a difference between the maximum complexity and the observed complexity of the organism. This is due to the fact that the cells are now constrained. The inner cells, with three topographic connections, cannot be freely substituted with the outer cells, which have only two topographic connections. Thus there is a departure from equiprobability. The entropy of the system at the four-cell stage is calculated as

$$H_{obs} = -4(1/4 \log_2 1/4) = 2 \text{ bits.}$$

Note that there is only a single class of cells (the class of two connections). In contrast, the entropy of the system at the six-cell stage is calculated as

$$H_{obs} = -4(1/8 \log_2 1/8) - 2(2/8 \log_2 2/8) = 2.5 \text{ bits.}$$

Note that there are two classes of cells with different probabilities. Subsequent growth to the eight-cell stage results in further constraints and a greater departure from equiprobability. Macroscopic information continues to grow (figure 8.2). Both the entropy and the organization of the system increase, but the observed entropy lags further behind the maximum possible entropy over time.

8.5 Evolution within Populations

I have alluded to the fact that the rules of population genetics are dynamical and that evolution at this level may be reversible. It may seem paradoxical that I should immediately move to this level of evolution. But dynamics and thermodynamics are complementary, and populations can serve to illustrate how it is possible to measure genetic (information) entropy and genetic phase space.

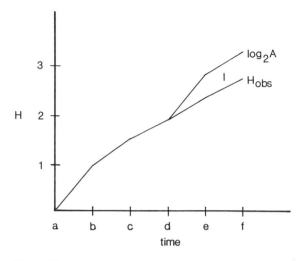

Figure 8.2
A graph of the values from table 8.1.

Populations represent a level of biological organization between that of individuals and that of species. A population is a local aggregation of individuals. Those of interest here belong to the same species. A population may be large or small, open (sharing genes with other populations) or "closed" (isolated from other populations). Occasionally a species may consist of a single population. More frequently, several to many populations comprise a species.

Information resides in a population in the form of genotypes and phenotypes. For simplicity, I shall restrict this discussion to genotypes. We may define the maximum evolutionary potential of a population as $\log A$, where A is the number of genotypes in the population. Consider a single locus. If our population consists of diploid individuals who are entirely homozygous at that locus (only a single allele is found), then no evolution is possible at that locus. The evolutionary potential is

$$A = 1, \qquad \log_2 A = 0.$$

Now, let us consider a population comprising 30 mating individuals that are homozygous for the allele X. In the next generation a mutation occurs such that one of the offspring is now heterozygous (i.e., its genotype is XX'). For simplicity of calculation, I shall keep the number of breeding individuals constant over successive generations. Our population has some evolutionary potential since $\log_2 A$ now equals 1. However, the distribution of genotypes is not random since only a single individual has the genotype XX', while all other individuals have the genotype XX. Thus, the

Table 8.1
Computed values of macroscopic information (I), complexity (H_{obs}), and maximum possible entropy ($\log_2 A$) for each stage shown in figure 8.1

Value	Time period					
	a	b	c	d	e	f
$\log_2 A$	0	1.0	1.58	2.0	3.0	3.5
H_{obs}	0	1.0	1.58	2.0	2.5	2.9
I	0	0	0	0	0.5	0.58

observed entropy of the population is very low:

$$H_{obs} = -(29/30 \log_2 29/30) - (1/30 \log_2 1/30) = 0.210.$$

Now, we allow the population to exist for several generations, and we allow the mutation to be spread. There are now three possible genotypes (XX, XX', and X'X'), and $\log_2 A$ has increased to 1.585. This is the maximum possible evolutionary potential for a single locus with two alleles. The dynamics of evolutionary change may subsequently follow a number of pathways including replacement of X by X', the disappearance of X', a stable polymorphism, etc. (as shown by numerous standard works in population genetics—cf. Wright, 1968, 1969, 1977, 1978; Dobzhansky, 1970; Wilson and Bossert, 1971; Lewontin, 1974; Futuyma, 1979). Plots of entropy changes in such a system are shown in Brooks and Wiley (1986, p. 136). In order for a population to reach maximum complexity (where $H_{obs} = H_{max}$), the population would have to consist of equal numbers of individuals of each genotypic class, an unlikely situation because of stochastic factors. Thus evolution is likely to be constrained even in very simple systems.

When we consider more complex systems, it becomes easy to see why evolution is constrained, even in potentially reversible systems. The list below shows the maximum number of genotypes for three different genetic models:

two-locus, two-allele model: 9 genotypes;
one-locus, three-allele model: 6 genotypes;
ten-locus, two-allele model: 59,049 genotypes.

Even the simplest organisms have many more than ten loci, and considering that as much as 10% of the loci in eucaryotic organisms have more than two alleles, the evolutionary potential of the average eucaryotic population must be high indeed. However, the large diversity that is potentially present in such populations presents potential problems for any investigator who wishes to obtain an estimate of complexity. Obviously, the investigator could not hope to count genotypes in natural populations for any feature controlled by more than a few loci. Fortunately, this problem can be overcome because entropy is directly related to variance (Brooks and Wiley, 1986).

We can understand this relationship by considering redundancy. Redundancy is a measure of the amount of information diversity that is present in a system. It is defined as

$$R = 1 - H_{obs}/\log_2 A. \tag{4}$$

In simple terms, the observed entropy of a system is inversely related to redundancy. A completely redundant population would be one in which all genotypes were identical ($R = 1$, $\log_2 A = 0$). In our population of 30 individuals, the redundancy of the population when the first mutant was born would be

$$R = 1 - 0.21/1 = 0.79.$$

As it turns out, variance (σ^2) is inversely related to redundancy. Variance increases as redundancy decreases. Thus, variance is directly related to entropy, and is, in fact, an estimate of information entropy. High variance populations (species, clades) are high entropy systems. Brooks and Wiley (1986) present a more formal treatment of the relationship between variance and information entropy that can be related directly to the computer simulation model of Brooks et al. (1984). The relationship between variance and information entropy is very important because it provides the basis of a protocol for measuring the entropy of populations by a means presently available to evolutionary biologists. We shall see in the next section that variance is also important in discussions concerning cohesion.

8.6 Cohesion

Individuals of a species are of evolutionary consequence only if they leave offspring. Individuals of sexual and parasexual species produce offspring who are the product of gamete fusion or some other sort of genetic exchange. We may distinguish between two sorts of cohesion. Vertical cohesion obtains between parents and offspring. Horizontal cohesion obtains between parents and between populations linked by gene flow (i.e., migration followed by successful mating). As stated earlier, cohesion permits some of the information present in parents to be passed on to offspring. In sexual species and between populations, cohesion performs an integrative function. (An analogous situation obtains between the cells of a multicellular organism; the cohesion in this case is cell cohesion, which also has a genetic aspect.)

Some critics of our early papers (Wiley and Brooks, 1982, 1983) apparently misunderstood how we proposed to measure cohesion and thus concluded that loss of cohesion is a negentropic rather than an entropic phenomenon (cf. Løvtrup, 1983; Bookstein, 1983; Wicken, 1983). Answers to these critics (regarding this point and other points) may be found in Wiley and Brooks (1983), Brooks and Wiley (1985), and Collier (1986). Basically, we present the idea that cohesion within a population is directly related to the variance of panmixis and that cohesion within a species (between populations) is inversely related to the degree of isolation of its populations (i.e., an entropy measure of cohesion is directly related to isolation). Brooks and Wiley (1986) discuss these points in more detail. We suggest that the cohesion that obtains between the populations comprising a species can be estimated by a measure that takes into consideration both the topological connections between populations (i.e., gene flow routes) and the relative isolation of each population. Thus

$$H_c = -\sum \hat{F}_i(p_i \log_2 p_i),\tag{5}$$

where $\hat{F}_i$ is a measure of isolation (Wright, 1968, 1978) for the ith population, and the remainder of the equation is identical to the H_{obs} used previously. We have discussed examples of how this measurement behaves (Brooks and Wiley, 1986, pp. 164–177). The following points can be made:

1. Species cohesion decreases with increasing isolation of populations.
2. Species cohesion decreases as gene flow routes are cut off.
3. So long as all populations are connected with each other, the species will exhibit a relatively high level of species cohesion (low cohesion entropy) that will tend to fluctuate around an equilibrium point.
4. Complete isolation of a population will cause the species to stop fluctuations and will decrease cohesion (increase cohesion entropy). The number of populations isolated is directly proportional to the increase in cohesion entropy.
5. The changes in (4) become irreversible to the extent that genetic isolation obtains or that continued geographic isolation obtains until establishment of new species.

8.7 Speciation and Clades

Speciation is associated with cladogenesis, the splitting of an ancestral species into two (rarely more) species. A clade is a historical entity to which the ancestor and its descendants belong as parts of a whole. It is easy to imagine a smooth reduction between the phenomena operating at the level of populations and the histories of clades. The disjunction between levels occurs when lineage splitting becomes irreversible. In some cases, irreversibility may be quite abrupt and readily observable because of particular changes in their information systems that cause genetic isolation. In other cases, the gene pools may be separated by geological events and remain potentially reversible for a long period of time, in spite of the fact that we can observe differences between them. Indeed, most newly evolved species are allopatric in their distributions (live in adjacent regions, but not in the same region), and many can form viable hybrids when crossed in the laboratory. The "fuzziness" of species is one of the characteristics of individuals and is to be expected (Hull, 1978, 1980). These characteristics have plagued attempts to formulate a universally applicable species concept. "Biological species" are supposed to be reproductively isolated, but many species can interbreed. Some that interbreed nevertheless represent irreversible systems because the hybrids are sterile or because the intermediates are selected against in the long run (genetic "sinks" along contact zones between species are an example). In general, the farther away the system moves from a cladogenetic event, the more irreversible the system becomes and the more irreversible the system appears to an observer. (For example, hybrids between species of different genera are rare and unexpected; hybrids between families come as a great surprise; and hybrids between phyla are unknown.) These observations reinforce our notions of the relationship between information, cohesion, and the second law. Variance between clades increases with time, and phylogeny is a special case of the operation of the second law.

If we move from the level of populations to the level of species and phylogenetic trees, we may calculate several types of entropy measures. Taking the tree itself as the macrostate, we may examine its entropic behavior using measures adapted by Karreman (1955). We may also examine the spread of information over the tree (Wiley and Brooks, 1983; Brooks and Wiley, 1985, 1986). We may examine two simple systems in which phylogenies are portrayed as directed graphs. In figure 8.3 we see two phylogenetic histories. The first (figure 8.3a) represents two peripheral isolation events, with the ancestral species X first giving rise to the descendant Y and then later to the descendant Z. We may calculate an entropy of topological information reflecting a summary of these lineage splits. On the left side of figure 8.3a we observe that X has two connections, one with itself and one with Y, for a total of three connections. H_{obs} can be calculated as

$$H_{obs} = -1(2/3 \log_2 2/3) - 1(1/3 \log_2 1/3) = 0.918.$$

On the right side of figure 8.3a there are more connections. Species X has given rise to species Z. If we perform a similar calculation, we observe that the entropy of the system has increased ($H_{obs} = 1.253$). On the left side of figure 8.3b we have an ancestor who gave rise to two descendants while becoming "extinct" (i.e., both of the descendants diverged from the original

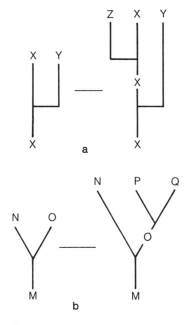

Figure 8.3
Cladogenesis in two groups of species.

ancestral information system). Thus, the ancestor M has two connections (one each with N and O), while the descendants have one each (with M). The H_{obs} is

$$H_{obs} = -1(2/4 \log_2 2/4) - 2(1/4 \log_2 1/4) = 1.5.$$

Carried through for another speciation event (O gives rise to P and Q, right side of figure 8.3b), we observe an increase in entropy ($H_{obs} = 2.236$).

These simple examples demonstrate that entropy does increase during speciation. A similar result is obtained when both information changes (in the form of evolutionary novelties plotted on the topology where they originate) and cladogenetic events are considered (summarized in Brooks and Wiley, 1986).

8.8 Conclusions

The concept of information used in the Brooks-Wiley theory of non-equilibrium evolution permits the calculation of physically interpretable measures of information entropy for biological systems. Biological processes working on irreversible systems produce positive increases in these measures. Examples that illustrate this are drawn from ontogeny, reproduction, and phylogeny. Evolution is a special case of the second law of thermodynamics. The hierarchial structure of many types of biological relationships is a consequence of these phenomena.

References

Bookstein, F., 1983. Comment on a "nonequilibrium" approach to evolution. *Syst. Zool.* 32:291–300.

Brillouin, L., 1962. *Science and Information Theory.* New York: Academic Press.

Brooks, D. R., and E. O. Wiley, 1984. Evolution as an entropic phenomenon. In *Evolutionary Theory: Paths to the Future,* J. W. Pollard, ed., New York: Wiley.

Brooks, D. R., and E. O. Wiley, 1985. Nonequilibrium thermodynamics and evolution: responses to Bookstein and Wicken. *Syst. Zool.* 34:89–97.

Brooks, D. R., and E. O. Wiley, 1986. *Evolution as Entropy: Towards a Unified Theory of Biology.* Chicago: University of Chicago Press.

Brooks, D. R., P. H. LeBlond, and D. D. Cumming, 1984. Information and entropy in a simple evolution model. *J. Theor. Biol.* 109:77–93.

Collier, J., 1986. Entropy in evolution. *Biol. and Philos.* 1:5–24.

Dobzhansky, T., 1970. *Genetics of the Evolutionary Process.* New York: Columbia University Press.

Frautschi, S., 1982. Entropy in an expanding universe. *Science* 217:593–599.

Futuyma, D. J., 1979. *Evolutionary Biology.* Sunderland, MA: Sinauer Assoc.

Ghiselin, M. T., 1969. *The Triumph of the Darwinian Method.* Berkeley: University of California Press.

Ghiselin, M. T., 1974. A radical solution to the species problem. *Syst. Zool.* 15:207–215.

Hennig, W., 1966. *Phylogenetic Systematics.* Urbana: University of Illinois Press.

Hull, D. L., 1976. Are species really individuals? *Syst. Zool.* 25:174–191.

Hull, D. L., 1978. A matter of individuality. *Phil. Sci.* 45:33–60.

Hull, D. L., 1980. Individuality and selection. *Ann. Rev. Ecol. Syst.* 11:311–332.

Karreman, G., 1955. Topological information content and chemical reactions. *Bull. Math. Biophys.* 17:279–285.

Landsberg, P. T., 1984a. Is equilibrium always an entropy maximum? *J. Stat. Physics* 35:159–169.

Landsberg, P. T., 1984b. Can entropy and "order" increase together? *Physics Letters* 102A:171–173.

Layzer, D., 1975. The arrow of time. *Sci. Amer.* 233:56–69.

Layzer, D., 1977. Information in cosmology, physics, and biology. *Int. J. Quantum Chem.* 12(suppl. 1):185–195.

Layzer, D., 1978. A macroscopic approach to population genetics. *J. Theor. Biol.* 73:769–788.

Layzer, D., 1980. Genetic variation and progressive evolution. *Amer. Natur.* 115:809–826.

Layzer, D., 1981. Quantum mechanics, thermodynamics, and the strong cosmological principle. In *Physics as Natural Philosophy*, A. Shimony and H. Feshbach, eds., Cambridge, MA: The MIT Press.

Lewontin, R. C., 1974. *The Genetic Basis of Evolutionary Change.* New York: Columbia University Press.

Lotka, A. J., 1924. *Elements of Mathematical Biology.* Reprinted 1956, New York: Dover Books.

Løvtrup, S., 1983. Victims of ambition: comments on the Wiley and Brooks approach to evolution. *Syst. Zool.* 32:90–96.

Morowitz, H. J., 1968. *Energy Flows in Biology: Biological Organization as a Problem in Thermal Physics.* New York: Academic Press.

Prigogine, I., 1980. *From Being to Becoming.* San Francisco: Freeman.

Prigogine, I., and I. Stengers, 1984. *Order Out of Chaos.* New York: Bantam.

Prigogine, I., and J. M. Wiame, 1946. Biologie et thermodynamique des phenomenes irreversibles. *Experientia* 2:451–453.

Prigogine, I., G. Nicolis, and A. Babloyantz, 1972. Thermodynamics of evolution. *Physics Today* 25(11):23–28, 25(12):38–44.

Rosenberg, A., 1985. *The Structure of Biological Science.* Cambridge: Cambridge University Press.

Schrödinger, E., 1944. *What Is Life?* Cambridge: Cambridge University Press.

Shannon, C. E., and W. Weaver, 1949. *The Mathematical Theory of Communication.* Urbana: University of Illinois Press.

Wicken, J. S., 1983. Entropy, information, and nonequilibrium evolution. *Syst. Zool.* 32:438–443.

Wiley, E. O., 1975. Karl R. Popper, systematics, and classification—a reply to Walter Bock and other evolutionary taxonomists. *Syst. Zool.* 24:233–243.

Wiley, E. O., 1980. Is the evolutionary species fiction? A consideration of classes, individuals, and historical entities. *Syst. Zool.* 29:76–79.

Wiley, E. O., 1981. *Phylogenetics: The Theory and Practice of Phylogenetic Systematics.* New York: Wiley.

Wiley, E. O., and D. R. Brooks, 1982. Victims of history—a nonequilibrium approach to evolution. *Syst. Zool.* 31:1–24.

Wiley, E. O., and D. R. Brooks, 1983. Nonequilibrium thermodynamics and evolution: A response to Løvtrup. *Syst. Zool.* 32:209–219.

Wilson, E. O., and W. H. Bossert, 1971. *A Primer of Population Biology*. Sunderland, MA: Sinauer Assoc.

Wright, S., 1968. *Evolution and the Genetics of Populations*. Vol. 1, *Genetic and Biometric Foundations*. Chicago: University of Chicago Press.

Wright, S., 1969. *Evolution and the Genetics of Populations*. Vol. 2, *The Theory of Gene Frequencies*. Chicago: University of Chicago Press.

Wright, S., 1977. *Evolution and the Genetics of Populations*. Vol. 3, *Experimental Results and Evolutionary Deductions*. Chicago: University of Chicago Press.

Wright, S., 1978. *Evolution and the Genetics of Populations*. Vol. 4, *Variability within and among Natural Populations*. Chicago: University of Chicago Press.

9

Dollo's Law and the Second Law of Thermodynamics: Analogy or Extension?

Daniel R. Brooks, D. David Cumming, and Paul H. LeBlond

9.1 Introduction

The fundamental unifying principle of biology is the recognition that biological diversity has evolved. Because the principle is so important, it is necessary for evolutionary explanations and theory to reflect closely current knowledge. The production of biological diversity is a genealogical phenomenon. Each generation represents a pool of phenotypic diversity. This potential is large but not unlimited due to unique genealogy, or *historical constraint*. Reproduction actualizes some of the phenotypic potential but filters out the rest as a *genetic constraint*. Ontogeny further restricts the range of phenotypes as *developmental constraints* operate to produce fewer phenotypes than genotypes. Finally, not all of the organisms produced can live to reproduce in the environment in which they occur; this *environmental constraint* is natural selection. This process is also directional in time. Despite the fact that biologists recognize and understand this sequential process (figure 9.1), evolutionary explanations are often couched in terms that suggest that natural selection is the sole constraint, or ordering force, operating in biology. But the theory of natural selection does not imply either directionality in time (Maynard Smith, 1970) or inherent ordering forces for biology. However, a second biological principle, called Dollo's Law, does embody both irreversibility and a general increase in complexity during evolution (see Collier, this volume). A relatively complete theory of evolution must integrate both Dollo's Law (irreversibility and inherent ordering constraints) and Natural Selection (environmental ordering). The *unified theory of evolution* (Brooks and Wiley, 1986) attempts to do this (figure 9.2).

Two aspects of the production of diversity shown in figure 9.1 are suggestive of a particular kind of lawlike behavior. The first is the temporal directionality and the second is the probabilistic nature of the process.

At present, the only natural law of which we know having a sense of time, or irreversibility, is the Second Law of Thermodynamics (Layzer,

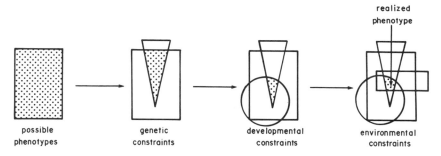

Figure 9.1
Schematic representation of the production of phenotypic diversity in biology.

1977). Thermodynamics is a field concerned both with the arrow of time and with probabilistic behavior. It has a history approximately as long as evolutionary theory, and has been beset by many of the same conceptual problems: irreversibility, teleological-appearing behavior, functional efficiency, and microscopic/macroscopic incommensurability. One of the early leaders in the field, Ludwig von Boltzmann, admired Darwin and wished to provide for physics something comparable to what Darwin had provided biology (Brush, 1983). The conceptual issues seem so similar that thermodynamics would seem a good starting point for investigating the possible effects of natural laws in evolution. Lotka (1924; 1956 reprint) and D'Arcy Thompson (1942) thought that organic evolution was the biological manifestation of the Second Law. Biology and physics have traditionally parted ways on the issue of thermodynamics because biology seems to follow a generally optimistic path, whereas thermodynamics carries a pessimistic air with it. Attempting to reconcile the organizing process of biological evolution with the increase in disorder apparently ordained by the Second Law of Thermodynamics has been a major focus of scientific thought for decades (Schrödinger, 1944; Prigogine and Wiame, 1946; Lotka, 1956; Blum, 1968). Similar concerns have arisen in cosmology on how to match large scale expansion of the observed universe with the structure of galaxies and of our solar system (Layzer, 1975, this volume; Frautschi, 1982, this volume; Davies, 1983).

The natural systems studied in physics, chemistry, and biology are made up of simple microscopic components. The laws describing the behavior of individual components are time invariant. However, macroscopic systems made up of these components always exhibit one of two forms of irreversible behavior. Those that follow the "arrow of time" (Eddington, 1928) move in the direction of decreasing order and organization. When such a system reaches a state of maximum disorder, it stays there. An example is a sugar cube placed in a glass of water. The cube dissolves, and

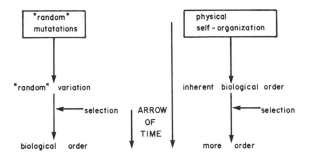

Figure 9.2
Schematic representation of some differences between traditional Darwinian and neo-Darwinian views of the generation of biological order (left) and the viewpoint of the unified theory of evolution (right).

the result is a homogeneous mixture of water and sugar molecules. Although no microscopic law forbids the reassembly of the sugar cube, it never occurs. Other systems follow the "arrow of history" (Layzer, 1975). They move spontaneously toward states of higher order and organization. These systems are called "self-organizing." For example, embryonic organisms develop into more complex adults. The reverse process does not occur.

What is the proper explanation for spontaneous increases in macroscopic order, or self organization? One model, based mainly in physical chemistry (Prigogine, 1980; Prigogine and Stengers, 1984), asserts that because open systems can exchange matter and energy with their surroundings ("conversations with the environment") fluxes of high grade (low entropy) energy from the environment can impose order on ("inform") a disordered system with concomitant local decreases in entropy. The arrow of time and the arrow of history point in opposite directions. Entropy increases in the surroundings due to the exportation of entropy from the system of equal or greater magnitude satisfy the overall requirements of the Second Law, but a paradox remains: If there is nothing inherent in the initial composition and configuration of the system that traps energy, how can this happen? Does this mean that the Second Law is indeterminate—is irreversibility merely a statistical artifact? The so-called "principle of order through fluctuations" (Prigogine, 1980; Jantsch, 1980) is sometimes invoked to compensate for this paradox.

A second model, based primarily in astrophysics (Layzer, 1975, 1977, this volume; Frautschi, 1982, this volume; Davies, 1983; Landsberg, 1984), asserts that it is the effects of the initial conditions ("conversations with the past") together with environmental exchanges that can lead to spontaneous increases in order. The uptake of energized particles by a low entropy initial configuration would increase the entropy of the system as well as that of the surroundings. If the entropy of the surroundings increases more than does the entropy of the system, the system will become more ordered relative to the environment (or any observer in the environment) as a result of increasing entropy. The arrow of time and the arrow of history point in the same direction. This eliminates indeterminism from the Second Law (though not from the evolutionary process), but creates a new paradox: initial conditions constraints are associated with kinetics or dynamics, which are not inherently irreversible (Layzer, 1981; Tisza, 1966). This debate in physics and physical chemistry concerns in great part the adequacy of environmental selection alone to account for macroscopic order, another parallel with current debates in biology. A recent convergence of views suggests that certain aspects of both cosmological and biological evolution behave according to this second view, in which both entropy and order can increase if the rate of expansion of a system ensemble is so rapid or extensive that the number of states occupied increases less rapidly than the maximum that become available (Layzer, 1975, 1977, 1978, 1980, this volume; Frautschi, 1982, this volume; Davies, 1983; Landsberg, 1984; Brooks et al., 1984; Brooks and Wiley, 1984, 1985, 1986). The biological arrow of history points in the same direction as the arrow of time. This suggests that we should be able to formulate Dollo's Law in a manner directly analogous to the Second Law.

There are several standard representations of the Second Law. If we are able to draw a direct analogy between Dollo's Law and the Second Law, we should be able to identify biological properties corresponding to the terms of these representations and derive similar predictions. We shall consider biological systems in terms of four of them. We shall compare two irreversible biological processes, ontogeny (development) and reproduction (population growth).

$$\Delta(PV/T) \propto S, \tag{1}$$

where for biology V = the volume of a developing organism or of a population of organisms (equivalent to the number of cells or of organisms), P = the environmental pressure on the organism, T = metabolic temperature, and S = entropy. Both development and reproduction increase V. T and P are essentially constant, or fluctuate only within a narrow range because metabolic activities are enzyme-mediated, and each species tends to live and develop at a fairly constant altitude/depth during ontogeny. Increasing V at constant P and T produces increasing S, or dS is greater than zero.

$$\Delta G = \Delta U + P\Delta V - T\Delta S, \tag{2}$$

where G = the Gibbs Free Energy and ΔG must be less than zero if the reaction is to proceed spontaneously, U = the chemical potential, and P, S, T, and V are as in equation (1). ΔV is positive for developing organisms and growing populations. T and P are essentially constant, as above. Increasing volume results from increasing the number of particles in the system. This also tends to increase U ($\Delta U < 0$). Thus, for ΔG to be less than 0, ΔS must be greater than 0. Increasing the number of particles in an ensemble (growth) also increases the statistical entropy according to

$$S = k(\log_e(W)),\tag{3}$$

where S = the statistical entropy, k = Boltzmann's constant, and W = the number of microstates accessible to the ensemble.

The above equations were originally developed for applications to closed systems, either isolated (no energy or matter exchange with the surroundings) or not (energy but not matter exchange with the surroundings). Living systems grow spontaneously, resulting in an entropic drive stemming from an increase in volume due to a net gain of particles. This means that they are open systems, capable of exchanging matter and energy with their surroundings. Characterizing entropic behavior in open systems requires a representation noting the flows (dS) of matter and energy from the surroundings into the system (d_eS) and from the system back into the system and its relevant surroundings (d_iS). Prigogine (1980) and Prigogine et al. (1972) summarized this relationship thusly:

$$dS = d_eS + d_iS, \qquad d_iS \geqslant 0,\tag{4}$$

where dS = change in entropy of the surroundings, d_eS = change in entropy due to exchanges between the environment and the system and d_iS = change in entropy due to irreversible processes within the system that export at least some entropy to the surroundings. If some of the entropy production by irreversible processes within the system is not exported to the surroundings, it may manifest itself by building and maintaining macroscopic structure. Growth processes are examples of this phenomenon. For our biological analogy, the entropy function in equations (1)–(3) corresponds to that part of d_iS that is dissipated within the system.

Thus, it appears that Dollo's Law can be formulated in strict analogy with four thermodynamic representations so long as one associates biological self-organization more with cosmological than chemical models. At first thought, it might seem inappropriate for one to look to cosmological principles rather than to chemical principles. However, the biological view espoused in this paper is an *internalist* view, which cosmological considerations, by definition, must also be. Classically, thermodynamic behavior has been judged by changes in the environment of the system, an *externalist* view. In a closed system, changes in the system must complement changes in the environment (total entropy is conserved), but this is not necessarily the case with open systems. Thus the suggestion has been made that so long as there is a positive amount of entropy being produced by, and dissipated from, the system, into the environment ($d_iS > 0$), we need not be concerned with the particulars of the system itself. The internal entropy of the system can increase or decrease without violating the Second Law. We do not disagree with this in principle, but we do believe that the initial conditions constraints affecting living systems are such that their internal entropy will show spontaneous increases rather than decreases. This can be more clearly seen by reference to our analog V in equations (1) and (2). The volume of the system is an internal property of the system, and it is fundamentally important in determining whether the internal entropy increases or decreases. This contrasts with classical thermodynamic treatments, in which volume is a boundary condition external to the system to which the system conforms.

If a system is open and dS is positive, the entropic drive need not stem from specific heat loss, a functional consideration, but from the increase in ensemble size, structural consideration (see Landsberg, 1984). This introduces an apparent paradox. Traditionally, thermodynamics has been invoked only to deal with problems of heat- or energy-flow. Matter-flow, including changes in the sizes of ensembles, has been handled by kinetics. It is true that every kinetics solution has a thermodynamic equivalent (Harrison, this volume), but without the thermodynamic component, kinetics equations are not inherently irreversible (see Prigogine and Stengers, 1984). This would seem to render this paradox more definitional than substantive (see also Harrison, this volume; Hopf, this volume; Tisza, 1966). The attempt to provide a unified view of energy-flow and matter-flow in thermodynamics parallels yet another conceptual issue in biology—the relationship between structure and function. This view suggests that we should look at irreversible matter-flow and its entropic behavior if we wish to find the influence of Dollo's Law in biological evolution.

If the particles being incorporated into the ensemble are homogeneous (H: Landsberg, 1984), then (3) holds. The evolution of such a system involves only an increase in what Wicken (1979) called *size complexity*. But if the particles are not homogeneous ($\bar{H}$: Landsberg, 1984), then

$$S = - \sum_i [(p_i) \log_e(p_i)], \qquad S \leqslant S_{max}, \tag{5}$$

where $p_i = $ the frequency of occurrence of the ith distinct kind of particle (or unit structure). In such cases, S can increase through time at a slower rate than $k(\log_e(N))$, which is S_{max} for any one-dimensional system of N particles. This allows the system to evolve increasing amounts of what

Wicken (1979) termed *heterogeneous complexity*. It is the generation, through replication, of hierarchically organized heterogeneous complexity that differentiates biological self-organization from other processes of self-organization. This form of complexity can be measured as "information" (I: Brillouin, 1962; Layzer, 1977; Gatlin, 1972), where

$$I = S_{max} - S, \tag{6}$$

or as "order" (Q: Landsberg, 1984), where

$$Q = 1 - (S/S_{max}). \tag{7}$$

Self-organizing phenomena are poorly understood, and there is much interest in the formulation of "a general mathematical theory to describe the nature and generation of complexity" (Wolfram, 1984c, p. 419). Attempts to investigate complex systems by modeling them with differential equations have met with limited success, for the following reasons:

1. Differential equations describe macroscopic, not microscopic, properties of systems.
2. For many natural systems, no differential equations are available.
3. Differential equations tend to be complicated, and the simulation of a complex system may require a large number of them. Such simulations can be difficult to implement and expensive to run.
4. Initial conditions specified by real numbers produce complex model behavior. This makes analysis difficult.

An additional problem is the lack of consensus on appropriate mathematical measures of "order," "disorder," "organization," "chaos," "simplicity," and "complexity."

Recently, an alternative modeling approach based on cellular automata has emerged. A cellular automaton consists of

1. a collection of identical cells,
2. a set of allowed cell states,
3. a neighborhood,
4. a transition rule.

The automaton evolves as follows. All cells are assigned initial states. The states of all cells are updated simultaneously at discrete time intervals. The transition rule specifies the next state of each cell as a function of the present states of all the cells in its neighborhood.

For example, consider an 11-cell, 1-dimensional automaton:

| | | | | | | | | | | | |.

Each cell, | |, can be in one of three states: $|0|$, $|1|$, or $|2|$. The neighborhood of a cell consists of the cell itself, plus the cells located immediately to its left and right. If the transition rule is as follows,

Neighborhood sum at time t	New cell state at time $t + 1$
0	0
1	2
2	1
3	1
4	0
5	2
6	1

and the automaton is initialized to

|0|0|0|0|0|1|0|0|0|0|0|,

then it will evolve as follows:

Time	
0	|0|0|0|0|0|1|0|0|0|0|0|
1	|0|0|0|0|2|2|2|0|0|0|0|
2	|0|0|0|1|0|1|0|1|0|0|0|
3	|0|0|2|2|1|2|1|2|2|0|0|
4	|0|1|0|2|2|0|2|2|0|1|0|

Cellular automata were originally introduced by von Neumann and Ulam (von Neumann, 1966; Burks, 1970). They were called "cellular spaces" and were intended to model biological self-reproduction. Cellular automata have been used to model systems in physics, chemistry, and biology. They have also proven useful in number theory, image processing, and visual pattern recognition. Wolfram (1983a,b, 1984a,b,c) has recently used cellular automata to construct systems whose behavior can be "tuned" to exhibit arbitrary degrees of complexity. These systems make use of local neighborhoods and simple transition rules. As general models of complex systems, cellular automata have the following advantages:

1. They provide a more direct simulation of the microscopic structure and behavior of systems.
2. Arbitrarily complex behavior can be produced using simple transition rules and local neighborhoods. Thus, models based on cellular automata are easy to implement and cheap to run.
3. The behavior of the models is easier to control and analyze.

Organizational features of systems composed of cellular automata can be expressed as discrete probability distributions. For example, in the case of the 11-cell automata, we can define a distribution $P = \{p_1, p_2, p_3\}$, where

p_1 = number of cells in state 0/total number of cells,

p_2 = number of cells in state 1/total number of cells,

p_3 = number of cells in state 2/total number of cells.

Consequently, these systems are amenable to analysis by the class of functions known as discrete information measures. The first discrete information measure was proposed by Shannon (Shannon and Weaver, 1949). Shannon defined his measure, called entropy, as follows. Given a discrete probability distribution

$$P = \{p_1, \ldots, p_n\},$$ (8)

the entropy H of P is

$$H(P) = -\sum_{i=1}^{n} [(p_i) \log_2(p_i)] \text{ bits.}$$ (9)

$H(P)$ is a measure of the "shape" of the distribution P. When P is equiprobable, (i.e., $p_1 = p_2 = \cdots = p_n$), then $H(P)$ attains its maximum value of $\log_2 n$. When P is farthest from equiprobability, (i.e., $p_j = 1$, $p_1, \ldots, p_{j-1}$, $p_{j+1}, \ldots, p_n = 0$), then $H(P) = 0$, its minimum value. Many other discrete information measures have been defined. Van der Lubbe et al. (1984) have recently shown that all known discrete information measures can be expressed using the (ρ, σ) certainty measure, defined as

$$G_n(P; \rho, \sigma) = \left[\sum_{i=1}^{n} (p_i)^\rho \right]^\sigma.$$ (10)

The simplicity and power of cellular automata, their connection with discrete information measures, and the new unified view of these information measures all suggest the possibility of constructing a general-purpose simulation program based on 1-dimensional cellular automata. Such a program would allow investigators to

1. construct systems composed of cellular automata,
2. specify evolution schemes for these systems,
3. define complexity measures by choosing discrete probability distributions and a (ρ, σ) certainty measure, and
4. use the complexity measures to monitor the systems as they evolve.

The Brooks-LeBlond-Cumming (BLC) analog of biological evolution is a specialized version of the program described above. Its results have inspired the formulation of Hierarchical Information Theory (HIT) a general framework accounting for simultaneous increases in entropy and order in complex systems. We will introduce HIT beginning with a précis of the BLC model, and an analysis of DNA structure.

9.2 The BLC Analog

A significant obstacle to the study of information and entropy in biology has been the absence of a model amenable to quantitative analysis that would be consistent with the molecular level of DNA base sequences and would also incorporate features of higher-level developmental processes that are an essential part of large-scale evolution. The BLC analog (Brooks et al., 1984) fills this gap.

The BLC model consists of populations of 1-dimensional cellular automata of length N whose time dependent cell values $x_i(t)$, $i = 1, 2, \ldots, N$, represent discrete developmental stages. Each automaton represents an epiphenotype, or developmental program. A species consists of a population of such automata that were all identical at some past time. Starting with a single initial species that includes Q automata $x_i(0) = 0$, random mutations add to the x_i according to simple developmental rules that introduce diversity within the species. Specifically, a successful mutation at position i occurs with probability $r_m(i) = 2^{-(N+1-i)}$ at each time step and increases x_i and all x_j, $j > i$, by unity. Whenever a mutation occurs, a bifurcation may also take place, with probability $r_b(i) = 2^{-i}$. This scheme assigns lowest bifurcation probability to those mutations that are most likely to happen, and hence are least fundamental. A bifurcation leads to the creation of a new species, composed of Q individual automata identical to that which bifurcated. This corresponds to the peripheral isolates, or "founder effect" allopatric modes of speciation (Wiley, 1981). A phylogeny of species thus gradually develops in time in a framework where entropy and information are readily quantifiable.

Entropy in the BLC model is coarse-grained, measured in terms of the possible arrangements of the x_i values, taken singly or in n-tuplet groups (up to $n = N$) (Gatlin, 1972). Thus,

$$H_n = - \sum_{i=1}^{A^n} [(p_i) \log_2(p_i)] \text{ bits,} \tag{11}$$

where H_n is the entropy of n-tuplets of values of x_i, A is the range of values of x_i within a species ($A = x_{\max,N} - x_{\min,1} + 1$), and p_i is the measured probability of finding a specified string of n elements within the Q automata of the species. The summation is over the total number of different n-tuplets possible over the range of the alphabet A. The increase in entropy with time for a population of 100 9-vectors starting with $x_i(0) = 0$ is shown in figure 9.3 for each of $n = 1, 2, \ldots, 9$. The entropy in each "word-length" or n-tuplet group increases continuously and rapidly, at first, as the mutation process increases the diversity of values of x_i. Entropy in the higher n-tuplets soon reaches a plateau for a given population size when all

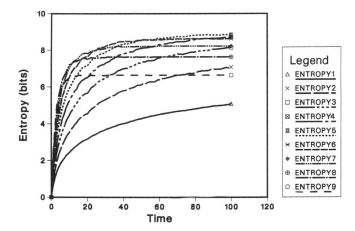

Figure 9.3
Entropy ($H_1, \ldots, H_9$) versus time (arbitrary units) for a population of 100 9-vectors.

occurring subvectors become different. The total number of possible configurations, however, continues to increase with A.

The difference between the maximum possible entropy and its actual value is the information defined as (Gatlin, 1972)

$$D_1 = \log_2(A) \quad H_1 \text{ bits}, \qquad n = 1; \tag{12}$$

$$D_n = nH_1 - H_n \text{ bits}, \qquad n > 1; \tag{13}$$

D_1 is the information residing in the departure of the distribution of single symbols from equipartition; D_n is the measure of the information contained in the failure of n-tuplets to be randomly distributed. The evolution of information content for the population described above is shown in figure 9.4. As A increases, the information content stabilizes first in the lower n-tuplets, where mutations increase the actual entropy at about the same rate as $\log_2(A)$. The possible diversity of longer n-tuplets rapidly outstrips that found in the more complex arrangements, i.e., in longer "words."

The order in each n-tuplet is defined as (Landsberg, 1984)

$$\text{ORDER}_n = 1 - (H_n/H_{\max,n}). \tag{14}$$

where $H_{\max,n}$ is the maximum entropy possible for n-tuplets in the range A, corresponding to equally probable occurrence of each possible configuration. It is clear that increases in order become rapidly associated with the longer configurations (figure 9.5). The progressive allocation of information and order to the longer substrings of the BLC model implies the emergence of higher levels of self-organization. If similar constraining rules affect changes in the DNA base sequences on chromosomes, we would

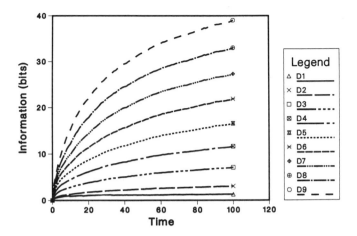

Figure 9.4
Information $(D_1, \ldots, D_9)$ versus time (arbitrary units) for a population of 100 9-vectors.

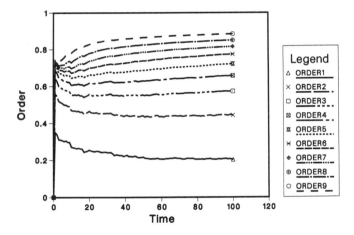

Figure 9.5
$ORDER_1, \ldots, ORDER_9$ versus time (arbitrary units) for a population of 100 9-vectors.

expect to find information structure in DNA sequences similar to that produced by the BLC analog.

9.3 DNA Information Measures

We may show the entropy, information, and order structure of the populations in the BLC analog at any time (figure 9.6 shows three such time slices for the information structure). Each of those time slices should be comparable to the genetic structure of organisms of different species. To test this, entropy, information, and order were calculated as above for 23 nuclear, mitochondrial, and chloroplast DNA sequences for a variety of species (see tables 9.1–9.3). (Sequences were obtained from the European Molecular Biology Laboratory Nucleotide Sequence Data Library; the sequences chosen were those of appreciable length that were complete and that represented a wide phylogenetic range of organisms.) In all cases there is progressive allocation of order and information to longer and longer segments of the DNA, in accordance with the expectations of the BLC model. Differences between the expectations of the BLC model and DNA structure suggest rules or constraints affecting DNA evolution that are not included in the BLC model. For example, D_2 is lower than D_1 for most sequences (figure 9.7), exceptions being mammals, birds, one slime mold sequence, and the tobacco chloroplast (figure 9.8). In addition, D_1–D_4 do not show appreciable departures from randomness for any of the

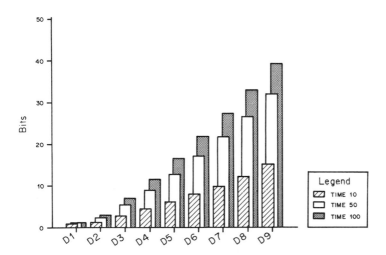

Figure 9.6
Information $(D_1, \ldots, D_9)$ calculated at times 10, 50, and 100 for a population of 100 9-vectors.

Table 9.1
$D_1, \ldots, D_6$ values calculated for 23 DNA sequences

Sequence	D_1 (bits)	D_2 (bits)	D_3 (bits)	D_4 (bits)	D_5 (bits)	D_6 (bits)
Cyanobacteria anabaena 7120 nifH gene (1271 bp)	0.013	0.010	0.070	0.235	0.797	2.030
Chloroplast Nicotiana tabacum (2165 bp)	0.005	0.024	0.065	0.152	0.503	1.500
Zea mays chloroplast gene (1803 bp)	0.028	0.011	0.046	0.138	0.523	1.568
Euglena gracilis chloroplast genes (1358 bp)	0.226	0.020	0.059	0.192	0.623	1.441
Mitochondrion bos taurus (16338 bp)	0.066	0.011	0.030	0.062	0.124	0.304
Mitochondrion Saccharomyces cerevisiae (10168 bp)	0.196	0.011	0.033	0.077	0.179	0.445
Xenopus laevis gene for 5.8S rRNA (1326 bp)	0.187	0.043	0.121	0.304	0.817	1.739
Bovine adult beta-globin gene (2072 bp)	0.009	0.070	0.166	0.311	0.681	1.619
Mouse genes mGK-1 and mGK-2 (fragment) (9433 bp)	0.003	0.089	0.187	0.301	0.471	0.828
Rabbit embryonic globin gene beta-3 (1905 bp)	0.013	0.053	0.129	0.260	0.645	1.621
Slime mold gene for 5.8S rRNA and 26S rRNA (6191 bp)	0.009	0.013	0.036	0.087	0.212	0.657
Human c-Ha-ras2 oncogene (1263 bp)	0.013	0.079	0.189	0.411	0.974	2.119
Human gene for fetal hemoglobin (11376 bp)	0.023	0.052	0.117	0.199	0.345	0.703
Chicken cytoplasmic beta-actin gene (5046 bp)	0.023	0.027	0.079	0.169	0.383	0.955
Grey seal myoglobin gene fragment (1187 bp)	0.026	0.073	0.192	0.399	0.993	2.153
Chicken ovalbumin gene (germ line) (7564 bp)	0.045	0.049	0.116	0.196	0.331	0.655
Chromosome of the human mitochondrion (16569 bp)	0.069	0.012	0.031	0.065	0.132	0.318
Hordeum vulgare chloroplast fragment (3819 bp)	0.043	0.013	0.034	0.085	0.272	0.890
Slime mold gene for actin 5 (658 bp)	0.246	0.105	0.336	0.730	1.441	2.474
Trypanosoma brucei basic copy gene (2217 bp)	0.060	0.034	0.086	0.198	0.549	1.386
Fruit fly: transposable element FB4 (4089 bp)	0.088	0.080	0.198	0.425	0.875	1.717
Zea mays gene encoding a zein gene (2938 bp)	0.039	0.013	0.048	0.143	0.410	1.174
Yeast (S. cerevisiae) gene HIS4 (4751 bp)	0.031	0.019	0.059	0.125	0.294	0.828

Table 9.2
Entropy$_1$,..., Entropy$_6$ values calculated for 23 DNA sequences

Sequence	Entropy$_1$ (bits)	Entropy$_2$ (bits)	Entropy$_3$ (bits)	Entropy$_4$ (bits)	Entropy$_5$ (bits)	Entropy$_6$ (bits)
Cyanobacteria anabaena 7120 nifH gene (1271 bp)	1.987	3.964	5.891	7.713	9.138	9.891
Chloroplast nicotiana tabacum (2165 bp)	1.995	3.966	5.921	7.829	9.472	10.471
Zea mays chloroplast gene (1803 bp)	1.972	3.933	5.870	7.750	9.337	10.265
Euglena gracilis chloroplast genes (1358 bp)	1.774	3.528	5.263	6.903	8.246	9.202
Mitochondrion *bos taurus* (16338 bp)	1.934	3.356	5.771	7.672	9.544	11.298
Mitochondrion *saccharomyces cerevisiae* (10168 bp)	1.804	3.597	5.379	7.139	8.841	10.379
Xenopus laevis gene for 5.8S rRNA (1326 bp)	1.813	3.583	5.319	6.949	8.249	9.141
Bovine adult beta-globin gene (2072 bp)	1.991	3.912	5.807	7.653	9.274	10.327
Mouse genes mGK-1 and mGK-2 (fragment) (9433 bp)	1.997	3.905	5.803	7.686	9.513	11.152
Rabbit embryonic globin gene beta-3 (1905 bp)	1.987	3.921	5.833	7.688	9.291	10.301
Slime mold gene for 5.8S rRNA and 26S rRNA (6191 bp)	1.991	3.970	5.937	7.877	9.743	11.289
Human c-Ha-ras2 oncogene (1263 bp)	1.937	3.896	5.773	7.539	8.963	9.806
Human gene for fetal hemoglobin (11376 bp)	1.977	3.902	5.814	7.710	9.541	11.160
Chicken cytoplasmic beta-actin gene (5046 bp)	1.977	3.928	5.852	7.739	9.502	10.907
Grey seal myoglobin gene fragment (1187 bp)	1.974	3.874	5.728	7.495	8.875	9.688
Chicken ovalbumin gene (germ line) (7564 bp)	1.955	3.860	5.748	7.622	9.442	11.072
Chromosome of the human mitochondrion (16569 bp)	1.931	3.850	5.761	7.658	9.523	11.268
Hordeum vulgare chloroplast fragment (3819 bp)	1.957	3.900	5.836	7.742	9.513	10.851
Slime mold gene for actin 5 (658 bp)	1.754	3.402	4.925	6.285	7.328	8.048
Trypanosoma brucei basic copy gene (2217 bp)	1.940	3.847	5.734	7.563	9.152	10.256
Fruit fly: transposable element FB4 (4089 bp)	1.912	3.744	5.538	7.223	8.684	9.755
Zea mays gene encoding a zein gene (2938 bp)	1.961	3.909	5.836	7.702	9.396	10.593
Yeast (*S. cerevisiae*) gene HIS4 (4751 bp)	1.969	3.919	5.849	7.751	9.551	10.987

Table 9.3
$ORDER_1, \ldots, ORDER_6$ values calculated for 23 DNA sequences

Sequence	$ORDER_1$	$ORDER_2$	$ORDER_3$	$ORDER_4$	$ORDER_5$	$ORDER_6$
Cyanobacteria anabaena 7120 nifH gene (1271 bp)	0.007	0.009	0.018	0.036	0.086	0.176
Chloroplast nicotiana tabacum (2165 bp)	0.002	0.008	0.013	0.021	0.053	0.127
Zea mays chloroplast gene (1803 bp)	0.014	0.017	0.022	0.031	0.066	0.145
Euglena gracilis chloroplast genes (1358 bp)	0.113	0.118	0.123	0.137	0.175	0.233
Mitochondrion *bos taurus* (16338 bp)	0.033	0.036	0.038	0.041	0.046	0.059
Mitochondrion *saccharomyces cerevisiae* (10168 bp)	0.098	0.101	0.103	0.108	0.116	0.135
Xenopus laevis gene for 5.8S rRNA (1326 bp)	0.093	0.104	0.114	0.131	0.175	0.238
Bovine adult beta-globin gene (2072 bp)	0.004	0.022	0.032	0.043	0.073	0.139
Mouse genes mGK-1 and mGK-2 (fragment) (9433 bp)	0.002	0.024	0.033	0.039	0.049	0.071
Rabbit embryonic globin gene beta-3 (1905 bp)	0.006	0.020	0.028	0.039	0.071	0.142
Slime mold gene for 5.8S rRNA and 26S rRNA (6191 bp)	0.004	0.008	0.010	0.015	0.026	0.059
Human c-Ha-ras2 oncogene (1263 bp)	0.006	0.026	0.038	0.058	0.104	0.183
Human gene for fetal hemoglobin (11376 bp)	0.011	0.024	0.031	0.036	0.046	0.070
Chicken cytoplasmic beta-actin gene (5046 bp)	0.011	0.018	0.025	0.033	0.050	0.091
Grey seal myoglobin gene fragment (1187 bp)	0.013	0.032	0.045	0.063	0.113	0.193
Chicken ovalbumin gene (germ line) (7564 bp)	0.023	0.035	0.042	0.047	0.056	0.077
Chromosome of the human mitochondrion (16569 bp)	0.035	0.038	0.040	0.043	0.048	0.061
Hordeum vulgare chloroplast fragment (3819 bp)	0.022	0.025	0.027	0.032	0.049	0.096
Slime mold gene for actin 5 (658 bp)	0.123	0.149	0.179	0.214	0.267	0.329
Trypanosoma brucei basic copy gene (2217 bp)	0.030	0.038	0.044	0.055	0.085	0.145
Fruit fly: transposable element FB4 (4089 bp)	0.044	0.064	0.077	0.097	0.132	0.187
Zea mays gene encoding a zein gene (2938 bp)	0.019	0.023	0.027	0.037	0.060	0.117
Yeast (*S. cerevisiae*) gene HIS4 (4751 bp)	0.015	0.020	0.025	0.031	0.045	0.084

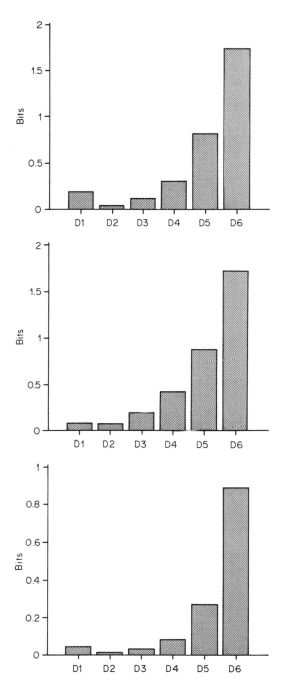

Figure 9.7
Information $(D_1, \ldots, D_6)$ calculated for 3 DNA sequences. D_2 is lower than D_1 for all 3 sequences. Top = *Xenopus laens* gene for 5.8S rRNA (1326BP); middle = *Drosophila melanogaster* transposable element FB4 (4089BP); bottom = *Hordenum vulgare* chloroplast fragment (3819BP).

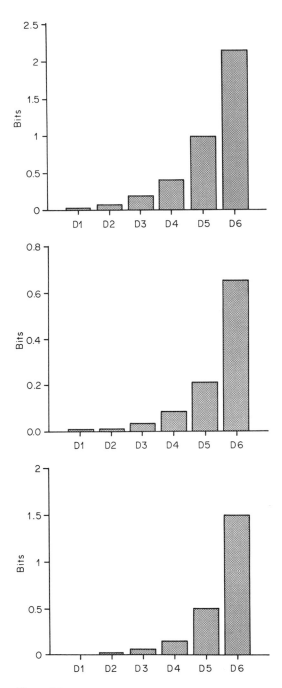

Figure 9.8
Information $(D_1, \ldots, D_6)$ calculated for 3 DNA sequences. D_2 is higher. Top = grey seal myoglobin gene gragment (1187BP); middle = slime mold gene for 5.8S rRNA and 26S rRNA (6191BP); bottom = *Nicotiana tabacum* chloroplast (2165BP).

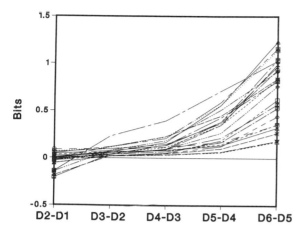

Figure 9.9
$D_n - D_{n-1}$, $n = 2, \ldots, 6$, calculated for 23 DNA sequences.

sequences, but there is an appreciable increase in information at the D_5/D_6 levels (figure 9.9). Because there is an average of 10.2 base pairs per complete spiral (i.e., 5–6 per half turn) in the helical DNA molecule, this increase in information content at the level of units of 5–6 bases is suggestive that our measure may be capable of detecting some topological information content. Karreman (1955) suggested an application of information theory to studies of topological order. Finally, differences in absolute magnitude of the $D_1, \ldots, D_6$ fractions in particular cases should not be affected by total sequence length; rather, they seem to reflect differences in the degree of randomization that has occurred at the $D_1, \ldots, D_4$ level.

9.4   Hierarchical Information Theory

Wolfram (1984c) has recently reiterated the need for "a general mathematical theory to describe the nature and generation of complexity." The insights gained from the BLC model and the DNA information measures led to the formulation of Hierarchical Information Theory (HIT). As recently summarized by Collier (1986) and Brooks and Wiley (1986), the word information has been used in a variety of ways. In communications theory the magnitude of the entropy of the system (the "message") is equated with its information content (Shannon and Weaver, 1949). In physical measurement theory, information is defined as the difference between the entropy of the observed state of the system and its maximum possible entropy (Brillouin, 1962). This is the sense in which $D_1, \ldots, D_n$ are measures of information.

Orthodox views in the physical and communications sciences treat information as quantifiable but not material. Information is used to denote the degree to which external forces have created structure in the system. An essential part of the Brooks-Wiley theory is that there is a material form of information inherent in biological systems. This "instructional information" resides in molecular structure as potential for specifying various kinds of homeostatic and ontogenetic activities. Energy taken up by the organism following the "entropy gradients" in the surroundings (embodied in $d_e S$) "forces" the actualization of this potential. The result is structure that can be described using conventional information measures. There is an entropic "cost" associated with this actualization, however. Over short time scales, such as those associated with ontogeny, the information expressed is a subset of the potential, the rest being dissipated as a result of work done by irreversible processes within the biological system ($d_i S$). Part of the actualization process involves faithful but imperfect replication of the chemical structure that defines the realm of potential. Over long time scales ("evolutionary time"), the accumulation of variations on that molecular structure increase the realm of the potential and thereby the diversity of the actual. Over short time scales, biological systems, from cells to ecosystems, behave like dissipative structures. Over longer time intervals, they behave like expanding phase space systems (for a more extensive discussion of scaling of entropy production in biological systems, see Brooks and Wiley, in press).

In biology, then, there seems to be information in the system as well as in the constraints or rules affecting the system and keeping it from maximum entropy. If the orthodox view of information is the only legitimate view, then not only the Brooks-Wiley theory but also all hereditary and molecular concepts of genetics fail. If biological information is material as well as quantifiable, we must show that time-dependent changes in that information conforms to the expectations of the second law. It has been shown that this view of information allows macrostate/microstate distinctions to be made, and embodies some degree of underlying indeterminism (Collier, 1986, this volume; Brooks, Collier, and Wiley, 1986; Brooks and Wiley, 1986, in press). As a result of the discussion above, it is apparent that we must also show that the information potential allowed by biochemical structure is greater than the information expressed as a result of biological functioning. It is in this regard that HIT becomes important.

9.5 Information Capacity

In any K-dimensional system composed of N^K irreducible parts, each of which can be in one of M distinct states, the total information capacity of the system is distributed hierarchically over N^K levels. We define an i-sized part as any combination of i irreducible parts. The ensemble consisting of all M^{N^K} possible distinct states of the system contains M^{N^K} (N^K CHOOSE i) i-sized parts, of which at most M^i are distinct (in this paper, (A CHOOSE B) denotes $A!/(B!(A - B)!)$). The information capacity of level i, $C_{I,i}$, is the Shannon-Weaver entropy (Shannon and Weaver, 1949) of the i-sized parts contained in the ensemble. That is,

$$C_{I,i} = - \sum_{j=1}^{M^i} [(p_{i,j}) \log_2(p_{i,j})] \text{ bits,} \tag{15}$$

where $p_{i,j}$ = relative frequency of occurrence of the jth distinct i-sized part in the ensemble. Because each member of the ensemble is distinct, we have $p_{i,j} = M^{-i}$, and (15) can be written

$$C_{I,i} = - \sum_{j=1}^{M^i} [(M^{-i}) \log_2(M^{-i})] \text{ bits}$$
$$= i(\log_2(M)) \text{ bits.} \tag{16}$$

C_I, the total information capacity of the system, is the sum of the information capacities of all levels in the hierarchy (Gatlin, 1972; Layzer, 1977). That is,

$$C_I = \sum_{i=1}^{N^K} [C_{I,i}] \text{ bits}$$
$$= \sum_{i=1}^{N^K} [i(\log_2 M)] \text{ bits} \tag{17}$$
$$= N^K((N^K + 1)/2) \log_2(M) \text{ bits.}$$

For example, consider an English phrase N letters long. If we restrict our alphabet to 26 letters and a space, then $M = 27$; $K = 1$. The system is composed of $N^K = N$ irreducible parts, which are single letters. Thus its information capacity is distributed hierarchically over N levels. The system has $M^N = 27^N$ possible states. The ensemble formed from these states contains $27^N(N$ CHOOSE $i)$ i-sized parts. There are $27^N(N$ CHOOSE $1) = N(27^N)$ 1-sized parts. 2-sized parts correspond to pairs of letters; there are $27^N(N$ CHOOSE $2)$ of them. Note that only $27^N(N - 1)$ of the 2-sized parts are composed of two letters that are positioned next to each other in the phrase. We denote these pairs as 2-tuplets, and all other 2-sized parts as 2-collections. In general, we define an i-tuplet as a (1-dimensional) i-sized part composed of i successive 1-sized parts. An English word of length i is an i-tuplet. Of the $27^N(N$ CHOOSE $i)$ i-sized parts in the ensemble, only $27^N(N - i + 1)$ are i-tuplets; the rest are i-collections. The information capacity of the single letters is $C_{I,1} = \log_2(27)$. The information capacity of the 2-sized parts is $C_{1,2} = 2(\log_2(27))$. The information capacity of the entire phrase is $C_1 = N((N + 1)/2) \log_2(27)$ bits.

We can think of M^i as the number of distinct possible states of a system composed of a single i-sized part, and $C_{1,i}$ as the information capacity of such a system. We can equate the Shannon-Weaver entropy, $\log_2(M^i)$, with the thermodynamic entropy, $X(\log_e(M^i))$, if the arbitrary constant X equals $(1/\log_e(2))$ (Brillouin, 1962). In this case, both entropies are expressed in bits. We adopt this convention, and hereafter refer simply to entropy.

If we set $K = 1$ and $M = 2$, our system reduces to a "string of bits" (zeros and ones) of length N. According to (17), the total information capacity of the system is $C_1 = N(N + 1)/2$ bits. If we set $K = 1$ and $M = 4$, our system reduces to a DNA sequence containing N base pairs. From (17), the total information capacity of the sequence is $C_1 = N(N + 1)$ bits. One might be tempted to object that "the standard definition of the entropy of a system implicit in the formulations of Boltzmann and Gibbs is the logarithm of the number of states accessible to the system (Kittel, 1969). The 'string of bits' has at most 2^N accessible states. Therefore the maximum possible entropy is $\log_2(2^N) = N$ bits."

Standard thermodynamics attempts at representing hierarchical systems fall short for the same reason. Khinchin (1957; see also Gatlin, 1972) suggested that hierarchical systems could be represented thusly,

$$H(AB) = H(A) + H_A(B), \tag{18}$$

where $H(AB)$ is the total entropy (or the information capacity), $H(A)$ is the macroscopic contribution (the entropy or the information content of the constraints—also macroscopic information), and $H_A(B)$ is the microscopic contribution (the entropy or the information content of the system—also microscopic information of Wicken, this volume). Let us consider a DNA sequence 32 bases long, with each base represented 8 times:

$$H(AB) = N \log_2(M)$$

$$= 32 \log_2(4) \tag{19}$$

$$= 64 \text{ bits;}$$

$$H_A(B) = \log_2[N!/N(C)!N(G)!N(T)!N(A)!]$$

$$= \log_2[32!/8!8!8!8!] \tag{20}$$

$$\simeq 56 \text{ bits;}$$

therefore,

$$H(A) \simeq 8 \text{ bits.} \tag{21}$$

From HIT [equation (16)],

$$C_{1,i} = i \log_2(M),$$

$$C_{1,32} = 32 \log_2(4) \tag{22}$$

$$= 64 \text{ bits.}$$

Thus, $H(AB) = C_{1,32}$. A strong reductionist program would decompose the topmost level of any macroscopic system (level 32 in this case) directly to its component parts $(H_A(B))$ and assume complete description. This would grossly underestimate the capacity and content of any truly hierarchical system.

Thus, Khinchin's formalism represents that special case under HIT in which the total information capacity of the system is determined only by the array as a whole and by its smallest parts. The question then arises as to whether or not the principle of hierarchical decomposition circumscribes the realm of applicability of information measures in physical systems. If so, then two paradoxes arise. The first is an empirical one. DNA, as a chemical array, does not function in an all-or-nothing manner in biological systems; it functions combinatorially. Furthermore, not all of the DNA even functions. Thus, the principle of hierarchical decomposition obscures some of the observed chemical activity of DNA. The second paradox is more theoretical. Using Khinchin's formalism, there is not enough structural information in DNA to account for ontogeny. HIT resolves both of these paradoxes. If we treat the information capacity and information content of DNA as a combinatorial hierarchy, corresponding to the chemical phenomenology observed, the total information capacity (total possibility) for the DNA sequences would be [from equation (17) of HIT]

$$C_1 = \sum_{i=1}^{N^K} C_{1,i}$$

and $S(AB)$ would be

$$C_1 = H(AB)$$

$$= N^K(N^K + 1/2) \log_2 M$$

$$= 32(32 + 1/2) \log_2 4$$

$$= 32(33/2)(2) \tag{23}$$

$$= 32(33)$$

$$= 1{,}056 \text{ bits.}$$

This is more than enough information potential; in fact, if all the potential were expressed, chaos (rather than ontos, the linguistic and biological antonym of chaos) would reign in biological systems. Because not all combinations of DNA sequences function, the instructional information needed to specify ontogeny and homeostasis can be seen as a subset of the structural information potential. Structure and function in this view are related to each other much as syntax and semantics are related in language. Both are products of the same process, but one is a context-dependent subset of the other.

The BLC analog and the DNA analyses presented herein confirm biological intuition that information exists in many levels in biological hierarchies. That even a "linear" molecule can exhibit hierarchical structure stems from different bonding affinities among different bases and among different combinations of bases, as well as from secondary, tertiary, and quaternary structure (see, e.g., the values for D_5 and D_6 in the DNA analyses).

It is important to distinguish between the information capacity of a system, which is maximum possible entropy, and the information content of a particular state of the system, which is the entropy of the single member of the ensemble corresponding to that state. The information content is bounded above by the information capacity. These quantities are independent of any semantic meaning assigned to the states of the system. The semantic content of any particular state should be bounded above by its information content (see also Collier, 1986). If we set $N = 3$, then $C_1 = 6(\log_2(27))$ bits. We can compute the information content of various states of the system.

$$\text{Total information content (qqq)} = \log_2(1) + \log_2(1) + \log_2(1) = 0.$$

$$\text{Total information content (dog)} = \log_2(3) + \log_2(3) + \log_2(1)$$

$$= 2(\log_2(3)).$$

$$\text{Total information content (dgo)} = \log_2(3) + \log_2(3) + \log_2(1)$$

$$= 2(\log_2(3)).$$

Note that even though the total information content of (dog) is equal to the total information content of (dgo), the semantic content of (dog) is greater than the semantic content of (dgo), because (dog) has meaning ascribed to it, and (dgo) does not. Our considerations so far deal solely with information capacity calculated over ensembles. We shall discuss the problems inherent in defining semantic content later.

9.6 Order and Disorder

Suppose constraints operate on a system in such a way that it is prevented from entering one or more of its M^{N^K} possible states. Those possible states that are no longer accessible are forbidden states, and those that continue to be accessible are permitted states. The permitted ensemble is that ensemble formed from all permitted states of the system. Those possible i-sized parts that do not occur in the permitted ensemble are forbidden i-sized parts, and those that do are permitted i-sized parts. The disorder capacity of level i, $C_{D,i}$, is the entropy of the i-sized parts contained in the permitted ensemble. The order capacity of level i, $C_{O,i}$ is

$$C_{O,i} = C_{I,i} - C_{D,i}. \tag{24}$$

This is the same as Gatlin's (1972) D_i measure. Information capacity $C_{I,i}$ thus comprises order capacity $C_{O,i}$ and disorder capacity $C_{D,i}$:

$$C_{O,i} + C_{D,i} = C_{I,i}. \tag{25}$$

The order capacity of the whole system, C_O, is

$$C_O = \sum_{i=1}^{N^K} [C_{O,i}], \tag{26}$$

and the disorder capacity of the whole system, C_D, is

$$C_D = \sum_{i=1}^{N^K} [C_{D,i}], \tag{27}$$

Thus, we can write

$$C_O + C_D = C_I. \tag{28}$$

In other words, information capacity appears in two forms, order capacity and disorder capacity. Order capacity, C_O, is referred to as "information," and disorder capacity, C_D, as "entropy" in physical measurement theory (see also Brooks and Wiley, 1986; Collier, 1986). The order capacity of level i is a measure of the degree to which the constraints manifest themselves on that level. If many i-sized parts are forbidden and/or the frequency distribution of the permitted i-sized parts is far from equiprobability, then $C_{O,i}$ will be close to $C_{I,i}$. If there are few forbidden i-sized parts, and the frequency distribution of the permitted i-sized parts is close to equiprobability, then $C_{O,i}$ will be close to zero.

Let us use our English phrase of length N to illustrate these concepts. The system constraints correspond to the rules of spelling and grammar of the English language. On level 1, no letter is forbidden, but the frequency distribution is not equiprobable. Letters such as 'e' and 'a' appear more frequently in the permitted ensemble than letters such as 'q' and 'z.' On higher levels, we need to distinguish between constraints on i-collections and those on i-tuplets. The former reflect the rules of grammar, while the latter reflect the rules of spelling. For example, no English word contains the 2-tuplet 'qq,' but there are valid sentences containing two q's. Thus the 2-tuplet 'qq' is forbidden, but not the 2-collection formed from two q's.

C_I, the total information capacity of the system, corresponds to the sum of the maximum possible values of the entropy on all levels when the system is unconstrained. C_D, the disorder capacity, corresponds to the same sum calculated when constraints are present. C_O, the order capacity, is the difference between C_I and C_D. Thus C_O is a measure of the total amount of "order" in the system, and C_D is a measure of the total amount of "disorder." Landsberg (1984) defined

$$\text{DISORDER} = C_D/C_I \tag{29}$$

and

$$\begin{aligned}\text{ORDER} &= 1 - \text{DISORDER}\\ &= C_O/C_I.\end{aligned} \tag{30}$$

We extend these classical concepts hierarchically as

$$\text{DISORDER}_i = C_{D,i}/C_{I,i} \tag{31}$$

and

$$\begin{aligned}\text{ORDER}_i &= 1 - \text{DISORDER}_i\\ &= C_{O,i}/C_{I,i}.\end{aligned} \tag{32}$$

9.7 Closed Systems

In thermodynamics, a closed system is defined as one having constant energy, constant number of particles and constant volume (Kittel, 1969). In our K-dimensional system, the volume is determined by N and K, the number of particles by N, and the energy by M. Our system corresponds to a closed system if N, K and M are held constant. From (28), we see that in a closed system, the total information capacity, C_I, or total entropy, is conserved as the sum of two parts, order and disorder, that may change from one to the other.

9.8 Noise

We define noise as any influence that causes the system to wander randomly among its possible states. If a closed system enters only permitted states, C_D, C_O, and C_I remain unchanged. However, if the noise causes the system to enter a hitherto forbidden state, the system constraints are weakened. Thus the order capacity of the system has been reduced. Because C_I is conserved, and $C_D + C_O = C_I$, the decrease in order capacity must be accompanied by an equal increase in disorder capacity. Noise converts order capacity to disorder capacity. An observer will notice an increase in DISORDER and a decrease in ORDER, even though the total information capacity of the system remains unchanged.

Hierarchical Information Theory allows the following informational analog of the Second Law of Thermodynamics for closed systems:

1. Total information capacity is conserved.
2. Order capacity plus disorder capacity equals total information capacity.
3. Disorder capacity always increases or stays the same.
4. Order capacity always decreases or stays the same.

This definition is entirely consistent with classical thermodynamic definitions.

At each level in a hierarchical system, the constraint strength, denoted $S_{o,i}$, is a measure of the degree to which the constraints resist the efforts of the noise to convert order capacity to disorder capacity. We do not explicitly define $S_{o,i}$, but note that it should reflect both the degree of initial resistance to the entry of forbidden states (initial conditions constraints), and the subsequent efforts to reestablish those states as forbidden (boundary conditions contraints).

Brooks and Wiley (1986) have associated initial conditions constraints with historical and developmental effects and boundary conditions constraints with environmental ("natural") selection effects in biological evolution. This suggests an outline of a general research program. As presented by Brooks and Wiley (1986), it comprises first partitioning out initial conditions effects from boundary conditions effects in any system of interest, and at any level in the biological hierarchy. This can be achieved at least partially by the use of phylogenetic systematic methods, because initial conditions effects are historical in nature and phylogenetics methodology discerns the maximum degree of historical constraint on a set of data (Brooks et al., 1986). Cheverud et al. (1985) used a combination of phylogenetic analysis and nested ANOVA to partition phylogenetic and developmental constraints from possible selective effects in the evolution of sexual dimorphism among primates. The new field of *historical ecology* (Brooks, 1985) uses similar reasoning in studying the evolution of ecological associations. Once this is done, explanations need to be provided for each class of effects, describing the manner in which each constraint keeps the evolving system from entering an equilibrium state. Analysis and explanation of the dynamics of boundary conditions effects is well advanced thanks to population biology (population ecology plus population genetics), and the thermodynamic basis of these effects is being developed (see Johnson, this volume). Initial conditions effects are likely to be efficiently described and explained by various kinetic formulations, some of which are already being articulated (see Harrison, this volume).

We denote the noise strength at level i by $S_{D,i}$. It is a measure of the amount of effort the noise brings to bear in order to violate the constraints and to prevent their reestablishment. We define $T_{O,i}$, the ordering tendency on level i, as

$$T_{O,i} = S_{O,i}/S_{D,i}. \tag{33}$$

In a closed system subject to noise, if $T_{O,i} < 1$, then as time approaches infinity, $C_{O,i}$ approaches 0, i.e., ORDER$_i$ approaches 0. If $T_{O,i} < 1$, then $C_{D,i}$ approaches 0, i.e., DISORDER$_i$ approaches 0.

9.9 Self-Organizing Systems

Hierarchical Information Theory defines a self-organizing system as one in which

1. Total information capacity, C_I, increases with time.
2. Information capacity on all levels ($C_{I,i}$, $i = 1, \ldots, N$) increases with time.
3. Total order capacity, C_O, and total disorder capacity, C_D, increase with time.
4. Order capacity on all levels ($C_{O,i}$, $i = 1, \ldots, N$) and disorder capacity on all levels ($C_{D,i}$, $i = 1, \ldots, N$) increase with time.
5. At low levels, disorder prevails; i.e., for small i, $C_{D,i} > C_{O,i}$; i.e., DISORDER$_i$ > ORDER$_i$.
6. At high levels, order prevails; i.e., for large i, $C_{O,i} > C_{D,i}$; i.e., ORDER$_i$ > DISORDER$_i$.

To satisfy 1 and 2, the system must be open; that is, one or more of K, N, and M must increase with time, and total entropy (= total information capacity) is not conserved. To satisfy 3–6, the system must be subject to both noise and constraints, such that the ordering tendency is <1 at low levels, and >1 at high levels (compare ORDER$_1$ and ORDER$_2$ with ORDER$_{3-9}$ in figure 9.5). The DNA sequences analyzed seem to indicate that this kind of self-organization occurs in biological systems.

A system is disordered if it satisfies 5 but not 6, and ordered if it satisfies 6 but not 5. Systems which satisfy both 5 and 6 are complex. If the ordering tendency is >1 at low levels, an ordered system of limited potential emerges, such as a crystal, or the geometric patterns found in some cellular automata (Wolfram, 1984c). If $C_{D,i} < C_{O,i}$ at low levels, entropy may decrease internally, but this produces limited amounts of complexity. Ergo, processes that decrease entropy would not seem to be reasonable models for biological evolution. If the ordering tendency is <1

at high levels, a disordered system results, such as gas in a box, or the chaotic patterns found in some cellular automata (Wolfram, 1984c).

9.10 Applications of HIT

We examine some examples of self-organization from the HIT point of view. In cosmological models, expanding space corresponds to increasing all parameters of phase space. Randomizing forces, or noise, tend to distribute particles throughout phase space. At low levels, the noise is stronger than the constraints, which take the form of short-range forces between particles, and gravitational forces between small numbers of particles. Thus the ordering tendency is < 1. At high levels, gravitational forces between large numbers of particles overpower the noise, and the ordering tendency is > 1 (Layzer, 1977).

In both Layzer's (1978, 1980) biological model and the BLC analog, replication errors and mutation of DNA correspond to noise. The system is open in that the length of the genome, the size of developing organisms, and the number of new organisms increase. In Layzer's model, natural selection acted as the sole constraint producing order, but the BLC model demonstrates that biological order will emerge in the absence of selection; selection is seen as one of a series of possible constraints. Biochemical rules governing DNA replication correspond to constraints that are weaker than noise at low levels (e.g., individual base pairs), resulting in an ordering tendency < 1. At higher levels, constraints include the historical burden of reproduction and higher-level functionality. Layzer (1978, 1980) apparently considered natural selection to be a form of "external noise" (we use the term "constraint") analogous to the force of gravity in self-gravitating systems. Sexual reproduction is a closer analog to gravity in biological systems (Brooks and Wiley, 1986; Wiley, this volume). At these levels, the ordering tendency is > 1. Table 9.4 lists a few examples of constraints on biological systems leading to self-organization. They are arranged according to whether they are due strictly to initial conditions effects (emergent self-organization), to initial conditions effects acting as boundary conditions (self-imposed organization), or to boundary conditions effects (imposed self-organization). The arena in which biological functioning (including selection and adaptation) emerges is one of hierarchical structural self-organization driven by processes that increase the entropy function of our form of Dollo's Law. Thus, it appears that the entropy function associated with Dollo's Law behaves like thermodynamic entropy for irreversible processes.

As a framework for understanding complex systems, HIT represents complexity by recognizing that the whole may be greater than the sum of its parts, and hence that information may be contained in a series of

Table 9.4
Examples of constraints on biological systems leading to self-organization

Organization type	Functional level			
	Molecular	Ontogenetic	Population	Community
Emergent self-organization	1° structure	DNA content (preformation)	Ontogenetic programs	Species composition
Self-imposed organization	2°–4° structure	Epigenesis	Sexual reproduction	Food webs
Imposed self-organization	?	?	——————Natural Selection——————	

interrelated but identifiably different levels in a hierarchy. The position adopted is thus intermediate between full reductionism, which would insist that all is explainable from the lowest level of the hierarchy, and a degree of holism that would attribute significance only to the highest level. HIT interprets the Second Law of Thermodynamics as a tendency toward disorder at low levels of a hierarchy that makes it possible for order to appear at higher levels. We think this corresponds to the intuitions of many who have grappled with this problem.

HIT needs to be expanded in two related areas. First, we must derive sets of kinetic equations explaining particulars of biological order more precisely, especially with regard to interlevel interactions in each hierarchical system. At the level of the hierarchical structure of DNA, this would amount to a genetic statistical mechanics (see Collier, this volume). The equations would undoubtedly be nonlinear and the mathematics difficult. One starting point might be Harrison's generalized wavelength equation presented in this volume, where

$$\lambda_i = 2\pi \, (\text{scrambling/coupling})^{1/2}, \tag{34}$$

which could be rewritten using HIT notation as

$$\lambda_i = 2\pi \, (1/T_{0,i})^{1/2}, \tag{35}$$

where $T_{0,i}$ is more precisely defined by kinetic couplings relationships. We would expect that for low values of i, $1/T_{0,i}$ would be greater than 1 and for higher values of i, $1/T_{0,i}$ would be less than 1. Qualitative changes in λ would indicate the level(s) in any complex system at which constraints were greater than the disordering tendencies (see figure 9.10 for an example drawn from the BLC model). Many attempts along these lines are presented in Lamprecht and Zotin (1978, 1983, 1985; see also Harrison, this volume).

Second, we need a means of examining semantic content. Total information capacity places an upper bound on information content. Total information content similarly places an upper bound on semantic content. Information capacity and information content, as we have defined them, are both structural and syntactic; hence, semantic content must be functional. If semantic content is bounded by physical information content, we should expect functional changes to be consistent with but more conservative than structural changes in the course of evolution, in the following sense.

The processes of DNA replication, growth and differentiation, and reproduction may produce parts of organisms or whole organisms that are structurally identical to or altered from previous states. If they are structurally identical, they are presumably functionally identical (at least in terms of functional capabilities). The information content has increased (N has increased) but the semantic content is the same (there are no new

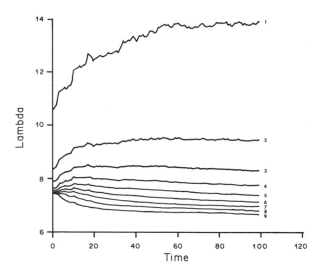

Figure 9.10
$\lambda_i (i = 1, \ldots, 9)$ versus time (arbitrary units) for a population of 100 9-vectors. Top = λ_1, bottom = λ_9.

functions). If they are structurally altered from precursor states, they may be nonfunctional, in which case the information content has increased without any increase in semantic content. If these structurally altered forms are functionally identical to the precursor states, information content has again increased while semantic content has not. If they are functionally different from the precursor states, then both information content and semantic content have increased. Thus, we would expect only some structural changes to produce functional changes. Cases in which the information content increases but the semantic content remains the same are reflections of persistent order capacity, whereas cases in which semantic content increases are reflections of the conversion of order capacity to disorder capacity.

Because in our view both disorder capacity and persistent order capacity must grow in order for a system to evolve arbitrarily high degrees of complexity, we would expect biological systems to be mixtures of historical and nonhistorical features, both structural and functional. From this deduction and the above discussion, we may predict that functional changes will occur less often than structural changes in the course of evolution. Empirical recognition of this state of affairs at the molecular level led to the formulation of the so-called *neutralist* theories of evolution (see King and Jukes, 1969; Kimura, 1979); if most structural variants are functionally equivalent, they are selectively equivalent as well. There is now empirical evidence supporting this prediction at the phylogenetic level (Brooks et al., 1985).

9.11 Conclusions

Deterministic (microscopic) systems have a "story" embedded in them. That is the reason their future behavior under a variety of conditions can be predicted. If biological order stemmed solely, or even predominantly, from deterministic effects of environmental perturbations (natural selection broadly construed), that order would be a representation of the environment. Because many environmental conditions are cyclical, we might expect to see cyclical evolutionary change rather than the hierarchical pattern of evolutionary diversification showing increasing complexity of structure and function, the particular instances of which are hierarchically organized as well (Collier, this volume). In other words, our empirical observations of irreversible processes in biology refute any doctrine of strict environmental determinism.

Macroscopic systems have an irreducible indeterminism, making them in some sense "storyless" physical manifestations. Some might equate "storyless" with "meaningless" in the same way that some have equated abstraction in art and music with statements about the meaninglessness of life. This is not the only interpretation, however. Storyless systems may be those that generate their own meaning as they evolve (or, in the case of art or music, as they are perceived by more and more people). Just as in the case of deterministic systems, "meaning" is manifested in the interaction between system and environment (or work of art and observer). In this case, however, the system's meaning is imposed *on* and not *by* the environment. That is, organisms define niches, not the reverse, and this allows the possibility for organisms to be produced whose niche requirements are inaccessible to them, leading to the "Malthusian instability" (Layzer, this volume) and natural selection as a corollary to the basic evolutionary dynamic determined by Dollo's Law. This view allows the environment to *affect* evolution while recognizing that other factors *effect* it. It is thus a conceptual framework that subsumes the Darwinian and neo-Darwinian influences in biology and integrates them with other factors.

The *unified theory of evolution* (Brooks and Wiley, 1986) represents an attempt to find a biological theory that explains (1) irreversibility in biology, (2) the manner in which organized biological variation is generated, and (3) the manner in which that variation is affected by natural selection. Furthermore, it attempts to help unify physics and chemistry with biology without reducing biology to physics and chemistry. Reactions to this attempt have varied.

The most persistent objection is that the entropy function in our formulation of Dollo's Law does not correspond to anything thermodynamically relevant. We suggest that Dollo's Law is a biological manifestation of the Second Law. It explains the lawlike behavior of entropy production by irreversible processes within biological systems, i.e., spontaneous growth phenomena. Others have suggested that it is only analogous, perhaps even a poor analogy. We hope we have shown that, at the very least, the analogy is tightly drawn. Collier (1986, this volume) has offered some ways of meeting these objections, and we shall add some observations of our own. First of all, because biological processes conform to the expected behavior of our version of Dollo's Law, biologists need not have the question of analogy or extension resolved in order to pursue research under the unified theory. Second, whether Dollo's Law stems only from the initial conditions of the origin of life or is the biological manifestation of the Second Law, the increasing entropy function means that evolution is inevitable. Third, if Dollo's Law is *not* the biological manifestation of the Second Law, the Boltzmann entropy function must not be entirely justified by the Second Law, but requires a principle more general than thermodynamics (Boltzmann, 1877), communications theory (Shannon and Weaver, 1949), topology (Karreman, 1955), and biological evolution (Brooks and Wiley, 1986). And fourth, if Dollo's Law is the biological manifestation of the Second Law, then it is already justified by a principle more general than biology. In addition, because selection theory has an apparent thermodynamic basis (see Johnson, Schneider, Wicken all in this volume), both Dollo's Law and the Theory of Natural Selection would have the same physical basis and the *unified theory* would contain no inherent dualism. Collier (this volume) suggests that the theory represents a nonredundant, nontrivial, and empirically tractable extension of some physical principles into biology. We certainly hope this is the case.

References

Blum, H. F., 1968. *Time's Arrow and Evolution*, 3rd ed. Princeton: Princeton University Press.

Boltzmann, L., 1877. Uber die Beziehung eines allgemeine mechanischen Satzes zum zweiten Hauptsatzes der Warmetheorie. *Sitzungsber. Akad. Wiss., Wien. Math.-Naturwiss. Kl.* 75:67–73.

Brillouin, L., 1962. *Science and Information Theory*. New York: Academic Press.

Brooks, D. R., 1985. Historical ecology: a new approach to studying the evolution of ecological associations. *Ann. Missouri Bot. Garden* 72:660–680.

Brooks, D. R., and E. O. Wiley, 1984. Evolution as an entropic phenomenon. In *Evolutionary Theory: Paths into the Future*, J. W. Pollard, ed., New York: Wiley.

Brooks, D. R., and E. O. Wiley, 1985. Nonequilibrium thermodynamics and evolution: responses to Bookstein and to Wicken. *Syst. Zool.* 34:89–97.

Brooks, D. R., and E. O. Wiley, 1986. *Evolution as Entropy: Toward a Unified Theory of Biology*. Chicago: University of Chicago Press.

Brooks, D. R., and E. O. Wiley, in press. *Evolution and Entropy: Toward a Unified Theory of Biology*, 2nd ed. University of Chicago Press.

Brooks, D. R., J. Collier, and E. O. Wiley, 1986. Definition of terms and the essence of theories: a reply to J. S. Wicken. *Syst. Zool.* 35:640–647.

Brooks, D. R., P. H. LeBlond, and D. D. Cumming, 1984. Information and entropy in a simple evolution model. *J. Theor. Biol.* 109:77–93.

Brooks, D. R., R. T. O'Grady, and D. R. Glen, 1985. Phylogenetic analysis of the Digenea (Platyhelminthes: Cercomeria) with comments on their adaptive radiation. *Can. J. Zool.* 63:411–443.

Cheverud, J. M., M. M. Dow, and W. Leutenegger, 1985. The quantitative assessment of phylogenetic constraints in comparative analysis: sexual dimorphism in body weight among primates. *Evolution* 39:1335–1351.

Collier, J., 1986. Entropy in evolution. *Philos. and Biol.* 1:5–24.

Cumming, D. D., D. R. Brooks, and P. H. LeBlond, 1987. Hierarchical information theory. *Nature*, in press.

Davies, P. C. W., 1983. Inflation and time asymmetry in the universe. *Nature* 301:398–400.

Eddington, A., 1928. *The Nature of the Physical World*. Cambridge: Macmillan.

Frautschi, S., 1982. Entropy in an expanding universe. *Science* 217:593–599.

Gatlin, L. L., 1972. *Information Theory and the Living System*. New York: Columbia University Press.

Jantsch, E., 1980. *The Self-Organizing Universe*. Oxford: Pergamon Press.

Karreman, G., 1955. Topological information content and chemical reactions. *Bull. Math. Biophys.* 17:279–285.

Khinchin, A. I., 1957. *Mathematical Foundations of Information Theory*. New York: Dover.

Kimura, M., 1979. The neutral theory of molecular evolution. *Sci. Amer.* 241:98–126.

King, J. L., and T. H. Jukes, 1969. Non-Darwinian evolution. *Science* 64:788–798.

Kittel, C., 1969. *Thermal Physics*. New York: Wiley.

Lamprecht, I., and A. I. Zotin, 1978. *Thermodynamics of Biological Processes*. New York: de Gruyter.

Lamprecht, I., and A. I. Zotin, 1983. *Thermodynamics and Kinetics of Biological Processes*. New York: de Gruyter.

Lamprecht, I., and A. I. Zotin, 1985. *Thermodynamics and Regulation of Biological Processes*. New York: de Gruyter.

Landsberg, P. T., 1984. Is equilibrium always an entropy maximum? *J. Stat. Physics* 35:159–169.

Layzer, D., 1975. The arrow of time. *Sci. Amer.* 233:56–69.

Layzer, D., 1977. Information in cosmology, physics and biology. *Int. J. Quantum Chemistry* 12 (Suppl. 1): 185–195.

Layzer, D., 1978. A macroscopic approach to population genetics. *J. Theor. Biol.* 73: 769–788.

Layzer, D., 1980. Genetic variation and progressive evolution. *Amer. Nat.* 115: 809–826.

Layzer, D., 1981. Quantum mechanics, thermodynamics and the strong cosmological principle. In *Physics as Natural Philosophy*. A. Shimony and H. Feshbach, eds., Cambridge, MA: MIT Press.

Lotka, A. J., 1956. *Elements of Mathematical Biology*. New York: Dover.

Maynard Smith, J., 1970. Time in the evolutionary process. *Studium Generale* 23: 266–273.

Prigogine, I., 1980. *From Being to Becoming*. San Francisco: Freeman.

Prigogine, I., and I. Stengers, 1984. *Order Out of Chaos*. New York: Bantam.

Prigogine, I., and J. M. Wiame, 1946. Biologie et thermodynamique des phenomenes irreversibles. *Experientia* 2: 451–453.

Prigogine, I., G. Nicolis, and A. Babloyantz, 1972. Thermodynamics of evolution. *Physics Today* 25(11): 23–28; 25(12): 38–44.

Schrödinger, E., 1944. *What Is Life?* Cambridge: Cambridge University Press.

Shannon, C. E., and W. Weaver, 1949. *The Mathematical Theory of Communication*. Urbana: University Illinois Press.

Tisza, L., 1966. *Synthese* 14: 110–131.

Thompson, D'Arcy W., 1942. *On Growth and Form*. Cambridge: Cambridge University Press.

van der Lubbe, J. C. A., Y. Boxma, and D. E. Boekee, 1984. A generalized class of certainty and information measures. *Inf. Sci.* 32: 187–215.

von Neumann, J., 1966. *Theory of Self-Reproducing Automata*. A. W. Burks, ed., Urbana: University Illinois Press.

Wicken, J. S., 1979. The generation of complexity in evolution: a thermodynamic and information-theoretical discussion. *J. Theor. Biol.* 77: 349–365.

Wiley, E. O., 1981. *Phylogenetics, the Theory and Practice of Phylogenetic Systematics*. New York: Wiley-Interscience.

Wolfram, S., 1983a. Cellular automata. *Los Alamos Sci.* 9: 2–21.

Wolfram, S., 1983b. Statistical mechanics of cellular automata. *Rev. Mod. Phys.* 55: 601–644.

Wolfram, S., 1984a. Universality and complexity in cellular automata. *Physica D* 10: 1–35.

Wolfram, S., 1984b. Computer software in science and mathematics. *Sci. Amer.* 251: 188–203.

Wolfram, S., 1984c. Cellular automata as models of complexity. *Nature* 311: 419–424.

IV

Evaluations and Implications

10

The Dynamics of Biological Order

John Collier

There are several things that are puzzling about biological order. The first and most fundamental is its nature. We have no trouble identifying it, yet its manifestations are so various that in the past otherwise sensible people have invoked a variety of occult entities to explain it. The second puzzle about biological order is where it comes from. It appears to originate spontaneously, unlike most things in the world, which if left alone, tend to disintegrate rather than organize themselves (though recently exceptions have been discussed). This peculiarity of biological order led Schrödinger (1944) to describe life as negentropic. This leads to a paradox: Why should life be negentropic if the physical and chemical processes that underlie it are entropic? The last puzzle about biological order is that it does not repeat itself (Dollo's Law). Not only this, but it seems to increase more or less monotonically with time, becoming more and more complex. In the past, puzzles like these led to speculations about a Creator with a Divine plan. Whether or not these speculations offer any sort of explanation, science requires an account of the underlying dynamics.

Since the rise of the neo-Darwinian synthesis, and especially with the successes of molecular biology since 1953, the genetic code is the key to understanding the nature and evolution of biological order. Biological organisms themselves do not evolve; they live and die. Nor does the material substance of organisms evolve; it becomes a part of some organism, and then ceases to be a part of that organism. Not even the forms of organisms evolve; forms appear and disappear as the organisms that have them are born and die. What evolves is a historical sequence of forms, each causally related to its predecessor. The continuity between forms is provided by the information transmitted to successors through replication. The medium of transmission (largely, if not exclusively) is the genetic code. Fundamentally, biological evolution is the evolution of genetic encodings, the physical embodiment of the information responsible for biological organization.

The genetic code has both a material and a formal aspect, each having implications for the role of information in evolutionary theory. The material basis of the genetic code is chemical and must obey the laws of chemistry and physics, including those of thermodynamics . It is possible to define the physical information content of a particular state of a chemical system in thermodynamic terms using the standard relationship between information and entropy developed by Szilard (1929) and Brillouin (1962). Inasmuch as evolution is a process involving physical information, it must be compatible with physical information theory and thermodynamics. In particular, since evolution occurs under nonequilibrium conditions, it must be accompanied by increases in entropy.

Formally, the genetic code is the major means by which the form of biological organisms is transmitted both in the development of the organism and in reproduction. It provides a set of open-ended instructions similar to a computer program, which the zygote interprets in order to develop into a mature organism. On this computational model, these instructions are encoded information, mostly inherited from ancestors, much of which is passed on to offspring. Transmission of information by a code falls within the domain of communications theory, as originally developed by Shannon and Weaver (1949). Another formal characteristic of evolution is a monotonic increase in the complexity and organization of successive forms. Evolution involves not only information transmission, but also changes and increases in that information. Dollo's Law, which is highly confirmed by observation, is a corollary: Successor forms do not repeat any of their predecessors.

It is not immediately clear how to reconcile the material and formal aspects of the genetic code. There are various arguments (discussed in more detail below) that imply that reconciliation is impossible, is impossible to achieve in any systematic way, or is of no interest to biology. The arguments for impossibility are best met directly by showing how the formal and material aspects of the genetic code are systematically related, or at least by giving a plausible theoretical account of how they could be related. This requires an account of how formal, or abstract, information can reside naturally in certain types of physical systems, of which the genetic system is one. A sketch of such an account is given below. The objection of the irrelevance to biology of reconciling structural and functional explanations of the operation of the genetic code is undermined by the paradox of biological order. The resolution of this paradox necessitates investigating the relation between the formal and material sides of genetics.

The increasing order produced by evolution is often attributed to the incorporation of random genetic variations into transmitted genetic encodings. At first glance, and even after a sober second look, this explanation appears to be inconsistent with the inevitable entropy increase of physical systems. It turns out that there are nonequilibrium physical systems called dissipative structures that spontaneously increase their order, albeit at the expense of increasing the entropy of the environment (see Prigogine, 1961;

Nicolis and Prigogine, 1977; Wicken, 1978; Jantsch, 1981). If biological organisms are dissipative structures, increases in structural order are inevitable. This still does not explain why the functioning of the genetic system should produce more order; it merely shows that it is possible. There must be some characteristic of the genetic system that manifests this possibility. Landsberg (1984), Layzer (1975, this volume) and Frautschi (1982, this volume) have pointed out that the entropy and order of a system can increase together if the size of the phase space of the system increases. Layzer (this volume) suggests that the evolutionary phase space is genetic phase space, and describes how it could increase. This gives a possible dynamics for increases in biological order.

The next step is to show that living systems actually obey this dynamics. Dan Brooks and Ed Wiley (Wiley and Brooks, 1982; Brooks and Wiley, 1984, 1986; Brooks et al., this volume; Wiley, this volume) present us with a theory of evolution, based on a dynamics of increasing entropy of the information stored in biological species, that they have applied to a wide range of biological issues and problems. If their theory is correct, it explains the nature and cause of biological order. It also resolves the paradox of biological order by showing that life is not negentropic. I shall examine their solution, in particular whether it is of any special interest to biologists. I believe that careful consideration of this issue will help in evaluating the relationship of the various proposals presented in this book. The application of physical concepts to biological problems tends to stir up animosities between scientists who favor such moves and those who do not. I believe that biologists are right in rejecting most reductionist tendencies, but also believe that they are too sanguine about the ability of theories that do not invoke physical notions to account adequately for everything of biological interest in evolution. One of the greatest strengths of the Brooks-Wiley theory is that it avoids both of these pitfalls. Quite apart from empirical evidence from particular applications, there are strong theoretical reasons to accept it.

There are two reductionist tendencies in biology that favor the material and formal aspects of biological order, respectively. Both can trace their contemporary form to positivistic trends in the philosophy of science (Rosenberg, 1985, pp. 21–25). The first, more commonly considered reductionist, attempts to reduce biology to the laws governing its physical and chemical components. The second, which is equally reductionist in spirit, though it is often represented as being opposed to reductionism, attempts to reduce biology to laws concerning the functions of biological entities. The extreme materialist holds that evolution is entirely a consequence of the activity of the chemicals that make up organisms, and that an adequate theory of evolution can be stated completely within the accepted laws of chemistry. The extreme functionalist, on the other hand, holds that evolution is a consequence of the random generation of biological forms and their selection according to their adaptive value, and that biological organization can be explained in terms of adaptive value. While I doubt that any biologist fully and consistently subscribes to either of these schools of thought, their opposition has tended to direct attention away from the advantages of synthesizing the persuasive insights of both. Both are fundamentally inadequate as they now stand; any sophisticated understanding of evolution borrows from both. Before discussing the requirements for a synthetic approach to the puzzles about biological order, I would like to point out the difficulties, first with proposed materialist reductionist solutions, and then with formalist proposals.

Living systems are composed of chemicals. Although there may be laws governing very complex systems like organisms that are difficult or impossible to anticipate from our knowledge of simpler chemical systems, there is no good reason to suppose that biological systems violate the fundamental laws applying to chemical systems in general. The only open question about the relevance of physical and chemical theories to biology is whether they place useful constraints on biological theory. There are three ways that fundamental laws and theories from outside biology could be uninteresting to biologists.

First, a law or theory is of little interest to biologists if it applies to every biological system in exactly the same way as it applies to nonbiological systems. These applications are biologically trivial. The law of gravitation is a good example. There is nothing special about the way biological systems obey the law of gravity. Although gravitational forces may be of interest to biologists when they consider the various strategies that, say, trees use to deal with these forces, biologists apply gravitational theory in exactly the same way as their colleagues in the physical sciences. By this I mean that biologists applying gravitational theory work within the same Kuhnian disciplinary matrix (Kuhn, 1970, 1977) as their colleagues in physics, using the same exemplars, models, and techniques.

Second, a law or theory is biologically uninteresting if it gives no predictions or explanations within the domain of biology that cannot be given with established biological theory. Such laws are biologically redundant. Some biologically trivial laws fall into this category because they apply to biological systems vacuously. Rosenberg (1985, p. 62) argues that there are functional explanations for which any physicochemical explanation would be biologically redundant: "Consider a complex teleological regularity, like 'plovers lay four eggs in order to maximize inclusive fitness.' Any attempt to provide an account of the directively organized subsystems of plovers to *fully* explain this regularity would be unmanageably long, baroque, and without further theoretical and predictive payoff beyond the functional explanation." A functional reductionist would hold that all physicochemical explanations for biological phenomena are redundant, but a more moderate position might hold that only some such explanations are redundant. I cannot think of any actual nontrivial applications of physical or chemical laws or theories that are unquestionably biologically redundant, but the objection of redundancy could be raised against Brooks and Wiley's application of nonequilibrium thermodynamics to evolution.

Last, a law or theory is irrelevant to biologists if it is obscure how to apply it to problems that interest biologists. Quantum mechanics applies to biological systems, and there is little doubt that special issues in quantum mechanics are raised by the formation of proteins and the replication of nucleic acids. Quantum mechanics is presently of little interest to biologists, however, since it is not clear how to apply it. Perhaps this will change in the future, but for the time being biologists are justified in largely ignoring quantum mechanics. In order to interest biologists, a proponent of applying a fundamental physical or chemical law or theory to biological problems must show not only that the application is nontrivial and nonredundant, but also that it is tractable. Biologists are justified in ignoring laws and theories that violate these conditions, even though they might be intrinsically interesting or show promise for unifying the sciences.

The laws of thermodynamics apply to all natural systems, including biological systems. Furthermore, since biological systems exist under nonequilibrium conditions, we can assume that they obey the principles of nonequilibrium thermodynamics. Prigogine (1961; also Nicolis and Prigogine, 1977; Jantsch, 1981) has observed that nonequilibrium conditions permit the spontaneous development and maintenance of self-organizing systems called "dissipative structures," which maintain their organization, in spite of an overall increase in entropy, by expelling matter and energy into the environment. A paradigm is the vortices produced by heating a pot of water. Assuming that biological systems are dissipative structures, the paradox of biological order seems to be resolved. Biological order can spontaneously increase locally at the expense of increased entropy in the whole system.

There are two closely related difficulties with this resolution of the paradox. First, although it is true that biological organisms, considered as chemical systems, almost certainly fall within the scope of dissipative structures as described by Prigogine, it is not clear how the chemical order that results is physically related to the biological order in evolving genetic encodings. We do not know nearly enough about organisms as chemical systems to be able to tell whether their functioning as dissipative structures has anything to do with the creation or even maintenance of inherited order. Furthermore, insofar as we can tell that organisms are Prigogine-type dissipative structures, no applications of the theory of dissipative structures are required that are peculiar to biology. There is no evidence from this quarter that the laws of nonequilibrium thermodynamics apply to biological systems nontrivially.

Second, although Prigogine's theory can account for the existence of increasingly complex chemistry in living systems (see Wicken, 1978, 1980, and this volume), it is not clear how dissipative structures can account for the peculiarities of biological order, which, unlike the order of the simple dissipative structures described by Prigogine, is (a) encoded and (b) hereditary. If thermodynamics is to explain biological order, it must account for these two features. To do this at the chemical level would require an account of the origins and development of the genetic code in purely chemical terms, along with an account of the chemical origins and operations of the mechanisms of inheritance. These are currently intractable problems, and are likely to remain so for the foreseeable future. Even if they can be solved, there may be an adequate explanation of the origin and development of biological order using only established biological theory together with trivial applications of physical and chemical principles. The chemical explanations required to apply Prigogine's theory to the problems of biological order seem likely to be similar to reductive explanations of the plover's four eggs (see above): They would provide little theoretical payoff. If biological order can be explained adequately by natural selection or some other functional account, explanations in terms of nonequilibrium thermodynamics are redundant.

In order to discuss the limitations of thermodynamic accounts at the molecular level, Wicken (1978, also 1985 and 1986) distinguished between order and organization, order being "a statistical concept referring to the regularity in a sequence of digits, the homogeneity and coherence of radiant energy, or the spatial periodicity of ions in an inorganic crystal," while organization "refers to the specific set of spatio-temporal and functional relationships among (a physical system's) parts." Biological order clearly involves Wicken's organization. He argued that thermodynamics can account for the generation of structural complexity, but not for functional organization. He also distinguished (1980, 1986; see also Layzer, 1975) between macroscopic information, which is thermodynamic, and microscopic information, deriving from specific molecular sequences. Wicken believes that sequential information is not amenable to thermodynamic treatment (for a contrary view, see Holzmuller, 1984), and that biological organization involves only microscopic information. Evolution results when reductions in macroscopic information in the environment are coupled to increases in biological organization (Wicken, 1980, 1986). He points out that the details of the direction of evolution cannot be predicted from the boundary conditions placed by external thermodynamic constraints. Wicken takes this to support his claim that biological organization involves only microscopic information, and cannot be dealt with directly using thermodynamics. This justification, however, presumes that external thermodynamic constraints are the only ones that are active, which further presumes that biological organization cannot be assigned a macroscopic information. Wicken's position turns on this last assumption, which he supports only circularly. (A different discussion of Wicken's view and reasons for questioning it can be found in Brooks et al., 1986).

If Wicken is nonetheless correct about the inapplicability of thermodynamics to sequential information, thermodynamics acts only as an external force required for the development of biological order. Like Prigogine and Jantsch, Wicken has consistently adopted and developed this externalist approach throughout his work. But there is nothing peculiarly biological about the application of thermodynamics to evolution in the externalist account. It is biologically trivial, as are all applications of external energetic or entropic criteria to biological systems, intesesting though they might be in their own right. If thermodynamics is to be applied nontrivially to explaining biological order it is necessary to define a macroscopic information for functional organization that has a direct physical interpretation. Interestingly, this can be done, as I shall describe below.

Since purely physicochemical explanations of biological order are incomplete or (perhaps irremediably) intractable, functional aspects of genetic encoding must be taken into consideration. It is empirically well-established that the genetic code is the basis for hereditary transmission, by means of gene replication and transcription. The inheritance of characters through reproduction, then, is the primary function of the genetic code. Using only the formal aspect of the code, there are in principle no problems with defining biological order. Using communications theory (Shannon and Weaver, 1949), it is in principle possible to determine the information capacity of each segment of genetic material. If we know how proteins are encoded for transcription, how these proteins are involved in developmental pathways, and how these developmental pathways eventually lead to expressed characters, we can in principle determine the amount of structural, developmental, and phenotypic information actually encoded. Even though we cannot carry this out in practice, it is often possible to make reliable comparisons of the relative complexity of various biological structures, if only on phenomenological grounds. This provides an estimate of the amount of information that must be transmitted through reproduction.

Communications theory allows us to make qualitative and (in principle) quantitative measurements of biological order, but it cannot explain the origin of the order it measures. Although communications theory explicitly permits sources of information, it gives no account of these, since it deals only with information transmission. In its classic form it is restricted to cases in which information either remains constant or degrades. Even if it is possible to account for the production of information in thermodynamic terms (as Wicken has sketched), classic communications theory requires that this account be externalist. In Wicken's terms, communications theory deals only with microscopic information, whereas the application of thermodynamics requires macroscopic information.

In standard evolutionary theory genetic variation increases the capacity of the genetic encoding, while natural selection determines which variations are informative (functional). On this model, all biological order is attributable to the action of the forces of selection. Random genetic variants may be either useless "noise" or survivable "messages," selected for their adaptive value (Cooper, 1981; Mayr, 1982, pp. 67–69). Biological order is a "reflection" of order in the environment in the sense that it is a consequence, via natural selection, of environmental order. Except inasmuch as it is affected by selection, the chemical level is entirely random with respect to biological order, and does not contribute to it. Although the contributions of the various characters of an organism to its fitness are the proximate causes of its reproduction rate, and might be thought to be the source of order in the organism, the degree to which a given character contributes to an organism's fitness depends ultimately entirely on the environment. The contributions of the characters of an organism to its fitness are contributions to its biological order only insofar as they are selected for.

The fundamental problem with this approach is that it requires that biological order varies solely according to the environment. If there were a circular succession of environments, the same gene might be first informative, then noise, and then again informative. This is inconsistent with the observation that biological order steadily increases. Since environmentally caused changes can be reversed by reversing environmental conditions, selection is not the source of irreversibility unless environmental conditions are irreversible. Although all environmental processes are irreversible, only some properties of these processes exert selective forces. Some properties of the environment change irreversibly, but many evolutionarily significant conditions, such as climate and food supply, are cyclic. It seems improbable, therefore, that irreversible environmental changes are the source of evolutionary irreversibility. Although selection is an important factor in determining how biological order is expressed, it cannot be the only source of biological order, since it cannot account for the irreversibility of evolution.

The most direct response to this objection is to maintain that biological order and the irreversibility of evolution are independent of each other. Irreversibility, on this account, is due to the fact that the genotype is constantly changing, and that if a need arises again for some capacity that has been previously lost, the capacity will be generated by a very different genotype than the original (Mayr, 1982, p. 609). The change in the genotype is partly due to selection, and partly due to random changes (i.e., changes that are not ordered with respect to selection). Granted, the reply goes, selection does not contribute to irreversibility, but irreversibility can be explained by the random changes that do not contribute to biological order.

The answer to this response is equally direct, if not quite so blinkered by theory. Explaining the irreversibility of evolution independently of biological order is impossible, since it is increases in biological order that need explanation. If order originates entirely in the environment, and is imposed on organisms via selection for functional adaptations, the amount of order would be just that imposed by the environmental conditions. Changing environmental conditions could just as easily decrease the total order as increase it. Cyclic environmental changes would result in the cyclic creation and destruction of order, contradicting our intuitive observation that biological order increases. Biological order is not just the product of natural selection. If Darwinism, which attributes evolution to genetic variation and selection alone, is to be maintained, genetic variation must also contribute to biological order. But genetic variation depends on the physicochemical structure of the genetic system. The extreme functional reductionist, who maintains that all biological order can be explained by adaptive value, is wrong.

There are several constraints on genetic variation that introduce order. Although it is sometimes thought that selectionists must assume that genetic variation is random, this is not true. Darwinian selection requires only that genetic variation is not causally linked to selective forces. For selection to work, genetic variations must be physically possible and even fairly likely, given the current genetic state. Two factors that constrain genetic variation, then, are physical likelihood and the current genotype. Since these two constraints apply throughout the whole history of a lineage, the potential for genetic variations in a population at a particular time is a result of the past history of genetic variations of the lineage and the statistical laws governing variation. Both contribute to biological order. Since the evolutionary increase of biological order is unlikely to be a historical quirk, we can be pretty certain that it can be explained systematically. Although the particular history of a lineage depends on chance events, and is not amenable to systematic analysis, the statistical laws governing variation must be incorporated into an adequate general theory of biological order. The theory can safely ignore the particular chance events determining the unique character of the biological order within a particular lineage, since this is not part of what is to be explained.

Genetic variation might produce biological order only in the presence of selection, or also in its absence. Perhaps independent contribution is possible under some circumstances, but in realistic cases it is negligible. Whichever case holds, the role of genetic variation is theoretically important because it is essential for explaining evolutionary irreversibility. It would be more interesting, though, if genetic variation can produce biological order even without environmental selection. This question needs to be thoroughly investigated.

Lionel Harrison (this volume) has suggested that increases of biological order can be understood in terms of kinetic theory as the result of diffusion and self-catalysis. These mechanisms seem promising, and are certainly worth further investigation. If the mechanisms of gene-kinetics can be understood entirely in terms of the underlying chemical processes, gene-kinetics can be reconciled with the laws governing these chemical processes, and the paradox of biological order can be resolved. Unfortunately, this sort of reduction is not possible now. A different approach would be to show that, solely on its own principles, gene-kinetics spontaneously and irreversibly produces biological order. This would be to develop a statistical gene-mechanics, with a derivative "gene-thermodynamics." Order would need to be suitably defined so that it would be statistically likely to increase in an arbitrary gene system. This requires the definition of macrostates of the genetic system, preferably in functional terms in order to avoid the intractabilities of genetic reduction. Whether we start from an externalist or an internalist perspective, a satisfactory explanation of evolutionary irreversibility seems to require that genetic configurations have macrostates.

It seems unlikely on information-theoretic grounds that a purely functional genetic statistical mechanics can resolve the paradox of biological order. Since biological order is measured by the information it bears, it obeys a law of information theory parallel to the second law of thermodynamics: The information transmitted by a channel cannot increase as it is transmitted through the channel; it can only decrease or remain the same. It seems that no matter how genetic information is reordered or varied, it cannot show an irreversible increase in content unless the additional information comes from outside the functional system (and hence from outside of the scope of a purely functional theory). This limitation applies generally to any theory of biological order that tries to deal with only the formal aspect. If we define macrostates internally in purely functional terms, the order of these states can only remain constant or degrade with time. This is true whether we take the functional system to be just the gene-reproduction system or whole ecosystems. Internalist accounts of biological order cannot explain irreversibility because they inherently deal with closed systems.

An adequate theory of biological order will give an internalist definition of biological order to avoid the problems of intractability and incompleteness, but will also be compatible with externalist accounts of order so that the system is not closed but can allow order to be incorporated from the outside. It is possible for such systems to increase their functional order by dissipating some of the information that flows through them while incorporating a small part of it, similarly to the way Prigogine's dissipative structures self-organize at the expense of dissipating some of the energy and matter that flows through them. An increase in functional order involving the incorporation of new information in which the genetic state produced is more likely can explain a spontaneous increase in order.

This is exactly what Brooks and Wiley do. They use both the physical concept of entropy and the formal concept of information, unified into a physical information theory (Collier, 1986), to predict spontaneous production of biological order by the incorporation of genetic variation into biological organization at the species level. Using this theory, they show that genetic variation that is captured and propagated by reproduction within a species increases a formally definable entropy. They postulate that this entropy increase both drives evolution and explains its irreversibility. The entropy they use is definable in purely physical terms, and is a component of the chemical entropy of the living system and its environment (Collier, 1986). The irreversibility of evolution, on this account, is a special case of the second law of thermodynamics, and biological order (or at least that component of biological order that is not due to environmental selection) is a consequence of this law. I shall briefly sketch some of the details of this theory, and then discuss its significance.

Any collection of things that mutually interact through forces will have a certain amount of organization. We can call the organized collection an array (Collier, 1986). An array has both macroscopic information, defined by its physical state in the usual way, as well as microscopic information, in virtue of its organization. The exact details of the definition of these informations is irrelevant here, except to note that the macroscopic information is necessarily greater than the microscopic information, since the organization contributes to the order of the array but there may be order that is quite accidental to the organization. This may seem paradoxical to those following Layzer (1975) and Wicken (1980), who discuss the conversion of macroscopic into microscopic information. The problem is a false dichotomy: Information that is "converted" into microscopic form can remain in macroscopic form, as long as it is capable of doing work in virtue of its organization. Wicken's claim that biological organization involves only microscopic information overlooks the potential for work that any organized system has. The equivalence of information and the ability to do work is central to the "exorcism" of Maxwell's Demon (Brillouin, 1962, pp. 162–183), as well as to a multitude of discussions of the thermodynamics of computation. The ability to do work, sort, or compute implies a thermodynamic debit that is restored as heat when the organization is destroyed.

Although the microscopic information of organization is correlated with a macroscopic information, as I said above the macroscopic information of the physical system is greater than the information of the organization. Thus, the physical entropy is not a measure of the entropy of the biological organization. If the organization itself has an entropy that is more than a mere artifact of the numerical comparison of the macroscopic and microscopic information, then it must have macrostates definable purely in terms of the physical properties taking part in the organization. Because these macrostates can carry information, in the sense of Shannon and Weaver, exactly equal to their microscopic information, I classify them as physical information systems (Collier, 1986). The entropy that Brooks and Wiley (1986, and Brooks et al., this volume) refer to as increasing in evolution is just the entropy of these systems.

Sets of physical things that persist for a fair length of time and interact in regular ways to form arrays are the elements of a physical information system. The information content of an array is the sum of the contributions of the individual elements. The (probabalistic) laws of combination of the elements are the constraints of the information system (see Shannon and Weaver, 1949, p. 38, for a simple example of constraints). Irregular interactions, either among elements or with external structures, are noise to the system, although they may contribute to the overall order of a system of elements. If we assume that there is a maximal array size (which might be defined statistically), we can define the microstates of the system to be the possible maximal arrays, and the macrostates are the actual arrays. In realistic systems there will be a limit to array size. These definitions permit us to define a macroscopic information and entropy of each array entirely internally to the system, but in a way that is completely compatible physically with the external entropy and macroscopic information (although the values will differ; see Collier, 1986, for details).

There is a nested hierarchy of information systems in biological systems with at least four levels: chemical, genetic, phenotypic, and species. These levels are distinguished by their functional role, being ordered by functional dependence and partial causal independence. The functional role of species level information is reproduction. This is why it is natural to define species in terms of their members' ability to reproduce. For sexual species, at least, the following definition of species works fairly well: For organisms A and B there are a number (perhaps 1 or 0) of minimal sets of characters that allow A and B successfully to interbreed. Call the union of these sets the fecundity characters of A and B. If this set is nonempty, we can say that A and B are mutually fecund. The closure of this relationship is (roughly) the relationship of conspecificity. The information expressed by a species is the information contained in the members of the union of all the fecundity characters of the pairs of its members. The species could probably get by on less information than it does, but it does not, so the information expressed at this level can display some unnecessary variety.

The above definition of conspecificity in terms of the closure of mutual fecundity won't work for asexual species. The opposite problem seems to be presented by hybrids. Since hybrids tend to revert to "wild" forms, and nonsexual species tend to be preserved in more or less the same form through many generations, it appears that stability of the form through reproduction is in some sense the basis of species identity. Some diachronic analogue to the synchronic definition for sexual species might be able to capture the central function of reproduction for the more general case.

The functional role of the phenotype is to expose information for selection, or at least (on the Brooks-Wiley view) for incorporation as species information. This is subordinate to the role of the species level information, since what is selected is what in the long run contributes to reproduction. The phenotypic information is structurally independent of the species information, though, to the extent that it can vary without interfering with reproduction. Similarly, the functional role of the genetic information, which is to permit phenotypic variation, is subordinate to the role of the phenotype, since phenotypic variation gives something for selection to work on. The genotype can of course vary considerably for a given phenotype. The extension of this pattern to the chemical level is fairly obvious.

The hierarchy can also be differentiated by causal dependence, with each level causally dependent on the level below for its structure and details of its expression, and causally dependent on the level above for its preservation. A property is widely thought to be functional biologically if and only if the cause of its preservation is what it does (see Wright, 1973), so this second criterion is perhaps equivalent to the first.

Not all of the information at a lower level is expressed at the higher levels; in fact most of it is not. Only a small amount of the total chemical information is expressed genetically; only a small proportion of the genetic information, which allows a vast multitude of possible developmental pathways, is actually expressed phenotypically, and only a small part of the characters of its members are involved in the propagation of the species. This filtering of information upward through the hierarchy allows some variations at lower levels to be quite irrelevant to activity at the higher levels, while other changes will be highly significant.

The main feature of interest about the biological informational hierarchy is that information at a lower level that is not expressed at higher levels can come to be expressed if conditions change. This change in conditions could be external, but might also, and probably more often does, involve changes in the interaction of the information with other information that is either lost or created. Chemical variation will often be expressed at the genetic level, which can alter the developmental "message," and possibly the phenotype. This can even (though it is not very likely in the short run) affect breeding behavior, and hence species cohesiveness. It is in principle possible, then, for random chemical variation to cause a speciation event without any external action. Other internally caused effects at the species level are more subtle, but more likely.

Most chemical variation, even that which is expressed at the phenotypic level, is not preserved, because most variations are as likely to disappear as appear, maintaining a rough equilibrium. Characters that are directly involved in reproduction, though, are preserved as long as the lineage is preserved. Any character that contributes to reproduction will be (in a sense) captured. When a new element is expressed at a certain level, for example, captured at the species level by aiding in reproduction, the size of the information system at that level increases along with the amount of information at the level, which is increased by the new addition. The increase in size of the information system results in an increase in the entropy of the arrays at that level (Brooks and Wiley, 1986; Brooks et al., 1984). The incorporation of information at the species level through its expression through capture of lower level information is therefore an entropic process. This entropy is a physical entropy (as argued above and in Collier, 1986), and is fairly well decoupled from other entropy flows, which explains why evolution is irreversible.

There are further details to the Brooks-Wiley theory involving the entropy of species cohesion and applications to ontogeny, but the above sketch is sufficient to establish the nontriviality, tractability, and non-redundancy of their theory. The nontriviality is established by the special application of the information-theoretic and thermodynamic principles to the biological processes of reproduction and heredity. Tractability is insured by the use of functional concepts in the definitions of entropy and information: No particular reductive analysis is presumed. Nonredundancy is ensured at least by the explanation of irreversibility, which resists explanation in purely functional terms. There is also the possibility of evolutionary change controlled by internal factors resulting from the past history of a lineage rather than being under the control of selection. This possibility includes the possibility of internally caused speciation events, totally independent of any environmental factors including geographical separation, though these are probably rare. It does, however, provide the most direct test of the Brooks-Wiley theory, although the nonexistence of such events does not prove the theory false.

The Brooks-Wiley theory is compatible with the essential Darwinian insight that evolution is due to genetic variation and selection. It differs from most purely selectionist theories in allowing the possibility that both evolution and speciation can occur without any selection pressure from the environment. Furthermore, it predicts that there will be evolution that cannot be entirely accounted for by selection pressure. Whether or not this actually occurs will probably remain hotly debated for some time. Even if it does not, the Brooks-Wiley theory is not thereby falsified. The characters contributing to reproduction that are incorporated at the species level in the informational hierarchy could owe their persistence entirely to selective forces, but the same Brooks-Wiley mechanisms would be at work. In particular, the incorporation of these characters increases entropy, which explains the irreversibility of evolution. Given the inability of functionally motivated selectionist accounts to explain irreversibility adequately, even if the Brooks-Wiley theory makes no successful new predictions it increases the explanatory power of biological theory. Furthermore, with its basis in physical information theory, it provides a good foundation for the unification of biology with the physical sciences. It does this without denying the special character of biological science, since it specifically incorporates at its most fundamental level the concepts of reproduction and heredity, which are not found in applications within the physical sciences proper.

References

Brillouin, L., 1962. *Science and Information Theory*. New York: Academic Press.

Brooks, D. R., and E. O. Wiley, 1984. Evolution as an entropic phenomenon. In *Evolutionary Theory: Paths to the Future*, J. W. Pollard, ed., London: Wiley.

Brooks, D. R., and E. O. Wiley, 1986. *Evolution as Entropy: Toward a Unified Theory of Biology*. Chicago: University of Chicago Press.

Brooks, D. R., J. D. Collier, and E. O. Wiley, 1986. Definitions and the essence of theories: a rejoinder to Wicken. *Syst. Zool.* 35:640–647.

Brooks, D. R., P. H. LeBlond, and D. D. Cumming, 1984. Information and entropy in a simple evolution model. *J. Theor. Biol.* 109:77–93.

Collier, J. D., 1986. Entropy in evolution. *Biology and Philosophy* 1:5–24.

Cooper, W. S., 1981. Natural decision theory: a general formalism for the analysis of evolved characteristics. *J. Theor. Biol.* 92:401–415.

Frautschi, S., 1982. Entropy in an expanding universe. *Science* 217:573.

Holzmuller, W., 1984. *Information in Biological Systems: The Role of Macromolecules*. Cambridge: Cambridge University Press.

Jantsch, E., ed., 1981. *The Evolutionary Vision, AAAS Selected Symposia*. Boulder, CO: Westview Press.

Kuhn, T. S., 1970. *The Structure of Scientific Revolutions*, 2nd ed. Chicago: University of Chicago Press.

Kuhn, T. S., 1977. Second thoughts on paradigms. In *The Structure of Scientific Theories*, 2nd ed., F. Suppe, ed., Urbana: University of Illinois Press, pp. 459–499.

Landsberg, P. T., 1984. Can entropy and "order" increase together? *Physics Letters* A102: 171–173.

Layzer, D., 1975. The arrow of time. *Sci. Amer.* 233:56–69.

Mayr, E., 1982. *The Growth of Biological Thought*. Cambridge, MA: Belknap Press.

Nicolis, G., and I. Prigogine, 1977. *Self-Organization in Non-Equilibrium Systems: From Dissipative Structures to Order through Fluctuations*. New York: Wiley.

Prigogine, I., 1961. *Introduction to Thermodynamics of Irreversible Processes*, 2nd ed. New York: Wiley.

Rosenberg, A., 1985. *The Structure of Biological Science*. Cambridge: Cambridge University Press.

Schrödinger, E., 1944. *What Is Life?* Cambridge: Cambridge University Press.

Shannon, C. E., and W. Weaver, 1949. *The Mathematical Theory of Communication*. Urbana: University of Illinois Press.

Szilard, L., 1929. *Z. Physic.* 53:840.

Wicken, J. S., 1978. Information transformations in molecular evolution. *J. Theor. Biol.* 72:191–204.

Wicken, J. S., 1980. A thermodynamic theory of evolution. *J. Theor. Biol.* 87:9–23.

Wicken, J. S., 1983. Information transformations in molecular evolution. *J. Theor. Biol.* 72:191–204.

Wicken, J. S., 1985. Thermodynamics and the conceptual structure of evolutionary theory. *J. Theor. Biol.* 117:363–383.

Wicken, J. S., 1986. Entropy and evolution: ground rules for discourse. *Syst. Zool.* 35:22–36.

Wiley, E. O., and D. R. Brooks, 1982. Victims of history—a nonequilibrium approach to evolution. *Syst. Zool.* 31:1–24.

Wright, L., 1973. Functions. *Philosophical Review* 82:139–168. Reprinted in *Conceptual Issues in Evolutionary Biology*, Elliott Sober, ed., Cambridge, MA: MIT Press/Bradford Books, pp. 347–369.

11

Observations on Evolution

John Olmsted III

Evolution, despite being one of the linchpins of modern biology, is an idea that has been embroiled in controversy throughout its history. Much of this controversy has grown out of attempts to deepen the scientific basis upon which evolutionary theory rests, to link the ideas of evolution with other landmark developments in science. While such linkages can both substantiate a theory and improve our understanding of it, inappropriate drawing of connections often leads to confusion rather than to clarity. The many recent debates about evolution suggest that confusion rather than clarity is being promoted by the interconnections that are being proposed. In this paper I shall critically evaluate several of these attempts to establish linkages and show that there are difficulties with many of them. In particular, Newtonian determinism, cosmological parallels, thermodynamic necessity, and information-theoretic analogies will each be shown to have significant shortcomings when applied to biological evolution. Following these criticisms, I shall outline what strike me as the two central issues confronting the development of a more robust and mature evolutionary theory, those of the emergence of life and of the evolutionary trend toward greater complexity. Finally, I shall argue that what is now needed is elaboration of evolutionary theory from a biological perspective, with more attention to the carrying out of crucial observations and experiments in the realm of genetics. My goal is to provide a perspective that may illuminate how evolution interrelates with disorder and information. The reader should interpret this perspective in the context of my background. I am an experimental physical chemist—more specifically a photochemist—with an interest in how macroscopic and microscopic, thermodynamic and kinetic quantities can get entangled. I mention this at the outset because the literature in the field illustrates forcefully that our perspectives, even as scientists, are unavoidably constrained by our disciplines. I agree with Kant that the human mind is organized in ways that restrict our perceptions. In addition, I think that our training in a specific discipline (as well as the proclivities that led each of us to select a particular discipline) imposes on each of us an additional mind-set, which we then take as self-evident. My remarks should be considered in the context of my own mind-set, but I hope that each reader will be encouraged by my critique to reexamine his/her own mind-set.

While some of the disagreements afflicting the subject area of evolution stem from misunderstandings about vocabulary, more of them seem to me to be the result of conflicting mind-sets. At the risk of stereotyping, I would characterize physicists as obsessed with mathematical models, chemists with experiments, and biologists with functionality. If the real issues in the information-entropy-evolution debate are to be profitably addressed, we must all surmount these mind-sets and see the subject in broader perspective. In this context, attention must be paid to the use of models—analogies—to simplify and make comprehensible exceedingly complex systems, especially those of the living world. Models are both powerful and indispensable, but they can all too easily mislead, particularly when the ancillary properties of the model are carried along and attributed to the system being modeled (DNA as information and information as negentropy seem to me to be misleading models, for reasons I shall state presently). A particularly unfortunate model is the elevation of the Newtonian set of laws to the paradigm form toward which all other formulations of natural laws should aspire. Scientists of the post-relativity, post-quantum theory generations should know better. Whether or not there is a single paradigm for scientific laws is a significant, still-open philosophical question, but that the Newtonian laws are that paradigm is an untenable view. The notion that forces operating in deterministically closed systems represent an appropriate universal paradigm is surely weakened, if not destroyed, by relativistic reformulations in terms of space-time curvature. In the same vein, the notion of clockwork systems as paradigms was rendered untenable by the quantum mechanical notions of indeterminacy and observer-system interactions. Indeed, Popper has developed the view that Laplacian determinism is incompatible with the space-time restrictions generated by the special theory of relativity, without having to introduce quantum restrictions (Popper, 1982). As we ponder entropy and evolution as scientific concepts, we need to bear in mind that models in which determinism is a central feature do not serve very well even in important areas of physics, let alone in biology.

Entropy, one of the central constructs of science, surely must be relevant to evolution. Where that relevance lies is difficult to judge, because unfortunately entropy is loosely understood, even by many who work with entropic expressions. The macroscopic physicochemical definition, $dS = dQ/T$, does not contribute to a better understanding, since it is hard to get a physical sense of what a heat-temperature ratio represents (compare this to energy as capacity to do work and work as force times displacement—all intuitive quantities). The Boltzmann formulation, $S = k \ln W$, is not much better. What is the physical sense of the logarithm of a probability?

To me, the clearest definition of entropy is in terms of randomness. From this perspective, entropy is a quantitative measure of the degree of randomness of a system. The Second Law of Thermodynamics, which defines the role of entropy, is then best expressed in the general, Clausius form: In any real process, the entropy of the universe increases. This general form of the Second Law is preferable to other formulations precisely because it is entirely general, but for specific subclasses of processes a more specific (hence less widely applicable) formulation is likely to convey more information. For engines, the classic formulation, that it is impossible to convert heat completely into work in a cyclic process, is more informative. For living systems, a formulation in terms of order is more informative. The creation of local order requires generation of global disorder. This formulation in terms of order applies equally well to any system, whether or not biological, that is evolving toward an ordered state. A growing ice crystal achieves crystalline order by dissipating the heat of crystallization as thermal disorder of the surroundings. Gravitational coalescence of cosmic dust into relatively ordered planets is accompanied by dissipation of the gravitational energy as highly disordered radiation.

Evolution in the most general sense refers to any process that shows a regular development with time. A growing ice crystal, coalescing planets, a living ecosystem, each evolves. We must, however, distinguish carefully among at least three distinct categories of evolving system, since thermodynamic constraints will apply quite differently to each. A *closed* system—one that is isolated from its surroundings—can only evolve in directions that increase its entropy. It moves inexorably toward a disordered equilibrium state. A gas expanding through an orifice into an evacuated chamber is close to a closed system. With time, the molecular distribution evolves to the disordered, equal pressure state. An *outputting* system—one that expels matter and/or radiation to its surroundings—may evolve instead to an ordered equilibrium. A star is an example of an outputting system, evolving toward ever-higher order as it spews out radiation and matter. A *processing* system—one that both absorbs from and emits to its surroundings matter and/or radiation—may evolve to an ordered steady-state that is *far* from equilibrium. Prigogine's development of nonequilibrium thermodynamics, particularly as it relates to systems that are very far from equilibrium, deals primarily with processing systems (Prigogine, 1980). A planetary atmosphere is a processing system, absorbing and emitting both matter and energy yet undergoing rather small excursions about a steady-state condition. Biology concerns itself entirely with processing systems. All life forms absorb and emit matter and radiation. Further, the earth is also a processing system. Hence it is not surprising that biological evolution has generated ordered steady-state systems. Contrariwise, it would be very surprising if either closed systems or outputting systems supplied useful insights into biological evolution.

Part of the debate over what constitutes an adequate theory of evolution is more philosophical than scientific. What nature of explanations should we be seeking for the ordered steady-state systems that we encounter as products of biological evolution? How shall we judge the appropriateness of theories of evolution? It is a long-held tenet of science that among possible explanations, the one containing the smallest number of components is to be preferred. Indeed, this principle is applied quite broadly; witness Occam's Razor. In physics, it reigns supreme, as demonstrated by the high value accorded attempts to develop a unified field theory and conversely by the unease caused by the proliferation of subatomic particles, which spurs efforts to discover their "underlying" structure. But as we move to fields whose subject matter seems to be more complex, this parsimony principle becomes strained, less clearly applicable. Still, the prestige accorded plate tectonics in geology and evolution in biology originates in large part from the relative parsimoniousness of these rather simple theories that nevertheless can be applied to a multitude of phenomena.

Despite the widespread application in science of the principle of parsimony, it is not a scientific principle at all. It is a metaphysical principle. That is to say, there are no experiments that could be carried out to show that the most parsimonious explanation is necessarily correct. Our *intellectual* satisfaction with the simple explanation must suffice. This identification of parsimony as metaphysical rather than scientific does not devalue the principle. It merely recognizes it as outside the realm of scientific exploration. I would call it "superscientific," in that the metaphysical principle constitutes part of the mental framework within which we evaluate scientific endeavors.

Without violating its requirements, we can move along the ruler of parsimony in two directions, one leading to reductionism, the other to teleology. Reductionism is a most parsimonious metaphysical position, asserting that all of biology (and chemistry, and psychology, and politics, ...) can be—ultimately *must* be—explained by the laws of physics (which in turn, I suppose, will be subsumed under the unified field theory). Teleology expresses a different view, that life entails a purposiveness that is extraphysical. Though seemingly opposed, these views are not mutually exclusive. One can believe that the unified field theory was crafted by God in order to generate the universe and its life-forms. One can also believe that life, though without purpose, is described by biological laws that cannot be derived from the laws of physics. While the principle of parsimony is metaphysical rather than scientific, reductionism and teleology are less clearly one or the other. Conceivably, an experiment might be designed that would critically test whether or not life is purposeful. Conceivably, a law of evolution might be derived from physical laws, or conversely it might be proved that such a law can never be so derived. Although neither of these demonstrations has yet been convincingly carried out, there is a rich general analysis arguing against reduction. Popper's very broad arguments relate not only to determinism but also to the general failure of attempts to achieve reduction, even within physics itself. Popper argues in favor of an "open" universe, "in which the future was in no sense contained in the past or in the present, even though they do impose severe restrictions on it" (Popper, 1982, p. 3). Similarly, he implicitly argues for an "open" structure of science, in which the more complex relationships in biology are in no sense *contained* in physics, even though physicochemical laws significantly *restrict* the avenues of development open to biological systems. I agree with this point of view.

Each of these interrelationships, future/present/past and biology/chemistry/physics, is an example of a hierarchy, in which the necessity of a consequent occurrence (a future event, or a biological entity) is at issue. Simon has introduced the powerful notion of the nearly decomposable hierarchy, sufficiently coupled that one level has *effects* on another but insufficiently coupled that one level *dictates* another (Simon, 1969). Both future/past and biology/physics strike me as being nearly decomposable hierarchies. Closer to home, Pattee has been a champion of the nonreducibility of biology to physics, presenting the view that information in biology is complementary but not reducible to physical laws (Pattee, 1979). Still more strongly, Mayr suggests an *enrichment* relationship between these fields (Mayr, 1985). All of these thinkers proclaim that the most parsimonious explanation—that of full reductionism—is insufficient to account for what we encounter in the real world. Nonetheless, Popper holds that attempts at reduction, despite being unsuccessful, are ultimately worthwhile because of new insights that their very failures yield. Reductionists seem to be doomed to failure, but not of a Sisyphean kind; the stone has been successfully moved, but the remaining path has meanwhile become longer.

The foregoing analysis suggests that at our present level of understanding, insistence on either reduction or teleology as a necessary component of evolutionary theory is premature. Worse yet, I believe that such insistence is bound to create confusion rather than clarity. Much more science needs to be done to accomplish what should be the primary goal—elaboration of a descriptive, predictive, rich, and self-consistent full theory of evolution. This elaboration ought to take place in conformity with the principle of parsimony and in correspondence with the requirements of physical laws but should ignore reduction and teleology. The theory is most likely to be parsimonious if it is developed entirely out of biological and biochemical observations. In particular, I caution against trying to model it after theories of physics, as that is likely to result in an inappropriate, inelegant theoretical structure. Equally, I caution against trying to force evolutionary theory to emerge from chemical or physical principles. A major weakness of the Brooks-Wiley approach (Wiley and Brooks, 1982) is that it seems to make both of these mistakes. It tries to force a deterministic theory to emerge from the Second Law of Thermodynamics.

While evolutionary theory need not *follow* from physicochemical laws, it surely may not *contradict* them. This is a statement of the correspondence principle, that any new theory must remain in correspondence with already well-established laws. Correspondence demanded that quantum theory be equivalent to classical mechanics when applied to macroscopic bodies, since classical mechanics quite accurately describes such bodies. Similarly, correspondence demands that biological theories be consistent with physicochemical laws, since those laws accurately describe the physicochemical features of biological systems. Correspondence, however, is a much weaker requirement than reduction. The latter would require that biological theory be *derivable* from physicochemical laws, while the former requires only that biological theory be *compatible* with those laws. Specifically, evolutionary theory need not be derivable from the Second Law of Thermodynamics, but it cannot contradict that law. As I have already pointed out, biological evolution describes systems of the sort I have called "processing," one of whose properties is that they can evolve to ordered steady-states without violating the Second Law. Hence correspondence will not be difficult to achieve, but it remains essential to recognize those constraints that thermodynamics does place upon evolutionary theory.

The point of the foregoing remarks is that it is unrealistic to expect that evolutionary theory can be *deduced* from the laws of thermodynamics. Another approach that seems to me to be equally unrealistic is to use analogies between cosmological evolution and biological evolution. I see two very good general reasons why theories of cosmological evolution should not be transferred, even analogically, to the biological realm. First, cosmological systems are outputting rather than processing, which means that the qualities of the states accessible to the evolving systems are quite different in the two cases. Whereas both types of systems achieve order at the expense of their surroundings, the cosmological system "spends" by expelling chaotic stuff, while the biological system "spends" by transforming less random inputs into more random outputs. The latter is a richer strategy with, necessarily, a richer range of possible outcomes. (Within the cosmological realm, this distinction suggests that post-formation planetary evolution will be richer than stellar evolution. It is too bad that we have only one set of planets against which to test this prediction, although I think that the evolutionarily quite different states of Earth, Mars, and

Saturn favor its correctness). Second, cosmological theory is not yet sufficiently self-consistent nor well enough tested to be elevated to law.

For example, the formulations of Layzer (Layzer, 1977) begin with a singularity at $T = 0$, $t = 0$, yet immediately achieve a very high temperature. I am at a loss to comprehend how this might come about. Admittedly, singularities are relatively incomprehensible, but one that seems to start at absolute rest entails for me either the suspension of the laws of physics or a unique definition of the meaning of temperature. Some such peculiarity may indeed be required at the inception of the universe, but that does not look like a model that will have fruitful potential for application elsewhere. The singularity at $t = 0$ is not the only example of incompleteness of cosmological theory. There seems in such theories to be an *assumption* that thermodynamics, which is easier to apply to outputting systems than is kinetics, of necessity will yield the same results as kinetics would. For systems at equilibrium, this assertion is correct, but as every undergraduate chemistry major learns, systems under kinetic control (e.g., far from equilibrium) can yield quite different products than systems under thermodynamic control (e.g., close to equilibrium). "It frequently happens that ... C is favored kinetically and D is favored thermodynamically; the relative yield of products then depends on whether there is kinetic or thermodynamic control" (Levine, 1983, p. 508). Additionally, thermodynamic restrictions are very weak for systems that are far from equilibrium. They do not constrain the possible paths very strongly. Kinetic restrictions provide much more information, at the expense of requiring rather detailed knowledge of the rates of the various processes involved.

A third example of the immaturity of cosmological theory is our incomplete knowledge of black holes, which for all their inaccessibility are likely to hold vital keys to cosmological understanding. Hawking has predicted that quantum mechanistic black holes emit tunneling radiation (Hawking, 1976). This is in principle a testable prediction whose verification or falsification would greatly increase our cosmological knowledge. Until it is experimentally tested—no doubt the experiments are fiendishly difficult—the Hawking analysis remains no more than a prediction. Whether or not black holes obey the Second Law of Thermodynamics also seems to me to remain an open question with profound cosmological ramifications. As Frautschi has pointed out (Frautschi, 1982), if black holes decay through Hawking radiation they are in conformity with the Second Law. However, if nothing escapes black holes, they may well represent increasing order without dissipation to the surroundings. Both Hawking and Frautschi state that since outside observers cannot gain information about black holes' internal states, all their states are equally probable, hence their entropies extremely large. This is not correct. The entropy of a black hole may be forever *indeterminate* because of our inability to observe its internal states, but the conclusion that all such states are equally *probable* does not follow from such indeterminacy. Indeed, a statement that all states are equally probable and computation of entropy therefrom is a piece of information about black holes. It appears that one is deriving information from a statement about which one cannot obtain information. That strikes me as logically untenable. Black holes are regions of space undergoing compression rather than expansion. Their interiors are unobservable by us. To my mind, their existence (if verified) opens up the intriguing possibility of a "breathing" universe, expanding in some regions while collapsing in others. Does a black hole eventually collapse far enough to encounter a bifurcation, at which it suddenly explodes in a Big Bang? Is our original singularity not unique (Dicke and Peebles, 1979)? Cosmology is replete with such intriguing speculative possibilities, but they are not germane to the equally intriguing issues of biological evolution, and they certainly are not well enough established to form a basis for biological theories.

If biological evolution cannot profit from analogies with cosmology, what about analogies between information theory and evolution? Is the information/entropy identification a fruitful notion to apply here? It is most unfortunate that Shannon chose to move from recognition that "quantities of the form $H = -\sum p_i \log p_i$ play a central role ... as measures of information, choice, and uncertainty. The form of H will be recognized as that of entropy ..." to the statement "We shall call H ... the entropy of the set of probabilities ..." (Shannon and Weaver, 1949). H, which measures information content, is described by a mathematical equation of the same form as that describing S, a measure of randomness in physical systems. As many have pointed out, this does not require that $H = S$. Jaynes, for example, notes, "The mere fact that the same mathematical expression— $\sum p_i \log p_i$—occurs both in statistical mechanics and in information theory does not in itself establish any connection between these fields" (Jaynes, 1957, p. 621). Jaynes, to be sure, attempts to establish a connection, but the result is to denude entropy of its physical meaning: "In the problem of prediction, the maximization of entropy is not an application of a law of physics, but merely a method of reasoning ..." (Jaynes, 1957, p. 630). I think entropy has become impoverished rather than enriched in this process.

That H and S are irreconcilably different should have been clear from Shannon's original identification of "the entropy of the set of probabilities." The thermodynamic entropy S is a state function property of a physical system. A crystal, an organism, a star, each has a value of S characteristic of it. H, on the other hand, cannot refer to a physical system since it is identified with a mathematical construct. Pursuing thermodynamics a step further, the quantity TS is an energy-related, well-defined physical parameter of any physical system at uniform temperature. What in the world is the quantity TH? For that matter, what is T for a "set of probabilities" or a sequence of symbols? If H and S are related in any way that is more profound than sharing a mathematical formalism, it should be possible to identify a temperature-analog that can be meaningfully and usefully applied to sets and sequences. Wicken has drawn biologists' attention to the incommensurateness of physical and informational "entropies": "One should begin then by distinguishing carefully between two distinct kinds of entropy.... First is thermodynamic entropy itself, which involves statisical ensembles of micro-structures.... Second is the entropy of a sequence of elements, which can be defined as the minimum algorithm or information required for its unambiguous specification.... It must be appreciated that sequence entropies are not thermodynamic entropies" (Wicken, 1983, p. 439). Wicken is correct, but he does not go far enough, in my view. Retaining the name "entropy" for the minimum algorithm of a sequence ensures that confusion will accompany attempts to interpret this quantity. Elsasser has expressed this problem very cogently. As he points out, "Gravitational and electrostatic equilibrium are characterized by the same (Laplace's) differential equation. Nobody would think that gravitational attraction and electrostatic attraction or repulsion are otherwise identical" (Elsasser, 1983, p. 107). The reason that nobody makes this mistake is that gravity and electrostatics have different names. Let us call the minimum information of a sequence by some other name than entropy. Perhaps 'information potential' would do, for reasons expressed below.

Although the two quantities (H and S) are quite different, they are described in terms of the same mathematical formalism. That formalism leads to a degradative principle in information theory that parallels, but is not the same as, the Second Law of Thermodynamics. That principle is Shannon's Law: In the transmission of information, errors will be generated and the message will tend toward randomness. This law has found fruitful application in signal transmission, but it is violated in genetic transmission, as revealed by the paleontological record. As Elsasser puts it, "The phenomenon of progressive scatter of hereditary characters is absent" (Elsasser, 1983, p. 109). The reason for this is to be found in the nature of biological entities as processing systems. Unlike transmission lines, which are closed or weakly outputting systems, biological systems process large amounts of energy to ensure that genetic messages remain intact.

A better analog than the electronic transmitter-receiver is newpaper production, in which considerable effort is expended (or should be) at proofreading, correcting the inevitable Shannonesque errors so that the final message, produced in millions of copies, is a faithful reproduction of the original. A system that is willing to expend enough effort can overcome Shannon's Law. We see here a very significant difference between Shannon's Law and Second Law of Thermodynamics. Appropriate effort can overcome the former, but no amount of effort can ever overcome the latter. One is a law applying to systems (closed ones, at that), the other a fundamental law of the universe. Biological organisms expend much effort in genetic proofreading, as is evident from the very high level of fidelity maintained in DNA replication. The error rate in this replication has been measured at less than one in 100,000,000, a factor of 100,000 lower than would be expected on kinetic grounds (Fersht, 1981). This discrepancy can only be explained by proofreading functions, which are known to occur both by editing of the strand end as it is built up and by postreplicative editing of remaining mismatches. Additionally, biological systems possess elaborate DNA repair capabilities to take care of errors generated at times other than those of replication (Kornberg, 1980). Living systems overcome Shannon's Law by these proofreading and correction mechanisms, but there are substantial energy and entropy costs accompanying these mechanisms.

Even though it is misleading to identify information with entropy, information theory nonetheless is powerful and valid in its own right. Certainly, DNA as a sequence of "letters" arranged in nonrandom order can be profitably viewed as containing information, and some aspects of information theory should be useful in analyzing genetic information. A major question asks which aspects might be useful. As already noted, genetic transmission is not subject to Shannon's Law because of proofreading. There are additional constraints on the applicability of information theory to biology, many of which have been profoundly explored at a philosophical level by Stuart (Stuart, 1985). I shall confine my observations to the practical question of how H relates to the biologically interesting property of information *content*. It was argued above that H is not entropy as understood by physical scientists. It also does not seem to be information content, for reasons given below. Perhaps it measures an upper limit, the maximum possible information content of a sequence. In that case, it could be called "information potential," as I suggested earlier.

Two examples drawn from ordinary language show that H is not information content. The first is the word "hype." Several years ago, "hype" was without meaning in the English language; the sequence h-y-p-e might as well be a random sequence, as it conveyed no message to a recipient. Today, that same sequence does convey a message. The information content of the sequence has undergone a change, yet the value of H for the sequence has remained constant. The second example is the sentence "Stop the car." This conveys to the recipient an explicit, perhaps even urgent message. Transposing the letters yields a sentence of identical H but without a message: "Tops het arc." Accepting the H measures something useful and seeing from these examples that the something cannot be the quantity of information conveyed to a recipient, it seems reasonable to identify H as a measure of the *potential* of a string to convey information. "Stop the car," then, understood in English, more nearly approaches the maximum conveyable information of the strings composed of permutations of "acehoprstt" than does "Tops het arc"; and "hype," through growth of our language, presently approaches the maximum conveyable more closely than it formerly did.

Implicit in the analysis of these language phrases are two fundamental notions: that the message carried by a sequence is dependent on an appropriately programmed recipient and that the quantity of interest to us is the message conveyed. These notions were not part of the original formulation of information theory, in which the concern was with the potential of a sequence to carry information and the accurate transmission of that sequence. Surely, though, they are of concern to biologists, for whom central questions involve what messages DNA actually conveys and how the recipient of the DNA sequence achieves an "understanding" of these messages. Just as evaluation of H for the two sentences "Stop the car" and "Tops het arc" sheds no light on the actual message content of the sentences, so evaluation of H for various DNA sequences will do us no good in trying to figure out what messages the sequences convey.

Two additional difficulties arise when an informational sequence can be nested and/or multidimensional, as is the case with DNA. As an example of nestedness, suppose that the earlier examples of sentences are embedded in a text, the first sentence of which is "In what follows, move the last letter of each word to the front of the word before reading it." The tables are now turned, "Tops het arc" becoming a message-conveying statement ("Stop the car"), while "Stop the car" is now the message-free sequence "Psto eth rca." In this instance, the information contained in part of a sequence pertains to the informational sequence itself. DNA sequences contain just such nestedness, of which the simplest examples probably are the "start" and "stop" codon sets. Furthermore, DNA has a three-dimensional conformation that clearly possesses some informational value. Since a given strand of DNA can exist in more than one conformation without any changes in its one-dimensional base sequence, the one-dimensional sequence by itself is insufficient to specify completely the information content of that strand. Information theory does not appear to be capable of treating the complexities introduced by either nestedness or additional dimensions.

The difficulties illustrated in the above examples were well-known to Brillouin, who was very careful to indicate what could and could not be expected of his concept of information: "We have selected ... a statistical definition of the word information.... We must exclude and ignore many of the usual connotations.... We define 'information' as distinct from 'knowledge,' for which we have no numerical measure. We make no distinction between useful and useless information, and we choose to ignore completely the value of the information (Brillouin, 1962, p. 9).

Let us now consider more closely the realm of biology. There are at least four levels of organization at which evolution-entropy-information questions may be entertained: the molecule, the individual, the species, and the ecosystem. It is at the molecular level that biological systems are most directly subject to physicochemical laws and therefore most likely to be elucidated by applying entropic constraints. It is also at the molecular level that biological complexity can be expressed in a sequential form to which some elements of information theory may be applied. Does this mean that higher organizational levels are equally susceptible to thermodynamic and/or information-theoretic analysis? At present, the answer seems to be no, at least in the case of species. From the thermodynamic perspective, Wicken observes, "Internal ordering depends on a system's ability to export entropy to its environment. Since species are not energy-transforming systems, it is not easy to see how they might accomplish this" (Wicken, 1983, p. 442). From the informational viewpoint, Løvtrup asserts, "Living beings prevail at a number of levels of organization above the molecular one. The existence and the reproduction of these levels imply a state of improbability, a kind of 'information' which cannot be dealt with by the current theory of information" (Løvtrup, 1983, p. 92).

Johnson has nonetheless attempted to develop a thermodynamic approach to *ecosystem* evolution (Johnson, 1981, and this volume). One major barrier to such development is the fact, first deduced by Prigogine, that dissipative structures (of which processing systems are prime examples) may evolve in two quite distinct entropic directions, toward *least* entropy production or toward *high* entropy production (Prigogine, 1978). Johnson struggles against this nonpredictive quality, attempting to characterize at least the dominant species in an ecosystem as being close to equilibrium. This is a misapplication of the equilibrium concept, for no biological system—molecule, individual, species, or ecosystem—is anywhere near equilibrium. Such systems can be, and in several cases considered by Johnson are, in stable steady-states, but there appears to be no necessity for such steady-states to be minimally dissipative. Ecosystem evolution may be more fruitfully approached from a kinetic viewpoint than from a thermodynamic one. Far from steady-state, one expects the race to be to the swift. New ecological niches are filled first by those species that can most rapidly propagate. At steady-state, in contrast, endurance is more important than speed. Efficient species with low rates of production but equally low rates of destruction are likely to predominate. In essence, this is a suggestion that biological systems function under kinetic, not thermodynamic, control. Thus the kinetic approach outlined by Harrison for the molecular level

(Harrison, 1981, and this volume) could be profitably expanded to the ecosystem level as well.

The approaches that I have criticized are attempts to deal with two very real problems that are inadequately addressed by current versions of evolutionary theory. These are how and why life originated in the first place and how and why life has evolved in the direction of apparently ever-increasing complexity. Let me now explore these problems.

The emergence of complex self-replicating forms from the prebiotic chemical soup is development of order out of chaos in what appears to be a most spectacular discontinuous step. It does not appear to have been necessitated by thermodynamics, the efforts of Wiley and Brooks, Wicken, and others notwithstanding. The emergence of life is *compatible* with thermodynamic principles but not *required* by them. As we have seen above, this is to be expected from the nature of thermodynamics, which deals with the limits on what is possible rather than with a determination of what will necessarily occur. We still must answer the question, what led to. this emergence of order out of chaos?

If we examine other instances of order emerging from chaos, we find forces and the energy released in the process of ordering under the influence of those forces as the source of the ordering. Cosmological ordering comes about in response to gravitational force. More compact, ordered bodies are at lower energy (are more stable) than dispersed, disordered bodies. Chemical ordering comes about in response to the Coulomb bonding forces expressed by the Schrödinger Equation. Molecules like H_2O, more ordered than their separated atoms, are lower in energy (more stable) than are the atoms. In both instances, the ordering process is a slide down into a potential energy well in the course of which energy is released in disordered form. But are these examples helpful as analogies? The assembly of prebiotic molecular fragments into more and more complex sequences, eventually resulting in a self-replicating form, does not appear to be a similar slide into a potential energy well. Once again, it is misleading to apply insights gained from *outputting* systems to the biosphere, which is constituted of *processing* systems.

A processing system is able to undergo a stochastic sampling of many configurations of varying complexity without deviating from physico-chemical laws. Indeed, in a system where the chemical energies of the various configurations are not very different, just such a sampling is to be *expected*, even as successive rolls of dice will sample all of their possible configurations. If the space being sampled includes a configuration that is self-replicating, then that configuration, once randomly generated, will replicate (exponentially, no doubt), and the system will be switched from a random sampling mode to a mode dominated by the replication. I am tempted to draw a loose analogy to a super-cooled liquid, whose molecules stochastically sample a multitude of relatively chaotic configurations until, by chance, a nucleation center is generated. Once this arrangement occurs, the crystal geometry persists and rapidly replicates, overwhelming all other configurations. The analogy remains loose because, whereas the growing crystal is an outputting system sliding down into a potential well, the self-replicating biotic form is a processing system that is apparently not undergoing such a slide.

In the parlance of biological evolution, self-replication conveys a selective advantage to the form that is endowed with that capability, and in this context we can view the emergence of life as closely similar to the emergence of a species. A stochastic sampling of configurations (random mutations) eventually generates one with enhanced survival potential (natural selection). Is this concatenation of a physical principle (random sampling in the absence of a clearly directing force) with a biological principle (persistence of a form with a replicative advantage) sufficient from both the scientific and metaphysical perspectives? We may be caught on the horns of a metaphysical dilemma. Occam's Razor favors this rather simple explanation for life's emergence, but reductionism shouts against elevating natural selection to a primary cause. Further elucidation of this dilemma seems to me to be squarely in the realm of metaphysics. This is not to say that scientists should shy away from pondering the issue. After all, one no less than Einstein spoke passionately and metaphysically in asserting "God does not play dice with the Universe." Nor are scientists in the field shy about making their metaphysical views known. Both Peacocke (Peacocke, 1979) and Wicken (Wicken, 1984) have recently braved this thicket in eclectic and thought-provoking presentations. One need not necessarily agree with their positions to derive food for further thought and analysis from what they say.

Once life appeared, its forms embarked on what seems to have been a consistent movement toward ever-increasing complexity. The initial emergence of life-forms from prebiotic conditions was an increase in complexity that can perhaps be explained by stochastic sampling coupled with selective advantage. Are random variation and natural selection also sufficient to account for the ever-increasing complexity of life with the passage of time? It should be obvious that complexity *per se* does not convey any advantage. The greater the complexity of a system, the more order it entails, hence the lower the system entropy and the greater the expenditure of entropy to the surroundings needed to construct it. Furthermore, the energy cost of maintaining complex systems is necessarily higher than that of maintaining simple systems. It appears that complex organisms must work harder both to replicate and to maintain themselves.

Selective advantage is not, however, limited to production advantages. In any dynamic steady-state, persistence of one component depends on its rate of disappearance being equal to its rate of appearance, so that in general any modification of a component that results in a lower rate of disappearance will lead to a higher concentration of that component. If organisms of greater complexity are, by virtue of new properties conveyed by that complexity, better able to prolong their lives, there will be a selective advantage for these organisms. If the disadvantages arising from the added costs of producing and maintaining the additional complexity are more than counterbalanced by the advantages conveyed by the complexity, natural selection will be sufficient cause for the new, more complex organism to persist.

From this perspective, systems of increased complexity may or may not be selected over simpler systems. What determines whether or not a complex system persists is whether the complexity conveys survival advantages and whether those advantages outweigh the disadvantages of the increased energy/entropy cost entailed by the complexity. That complexity alone is insufficient for survival is illustrated by the loss of sight by species inhabiting totally dark caves. The cost of maintaining sight under conditions of total darkness is without any balancing advantages, so this complexity has in time disappeared. Such regression away from complexity, as exemplified by blind cave-dwellers, can only occur when environmental change removes the advantage that allowed the complexity to emerge in the first place. Still, it serves to demonstrate that biological evolution is not inexorably complexity-increasing. The first organisms were relatively simple, for obvious reasons. Evolution has therefore in general shown a tendency toward increasing complexity, but it is unfortunately all too easy to conjure up a vision of environmental change that would precipitate at least temporary reversal of the trend. A post-nuclear-holocaust Earth could easily be uninhabitable by any creatures more complex than the cockroach.

Leaving dark caves and radioactive atmospheres aside as aberrations, there remain problems with the notion that variation and selection are sufficient, without any additional principle, to account for the general trend of biological evolution toward ever-greater complexity. Even granting that natural selection may be sufficient to account for the *survival* of more complex forms once generated, it is not clear that stochastic variation alone is enough to *generate* forms of high complexity. One problem is that accurate proofreading, necessary to guarantee genetic fidelity, surely is a two-edged sword that minimizes—if it does not eliminate—the possibility of genetic changes. This problem is due to our incomplete knowledge of the mechanisms of genetic variation. The proliferation of species demonstrates that such variation has occurred, yet the genetic fidelity of existing species makes it difficult for us to determine how speciation occurs, either in the present or in the paleontological record.

A second problem is that it is hard to imagine gradually developing complexity being advantage-conveying at every step of its development, while it is clear that every step of that development must have been disadvantageous from the energy/entropy standpoint. Here, perhaps, we confront a need for an additional basic principle. Either (1) some kinds of increased complexity always convey advantage, or (2) normal "survival of the fittest" is suspended under certain conditions, allowing energy-squandering intermediate forms to persist until they evolve further, or (3) complexity emerges in "quantum jumps," somehow bypassing disadvantageous forms. I can imagine that any of these principles might be correct. Sensory complexity, no matter how rudimentary, may always carry survival advantages that outweigh its disadvantages. Catastrophic species extinction might periodically "clear the decks," allowing inefficient species to survive relatively free of selection pressure long enough for fully developed new complexities to evolve. Genetic variation might occur through gene splicing, whereby whole new chunks of genetic capability were added at once.

These questions—whether an additional principle is needed to account for increasing complexity, and if needed, what its proper statement is— seem to me to be the stuff of which the evolution-entropy-information debate is made. At the present stage of biology, I doubt that analysis of the existing body of data will be sufficient to resolve these questions. I doubt also that metaphysical speculation will resolve them. What analysis *may* provide is a framework within which to carry out critical new evolutionary observations and/or experiments. What metaphysics *should* provide is clarification of our present speculations, revealing what is tenable and what is untenable. What biologists should be striving for, then, are new experiments and observations—as well as new paradigms—that will shed light on these difficult questions. Recent attempts to apply reductionist methods to the problems posed by evolution have not moved us significantly toward these goals. They have generated more controversy than enlightenment.

I see two major impediments to enlightenment: the incompleteness of our biological information base, and the failure of existing theories and models to recognize the existence and importance of hierarchical levels in biology. The first of these suggests that critical new experimental evidence must be uncovered before ground-breaking new theoretical advances can be made. The second dictates that we develop paradigms that are unique to biology, or at least to hierarchies. The efforts of Dyke to construct a top-down paradigm are noteworthy in this regard (Dyke, 1985). On the one hand, then, we need new paradigms, more boldly biological theoretical constructs within which to order our observations. On the other hand, we need more incisive observations to guide our theoretical development. In this milieu, biological theoreticians should not shrink from proposing new constructs, but these should be developed with the intent of making predictions whose testing will generate incisive new evolutionary data. An example of such a construct that, while probably incomplete, nonetheless is highly provocative is the Saunders and Ho principle of minimum increase in complexity (Saunders, 1984; Saunders and Ho, 1981). Briefly, they argue that evolution is fully pragmatic, working of necessity with the genetic material already present in the species and selecting variations that require the minimum increase in complexity in order to convey survivability. The mimicry of the monarch butterfly by the viceroy is cited as an example supporting this principle, the assertion being that wing-pattern changes entail far less genetic modification than would chemical modification of the body.

Without assaying too great an excursion into the realm of experimental design in biology, I can see two lines of research that this potentially rich theoretical notion immediately suggests. The first is a critical testing of the butterfly example: Can it be shown that the differences in DNA sequences between otherwise closely related butterfly species having different wing patterns are indeed fewer than the differences in DNA sequences between otherwise closely related butterfly species that taste different (presumably, predator choice is an adequate measure of taste)? For the principle of minimum complexity increase to be more than just another "just so" story, such data must be obtained. The second line of research is a critical test of the principle against some appropriate far-from-paradigm case. For instance, the 100,000,000 base pairs of DNA possessed by the South American lungfish, compared to about 3,000,000 in humans, appears to be incompatible with the principle that genetic variation always leads to minimum increase in complexity. Even granting that there is tremendous redundancy in lungfish DNA, what is the point of having all those base pairs, which the organism must replicate and maintain? Here is fertile ground to test the minimum complexity increase idea. Can Saunders and Ho suggest a scenario, consistent with their principle, that loads the lungfish with so much DNA? If they can, can experimental molecular geneticists carry out comparative DNA sequencing that will test that scenario?

These brief examples are intended to illustrate the directions that I think evolutionary research needs to take as next steps in its development. To recapitulate, these steps involve the elaboration of new, more biologically oriented models and the carrying out of more ambitious genetic experiments. The theory of evolution as an entropic phenomenon only partially meets these criteria and, as I have argued above, seems to be conceptually flawed in ways that make it untenable. Nonetheless, that theory has considerable value, first because by proposing the connection, Brooks and Wiley have forced others to examine the possibility in critical detail, and second because the theory has led them to propose appropriate tests and research programs that, once carried out, will add substantial new biological information to the evolutionary data base (Brooks and Wiley, 1984). In the final analysis, my critique of them and of others who are trying to reduce evolution to an entropic or informational phenomenon is not that they are too bold. Rather, I think biologists are being insufficiently bold. Instead of trying to make evolution a consequence of thermodynamics and/or information theory, they need to develop it more fully in its own right.

References

Brillouin, L., 1962. *Science and Information Theory*, 2nd ed. New York: Academic Press.

Brooks, D. R., and E. O. Wiley, 1984. Evolution as an entropic phenomenon. In *Evolutionary Theory: Paths into the Future*, J. W. Pollard, ed., Chichester: Wiley, pp. 141–171.

Dicke, R. H., and P. J. E. Peebles, 1979. The big bang cosmology—enigmas and nostrums. In *General Relativity, an Einstein Centenary Survey*, S. W. Hawking and W. Israel, eds., Cambridge: Cambridge University Press, pp. 504–518.

Dyke, C., 1985. Complexity and closure. In *Evolution at a Crossroads: The New Biology and the New Philosophy of Science*, D. J. Depew and B. H. Weber, eds. Cambridge, MA: MIT Press, pp. 97–131.

Elsasser, W. M., 1983. Biological application of the statistical concepts used in the second law. *J. Theor. Biol.* 105:103–116.

Fersht, A. R., 1981. Enzymic editing mechanisms and the genetic code. *Proc. R. Soc. Lond.* B212:351–379.

Frautschi, S., 1982. Entropy in an expanding universe. *Science* 217:593–599.

Harrison, L. G., 1981. Physical chemistry of biological morphogenesis. *Chem. Soc. Rev.* 10:491–528.

Hawking, S. W., 1976. Black holes and thermodynamics. *Phys. Rev.* D13:191–197.

Jaynes, E. T., 1957. Information theory and statistical mechanics. *Phys. Rev.* 106:620–630.

Johnson, L. 1981. The thermodynamic origin of ecosystems. *Can. J. Fish. Aquat. Sci.* 38:571–590.

Kornberg, A., 1980. *DNA Replication*. San Francisco: Freeman.

Layzer, D., 1977. Information in cosmology, physics, and biology. *Int. J. Quantum Chem.* 12 (Suppl. 1):185–195.

Levine, I. N., 1983. *Physical Chemistry*, 2nd ed. New York: McGraw-Hill.

Løvtrup, S., 1983. Victims of ambition: comments on the Wiley and Brooks approach to evolution. *Syst. Zool.* 32:90–96.

Mayr, E., 1985. How biology differs from the physical sciences. In *Evolution at a Crossroads: the New Biology and the New Philosophy of Science*, D. J. Depew and B. H. Weber, eds., Cambridge, MA: MIT Press, pp. 43—67.

Pattee, H. H., 1979. The complementarity principle and the origin of macromolecular information. *BioSystems* 11:217—226.

Peacocke, A. R., 1979. Chance and the life game. *Zygon* 14:301—321.

Popper, K. R., 1982. *The Open Universe: An Argument for Indeterminism*. Totowa, NJ: Rohman and Littlefield.

Prigogine, I., 1978. Time, structure, and fluctuations. *Science* 201:777—785.

Prigogine, I., 1980. *From Being to Becoming: Time and Complexity in the Physical Sciences*. San Francisco: Freeman.

Saunders, P. T., 1984. The complexity of organisms. In *Evolutionary Theory: Paths into the Future*, J. W. Pollard, ed., Chichester: Wiley, pp. 121—131.

Saunders, P. T., and M.-W. Ho, 1981. On the increase in complexity in evolution II, the relativity of complexity and the principle of minimum increase. *J. Theor. Biol.* 90:515—530.

Shannon, C. E., and W. Weaver, 1949. *The Mathematical Theory of Communication*. Urbana, IL: University of Illinois Press.

Simon, H. A., 1969. *The Sciences of the Artificial*. Cambridge, MA: MIT Press.

Stuart, C. I. J. M., 1985. Bio-informational equivalence. *J. Theor. Biol.* 113:611—636.

Wicken, J. S., 1983. Entropy, information, and nonequilibrium evolution. *Syst. Zool.* 32:438—443.

Wicken, J. S., 1984. The cosmic broth: reflections on the thermodynamics of creation. *Zygon* 19:487—505.

Wiley, E. O., and D. R. Brooks, 1983. Victims of history—a nonequilibrium approach to evolution. *Syst. Zool.* 31:1—24.

12

Entropy and Evolution: Sorting through the Confusion

F. A. Hopf

I begin by defining the term zeroth order, which I use frequently. Under examination, natural systems are observed to have properties, some special to particular cases, some quite general. The term refers to general, obvious properties of the system. A zeroth order explanation of such phenomena may ignore details, perhaps even important ones, for the sake of simplicity in presentation. A zeroth order phenomenon of physics is that matter is stable and is composed of charged particles. This phenomenon is irreconcilable with the laws of physics as understood at the turn of the last century. It needs the uncertainty principle of quantum mechanics for explanation (ignoring details like the precise composition of individual materials). In this paper, I limit my remarks to zeroth order phenomena in nonequilibrium systems in physics and biology, and to zeroth order levels of the relevant theory, both in biology and in physics.

In trying to communicate with biologists, I find it useful to remind myself that they have, for a very long time, been doing a credible job understanding the workings of a complex system far from equilibrium. In the days when biomathematicians were developing theories of genetics and ecology (Roughgarten, 1979, has references), physicists were just beginning to solve their own zeroth order problems. While physics has made substantial strides in the last two decades in understanding systems far from equilibrium, this understanding is still far from complete.

A great difficulty confronting an interdisciplinary effort that includes biologists and physicists (I take chemistry to be a part of physics) is one of language. While it may be intuitively clear that the disciplines deal with common problems, it is difficult to clear away semantic issues and deal with similarities in a meaningful way. I doubt that there are any concepts in natural science that are more likely to engender semantic difficulties than entropy and irreversibility. The physics of ordinary (nonrelativistic) matter is structured as a hierarchy of phenomenologies. The highest level is thermodynamics. It is also the oldest, the most phenomenological, the most restricted, least mechanistic, and simplest. The lowest level is quantum electrodynamics, which is the most mechanistic, general, detailed, and difficult. I illustrate intermediate levels using physical chemistry, which has a complicated hierarchy. In this hierarchy, moving upward involves assumptions and approximations, leading to powerful generalizations applicable within strictly defined limits. Moving downward is dangerous. In thermodynamics, an increment dS of entropy is defined as

$$dS = \frac{\bar{d}Q}{T},\tag{1}$$

where T is temperature and $\bar{d}Q$ is an increment of heat. At this level in the hierarchy, entropy is well defined only if temperature is well defined. At thermodynamic equilibrium, i.e, the state of maximum disorder, temperature is defined. Prigogine (e.g., Glansdorff and Prigogine, 1971) has been the main advocate of using thermodynamics as a predictive tool away from equilibrium. He has used some generalizations of thermodynamics that solve some problems very close to thermodynamic equilibrium, but it is not yet clear what the ranges of validity of these principles are. Some cases close to equilibrium do not work (Landauer, 1975, 1981).[1] Far from equilibrium, this research program has proved to be largely sterile, in part because temperature is often ill defined. At the most fundamental level, I have found the second law of thermodynamics to be redundant. Quantum electrodynamics seems to predict its consequences without the need to invoke entropic principles explicitly.[2] Because second-law consequences remain valid at thermodynamic equilibrium at all hierarchical levels, its results are often embedded in developments based on quantum electrodynamics for reasons of expediency (Sargent et al., 1974).[3] Reversibility and its converse are a rich source of confusion. For example, the chemical symbol for reversibility, $\rightleftharpoons$, means different things at different levels of the hierarchy.[4] Arguments based on reversibility require knowing the level of the hierarchy that is appropriate to the problem. Once a level is determined, it is dangerous to embed in the development ideas or formulas that come from higher levels.

As one moves upward in the hierarchy, entropy remains useful as a diagnostic rather than predictive tool, even for nonequilibrium problems. When simplifications are made, there is always the risk of obtaining a perpetual motion machine of the second kind. Examining entropy avoids this risk. Diagnostic entropies can take many forms, can be applied in diverse cases, and can give rise to more confusion. Biologists did not use the term entropy when they developed diagnostic entropies for their own use. Consider, for example, the following derivation starting with the Shannon entropy H:

$$H = -\sum_i f_i \log_e f_i = -\sum_i f_i \log_e (1 + (f_i - 1)).\tag{2}$$

If f_i is not too small, H can be crudely approximated by using $\log_e(1 + x) \simeq x$:

$$H \simeq -\sum_i f_i(f_i - 1) = -\sum_i f_i^2 + \sum_i f_i. \qquad (3)$$

Since the census fractions f_i sum to one,

$$H \simeq D \equiv 1 - \sum_i f_i^2. \qquad (4)$$

D is one form of the measure proposed by Simpson (1949) for examining diversity, i.e., complexity, in biology, a point emphasized by Wicken. The Shannon entropy has certain mathematical features that make it superior to Simpson's measure, but both are usable as measures of diversity. I find Simpson's measure somewhat easier to interpret (Hopf and Brown, 1986).

Since the arrow-of-time metaphor (Brooks et al., this volume; Wiley, this volume) all too often hurts working scientists, I prefer to ignore it. Nonetheless, Brooks and Wiley make many false claims using the metaphor and these should be dispelled. Thermodynamic entropy does not compel irreversibility. Irreversibility arises from kinetics. Kinetic processes must be reversible on microscopic scales. Otherwise, the kinetic description would erroneously predict a final state in thermodynamic equilibrium that differs from the state of maximum entropy, a point touched on briefly by Harrison (this volume). Reversibility in principle does not mean reversibility in practice. Irreversibility occurs when actual reversal at the system level becomes so improbable that it can be taken to be impossible. Irreversibility is consistent with determinism. It was so developed by Poincaré (1956), who investigated various deterministic mechanisms leading to irreversibility. While modern physics is constructed around indeterministic principles of quantum mechanics, determinism can predict the irreversibility that occurs in ideal gases.

Analogies drawn between biological evolution and cosmology seem to me to be inappropriate. For one, the whole cosmological discussion may be an artifact of our ignorance as to how to handle thermodynamics when gravitation is important. Taken literally, the cosmological analogy demands that the state of maximum entropy on the surface of a planet should change monotonically in time, which is unlikely to be true. The cosmological analogy is a superfluous element in the analysis of Brooks and Wiley, which is kinetic analysis of trajectory divergence. Trajectory divergence analyzes kinetic changes within local volumes of a larger space. Global analyses involve examining kinetic changes over the entire space. These traditional approaches to examining the behavior of systems are complementary. I am confused by Brooks and Wiley's insistence that these approaches are fundamentally different. The study of trajectory divergence in stochastic systems is currently very fashionable. It uses measures devised by Shannon other than H itself (Crutchfield and Packard, 1983); H is used in global analyses.

It also seems to me that Brooks and Wiley's (Brooks et al., this volume; Wiley, this volume) and Layzer's (this volume) attempt to distinguish between initial and boundary conditions is pointless. Kinetic systems have constraints; one wants to know what the consequences of those constraints are—end of story. The claim made by Layzer that the Bernard convection problem (Glansdorff and Prigogine, 1971; Velarde and Normand, 1980) is a boundary condition problem is tricky. The interaction of the surface of a liquid with the environment imposes important selective biases on the competition among flow patterns. However, the boundaries do not enforce the outcome in the sense that there is only one pattern that conforms to the boundary. Hexagonal convection patterns occur over a wide range of boundary conditions in the laboratory, and are found in nature under widely different circumstances. Hence an imposed effect of special boundaries is unlikely. Roll patterns depend more critically on boundaries. They are also critically sensitive to initial conditions; under otherwise identical circumstances, different roll patterns are observed depending on different initial conditions. Is this a boundary condition problem or an initial condition problem?

I am generally skeptical of sweeping theoretical assumptions in biology, but I am willing to risk the following: The proper hierarchical level of biology lies above quantum electrodynamics. If true, I avoid making logical errors by starting with quantum electrodynamics since I then work upward in the hierarchy. I think that, at the level of quantum electrodynamics, the issues of reversibility and irreversibility are clear (Prigogine, 1980, chapter 3, disputes this). The fluctuation-dissipation theorem demands an association of a dissipative mechanism with a randomizing force such that their functional forms are derivable from each other (West and Lindenberg, 1984), and references therein). The theorem remains valid as one moves upward in the hierarchy, and I regard it as the kinetic counterpart to the second law. At the level of biology, I confess total ignorance regarding the proper functional forms. I assume their existence and fall back on speculation. Mortality is not directly a dissipative mechanism, but it leads directly to dissipation. In nature it has chance elements. I sketch here a model intended as a starting place from which a language might be developed (the ideas are similar to Wicken's). Let us denote by z and Z two DNA bases at a common location in a nonencoding portion[5] of the genome. Assume that these develop in time according to the principles of genetic drift[6] of neutral alleles at a locus. At any time, any one population subject to drift will have a fixed fraction f of Z, but an ensemble of reproductively isolated populations will have a distribution of f's, denoted $P(f)$.

$$H = -\int df P(f) \log_e(P(f)) \tag{5}$$

is proportional to the log of the standard deviation of $P(f)$ (assuming normal distributions). As drift proceeds, the standard deviation of $P(f)$ increases. The ensemble allows us to speak about an increase of macroscopic entropy. The description encounters difficulties as the bases fix in the populations at $f = 0$ or $f = 1$, but there should be many such events going on, and perhaps, in a complete description, the details will work out. If enough bases change, then intrapopulation sequence homology is gradually lost, which inhibits pairing in meiosis, leads to postmating reproductive isolation, increases the number of species, and hence increases the level of complexity of the biota. Next consider metabolism, a real dissipative mechanism. Metabolism produces reactive chemical species that are known to damage DNA. Damage appears to be a matter of chance. Recombinational repair of damage during meiosis leads to genetic variation, unequal crossing over, gene conversion, etc. This case is more difficult but perhaps more realistic than the previous one. Its mathematics is so formidable that I refuse to write down a symbol. It is, however, logically and entropically no different from the previous case and leads to the same sorts of conclusions.

Recently, there have been considerable efforts, often interdisciplinary, to see whether there are general principles that apply to nonequilibrium systems. The various problems of interest, lasers, hydrodynamics, chemical waves, biological waves, naked genes, cell membranes, brain function to name a few, have fundamental differences. There are, however, also similarities. Within these problems there is a subset that develops according to autocatalytic mechanisms that give rise to a Malthusian instability. Naked genes develop this way as does the light in a laser (Lamb, 1964). Living systems are also autocatalytic and this autocatalysis involves genes. Are they part of this class, or are they irreconcilably different? To be sure, living organisms have properties of individuality, age, and parentage that are properties forbidden to photons and, to a large extent, to naked genes (Demetrius, 1983).[7] By basing his theory of evolution on the Malthusian instability, Darwin (1859/1964) offers an enticing possibility of unifying physics and biology.

There is, however, a difficulty with evolution based on Malthusian concepts, which Darwin called the "dilemma of transitional forms," often referred to as "missing links." He observed that most living organisms are organized into species; i.e., a very large number of individual organisms are organized into a comparatively limited number of interbreeding groups, defined here as groups in which panmixis is possible over geological times. This organization is not what is expected when a system with a heterogeneous set of resources develops according to a Malthusian instability.

Instead, while some species should be common, the modal number of individuals per species should be very small—exactly how small depends on specific assumptions in the model. (My current best guess is 20–200 individuals.) As Darwin put it, "Why is not all nature in confusion instead of the species being, as we see them, well defined?" (1859/1964, first page of chapter 6 in all editions).

Note that Darwin is referring to difficulties in reconciling his mechanism with existing ecological features of the biota. Expressed in terms of entropies, he recognizes that local ecological systems have far fewer reproductively isolated populations than are inferred from the Malthusian instability. There are then far fewer nonzero census fractions f_i, a smaller information entropy, and more order than can be accounted for by theory. To confound the issue further, it is now known that autocatalytic physical systems with heterogeneous resources have the transitional forms that Darwin envisioned (Menegozzi and Lamb, 1978, and references therein). Not only do physical systems validate Darwin's conclusion; they also allow an alternative formulation of the dilemma. Since physical systems are subject to far fewer mechanisms than biological systems, and since these mechanisms are under much better control, one would expect autocatalytic physical systems to have more order (lower information entropy) than the much messier biological ones. However, the opposite is true.

Darwin attacked this dilemma by postulating that the rate of biotic evolution should, on the average, be governed by the rate of generation of favorable mutation. He assumed that the rate of favorable mutation was, on the average, the same for all individuals. He then deduced that the rate of evolution should be most rapid in interbreeding populations with large numbers of individuals, since many individuals generate many favorable mutations that can spread within the species. He also intuited, on much shakier grounds, that such evolution should be gradual in time. He argued, I believe correctly, that rapid evolution in large populations should lead to a biota organized into relatively few interbreeding groups. He also deduced that there should be ample evidence of evolution in the fossil record: Large populations should leave the most fossils, and they are where evolution is supposed to be occurring most rapidly. He acknowledged that the fossil record, as he saw it, refuted this consequence. As he put it, "As by this theory innumerable transitional forms must have existed, why do we not find them embedded in countless numbers in the crust of the earth?" (Darwin, 1859/1964, second page of chapter 6 in all editions).

I have found no paleontologist who claims that recent data support the claim that there are countless numbers of transitional forms. The present argument over gradualism versus punctualism is somewhat off this point. Simpson (1944) drew the obvious conclusion from the relative scarcity of transitional forms in the fossil record: Evolution is most rapid in small populations. If this result is valid, Darwin's explanation for the observed abundances of individuals within species collapses, and, at least by his own criteria, he has been refuted. The attempt to unify biology and physics fails.

A physicist, looking at the surface of the earth, finds many highly-ordered phenomena—weather, ocean currents, etc. These phenomena have low entropies, and the Second Law of Thermodynamics allows their use as energy sources. The earth also has life, which has low entropy and provides energy sources. All of these phenomena are driven by solar energy. All involve instabilities that are autocatalytic and hence Malthusian. The standard refutation suggests that all these common features are simply coincidence.

I do not believe in the coincidence, but to explain why, I need some terminology. It has long been observed that qualitative changes can occur in systems in thermodynamic equilibrium as parameters change. Ice turns to water at 0°C, water to steam at 100°C, etc. These changes in phase have parallels in nonequilibrium systems, but so much nomenclature has been used for these (e.g., threshold) that I prefer to call the general case a bifurcation, the terminology used by mathematicians. A bifurcation occurs when a bifurcation parameter (e.g., temperature) is changed through a bifurcation point (e.g., 0°C for H_2O), in such a way that the behavior of the system undergoes a qualitative change (e.g., ice to water). Eigen and Schuster's (1978) insight was to recognize that there is a bifuraction structure in the laws of evolution of autocatalytic systems, and that the bifurcation point is the law of Malthus (Eigen and Schuster, 1978). Strange things occur at bifurcation points, and systems become extremely sensitive to very small effects (see Kondepudi, this volume). In biology, the law of Malthus is, at best, approximate. In light of Eigen and Schuster's discovery, it no longer makes sense to speak of a single but approximate law of Malthusian evolution, any more than it makes sense to describe H_2O at approximatly O°C as being approximately ice. Physical systems are exactly Malthusian, so that Darwin's analysis is valid when applied to lasers (Hopf and Hopf, 1986). Is it possible that the zeroth order discrepancies between physical and biological systems are due to this bifurcation?

I think that this is a possibility that needs to be explored. There is, as yet, no organized Eigen and Schuster school of nonequilibrium systems, in the sense of there being a Brussels school or a Haken-Synergetics school. Moreover, Eigen and Schuster made a number of errors in their initial work (Szathmary, 1984) and imposed constraints on their kinetics that are reasonable for the experiments they envision doing, but do not apply comfortably to natural systems (Bernstein et al., 1983, Szathmary, 1984). These difficulties were the subject of most of the early criticisms of their work. The literature showing the interesting, positive consequences of their work is very recent; much is still in preparation or in press. Since this recent work has not yet been subject to systematic critical examination, it is premature to call any of it a success.

Bernstein et al. (1984) have argued that Eigen and Schuster's models lead naturally to the idea that sexual reproduction, a zeroth order feature of life, is primitive. It began originally, as it continues today (Bernstein et al., 1985), as an effective method by which parents repair damages in their DNA and maximize the likelihood of transmitting chemically intact DNA to offspring. This is a microevolutionary revival of the rejuvenation theory of sex, which we think offers a better zeroth order explanation of the facts than do more recent hypotheses based on variation (Bell, 1982). Sex drives biotic evolution into the part of the bifurcation space that Eigen and Schuster call hyperbolic.[8] The name comes from its paradigmatic example—second order autocatalysis—which is discussed by Harrison (this volume). Hyperbolic evolution causes organisms to coalesce into a limited number of species, even when the resources are heterogeneous (Hopf and Hopf, 1985).[9] Organisms that cannot reproduce sexually should not obey hyperbolic principles and should not, to zeroth order, exhibit the kinetic features associated with that coalescence. As far as we can tell, this claim is empirically sustained (Hopf and Hopf, 1986) for parthenogens, but much more data is needed.

Hyperbolic evolution is punctual. Eigen and Schuster refer to it as "once and forever evolution"; I refer to it as the principle of the survival of the first. Whatever gets there first wins, so long as it is decently adapted. To zeroth order, evolution proceeds by the destruction of established common forms, followed afterward by the emergence of new forms. Extinction through competition by rare, new, better adapted forms is a higher-order process[10] that should occur only occasionally. On the hyperbolic side of the bifurcation, Darwin's dilemma disappears, but the tempo and mode of evolution is quite different from what he envisioned. History is now all-important; what arrives first is a matter of chance.

The other side of the bifurcation is "linear" evolution, which I refer to as the principle of the survival of everything. Slight differences in fitness may have slight influences on the pattern of rarity and commonness, but competition does not lead to extinction. The final states are characterized by all species being very rare—i.e., rarity is now the general condition, not just the modal condition. Linear evolution implies that the constraints on the system play almost no role in the statistics of the final state. In its raw form, linear evolution demands spontaneous creation of living forms and is not interesting for biology. However, mechanisms abound within the biota that should cause final states to have some linear properties. Darwin pointed to epidemics as a mechanism that would do this. Other mechanisms are host-parasite, host-fungus, plant-insect, etc., interactions.[11] These interactions develop over time and are hence historical.

Because living organisms are not created spontaneously, linear evolution in biology does not lead to the history-independent result. Mechanisms leading to linear evolution are important at high population densities. Should they drive the host population to low densities, sexual reproduction in the host becomes costly and both host and exploiter risk extinction. Hence low density interactions should not, to zeroth order, be observable except perhaps when host populations reproduce asexually or through selfing. If it is assumed that this part of the bifurcation applies, to zeroth order, to species with many individuals, then increases in bioproductivity should result in an increase in the number of species with a roughly constant number of individuals per species (Brown and Gibson, 1983). Hyperbolic evolution alone implies that increases in bioproductivity should leave the number of species roughly fixed, with an increase in the number of individuals per species. Linear evolution predicts zeroth order phenomena like diversity gradients (MacArthur, 1972).

In brief, I have sketched a system that is historical. Nowhere have I relied upon properties of the biota that are fundamentally discrepant with physical systems. Physical systems are just too simple in their mechanisms to move back and forth in the bifurcation space in the way I have just described. The sketch is rudimentary, and in time, more details will be available. It is hoped that some of this will turn out to be valid; some will turn out to be wrong. At a minimum, I hope these insights can be developed to the point that they will damp out some of the more pointless arguments going on in evolutionary biology and ecology today, in which two empiricists studying system son differing sides of the bifurcation suspect each other's data, integrity, and sanity because the two systems seem so different. Give one scientist ice, the other water. Tell them it is the same substance. Give them imprecise thermometers and confusion will ensue.

Acknowledgments

I would like to thank H. Bernstein, H. Byerly, S. Hopf, and J. Wicken for critical readings of this manuscript and W. Miller for useful suggestions regarding physical chemistry.

Notes

1. Landaver (1981) is worth reading for anyone interested in interdisciplinary work involving physicists and biologists. Most physicists working in nonequilibrium statistical mechanics (also all chemists that I have worked with) restrict the term thermodynamics to cases in which temperature is well defined. I followed this usage in this paper.

2. A current standard device in the kinetics business is to formulate problems at higher levels

in the hierarchy according to the dictates of quantum electrodynamics, thus insuring a kinetics that is compatible with the first and second laws. I do not recommend this for biology except as an exercise in desperation.

3. Hollinger and Zenzen (1985) have made a beginning at discussing some of the different usages of the terms reversibility and irreversibility in physics (see especially chapter 5). Their discussion is limted to issues in principle. Further confusion can arise from usages in practice.

4. Near fundamental, mechanistic levels, the expressions $A + B \rightleftharpoons C$ and $2A + 2B \rightleftharpoons 2C$ are different. The former says that one molecule of A and one molecule of B undergo a two-body collision in which a microreversible reaction occurs that produces on C. The latter says that two molecules of A and two molecules of B undergo a four-body collision in which a microreversible reaction occurs that produces two C's. Four-body collisions are much less likely than two-body collisions, so the latter reaction is likely to be much slower than the former. At higher, mass-action levels the double arrow refers to a reversible reaction equilibrium and the two expressios are logically but not algebraically equivalent.

5. The problem of defining the microstates on which probabilities are to be defined is fraught with difficulty. It would be useful if someone would systematically discuss the question of how the base sequences within the DNA molecule can be used to define states. The Brooks-Wiley-Wicken argument (possibly also Layzer's distinction between biotic and chemical entropy) may be related to the use of enzymes as substitute measures of base sequences. Only encoding portions of the genome are tested this way Non-encoding portions must, however, maintain enough sequence homology for pairing in meiosis to occur. It is not clear to me whether enzymes are a general enough substitute for sequence.

6. Genetic drift corresponds to diffusion in physics; drift, in physics, is directional. The drift of individual bases is microreversible in the sense that f can change from a value a to a value b and then back to a again. A system in which many bases are drifting this way is irreversible in the sense that it is overwhelmingly unlikely that each and every base will simultaneously reverse itself in this fashion.

7. If Brooks and Wiley wish to pursue the theme that life is an irreconcilably unique phenomenon, then they must at least use an entropy that incorporates these unique properties (Demetrius, 1983). Since they have not done so, they are proceeding along shaky grounds.

8. Eigen and Schuster's (1978) terminology comes from the solutions of a rate equation in which one term contains a factor $x\mu$, where x is a variable that develops in time and μ is a coefficient. The equation $x = x\mu$ oversimplifies the argument but gives the terminology. The bifurcation occurs at $\mu = 1$, which gives the law of Malthus, i.e., $x \propto \exp(t)$, which is the law of exponential growth. For $\mu < 1$, all systems are qualitatively similar. The paradigmatic case is taken to be $\mu = 0$, which is solved by a straight line $x \propto t$. All systems with $\mu > 1$ are similar. The paradigmatic case is taken to be $\mu = 2$, in which x takes the form of a hyperbola. Eigen and Schuster use the term "Darwinian" for $\mu = 1$, which is unfair (see below). I prefer the term Malthusian.

9. In the original version of Hopf and Hopf (1985) the bifurcation structure of the laws of evolution was presented in some detail. Eigen and Schuster's analysis oversimplifies matters somewhat. This discussion was removed at the insistence of the editors. It is currently in a new document, available on request, that may some day be finished. The bifurcation actually occurs at a surface in "evolution" space that is determined by the set of all simple generaliza-

tions of mathematical ecology that use Lokta-Volterra (r and K) parameterizations. The law of Malthus is just an important special case on this surface.

10. Physicists have used the term multistable to refer to systems, like the one sketched in the text, with many stable final states. The channel dial on most television sets is an example. The process by which multistable systems change through internal stochastic mechanisms is referred to as tunneling. The book in which West and Lindenberg (1984) appears contains many papers discussing the current state of the art of tunneling analysis. Not all historical biotic events are tunnelings, e.g., events following the collision of North and South America. This collision event involves a coupling of two independently established systems. In such cases competition might be quite important. The principle of the survival of the first is not absolute. A newly emergent type can outcompete a previsously established one if it is substantially better adapted. This case is also not a tunneling.

11. I have been bothered by the way Darwin's ideas on competition are treated in the literature. His understanding of competition as a natural process was astute; he recognized the need for and the consequences of linear and hyperbolic processes in evolution. Eigen and Schuster have just systematized an analysis that is anticipated both in *The Origin* and in the works of many subsequent biologists. Most criticisms directed at Darwin should be directed toward his successors who tried to "clarify" his "fuzzy" ideas with simplistic principles like competitive exclusion.

References

G. Bell, 1982. *The Masterpiece of Nature*. Berkeley: University of California Press.

Bernstein, H., H. C. Byerly, F. A. Hopf, and R. E. Michod, 1984. The origin of sex. *J. Theor. Biol.* 110:323–351.

Bernstein, H., H. C. Byerly, F. A. Hopf, and R. E. Michod, 1985. Genetic damage, mutation and the evolution of sex. *Science* 229:1277–1281.

Bernstein, H., H. C. Byerly, F. A. Hopf, R. E. Michod, and G. K. Vemulapalli, 1983. The Darwinian dynamic. *Quart. Rev. Biol.* 58:185–207.

Brown, J. H., and A. C. Gibson, 1983. *Biogeography*. St. Louis: C. V. Mosby.

Crutchfield, J. P., and N. H. Packard, 1983. Noise scaling of symbolic dynamical entropies. In *Evolution of Order and Chaos in Physics, Chemistry, and Biology*, H. Haken, ed., Berlin: Springer-Verlag, pp. 215–227.

Darwin, C., 1859/1964. *The Origin of Species by Means of Natural Selection* (facsimile of the first edition, 1859). Cambridge, MA: Harvard University Press.

Demetrius, L., 1983. Selection and evolution in macromolecular systems. *J. Theor. Biol.* 103:619–643.

Eigen, M., and P. Schuster, 1978. The hypercycle, a principle of natural self-organization part B. *Naturwissenschaften* 65:10–14.

Glansdorff P., and I. Prigogine, 1971. *Thermodynamic Theory of Structure, Stability, and Fluctuations*. London: Wiley.

Hammes, G. G., 1978. *Principles of Chemical Kinetics*. New York: Academic Press.

Hollinger, H. B., and M. J. Zenzen, 1985. *The Nature of Irreversibility*. Dordrecht: Reidel, chapter 5.

Hopf, F. A., and J. H. Brown, 1986. The bull's-eye method for examining randomness in ecological communities. *Ecology* 67(5): 1139–1155.

Hopf, F. A., and F. W. Hopf, 1985. The role of the allee effect in species packing. *Theor. Pop. Biol.* 27: 27–50.

Hopf, F. A., and F. W. Hopf, 1986. Darwinian evolution in physics and biology. In *Frontiers of Nonequilibrium Statistical Physics*, G. T. Moore and M. O. Scully, eds., New York: Plenum.

Lamb, W. E., Jr., 1964. Theory of the optical maser. *Phys. Rev. A*: 1429.

Landauer, R., 1975. Inadequacy of entropy and entropy derivatives in characterizing the steady state. *Phys. Rev. A* 12: 636–638.

Landauer, R., 1981. Nonlinearity, multistability, and fluctuations: reviewing the reviewers. *Am. J. Phys.* 241: R107–R113.

MacArthur, R. H., 1972. *Geographical Ecology: Patterns in the Distribution of Species*. New York: Harper and Row.

Menegozzi, L. N., and W. E. Lamb, Jr., 1978. Laser amplification of incoherent radiation. *Phys. Rev. A* 17.

Onsager, L., 1931. Reciprocal relations in irreversible processes I. *Phys. Rev.* 37: 405.

Poincaré, H., 1956. Chance. Reprinted in *The World of Mathematics* 2, J. R. Newman ed., New York: Simon and Schuster, 1384.

Prigogine, I., 1980. *From Being to Becoming*. San Francisco: Freeman.

Roughgarten, J., 1979. *Theory of Population Genetics and Evolutionary Ecology: An Introduction*. New York: Macmillan.

Sargent, M., III, M. O. Scully, and W. E. Lamb, Jr., 1974. *Laser Physics*. Reading, MA: Addison-Wesley, chapter 14.

Simpson, G. G., 1944. *Tempo and Mode in Evolution*. New York: Columbia University Press.

Simpson, E. H. 1949. Measurement of diversity. *Nature* 163: 688.

Szathmary, E., 1984. Hyperbolic growth in molecular and biological populations I. *Abstracta Botanica* 8: 137–161.

Velarde, M. G., and C. Normand, 1980. Convection. *Sci. Amer.* 243: 92–108.

West, B. J., and K. Lindenberg, 1984. Non linear fluctuation dissipation relations. In *Fluctuations and Sensitivity in Nonequilibrium Systems*, W. Horsthemke and D. K. Kondepudi, eds., Berlin: Springer-Verlag.

Zermanslcy, M. W., 1957. *Heat and Thermodynamics*. New York: McGraw-Hill.

13

Evolution as Nonequilibrium Thermodynamics: Halfway There?

John H. Campbell

Evolution centers on organization and time. These are the most elusive aspects of our natural world. Time has not one but three components that escape our understanding. For unknown reasons the immediate present, the past, and the future become more abstract and elusive in that order. A popular approach to objectifying analyses is simply to ignore the abstract extensions of time and pretend that only the present is real.

This is the case with our current evolutionary orthodoxy, neo-Darwinism. It narrows evolution to a process of the immediate present. Evolution is defined as the microscopic change in gene frequencies in the instantaneous present. These are caused and directed by selective forces of the environment acting upon the species, *now*. Yesterday's predators are as utterly irrelevant to today's evolution as are tomorrow's temperatures.

Neo-Darwinism reduces evolution to a master equation:

$$\Delta Q = \text{Sc} \cdot Q.$$

Q represents the frequency of a gene (or more properly a gene allele) in a population, ΔQ is its instantaneous change (usually taken over a single complete generation to skirt the abstractions of a differential), and Sc is the selection coefficient, a constant defined for the present instant by the equation. Note that this mathematical definition gives no representation of past or future time or of biological complexity. The neo-Darwinist would be happy if there were only one generation or if the species was nothing more than a bowl of alphabet gene soup.

The appeal of this temporal simplification is so strong that the "new Darwinism" has been able to displace the historical perspective from the center stage of evolutionary science. For the neo-Darwinist, the historical development of life through geological time is merely a by-product of the evolutionary process. It is but the tailings of the instantaneous selective process much as the pile of sawdust is the accumulated residue of the cutting action of a saw blade upon logs in a saw mill. Evolution is the powered bite of steel on wood. Long term consequences of evolution are merely the exact mathematical summation of the evolutionary processes over each instantaneous cross section of time during that interval.

The significance of this view is that if there is not such a thing as long term evolution in its own right then, obviously, there cannot be *real* long term evolutionary properties. For example, evolutionary mechanisms cannot cause trends across time, because a "trend" in gene fluctuation over the single generational unit is semantic nonsense. Trends, as they appear in, say, the fossil record, are not components of the evolutionary process but only manifestations of how the sawdust piled up under the blade. We should look to persisting properties in the outside environment and not to the mechanics of evolution to explain trends and directions in the results of evolution.

One can account for the sway of neo-Darwinism over the evolutionary community only by the charisma of the mathematical statement. Every one of its underlying biological tenets has proven to be a misconception. The fossil record shows that species do not evolve in the continuous incremental fashion predicted by the neo-Darwinists (Stanley, 1979). Molecular biology has shown that genes are utterly different sorts of entities than proposed by neo-Darwinists (Hunkapiller et al., 1982; Dover, 1982; Campbell, 1982, 1983). Population geneticists themselves have shown that gene frequencies surge back and forth from year to year with no enduring evolutionary consequences (Dobzhansky, 1951). Indeed, the rates of phenotypic change that characterize long term evolution imply that any changes rapid enough to be measured from year to year can *only* be noise in the overall process (even if due to selection). The great majority of changes in gene structure that accumulate over geological time probably are not fixed by Darwinian selection at all, but represent physiological processes such as mutation pressure and gene correction mechanisms (King and Jukes, 1969). Finally, ecologists have shown that a species is anything but the granfalloon (Vonnegut, 1971) panmixic gene pool assumed for the neo-Darwinist's equations. Species are internally organized into various levels of demes with genetic factor regulating gene flow between them and mating patterns within them. Also, much of the physiologically significant genetic variation of the species is organized as polymorphisms with linkage disequilibrium and special mechanisms to preserve it from erosion by selection.

The disparities between neo-Darwinism and reality are so overwhelming that current biologists are scrambling for a completely fresh conceptual framework for the evolutionary process. Paradigms under consideration today are being recruited from sciences as diverse as cybernetics (Kauffman, 1985), molecular biology and DNA genetics (Hunkapiller et al., 1982), and paleontology (Gould, 1980). Nonequilibrium thermodynamic evolution is one of these candidate approaches, and perhaps an important one. Its success will be measured by how well it captures the attention of the community of evolutionists away from other alternatives.

Nonequilibrium thermodynamic evolution is a notable advance over neo-Darwinism in two ways. First, it addresses a second component of time, the past. Second, it deals with organization as such. Evolution becomes fundamentally a historical process occurring over time and not an instantaneous one. The way change accumulates determines the evolution of Brooks and Wiley's sawdust pile. Instantaneous natural selection is not too important other than to produce grist. Evolution is the process of adding new grains to past structure over time. A new set of statements becomes important to account for this cumulative process, dealing with the dissipation of order, free energy fluxes, and entropy of organization. The individual unit change itself is inconsequential, since with time it will be submerged into statistical statements.

The radical departure of this view from traditional neo-Darwinism is evident in the polarization of the two camps, a polarization fostered by both the innovators and the traditionalists. The new call is to realign evolutionary theory with physical reality. However, it goes only halfway. While recognizing the undeniable role of the past in evolution, it falters at admitting the other half of the time dimension. Also, it focuses on the growth of organization in biological systems rather than just change in numerical frequencies and it recognizes that organizational qualities follow entirely different dynamics than quantitative change. Yet, it neglects the sorts of organization that are central to biology. Let us examine these two halfway advances beginning with the simpler case of organization.

Thinkers such as Wicken go beyond the superficial Darwinian question of how evolution produces organization to the core issue of what roles organization has in the evolutionary process. Unfortunately, the organizational features discussed in this present volume as analogous to physical systems are not very relevant to most of biology. Packing densities of species, branching order of taxonomic cladograms, and the like may be of interest to certain specialties at the periphery of biology but surely they are secondary to *functional* organization—the cameralike structure of the eye that allows an animal to see the world, the synaptic connections among ten billion neurons that coordinate a score of muscles of a baby's face into a smile, the sophisticated genes and enzymes that enable a person's cells to rearrange his DNA to make, on demand, specific antibodies against *any* foreign molecule, even artificial ones that his ancestors never before encountered. Functional structures are the meaningful characteristics of organisms, and any adequate theory of evolution must center upon them. It may be natural for theorists to turn first to very formalistic organization, such as cladograms, that can be squeezed into simple thermodynamic equations. Yet the success of this approach will depend upon whether it can be extended to significant biological organization. For this, the profound role of natural selection cannot be minimized or ignored. Today's extraordinary organisms were not created by just the statistical laws of how changes pile up with the passage of time. The nature of those changes and of the selection pressures that caused them in the instantaneous present also are essential creative ingredients.

It may be possible to treat selection of the fittest as a thermodynamic process. For example, the excess of less fit organisms that are winnowed at each generation may represent the dissipation of "entropy" (akin to the radiation of low frequency radiation from the earth) that drives the survivors to a "less probable" and hence lower entropic form. Natural selection would correspond to an entropy pump (Campbell, 1967). However, the possible relationship between the minuscule increases in entropy that Brooks and Wiley associate with events such as speciation, on the one hand, and the enormous fluxes of energy through open ecosystems, on the other hand, is far too tenuous to be captured by quantitative analysis. In an open system any particular aspect of organization may increase or decrease in entropy content, depending upon how the system is organized and not by thermodynamic constraint. The question is how much a thermodynamic formalism adds to our study of biology. Will it be mainly ceremonial like so much other hollow systems theory (Berlinski, 1977)? Its purpose seems more directed to showing that evolution does not contradict the laws of thermodynamics than to illuminating the actualities of the process. That an abstract principle is true does not mean that it is relevant or useful. I suspect that nonequilibrium thermodynamic evolution has brighter prospects for contributing to the science of thermodynamics than to biology.

This effort to rationalize the most complex biological process with the most elementary physical principles, skipping over insights at intermediate levels, continues a long, undistinguished tradition. The Newtonian revolution excited certain physicists with the prospect of deriving all natural and even human phenomena from the mechanical formula $f = ma$. The flame has long gone out of this idealistic naiveté. In fact, it is now clear that the fabric of existence is not compatible even in theory with this sort of calculatable determinism for complexly organized matter (Davies, 1980). The second law bugles a new call to reductional fundamentalists, this time to derive all of sociology, human culture, economics, and world politics from initial thermodynamic premises (Iberall, 1985; Wilkinson and Iberall, 1985; Dyke, this volume). Biologists, understandably, have uncomfortable feelings of *dejà vu* after centuries of empty promises by physicists to reduce biology to an all encompassing equation. The new arch-reductionism is based on an even more tenuous physical relationship than its predecessor. Instead of an equation based on ponderables of mass and movement its source is a mathematical *inequality* concerning a most abstract quality, entropy. Even the contributors to this volume have quarreled over whether its amount increases or decreases during evolution, a disastrous confusion for the mathematical formulation Δentropy > 0 (Wiley and Brooks, 1982; Løvtrup, 1983; Wicken, 1983).

The direction of this reductionist thermodynamic effort is retrograde to the current revolution to liberate evolutionary theory from the mathematical twaddle of neo-Darwinism. Molecular mechanism is proving to be a stunningly successful reductionistic format for explaining biology. Only the most spectacular discoveries by nonequilibrium evolutionists will persuade biologists to turn their backs now on this biological paradigm, especially for the most central of all biological processes, evolution. I predict that evolutionary theory will continue to go in precisely the opposite direction to thermodynamic reductionism, becoming more biological, more concerned with actual mechanisms, and more wedded to structure-function relationships.

A case in point is the role of organization in the further complexification of structure. In recent years thermodynamicists have developed a number of concepts for the causal role of organization in its own formation, including Wicken's autocatalytic cycling (Wicken, 1984), Prigogine's self-organization (Prigogine, 1980), and Zeleny's autopoiesis (Zeleny, 1980). These are exciting concepts. The challenge now is to figure out appropriate ways to describe how *biological* levels of organization act self-generatively. I suggest that this challenge will not be met by extending concepts developed to account for degrees of organization shown by nonbiological matter. More likely the understanding will come from such thoroughly biological concepts as selfish DNA (Dawkins, 1976; Orgel and Crick, 1980; Doolittle and Sapienza, 1980), runaway sexual selection (Fisher, 1930), the Baldwin effect (see Mayr, 1963), automodulating genes (Campbell, 1982), and the like. We are even beginning to realize that biological structures can assume *functional* roles in their own evolution (Doolittle and Darnell, 1986).

The second outstanding task, of incorporating the full dimension of durational time into evolution, is even more Herculean than coming to grips with biological organization. The yawning gap between the causal roles of future and past time in present activities is much greater than the conceptual gulf between causality in cross sectional and durational time. In fact, the near universal dismissal of the relevance of the future to dynamics as antiscientific metaphysics probably leaves us even less equipped than the early Greek intellectuals to handle the full dimensionality of time (Rosen, 1985). It is to their credit that the advocates of a thermodynamic interpretation (especially Wicken, 1984 and this volume; and O'Grady and Brooks, this volume) are among the most intellectually active scientists exploring the relationship of future time to evolution. The tenor of their approach, however, is to explain *away* the embarrassment of future involvement instead of seeking its meaning, much as neo-Darwinists sought objectivity by developing a format that dismissed the causal role of the past.

It is evident that several major advances must occur before we can positively approach the role of future duration in the activities of complexly organized systems. One prerequisite is to develop a scientifically acceptable formalism for *how* future conditions actually can bear causally on a prior instantaneous present. This is a call for teleological *mechanisms*. I have asserted above that organisms can carry out evolutionary processes as biological functions. This idea is fundamentally future oriented. The concept of evolutionary function gives a biologically traditional foundation for roles of future considerations in the evolutionary process. Evolutionary *strategies* in the sense of games theory is another approach that, interestingly enough, is enthusiastically embraced by neo-Darwinists (Maynard Smith, 1974). At a more global level, I have described elsewhere a concrete mechanism for true future causality consistent with scientific reality and relevant for evolution (Campbell, 1985).

A second prerequisite is to catalogue and describe actual *examples* in which the future assumes an integral role in evolution. Determinents of mutation rates, sexuality, recombination mechanisms, and altruistic strategies are promising traits for such analysis. The incisive techniques of molecular biology allow one to describe such examples in the unequivocal terms of the molecular physiology and so skirt the abyss of metaphysics.

Third, it is essential for the biologist to sort out the various levels of future involvement in present action. We now realize that all teleology does not lump together with the same metaphysical status. Mayr (1974), in particular, has clarified and directed processes by dissecting them into a heirarchy of teleological categories.

Table 13.1 lists three classes of forward directed processes described by Mayr. Briefly, teleomatic refers to processes that reach predictable future end states through ordinary physical processes, such as when a ball tossed into the air ends up on the ground. Teleonomic systems proceed to end states directed by internal goal-directed *programs*. The end state is achieved by teleomatic processes, but is specified and predictably determined only by the internal program. The development of a chicken egg into a chick instead of a penguin or unicorn or pickled onion under the specification of its genetic program epitomizes a teleonomic process in biology. A computer working its way to a final output condition under control of a software program is an abiological equivalent.

The interested reader should consult Mayr's incisive discussion for details and for the importance of these distinctions to biology. Mayr advises that his classification of teleological behaviors is not complete. To emphasize this point I have further subdivided these categories. Thus, teleomatic includes two distinct types of processes. A ball rolling down hill arrives at its predestined final location for different reasons than a thermodynamic system's inevitable approach toward maximum entropy. Both processes

Table 13.1
Some categories of future-directed causation[a]

Teleological category	Aristotelian cause
Physical existence	*Essential* cause
Teleomatic	*Efficient* cause
Mechanical	
Statistical	
Teleonomic	*Formal* cause
Simple	
Open	
Closed	
Complex	
Teleological	*Final* cause
Human intentionality	
Future causality	

a. See text for details.

might be called teleomatic, even though the "drive" or "attraction" toward their goals is unrelated. A major distinction between the evolutionary perspective advocated in this volume and Darwinism lies in the analysis of teleomatic subcategory that each presumes. The thermodynamicists call for explanation by statistical laws rather than by physical mechanisms—a point that Wicken (1985) considers fundamental.

Similarly, there are at least two sorts of simple teleonomic programs. A closed teleonomic program guides a system toward a prespecified end point. An open program instructs the system where to proceed from moment to moment or from one intermediary state to the next, but does not otherwise presuppose the ultimate goal. Open teleonomy is without finalism. In theory an open teleonomic system can progress indefinitely in a programmed mode of action. Evolution clearly exhibits teleonomic mechanisms in this open sense. Closed teleonomic evolutionary mechanisms are more speculative.

In addition one can imagine complex teleonomic processes whose programs (open or closed) are related to the creation of their goals. We may well encounter such complex extensions of Mayr's rather simple "teleonomy" when computer scientists develop artificial intelligence into a true science, when psychobiologists discover the neurological mechanisms for the formation of the psyche, when (possibly) geneticists succeed in finally discovering how the eucaryotic genome physically specifies onto-geny, and perhaps when we come to grips with the evolutionary role of very complex biological phenotype and genotype. Complex teleonomy promises all of the paradoxical implications of self reference that Hofstadter (1979, 1981) has popularized so brilliantly. Maybe these forward looking processes fit better under teleology than under teleonomy in our table. They certainly admit a quantum leap in end-directedness.

Mayr's category of the truly "teleological" also allows subcategories. Man's intentional realization of preconceived desires surely represents a lower level of teleology from the movement of a system by an entity that would exist only in the future. We have only to turn to Darwin (1859) for instruction that teleological mechanisms do cause evolutionary change. Any adequate theory of evolution must encompass end-directed evolution by artificial selection. Without a doubt, the most rapid, radical, distinctive, and significant evolution in today's world is occurring in this teleological way. It is even possible to argue that this is an inevitable implication of a process that creates ever more complexly organized forms of life (Campbell, 1985). Eventually, teleological mechanisms are bound to arise and then to capture the evolutionary process. What impresses me the most about teleological analyses is that as one classifies goal-directed activities into discrete categories, more and more of their range seems realizable by plausible natural processes, such as evolution.

Wicken, Brooks, Wiley, and their followers have begun to climb the ladder of teleological categories. Even though their vision is to go only from one subcategory of teleomatics to another this is a beginning in the quest to accommodate the full dimensionality of time in evolution. It is hoped that it will be continued by the infusion of ideas about more complex physical causality, e.g., as discussed by Rosen (1985).

In summary, the advocates of a nonequilibrium thermodynamic approach to evolution propose a physical principle to break out of the confines of neo-Darwinism. This goal is one that other evolutionists are attempting from a variety of other perspectives new and old (Langridge, 1986). The measure for any approach, especially one abstracted from physics, is how well it relates to biology. Evolutionists are interested in the actualities of organisms and not theories of chaff.

Acknowledgment

This work was supported by NSF grant PCM81-20923.

References

Berlinski, D., 1977. Adverse notes on systems theory. In *Applied and General Systems Hierarchy*, G. J. Klir, ed., New York: Plenum.

Brooks, D., and E. O. Wiley, 1986. *Evolution as Entropy: Toward a Unified Theory of Biology.* Chicago: University of Chicago Press.

Campbell, B., 1967. Biological entropy pump. *Nature* 215:1308.

Campbell, J. H., 1982. Autonomy in evolution. In *Perspectives on Evolution*, R. Milkman, ed., Sunderland: Sinauer Assoc., pp. 190–200.

Campbell, J. H., 1983. Evolving concepts of multigene families. *Curr. Top. Biol. Med. Res.* 10:401–417.

Campbell, J. H., 1985. An organizational interpretation of evolution. In *Evolution at a Crossroads: The New Biology and the New Philosophy of Science*, D. J. Depew and B. H. Weber, eds., Cambridge, MA: MIT Press/Bradford Books.

Campbell, J. H., 1986. The new gene and its evolution. In *Rates of Evolution*, K. S. W. Campbell, ed., Canberra: Australian National Academy of Sciences.

Darwin, C. R., 1859. *On the Origin of Species by Means of Natural Selection, or Preservation of Favored Races in the Struggle for Life.* London: Murray.

Davies, P., 1980. *Other Worlds.* New York: Simon and Schuster.

Dawkins, R., 1976. *The Selfish Gene.* Oxford: Oxford Press.

Dobzhansky, T., 1951. *Genetics and the Origin of Species*, 3rd ed. New York: Columbia University Press.

Doolittle, W. F., and J. E. Darnell, 1986. Understanding introns: origins and functions. *Science.*

Doolittle, W. F., and C. Sapienza, 1980. Selfish genes, the phenotype paradigm and genomic evolution. *Nature* 284:601–603.

Dover, G. A., 1982. Molecular drive: a cohesive mode of species evolution. *Nature* 229:111–117.

Fisher, R. A., 1930. *The Genetical Theory of Natural Selection.* Oxford: Clarendon Press.

Gould, S. J., 1980. Is a new and general theory of evolution emerging? *Paleobiology* 6:119–130.

Hofstadter, D., 1979. *Godel Escher und Bach: An Eternal Braid.* New York: Basic Books

Hofstadter, D., 1981. *The Mind's Eye.* New York: Basic Books.

Hunkapiller, T., H. Huang, L. Hood, and J. H. Campbell, 1982. The impact of modern genetics on evolutionary theories. In *Perspectives on Evolution*, R. Milkman, ed., Sunderland: Sinauer Assoc., pp. 164–189.

Iberall, A. S., 1985. Outlining social physics for modern societies—locating culture, economics and politics: the Enlightenment reconsidered. *Proc. Natl. Acad. Sci.* 82:5582–5584.

Kauffman, S. A., 1985. Self-organization, selective adaptation and its limits: a new pattern of inference in evolution and development. In *Evolution at a Crossroads: The New Biology and the New Philosophy of Science*, D. J. Depew and B. H. Weber, eds., Cambridge, MA: MIT Press/Bradford Books, pp. 133–167.

King, J. L., and T. H. Jukes, 1969. Non-Darwinian evolution: random fixation of selectively neutral mutations. *Science* 164:788–798.

Langridge, J., 1986. Old and new theories of evolution. In *Rates of Evolution*, K. S. W. Campbell, ed., Canberra: Australian National Academy of Sciences.

Løvtrup, S., 1983. Victims of ambition: comments on the Wiley and Brooks approach to evolution. *Syst. Zool.* 32:90–96.

Maynard Smith, J., 1974. The theory of games and the evolution of animal conflicts. *J. Theor. Biol.* 47:209–221.

Mayr, E., 1963. *Animal Species and Evolution*. Cambridge, MA: Harvard Press.

Mayr, E., 1974. Teleological and teleonomic, a new analysis. In *Methodological and Historical Essays in the Natural and Social Sciences*, vol. 14, R. S. Cohen and M. W. Wartofsky, eds., Boston: D. Reidel, pp. 91–117.

Orgel, L. F., and F. H. C. Crick, 1980. Selfish DNA: the ultimate parasite. *Nature* 284:604–607.

Prigogine, I., 1980. *From Being to Becoming: Time and Complexity in the Physical Sciences*. San Francisco: Freeman.

Rosen, R., 1985. Organisms as causal systems which are not mechanisms: an essay into the nature of complexity. In *Theoretical Biology and Complexity*, R. Rosen, ed., New York: Academic Press, pp. 165–203.

Stanley, S. M., 1979. *Macroevolution: Pattern and Process*. San Francisco: Freeman.

Vonnegut, K., 1971. *Cat's Cradle*. New York: Dell.

Wicken, J. S., 1983. Entropy, information and nonequilibrium evolution. *Syst. Zool.* 32:438–443.

Wicken, J. S., 1984. Autocatalytic cycling and self-organization in the ecology of evolution. *Nature and System* 6:119–135.

Wicken, J. S., 1985. Thermodynamics and the conceptual structure of evolutionary theory. *J. Theor. Biol.* 117:363–383.

Wiley, E. O., and D. R. Brooks, 1982. Victims of history—a nonequilibrium approach to evolution. *Syst. Zool.* 31:1–24.

Wilkinson, D., and A. S. Iberall, 1985. From physics to world politics. Manuscript.

Zeleny, M., ed., 1980. *Autopoiesis, Dissipative Structures and Spontaneous Social Orders*. Boulder: Westview Press.

14

Teleology and Biology
Richard T. O'Grady and Daniel R. Brooks

Evolutionary theory did away with teleology, and that is that. (Hull, 1973)

What is most challenging about Darwin is his reintroduction of purpose into the natural world. (MacLeod, 1957)

Teleological notions are among the main obstacles to theory formation in biology. (Lagerspetz, 1959)

Let us recognize Darwin's great service to Natural Science in bringing back to it Teleology: so that instead of Morphology *versus* Teleology, we shall have Morphology wedded to Teleology. (Gray, 1874)

What you say about Teleology pleases me especially, and I do not think any one else has ever noticed the point. I have always said you were the man to hit the nail on the head. (Darwin's reply to Gray: see Darwin, 1959)

Teleology is a lady without whom no biologist can live; yet he is ashamed to show himself in public with her. (Van Brücke: see Davies, 1961)

We are primarily concerned here with two considerations that must be recognized when studying biological systems: (1) Organisms can be viewed from either a nonhistorical or a historical perspective, and (2) explanations for structural and functional properties should be approached differently. The subject of functionality leads to an analysis of the three types of end-attaining activity found in biological systems: teleomatic, teleonomic, and teleological. We suggest that many disagreements over the validity of causal explanations are the result of not only an insufficient delineation of the effects of these three factors, but also an excessively broad definition of teleology. The passages at the beginning are intended not to show that the authors are unclear as to what they mean by teleology, but that the term has been applied to different phenomena. We examine hierarchic causality in physical systems, and then use this framework to assess the explanatory strengths and weaknesses of neo-Darwinian theory. For our purposes, this is defined as those evolutionary explanations that look to natural selection as the *primary* cause of evolution, or the explanation of *first choice*.[1] We argue that neo-Darwinian explanations are weakened by the explanatory emptiness of the adaptational teleology that can occur under certain circumstances. These arise from certain of the theory's properties that (1) allow it to be applied to phenomena with which it is not capable of dealing and (2) confound its language of investigation with that of nonevolutionary studies.

14.1 Causality

We take it as a premise that a theory should be isomorphic with the processes and patterns it is intended to explain. If there are two causes operating in a natural system, then the theory dealing with it should also appeal to two causes. If there are multiple causes operating at different levels of generality and temporality—i.e., if some causes operate upon the effects of others—the most useful theory will appeal to causes related in a similar manner. The goal is to attribute the correct powers to each cause.

Temporal Perspectives

A physical entity or system can be examined from either a nonhistorical or a historical perspective. (O'Grady, 1984, referred to the nonhistorical as "ahistorical." It has since become necessary to distinguish between the nonhistorical, which does not consider historical phenomena, and the ahistorical, which actively denies their importance. See the section "Ahistorical Perspectives.") Some questions, such as "What is it made of?" and "What does it do?" are nonhistorical; they are interested in the properties of the thing *now*, not in its etiology. Other questions, such as "How did it come to be?" are historical; they are concerned with causes operating in the past that are responsible for the thing existing now. Still others, such as "What causes it to be as it is?" and "Why is it as it is?" look for either nonhistorical or historical answers, depending upon the completeness of explanation desired. (We seek to minimize the use of "why" questions because of the extreme ambiguity of that adverb. See the section "A Comment on 'Why' Questions.") Consider a rock falling from a height and breaking a window. The nonhistorical question is "What breaks the window?" and the answer cites the moving rock. The corresponding historical questions can address many levels of past causality, such as "How did the rock come to be moving?" "How did it come to be a rock?" and "How did gravity come to have such an effect upon rocks?"

Internested Causality

Not all causes operate upon a particular entity at the same level of generality. Some affect it independently, as in a canvas coming to have two colors because of the application of two paints. Others operate upon the effects of a preceding cause. Our rock, for example, may be covered with ferrous oxide particles. This property can be examined from either a nonhistorical or a historical perspective, as discussed above, but it can also be examined as a property of only certain types of rocks. All rocks fall, but not all rocks form ferrous oxide rust. The more general property of this particular rock is its susceptibility, as a heavier-than-air object, to gravitational attraction; it is within this context that the oxidation of its iron content occurs. This second process is nested, in a hierarchical manner, within the first. A theory of "rock-ness" must recognize this, and avoid trying to explain the falling of rocks by reference to the causal agents of oxidation, or vice versa.

For any physical system, then, there are a number of internested levels of causality operating. They range from the maximally general (universal) to the maximally particular (singular) (see Hull, 1983). Universal causes, operating upon all physical entities at all times and all places, are natural laws. Less general causes operate on a contingency basis and are thus manifested only under certain conditions. When this internested causality exists within a single system, it seems appropriate to refer to the more general causes in the hierarchy as ultimate, or primary causes, in the mechanistic sense (in contradistinction to the supernatural sense), and to the more particular causes as proximate, or secondary, causes.

14.2 Biological Systems: Structure, Function, and Evolution

Biological systems are specifically configured physical systems, so they are also subject to the causal considerations discussed above. Cats, after all, fall from heights just as rocks do, and it has nothing to do with their cat-ness. But there are two additional properties of biological systems that are relevant to our concerns. These are functionality and evolution.

At any moment of an organism's existence it must maintain a particular organization of its components in the face of potentially disruptive forces (heat, cold, energy flows, etc.). Living systems must always be "doing" something. They cannot *passively* exist, as do nonliving entities. Any physical object has *structure*, and thus some degree of order. A living system must have its structure *organized* in a manner that performs particular *functions* that attain the end-state of continuing the organism's existence. Functional properties are therefore nested within structural properties. There can be structure without function, but no function without structure (for us, structure simply refers to the physical existence of entities in a particular configuration).

Organisms do not function in order to survive. Rather, it is trivially true that they will not survive if they do not function. Organisms must *actively* exist. If they die, their constituent elements will still exist and still possess basic physical properties—dead cats fall from heights just as live cats do— but the organisms will no longer have the organizational properties of living things.

The second property of organisms that is of concern here is their evolutionary capacity. This comes from their reproductive abilities. We are referring to *biological* evolution, not just *physical* evolution or historical existence. Anything that *exists* through time has a history. If it also *changes* through time it can be said to physically evolve (Brandon, 1981, gives the example of a painting changing appearance because of the differential fading of its pigments). All evolving entities, therefore, have a history, but not all historical entities evolve. In biological evolution, in addition to history and change, there is descent with modification: An ancestor-descendant continuum is established through acts of reproduction. As this continuum is produced, whether intraspecifically or transspecifically, the causes responsible for ancestral properties become incorporated into the causality of the descendant. Every new descendant, every new ontogeny, does not, so to speak, start from scratch. It inherits many of its characters from its ancestors, which inherited many of theirs from their ancestors. And so on. This has two consequences. The first is that a character that arises for the first time in a species (i.e., unique, and contingent upon previously unrealized circumstances) may become part of the fixed, inherited causality of the properties of the descendants of that species. The second consequence is that an investigation of an organism's existence must deal with more than questions about ultimate origins, that is, about the origin of life on earth. It is also necessary to ask questions about any subsequent evolution, for a long series of causal events, spanning millions of years, is responsible for the organism appearing as it does now. This incorporation of contingent causality into inherited causality creates a time-vertical (or time-extensive: Vrba and Eldredge, 1984) hierarchy of causes. Phylogenetic history is not a passive "trace" of organisms' existence through time. It is a succession of causes.

Organic properties are thus nested not only within those of physical objects, but, even more restrictedly, within those of evolved objects. Our ubiquitous cat has three properties caused by three historical events during its evolution: It has inherited a nuclear membrane from the common ancestor of eucaryotes, it has inherited an internal skeleton from the common ancestor of vertebrates, and it has inherited fur from the common ancestor of mammals. Each of these properties originated as a unique, contingent character of a particular species, and each became an inherited character through the subsequent evolution of descendant species.

A nonhistorical study of cats can, of course, claim that all three of these characters are caused by the existing animal's ontogeny. This is quite true, and these contemporary proximate causes may be of greater interest to a particular investigator, such as a veterinarian. Centuries of nonevolutionary research in areas such as anatomy, physiology, and embryology have produced a great deal of valid data for contemporary nonhistorical analyses. So long as they are limited to nonhistorical interpretations, these studies need not be explicit about their assumptions of how the objects they work with came to be.

14.3 End-Attaining Activity

Some processes reach states at which the process ceases, or is altered in that it tends towards another state. We believe that it would be a mistake to always call such end-states goals, and the activities that attain them teleological. There are three categories of end-attaining activity that pertain to evolutionary biology.

First, natural entities or systems (i.e., not made by humans) may attain end-states because of the operation of processes whose existence depends not on the entity being alive, or being purposefully designed, but on the properties of the constituent matter. Some of these properties, such as gravity or entropic decay, operate universally, and are thus known as laws of nature. Others, such as radioactive decay and reaction gradients, are more restricted in their operation. All of this is teleomatic activity (Mayr, 1974; Wicken, 1981a, b). The end-state, such as a rock coming to rest at the bottom of a cliff, can simply be said to result from the properties of the entity. There is no "control" or "purpose" involved (excluding an unassailable belief in cosmological purpose). We refer to this activity as *end-resulting*.

Second, the functionality of living systems is caused by the operation of inherited genetic and epigenetic factors. These factors determine the end-states of processes such as homeostasis (maintenance of a species-specific physiological state), ontogeny (development into an adult of members of that species), and reproduction (replication of the progenitor(s) in that species). (This is not to suggest that all organic functionality is "coded-for" in inherited factors. Inheritance sets the context for further, emergent properties; it is necessary but not sufficient.) This is teleonomic activity (Pittendrigh, 1958; Mayr, 1961, 1974). The end-states are reached because of internal controlling factors. It is *end-directed*.

The third category is that of purposeful behavior, in which certain outcomes occur because events were deliberately brought about so as to produce them. This behavior requires some degree of cognition. It is most prevalent in humans, and exists to various extents in other animals. The end-state is a deliberately sought goal. O'Grady (1984) referred to this activity as goal-directed; it is perhaps better to call it *goal-seeking*, so as to make it clear that such behavior is the result of a consciousness capable of some amount of premeditation and choice. We think that only *this* type of end-attaining activity should be called teleological. Our position is a departure from earlier use of the term. Traditionally (see, e.g., Wicken, 1985), teleology has been used as a blanket term for all activities that achieved an end or goal. Thus, not only have the teleomatic and the teleonomic been considered to be teleological, but so have function, adaptation, and organization. From this position, for example, Gray (1874) was correct in saying that Darwin had wedded morphology to teleology—because Darwin's theory deals with functionality. We feel that the lack of precision in such terminology interferes with the search for, and the study of, different end-attaining processes in biological systems.

With respect to Aristotelian causality, which is in some ways responsible for much of the confusion over the status of teleological explanations (see Jaki, 1966), it seems that the following observations apply. (1) All three types of end-attaining activities have material causes (that in which change occurs) and efficient causes (that by which change occurs). (2) Teleonomic and teleological activity also have formal causes (internal representations: that into which something changes). (3) Only teleological activity also has final causes (that for the sake of which change occurs). Although the nature of the internal representations in teleonomic and teleological activity is different, it can be said that in both there is something within the organism that has a representation of the end-state and is involved in the taking of steps that have the effect of attaining that state. (The reader should note that we are avoiding the use of strictly teleological phrases such as "in order to" "so that.")

While not all physical entities show all three types of end-attaining activity, those that do are simply a subset of those that do not (figure 14.1). All physical entities show some type of teleomatic activity; a subset also shows teleonomic activity (biological systems); and a subset of those also shows teleological activity (cognitive biological systems). Thus, while the act of a rock falling to earth is teleomatic (gravity) and the act of a kitten becoming a cat is teleonomic (ontogeny), the act of a kitten falling to earth is teleomatic. To complete the example, a parachutist teleologically reaches for the ripcord as his teleonomically maintained body plummets teleomatically to the ground below.

Now, in order to put the internesting discussed above into a *historical* perspective, it is necessary to provide explanations for the origins of the entities showing the different types of end-attaining activity. It is at this

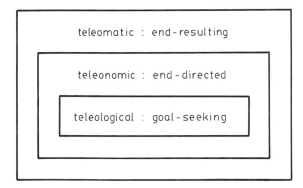

Figure 14.1
The relationships of three types of end-attaining activity in biological systems. They are internested, rather than mutually exclusive. All physical systems show teleomatic activity; a subset (biological systems) also shows teleonomic activity; a subset of those (cognitive biological systems) also shows teleological activity.

point that there is a risk of introducing inappropriate teleology by incorporating the attainment of the future end-state into the causal explanation for the activity coming to exist. Evolutionary theory seeks to provide mechanistic explanations for the etiology of organic structure and function, and to keep such ideas distinct from teleological explanations for the existence of man-made objects. Critics of evolution, such as William Paley, blurred this distinction when they presented their arguments from design. Paley's teleology of the designer appealed to external, imposed causality. Hull (1973) has called this Platonic teleology. Other writers, such as those orthogeneticists who approved of teleology (discussed later), appealed to internal, immanent causality. Hull (1973) has called this Aristotelian teleology. It seems to result from mistaking formal causation for final causation. That is, the properties of the state into which something changes are seen as the reason *why* that state was attained. Later in this section we suggest that this line of argument can be partly attributed to an inappropriate analogy of evolution with ontogenetic development. Both Platonic and Aristotelian teleology assume that the existence of functionality in organisms is indicative, as it is in human works, of purpose. They assume that it must have come to exist *for* some use and *for* some reason.

For evolutionary theory, the recognition of teleonomic activity solves half the problem of explaining what it is that causes an organism to be as it is. It provides a mechanistic nonhistorical explanation for organic functionality, and thus adequately deals with the "organic teleology" of design discussed by writers such as Russell (1916) and von Bertalanffy (1962). (See also Pittendrigh's letter to Mayr, in Mayr, 1974.) But this does not address the question about where those factors came from. What produced teleonomic systems in the first place, and what causes the evolution of one species-specific teleonomic system into another? Unless a mechanistic explanation can be found for these historical questions, teleonomy will mean nothing more than "purposefully designed but currently unattended organic activity," like a machine with servo-mechanisms.

The solution seems to lie in seeing teleonomic activity as the result of certain types of teleomatic activity. With respect to the origin of teleonomic systems—the origin of life on earth—this means that the living emerged from the nonliving through processes of self-organization, such as those proposed by Eigen (1971) (see also Wicken, this volume). With respect to the transformation of one teleonomic system into another—the evolution of species—this means that evolution is caused by teleomatic changes in inherited teleonomic properties during reproduction and ontogeny. Genetic drift (King and Jukes, 1969; Kimura and Ohta, 1971) and molecular drive (Dover, 1982a,b) are examples of such changes. More generally, we are simply referring to mutations, which are errors in the reproductive message from one generation to the next. The impact of this activity upon the teleonomic system in which it occurs may exceed that system's homeostatic capabilities enough to cause the death of the individual, or even the extinction of the species. If the system remains together, but nevertheless changes to a certain degree, then speciation occurs. This may come solely from species-internal changes (sympatric speciation), or it may be intensified by environmental events (allopatric speciation).This view appears to be consistent with Paterson's (1980, 1981, 1982) argument that speciation is an incidental effect of breakdowns in species-maintaining systems. Brooks and Wiley (1986) have argued that this process is the result of entropic dissipation of species-cohesive factors.

There is no immutable *telos* in the teleonomic activity of biological function. There is only an end-state that, although stable for generations of intraspecific reproduction, evolves into the end-state of a descendant species. The teleomatic processes responsible for this transformation attain their end-states because of the natural properties of the physical entities involved. They do not do so *for* the sake of the organism in which they happen to occur. Teleomatic activity does not occur *for* anything. The teleomatic produces the teleonomic (origin of life), whereupon the teleonomic sets the context of operation for, but does not direct or control, further teleomatic activity (evolution). Teleonomic activity is an *intraspecific* phenomenon. We see no evidence for *transspecific* teleonomic activity, in which controlling factors direct the attainment of an end-state that is evolutionarily beyond the maintenance of the existing species. The transspecific process of evolution is therefore *not* analogous to the intraspecific process of ontogeny, for only the latter is *directed toward* an end-state.

Ontogeny, a teleonomic activity, operates with an internal representation of the end-state(s) to be attained. It cannot be said that evolution operates with a similar, controlling representation of what is to be. This false analogy between evolution and ontogeny would seem to be responsible for many of the shortcomings of orthogenetic theory at the turn of the century. As with any end-attaining activity, this analogy has also attracted teleological interpretations of evolutionary change, such as the *élan vital* of Bergson's (1911) "creative evolution" and the "progressive evolution" of some neo-Lamarckians (see Bowler, 1983).

14.4 Nonhistorical and Historical Approaches in Biology

The intrusion of teleological explanations into what should be mechanistic explanations in biology is prevented by maintaining a proper distinction between nonhistorical and historical perspectives. Even though the questions may be phrased in similar ways, each is looking for a different type of answer. Each is usually associated with particular biological disciplines, and disagreements over what constitutes a valid explanation of a phenomenon may arise because nonhistorical and historical perspectives are being mixed. In addition, some disciplines are more interested in structural properties, while others are more interested in functional properties. These criteria give four ways of looking at biology: nonhistorical structuralism, nonhistorical functionalism, historical structuralism, and historical functionalism.

Nonhistorical Structuralism and Functionalism

Studies of this type take the existence of an organism for granted, and then ask questions such as "What is it made of?" and "What does it do?" These are usually known as form-and-function studies. Anatomy, physiology, molecular biology, biochemistry, biomechanics, and medicine, for example, are nonhistorical disciplines. By this we mean not that one *cannot* do evolutionary research from within these areas of study, but that one does not *have* to do such research in order to study these subjects. Embryology is also nonhistorical, for even though it studies organic development through time, it does not necessarily address the evolutionary origin of ontogenies. Even much of population biology is nonhistorical, for the same reason that it does not address evolutionary origins. Kettlewell's (1955, 1961, 1965) classic studies on industrial melanism in *Biston betularia*, for example, were concerned with changes in the relative frequencies of pigmentation patterns in a *given* system, and not with how the pigmentation properties themselves came to exist.

By disassociating themselves from the question of historical origin, nonhistorical studies can take either a mechanistic or a teleological approach without creating any problems. The questions "What is it made of?" and "What does it do?" are mechanistic. But it may be possible to discover more about the properties of the organism by asking the teleological "What is this for?" From a *nonhistorical* perspective, "what for" questions are perfectly legitimate. *This* is the proper place of teleology in biology. But there is a price paid, for it must be acknowledged that such teleological causation plays no role in the origin of the organism.

An anatomist looks at a heart, asks "What is it for?" and answers "For circulating the blood." A zoologist looks at protandrous development in hermaphroditic organisms, asks "What is it for?" and answers "For preventing self-fertilization." This approach treats organisms *as if* they were machines; it looks for explanations for functions and structures in the same way that a mechanic would examine an oil pump or the timing system of an engine. It treats the end-directed activity of teleonomic systems *as if* it were the goal-seeking activity of a teleological system. The teleology in nonhistorical studies is not problematic because it is divorced from mechanistic causal explanations for the existence of organisms and is used as only an explanatory analogy (after all, the heart *is* a pump).

This decoupling is one reason why centuries of data on the properties of organisms can still be used today, even though most of them were collected not only before evolutionary theory was developed, but under implicit or explicit assumptions of purposeful design. Biology today makes use of the findings of Harvey, Vesalius, Owen, and Agassiz, and it does not matter how those people thought living systems came to be.

Historical Structuralism
We apply this term to the view of evolution advocated in this paper. In this view, function emerges as an effect from structure, and therefore has no causal power of its own; evolutionary change is structural change, with functional change coming afterward, if at all; and any end-attaining aspects of these changes come from teleomatic processes operating within, but not because of, a teleonomic context. In no sense of the word does evolution occur *for* something. "What for" questions are not applicable in historical structuralism. This last point touches upon an advantage that one gains by keeping historical structuralism in mind when doing nonhistorical studies: Historical structuralism recognizes that some properties of organisms may not have any function at all. Organic structure simply changes during evolution, and it may be pointless to search for a use for a new bone configuration, or tissue organization, or biochemical product.

Historical Functionalism
This approach looks to function, rather than to structure, for the explanation of how things came to be. In doing so, it looks for causal powers in

what are, in fact, effects. Other authors have noted the shortcomings of such a viewpoint in morphological (e.g., Lauder, 1981, 1982; Smith, 1982) and behavioral studies (Jamieson, 1986). *The inability to find mechanistic evolutionary causes in functionality results in the extension of the teleological causality of nonhistorical studies into the historical realm.* This extension is not valid because the causal powers of such a teleology do not really exist. If the extension is made, the result is a historical teleology that asks a *second* type of "what for" question. This type is unacceptable in any scientific context. It asks "What did this *originate* for?" or "For what *purpose* did this come to be?"

Historical functionalism does not necessarily recognize a process of evolution through descent with modification. If it does, then the question becomes "What did this *evolve* for?" and the historical teleology of the answers becomes an evolutionary teleology of the type "The heart evolved in order to circulate the blood." If historical functionalism does not include a recognition of evolution, then its teleology is nothing more than an argument from design: This performs a function, therefore it must have come to be so as to perform that function.

14.5 Natural Selection

Although we have suggested that the transformational causes of historical structuralism are necessary and sufficient for *some kind* of biological evolution to occur, we are not suggesting that they are the only causes affecting the appearance of the organisms that have *actually* evolved on earth. Functionality *does* play a role in certain evolutionary phenomena. This is the basis of Darwin's theory.

In addition to being *effected* by the *generative* processes of historical structuralist causes, biological systems can be *affected* by imposed *eliminative* processes acting upon certain criteria. Natural selection is an eliminative force. It involves the survival of a subset of organisms from a heterogeneous grouping according to the relative functional efficiency of the organisms in a particular environment. Those organisms that function best (attain and maintain their teleonomic end-state best) will be in a position to leave more offspring than those that perish. Natural selection is the incidental survival of those morphs that were not actively eliminated. Natural processes eliminate some forms, and thereby passively promote the survivors. There is no active selection of morphs. This should be kept in mind when making comparisons to human selection, in which teleological actions actively choose certain forms.

Lewontin (1980) gave three factors that he considered necessary and sufficient for evolution by natural selection: (1) variation, (2) heritability of that variation, and (3) differential fitness of the inheritors of that variation.

We ask what would happen if there were *nothing but* heritable variation, with no subsequent selection. Would there be any evolution? We suggest that there would be. Selection can act only upon what already exists, and it is not necessary for creating order in that which it affects. There is no need to introduce an eliminative, imposed factor such as natural selection as a *necessary* cause of biological order. There are generative, intrinsic processes already in operation that produce descendant order from ancestral order. Natural selection can thus be said to act as a proximate cause operating *among* biological systems, each of which is a hierarchy of ultimate and proximate *within*-system causality (figure 14.2). Selection can have a major impact during the evolutionary history of a lineage, but because its among-system causality is extrinsic to any particular biological system, it cannot become incorporated into the historical causality of the lineage. Investigations of selection may therefore address the history of the evolution of an organism, but not the historical, transformational processes that caused the organism to exist.

We are not suggesting that any evolutionary biologist today would argue that all biological order is the result of natural selection operating upon totally unordered variation. Futuyma (1984) considered such an unqualified concept to be "simplistic." But there exists a tendency to lean toward this position, and it appears to be a relict of the controversies of the 1860s to the 1920s. There was at that time a struggle, first for the acceptance of Darwinian evolutionary theory, and then for the primacy

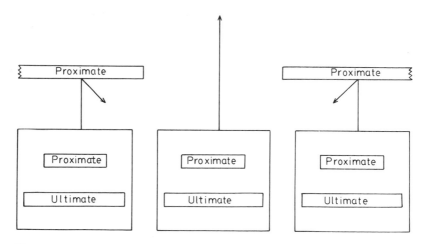

Figure 14.2
Three organisms composed of a hierarchy of within-system ultimate and proximate causality, subsequently differentially eliminated by an among-system proximate cause: natural selection.

of neo-Darwinian, mutationist, orthogeneticist, or neo-Lamarckian explanations (see Bowler, 1983). One of the major disputes was whether evolution was in any way predetermined or directed toward a goal. Orthogeneticists and neo-Lamarckians had difficulty keeping their proposed mechanistic explanations free from teleology. In addition, mystically minded critics of evolution offered blatantly teleological alternative explanations. The concept of purposeless change with which the Darwinians and neo-Darwinians attempted to introduce mechanistic causality advocated natural selection acting upon undirected variation. This means that variation is not directed toward the future needs of organisms. It can thus be said to be "random" with respect to those needs, but it cannot be said to be random with respect to the sources that produced it. Restricted variation and morphological trends in evolution are not indicative of predetermination; they result from historical events, and there are few things more determined and fixed than the past. When future change must take place within the context of these past events, it can be said to be *past-determined*. This is not the same as *future-determined* change that serves the needs of the organism.

14.6 Putting Natural Selection and Historical Causality into One Explanatory Framework

Natural selection and historical causality can be brought together in a single explanatory framework that factors out the relative contributions of causes by considering the most general causes first, and then the more particular causes only if necessary. As an extreme example, one would not look to a selection level cause to explain why a cat walks upon the ground (selection against those that disobeyed gravity and rose into the air?). By extension, it may not be justifiable to look immediately to selection when trying to explain why cats have four limbs, or a placenta, or retractile claws. This internesting of causes in historically produced systems indicates a *primacy of action* of some causes over others. It follows that explanations attributing phenomena to lower level causes have *logical primacy* over those dealing with higher level causes. The lower level causal explanation is to be treated as a *null hypothesis* of sorts. It is the most parsimonious explanation, the explanation of *first choice*. Its acceptance gives the least departure from the data at hand and the greatest consistency with the causes known to be capable of producing the effects in question. It is to be retained so long as additional data do not show it to be inadequate.

Intraspecific Investigations
Suppose one wanted to explain the evolution of a species of green frogs. Biotic or abiotic selection may have acted as a proximate cause (C1) by

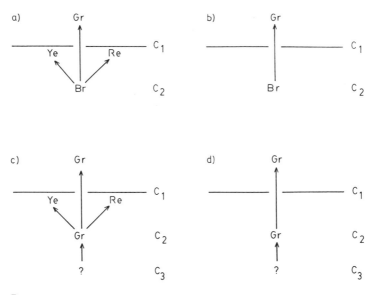

Figure 14.3
Four evolutionary histories for four skin colors of a species of frog: brown (Br), yellow (Ye), red (Re), and green (Gr). The causes involved are natural selection (C1), and inheritance at two levels (C2, C3).

eliminating nongreen frogs from a polymorphic state produced by a non-green immediate ancestor (figure 14.3a). If so, the developmental alteration that first produced the color change is the ultimate cause (C2), and the complete evolutionary explanation for green coloration must refer to both the developmental and selectional causes. There are, however, at least three other means by which the species could come to be green and only green: (1) the nongreen immediate ancestor may have produced only green descendants that were not subject to any selection (figure 14.3b), in which case only the developmental explanation would be necessary; (2) selection may have acted upon a polymorphic state produced by a green immediate ancestor (figure 14.3c); or (3) the current green species may simply be descended from a green immediate ancestor, and be unaffected by selection (figure 14.3d). The last two cases do not address the question of the origin of green coloration, and so the answer must be sought further back in the phylogeny, in even more general levels of causality (C3). However, for the species whose characters prompted the study, the cause of green coloration has been determined.

In all four cases above, the complete causal explanation for the condition of the species includes a component of historical causality. This component, which has *produced* the objects that selection may act upon, is the null hypothesis. It is to be accepted in the absence of additional data suggestive of selection. Historical causality is thus the explanation of *first choice*, while historical *plus* selectional causality is the explanation of *second choice*. This relationship among causes in an internested system differs from the more traditional either/or method of analysis. It is not a question of history *or* selection, but one of whether selection has acted upon a system already affected by more ultimate causes. This necessity to start investigations at lower hierarchic levels has been recognized by workers concentrating on levels of selection. For example, Williams (1966, p. 124) argued that one should look to individual selection to explain organic form before looking to group selection. We are suggesting that this argument be extended a few levels lower.

Phylogenetic Investigations
When inferring the evolutionary relationships of a group of organisms, the application of the null hypothesis takes the form of Hennigian phylogenetic analysis (Hennig, 1966). This technique infers genealogy by internesting the similarities caused by shared derived characters within the similarities caused by shared primitive characters. It attributes the maximum amount of ancestor-derived causality to the explanation of a character. An analysis of, say, four taxa (figure 14.4a) begins with any basal synapomorphies, and any autapomorphies, and the null hypothesis that the taxa are equally related to one another. This hypothesis may be rejected when additional data are considered (figure 14.4b), but it is replaced by one that still explains the data with as much appeal as possible to historical causality (figure 14.4c). The result is an internesting of characters and their causes (figure 14.4d). When a character is discovered to have a distribution that cannot be immediately attributed to a single historical origin and subsequent inheritance in the descendants, it is necessary to look to the next higher causal level: convergent and parallel evolution, possibly involving selection.

The search for maximal historical causality in the inference of evolutionary relationships extends to analyses of ecological properties of organisms. Dobson (1985) and Jamieson (1986), for example, have argued for the necessity of first determining the historical contribution when studying the evolution of behavior (see also Brooks, 1986).

Community Ecology Investigations
Logical primacy and null hypotheses have been examined in explanations of community structure (e.g., Quinn and Dunham, 1983; Roughgarden, 1983; Simberloff, 1983; Strong, 1983). The question has been whether one hypothesis has primacy of consideration over another, or whether there is

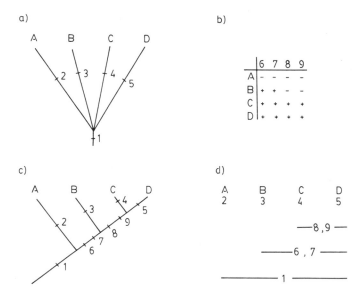

Figure 14.4
Hennigian phylogenetic analysis of four taxa, showing the application of the null hypothesis and the appeal to maximum historical causality. With only autapomorphies and basal synapomorphies considered, the null hypothesis (a) is that of a polytomy, in which all taxa are equally related. When additional data, if they exist, are considered (b), the revised hypothesis (c) explains all of the data with as much internested historical causality as possible (d).

such a multiplicity of impinging causes of equal status that one hypothesis is as reasonable a starting point as any. We suggest that neither of the hypotheses discussed so far, random dispersal or competition effects, is a suitable null hypothesis for biological systems.

The assumption of historically determined relationships appeals to the most general relevant causes in community structure analysis. Of course, this is not to say that factors such as colonization and competition have not affected communities. It simply means that the historical contribution must be factored out first (figure 14.5). Simberloff (1983) and Strong (1983) presented arguments that can be interpreted to support this approach. They noted the need to examine intraspecific, autecological factors, such as vagility, before dealing with interspecific, synecological factors, such as competition. Strong (1983, p. 639) came close to attributing this requirement to the historical nature of biological systems. It would seem that these goals are best met by formulating null hypotheses of historical causality. This can be accomplished with a method such as the historical ecology approach advocated by Brooks (1979a,b, 1980, 1981a, 1986; see also

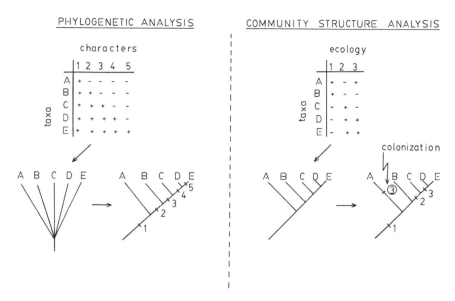

Figure 14.5
The application of the null hypothesis of historical causality to community structure analysis. The pattern of inheritance suggested by a phylogenetic analysis is used as the null hypothesis for explanations of ecological traits. Departures from congruence between the phylogeny and those traits are indicative of nonhistorical causation, such as colonization.

Brooks and Mitter, 1983; Mitter and Brooks, 1983; Cressey et al., 1983; Collette and Russo, 1985).

14.7 Adaptation

Darwin's theory recognized a particular type of organic functionality, the relative efficiency of which allowed survival from the eliminative forces of natural selection. This functionality is *adaptation*. (We do not address the use of the term adaptation to refer to intragenerational adjustments to new conditions.) Some workers, such as Bock (1967, 1979, 1980), have taken the view that "on theoretical grounds, all existing features of animals are adaptive" (1967, p. 63). Others, such as Williams (1966) and Gould and Vrba (1982), have argued that the designation of adaptation should be reserved for features that have been affected by natural selection. We agree with Brandon (1981), van der Steen (1983), and van der Steen and Voorzanger (1984) that the tight coupling of cause and effect in the latter approach is preferable. We do not, however, accept Williams' (1966, p. 9) argument that only adaptive characters have "functions," while any remaining characters have "effects." *All function is an effect of structure, regardless of whether selection is involved.* Adaptive functionality is simply one type of organic functionality, and adaptive structural changes must occur within the context of organic structural changes.

Adaptations are "useful" to the organism in that they have survived selection because of a relative superiority of function. (We find it difficult to define organic usefulness as much more than that which contributes to the organism's continued existence. This is not very satisfying. The designation of usefulness may be one of degree, and not of kind.) But no matter how useful a character is, it has not necessarily become that way because of selection. It could have been produced by genetic and epigenetic associations with other characters that have been selected. (Brandon, 1981, termed these epiphenomenal traits, and included gene linkage and pleiotropic effects with them.) It could have evolved as a monomorphic derivative of an ancestral condition (figure 14.3b), or it could have been inherited, unchanged, from an ancestor (figure 14.3d). It could have been caused by allometric and heterochronic alternations in body shape, or by history-independent physical effects upon structure (see the section "Ahistorical Perspectives").

Selection can be cited as a contributing cause of character usefulness only when there are grounds to believe that there has been a process of differential survival from a polymorphic stage because of functional differences. Otherwise, there is the risk of trivializing the adaptation into a synonymy with "character" or "biological organization." This would cause some of the perceived evidence for natural selection to come, in fact, from the fallacy of Affirming the Consequent: From the statement "If adaptation through selection, then usefulness and functionality" it is concluded "Usefulness and functionality, therefore adaptation through selection."

Some authors appear to have adopted this line of argument. Bock (1967, p. 63), for example, stated, "If [all existing features of animals] were not adaptive, then they would be eliminated by selection and would disappear." Ayala (1976) and Simpson (1958) have presented similar arguments that equate biological organization and functionality with adaptation. Once the *state* of adaptation has been thus synonymized, the *process* of adaptation is easily synonymized with the process of evolution (see Eldredge, 1985, p. 107). Such a perspective confounds studies of causes and their effects. It also ensures a continuous but specious supply of confirmations of the efficacy of neo-Darwinian theory.

14.8 Adaptational Teleology

This is a form of the evolutionary teleology of historical functionalism discussed above. It comes from uncertainty about the degree to which adaptive functionality can be used in evolutionary explanations. This uncertainty comes from (1) the incompleteness of neo-Darwinian theory for dealing with evolution, and (2) the ambiguity of some neo-Darwinian terms.

The Incompleteness of Neo-Darwinian Theory
With little or no sense of historical causality, neo-Darwinian theory does not have the components to explain fully the origins of structurally and functionally integrated evolutionary entities. In fact, as discussed by Wicken (1985) and O'Grady (1984), Darwinian theory was established by deliberately ignoring questions about the origins of biological organization. As a result, it must attribute evolution either to natural selection, which it knows to be capable of producing some sort of order, or to chance mutational events. Not surprisingly, natural selection is preferred. But as a proximate, among-system cause, natural selection is secondary to within-system causality. Its use as the explanation of first choice reverses the direction of explanation of the hierarchy of causes and tries to explain the system not from the bottom up, with upward causation, but from the top down, with downward causation. Such a procedure attempts to use the causal powers of a proximate cause to explain the effects of what is, in fact, a more ultimate cause. This will not work in historically produced systems because their causal relationships are temporally asymmetric. The higher levels have emerged from the lower levels. Higher level causes act upon a system already shaped by lower level causes. They cannot be responsible for the origin of lower levels because the lower levels came into existence first.

We acknowledge that we are using the term "downward causation" in a different sense than that of its originator, D. T. Campbell (1974), as well as that of authors such as Petersen (1983) and Vrba and Eldredge (1984). These writers have been concerned with the *amount* of organic variation, the causes of its elimination by selection, and the consequences that this has for any progeny. They are thus looking at the effects of higher level phenomena on the lower level properties of *subsequent*, or descendant, biological hierarchies. As such, the causality they deal with always goes forward in time, in the direction of reproduction. We, on the other hand, are concerned with how one explains the *origins* of organic form in a single organism. Thus, the higher and lower levels with which we deal exist at the same time, and we are asking whether or not it is useful to look to higher level properties (functions) for an explanation for the origin of lower level properties (structures). In this sense, our approach is closer to that of Churchland (1982), who advocated analyses that are structuralist and bottom-up, rather than functionalist and top-down (O'Grady, 1984).

When a bottom-up direction is taken in evolutionary explanations, an inability to subsume higher level properties with lower level causes indi-

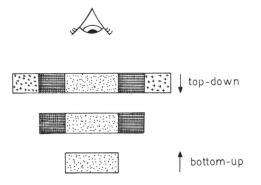

Figure 14.6
A schematic three-level hierarchy with three properties: dots, hatchings, and crosses. An observer sees all of the properties at once, and attempts to determine their respective causes by explaining the system from either the bottom up or the top down.

cates a need to expand the theory structure and consider higher level causes. These may be within- or among-system. However, when a top-down explanatory direction is taken, higher level effects can become part of the explanation for the existence of lower level processes. This is illustrated in figure 14.6, which shows a schematic three-level hierarchy. In addition to its own properties, each level possesses the properties of any lower levels. An investigator must try to find the causes of all three properties: dots, hatchings, and crosses. Proceeding upward, a bottom-up explanation incorporates higher level causes as unexplained phenomena are encountered. On the other hand, a top-down explanation begins with all the properties of the system, and then attempts to find their respective causes.

When natural selection is taken to be the primary cause of evolution, its effect, adaptation, becomes incorporated into explanations of why organisms, or parts of organisms, evolved. The result is a teleological causality that is *relied* upon to explain the phenomena concerned. This teleology is a form of historical functionalism, and it is not difficult to find examples of it in the research literature (see O'Grady, 1984). Organisms are imbued with powers of foresight and action. Questions such as "Why does this frog have green skin?" are given answers such as "*In order to* be better camouflaged," "*So that* it could not be seen by predators," and "*In response to* environmental demands for protective coloration." The claim that this phraseology is only an explanatory shorthand wears thin when no explanation for the origin of structures is forthcoming.

Teleological causality comes to bear the entire explanatory burden when adaptational status is used to explain evolutionary origins. This can be demonstrated by removing the teleology from the first explanation above by restating it as "This frog is better camouflaged because it is green" (see also Brooks, 1981b, and O'Grady, 1984). Such a statement is no longer teleological, but neither is it causal; it is simply a statement of fact that describes but does not explain. There is no causal explanation left at all once the teleological causality has been removed. Even if one attempts to introduce nonteleological causality by restating the explanation mechanistically as "This frog is green because yellow and red frogs were eliminated in the past," the only causality introduced is that of selection from an unaccounted-for polymorphism. There is still no explanation offered for how the green frog came to exist.

Ambiguous Terms

Any new theory must use some of the terms of the previous theory or theories. This is a requisite for the continuity of thought and language. But ambiguity can arise when terms carrying earlier connotations are used to refer to new concepts. Darwin's theory, and its derivative theory, neo-Darwinism, use at least two such terms. One is *selection*. It produces ambiguity in evolutionary explanations, despite the use of *natural* in front of it, because of its connotations of an active, deliberate choice of something from a larger group. It was argued in O'Grady (1984) that uncertainty over the causal powers of selection results from an overextension of Darwin's metaphor of the breeder, an analogy taken too literally. This is *selectional* teleology (e.g., "guiding": Stebbins, 1950; "scrutinizing": Darwin, 1859). Although distracting and easily avoidable, it presents no real problem. Unlike adaptational teleology, there does not appear to be a *reliance* upon it to explain evolution. If a statement containing selectional teleology is rewritten so as to have a mechanistic-causal format, there will be no loss of explanatory power. An example of this is rewriting "The jungle environment selected the tiger's camouflaging stripes" as "The camouflaging properties of the tiger's stripes contributed to the animal's survival from selection in the jungle environment."

The other loaded term is *adaptation*. It is very difficult to get away from this word's usual meaning of deliberate modification of a structure *for* some function. The issue is clouded further by the connotations produced by the use of the term adaptation to describe intragenerational adjustments to new conditions. The avoidance of teleology when using this term to study evolution is hampered by two aspects of neo-Darwinian theory.

The first is that selection/adaptation investigations pose a *third* and valid form of "what for" question. As noted by Brandon (1981), if adaptation results from selection among relative functional efficiencies, then the superior functionality of the survivors has to be part of the explanation for their existence. It is legitimate to ask "what for" questions about an adaptive structure's selected function and to give an answer of "for doing x" because the complete question is actually "*What* is the function of this structure that was selected *for* in the polymorphic stage?" This phraseology does contain selectional teleology, and it could be restated as "What is the function of this structure that produced a relative advantage during a period of selection?" but it is not future directed, in that it does not impart teleological causation to the processes that produced the polymorphism. This question and answer format is inappropriate for characters not acted upon by selection, for it is *only* when referring to the function of a character whose relative efficiency allowed survival from selection that the non-historical question of what something does has a valid connection to certain aspects of the historical question of how it came to be.

The delineation of these three types of "what for" questions appears to settle the disagreement between Brandon (1981) and Mayr (1961) over the acceptability of using such questions in biology. Brandon accepted them, Mayr rejected them. We suggest that Brandon was referring to the selection/adaptation form, while Mayr was referring to the historical func-tionalist form (see the section "A Comment on 'Why' Questions").

The second aspect of neo-Darwinian theory that leads to problems with the ambiguity of the term adaptation is that selection/adaptation "what for" questions deal with the *same* functional properties as do nonhistorical studies. As already noted, these nonhistorical studies have their own type of "what for" question and answer format, a format that *does* rely upon teleology, but only as an explanatory analogy. It is the failure to distinguish between these two types of questions, and the two types of answers they anticipate, that prevents recognition of the times when the existence of adaptation is used to explain the origin of organic form. It prevents sig-nals of the error of a top-down direction of explanation, of a loss of iso-morphism between theory and phenomena, and of an attempt to explain a lower level cause with an upper level effect. *These errors transform the acceptable teleology of the machine analogy in nonhistorical studies into the unacceptable adaptational teleology of historical functionalism.* The result is an explanation of the type "Character x evolved in order to adapt the or-ganism to condition y."

14.9 Ahistorical Perspectives

Neo-Darwinism is not the only explanatory framework dealing with evo-lution; it is simply the most prevalent. Another is that initiated by D'Arcy Thompson (1917), and recently expanded by Goodwin (1982), Webster and Goodwin (1982a,b), and others (e.g., Hughes and Lambert, 1984). It does not appear to encounter problems with teleology, at least as far as teleology induced by the theory's explanatory framework is concerned. (There is no defense against a teleology produced by a belief in cosmological purpose.) It avoids theory-induced teleology by concentrating on structure rather than function. It does this, however, by totally discounting history.

The above authors have argued against what they perceive to be the unique and contingent nature of historical events. They advocate the search for more lawlike, general causality in evolution, and suggest that it can be found in regular, time-independent forces affecting the structure of all physical objects (gravity, surface tension, diffusion constants, etc.). We refer to this view as *ahistorical structuralism* because of its active denial of the importance of historical phenomena. Supporters of this approach have tended to call it simply "structuralism"; Brooks and O'Grady (1986) referred to it as "nonhistorical structuralism," but that term is not precise enough for the present paper. Goodwin (1982) states the ahistorical structuralist viewpoint clearly when he argues for an abandonment of the genealogical concept of homology, and for the establishment of a taxonomy constructed like the periodic table of the elements. Groupings would be determined by contemporary physical properties alone, with no consideration of the order of historical appearance.

This approach does not at first appear to fit as smoothly into the organic causal hierarchy developed in this paper as does neo-Darwinian theory. This is because some of the forces with which ahistorical structuralism is concerned are, indeed, capable of "overriding" any historically accrued formative forces within organisms. But this simply amounts to recognizing that there are physical forces operating at a level more inclusive than that of biological systems. These are the teleomatic processes discussed earlier. Some teleomatic activities may be less restricted by their teleonomic context than others, and an expanded explanatory framework may be necessary to factor out these ahistorical contributions. Writers such as Alberch (1985) and Maynard Smith et al. (1985) address this point with their discussions of universal and local developmental constraints. A fuller synthesis of these ideas lies in the future. To this end, historically contingent events need not be seen as being incapable of acting as general causes.

Given that ahistorical structuralist arguments have primarily been directed at Darwinian and neo-Darwinian theory, it would appear that the reason a need was perceived for a dichotomy between historical and structural explanations was that in a theory utilizing natural selection as the explanation of first choice, historical events are indeed not associated with the causes of organic form or transformation. We noted earlier that as a proximate, among-system cause, natural selection can play a role in the *evolutionary history* of a lineage, but it cannot be incorporated into the *historical causality* of a lineage. The effects of natural selection are just that—effects; they are always contingent.

We suggest that a consideration of the manner in which teleomatic processes operate in a biological context eliminates the necessity for ahistorical structuralism to argue for a dichotomy between historical explanations and structural explanations. The biological context has come to exist through within-system causality involving the incorporation of ancestral contingent causality into the fixed, inherited causality of descendants. Biological "laws" of development can therefore arise from singular events. An example of this is the eucaryotic cell, a structure whose origin was a unique occurrence, but whose subsequent persistence has been expressed in Virchow's cell doctrine: *omnis cellula e cellula*. We put "law" in quotation marks here because such biological regularities are not spatio-temporally unrestricted, and are therefore not universal, as a natural law must be. Such regularities are, however, responsible for the production of organic form.

The ideas presented in this section can be illustrated with a graphic representation of the increase in the inherited information content of an evolving lineage over time (figure 14.7). The graph is empirically justified by analyses of entropic changes in open information systems (Brooks and Wiley, 1986; Brooks et al., 1984). The bottommost area contains those morphotypes that have actually existed. It is from *only* these organisms

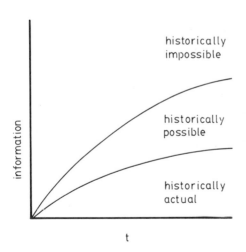

Figure 14.7
A characterization of different components of evolutionary dynamics in open information systems evolution. The bottom most area contains the historically actual: those organisms that have actually existed and reproduced. The middle area contains the historically possible: those organisms that could have existed had the appropriate matings taken place, as well as those organisms that did exist but never reproduced. The topmost area contains the historically impossible: those organic configurations that, although consistent with physical laws, have always been inaccessible because of the initial conditions established by the evolution of life on earth and the subsequent necessity for descendant order to come from ancestral order.

that subsequent organisms will evolve. All historical causality, therefore, comes from this area. The middle area of the graph contains those morpho-types that *could* have existed had the appropriate matings taken place. It also contains those organisms that did exist but died before they could re-produce and contribute to historical causality. This middle area is the re-mainder of morphospace. Finally, the topmost area of the graph contains those organic configurations that, although consistent with physical laws (e.g., silicon-based life), have always been inaccessible because of the *initial conditions* established by the evolution of life on earth and the subse-quent necessity of descendant order to come from ancestral order.

Ahistorical structuralism can be said not to recognize the top curve in figure 14.7. It does not distinguish between the historically possible and the historically impossible, for it is concerned only with general physical laws as they apply to any biological system, and not with the genealogies of particular organisms. On the other hand, historical functionalism can be said not to recognize the bottom curve in figure 14.7. It does not distin-guish between the historically possible and the historically actual. It tries to draw its explanatory power from the area of excluded morphotypes, in that it sees the forces that eliminated those forms as being responsible for the morphotypes that do exist. Only historical structuralism, as we have dis-cussed it in this paper, draws all of its explanatory power from those organisms, and those historically accrued causes that have actually existed, and have thus been in a position to be involved in changes in organic form. In this manner, historical structuralism (1) unites the historical and structural causality that ahistorical structuralism separates, (2) avoids the teleology that neo-Darwinism encounters through its reliance on functional criteria in historical explanations, and (3) deals with the evolutionary questions inaccessible to nonhistorical structuralist and functionalist studies.

14.10 A Comment on "Why" Questions

The recognition of the different types of biological questions with which this paper is concerned is made all the more difficult when the adverb "why" is used. Although questions are sometimes categorized according to the interrogative adverb they use, we suggest that there are no distinct classes of "what" questions, "how" questions, or "why" questions in biol-ogy. The form of the question sentence is more important than the adverb (table 14.1). The adverb "why" is problematic because the same sentence can be used to ask questions that anticipate nonhistorical, historical, adap-tational, or even teleological answers. For example, the question "Why do cats have fur?" can be answered with "Epidermal derivation," "Common inheritance from a mammalian ancestor," "Common inheritance from a mammalian ancestor whose fur gave it a relative functional advantage

Table 14.1
The language of evolutionary questions, as it pertains to the interrogative adverb used[a]

Type of process	Form of question
Nonhistorical	
Structural	What does it consist of
	How is it put together
Teleological	What is it for (a)
Functional	What does it do
	How does it work
Teleological	What is it for (a)
Historical generative	
Structural	What caused it to be
	How did it come to be
Functional	
Historical teleology	What did it originate for (b)
Evolutionary teleology	What did it evolve for (b)
Adaptational teleology	What did it evolve for (b)
Selectional eliminative	What was it selected for (c)

a. Note that there are three types of "what for" questions: (a) and (c) are acceptable, (b) is not. All of the processes can be addressed with the ambiguous "Why is it as it is?"

during a period of selection," or "So that they can keep warm." Mayr (1961) avoided this ambiguity by noting that the "why" questions of evolutionary (historical) biology—in contradistinction to the "how" questions of functional (nonhistorical) biology—should be taken to mean the mechanistic "how come," and not the finalistic "what for." We recommend our approach because it recognizes three types of "what for" questions—two of which are valid, one of which is not—and because it avoids the use of "why" questions altogether.

14.11 Summary and Conclusions

The causes responsible for the existence of an organism are interested in levels of generality. As specific configurations of physical elements, organisms are subject to general, physical causes, and then to particular, biological causes. Within this hierarchy are evolutionary causes that were once contingent for a particular species, but have subsequently been incorporated into the historical causality of its descendant species. This internesting of proximate and ultimate causality is best studied with a theory that appeals to similarly internested causes. The more general, historical causes have operative and thus logical priority over the less general causes.

The interactions of the structures in biological hierarchies produce functions that contribute to the survival of the organism. Organisms *must* function if they are to continue existing as organisms, rather than as collections of structured, but inanimate, matter. Function is an effect of structure. There can be structure without function, but no function without structure.

There are three types of end-attaining activity that can exist in biological systems: teleomatic, or end-resulting; teleonomic, or end-directed; and teleological, or goal-seeking. Organic functionality attains end-states, but these are not goals, and the functionality is not teleological.

A historical lineage of organisms persists over generations of teleonomic activity until teleomatic disruptions in species cohesion result in the evolution of new species with derived, but altered, structural properties. Function may change also, but this is not a necessary consequence. Teleomatic processes occur because of the physical properties of the matter constituting the organism, and not because of any effects they might have on the teleonomic system in which they take place.

At any point in this evolutionary process, natural selection can eliminate those organisms whose relative functional efficiency is inadequate for survival in their environment. Although it can become part of the evolutionary history of a lineage, selection acts as a proximate cause operating among organisms; it is not responsible for the within-organism historical causality that produces changes in organic form.

The resulting adaptation of the surviving organisms is an effect, not a cause, of their evolution. Only natural selection produces adaptation. An adaptive character is useful to the organism that possesses it, in that it has allowed survival of selection, but not all useful characters, no matter how indispensable to continued survival, are necessarily adaptations. Selection and adaptation are not necessary for the existence of functionality, usefulness, organization, or teleonomic activity.

Organisms can be studied from either a nonhistorical or a historical perspective. The first is interested in current properties, and does not ask where they came from. The second is interested in how organisms came to be. *Nonhistorical studies can be structuralist or functionalist*, and can ask mechanistic or teleological questions. The latter are a form of "what for" question, but the teleology creates no problems because it comes from a machine analogy and is not to be extended to historical explanations.

Historical structuralism is the term we give to the view advocated in this paper: Evolutionary change is structural change, with functional change coming afterwards, if at all. In no sense of the word does evolution occur *for* something; "what for" questions are not applicable in historical structuralism.

Historical functionalism is the result of attempting to use current functions to explain the origins of the structures that make those functions possible. This places effect before cause in the explanatory sequence, and produces an unacceptable teleology. This is adaptational teleology, and it has its own type of "what for" question: It asks "What did this evolve for?" and it answers "In order to adapt the organism to x."

Adaptational teleology is not the inevitable result of selection/ adaptation explanations, for such explanations are mechanistic as long as they are restricted to dealing with proximate among-system causality. Adaptational teleology is the result of improperly extending selection/ adaptation explanations to the realm of historical, more ultimate, within-system causality. The detection of adaptational teleology in evolutionary explanations is complicated by the use of a *third* type of "what for" question. This type is valid because it only addresses the reasons for a morph's survival from a period of selection. It is of the form "What function was this selected for?"

Each of the three types of "what for" questions is looking for a different kind of answer. Neo-Darwinian approaches encounter problems distinguishing these types of questions because, on the one hand, natural selection acts upon the *same* functional properties with which teleological nonhistorical studies deal, and, on the other hand, its explanatory framework does not include those causes responsible for the production and transformation of organic form. The recognition of these types of questions is made all the more difficult by the ambiguity produced with the use of the adverb "why."

Another evolutionary theory is that of *ahistorical structuralism*. In its search for more general causality in evolution, it argues for the importance of spatiotemporally unrestricted physical forces that operate on a broader level than that of just biological systems. We recognize these as teleomatic processes, and suggest that the contingent historical events that ahistorical structuralism rejects are those of the proximate among-system causality of natural selection. This dichotomy between historical explanation and structural explanation can be avoided by adopting a historical structuralist approach and thereby seeing that unique, contingent events occurring within an evolving lineage can become part of the fixed inherited historical causality of descendent organisms.

Acknowledgments

We thank Robert Brandon, John Collier, David Lambert, and Marjorie Grene for their comments on some of the ideas presented here. Maggie Hampong prepared the diagrams. The *Canadian Journal of Zoology* gave permission to reproduce figures 14.1–14.5. ROG thanks the MacMillean Family for fellowship support at the University of British Columbia. Research support was provided by operating grant A7696 to DRB from the Natural Sciences and Engineering Research Council of Canada.

Note

1. Neo-Darwinism is thus not a label that can applied to any evolutionary theory that recognizes natural selection *somewhere* in its framework. We suggest that the nature of a theory depends upon the way in which its components are structured, and not simply upon an enumeration of the components contained.

References

Alberch, P., 1985. Developmental constraints: why St. Bernards often have an extra digit and poodles never do. *Amer. Nat.* 126:430–433.

Ayala, F. J., 1976. Biology as an autonomous science. In *Topics in the Philosophy of Science*, vol. 27, M. Grene and E. Mendelsohn, eds., Boston: D. Reidel.

Bergson, H., 1911. *Creative Evolution*. Trans. Arthur Mitchell. New York: Henry Holt.

Bock, W. J., 1967. The use of adaptive characters in avian classification. *Proc. XIV Int. Ornith. Cong.*

Bock, W. J., 1979. A synthetic explanation of macroevolutionary change—a reductionist approach. *Bull. Carnegie Mus. Nat. Hist.* 13:20–69.

Bock, W. J., 1980. The definition and recognition of biological adaptation. *Amer. Zool.* 20:217–227.

Bowler, P. J., 1983. *The Eclipse of Darwinism*. Baltimore: Johns Hopkins University Press.

Brandon, R. N., 1981. Biological teleology: questions and explanations. *Stud. Hist. Phil. Sci.* 12:91–105.

Brooks, D. R., 1979a. Testing the context and extent of host-parasite coevolution. *Syst. Zool.* 28:299–307.

Brooks, D. R., 1979b. Testing hypotheses of evolutionary relationships among parasites: the digeneans of crocodilians. *Amer. Zool.* 19:1225–1238.

Brooks, D. R., 1980. Allopatric speciation and non-interactive parasite community structure. *Syst. Zool.* 29:192–203.

Brooks, D. R., 1981a. Hennig's parasitological method: a proposed solution. *Syst. Zool.* 30:229–249.

Brooks, D. R., 1981b. Review of Price, P. W., 1980. *Evolutionary Biology of Parasites*. Princeton: Princeton University Press. *Syst. Zool.* 30:104–106.

Brooks, D. R., 1986. Historical ecology: a new approach to studying the evolution of ecological associations. *Ann. Miss. Bot. Garden* 72:660–680.

Brooks, D. R., and C. Mitter, 1983. Analytic approaches to studying coevolution. In *Fungus-Insect Relationships*, Q. Wheeler and M. Blackwell, eds., New York: Columbia University Press.

Brooks, D. R., and R. T. O'Grady, 1986. Nonequilibrium thermodynamics and different axioms of evolution. *Acta Biotheoretica* 35:77–106.

Brooks, D. R., and E. O. Wiley, 1986. *Evolution as Entropy: Toward a Unified Theory of Biology.* Chicago: University of Chicago Press.

Brooks, D. R., P. H. Leblond, and D. D. Cumming, 1984. Information and entropy in a simple evolution model. *J. Theor. Biol.* 109:77–93.

Campbell, D. T., 1974. "Downward causation" in hierarchically organized biological systems. In *Studies in the Philosophy of Biology*, F. J. Ayala and T. Dobzhansky, eds., London: MacMillan.

Churchland, P. M., 1982. Is *thinker* a natural kind? *Dialogue* 21:223–238.

Collette, B. B., and J. L. Russo, 1985. Interrelationships of the Spanish mackerels (Pisces: Scombridae: *Scomberomorus*) and their copepod parasites. *Cladistics* 1:141–158.

Cressey, R. F., B. B. Collette, and J. L. Russo, 1983. Copepods and scombrid fishes: a study in host-parasite relationships. *Fish. Bull.* 81:227–265.

Darwin, C., 1859. *On the Origin of Species.* London: John Murray. (Republished 1958, New York: Mentor).

Darwin, F., 1959. *The Life and Letters of Charles Darwin*, vol. 2. New York: Basic Books.

Davies, B. D., 1961. The teleonomic significance of biosynthetic control mechanisms. *Cold Spring Harbor Symposium on Quantitative Biology* 26:1–10.

Dobson, F. S., 1985. The use of phylogeny in behavior and ecology. *Evolution* 39:1384–1388.

Dover, G. A., 1982a. A molecular drive through evolution. *Biosci.* 32:526–533.

Dover, G. A., 1982b. Molecular drive: a cohesive mode of species evolution. *Nature* 299:111–117.

Eigen, M., 1971. Self-organization of matter and the evolution of biological macromolecules. *Naturwissenschaften* 58:465–522.

Eldredge, N., 1985. *Unfinished Synthesis: Biological Hierarchies and Modern Evolutionary Thought.* New York: Oxford University Press.

Futuyma, D. J., 1984. Review of *Beyond Neo-Darwinism: An Introduction to the New Evolutionary Paradigm*, M. Ho, and P. T. Saunders, eds. Orlando: Academic Press. 1984. *Science* 226:532–533.

Goodwin, B. C., 1982. Development and evolution. *J. Theor. Biol.* 97:43–55.

Gould, S. J., and E. S. Vrba, 1982. Exaptation—a missing term in the science of form. *Paleobiol.* 8:4 15.

Gray, A., 1874. Scientific worthies. III. Charles Robert Darwin. *Nature* 10:79–81.

Hennig, W., 1966. *Phylogenetic Systematics.* Urbana: University of Illinois Press.

Hughes, A. J., and D. M. Lambert, 1984. Functionalism, structuralism, and "ways of seeing." *J. Theor. Biol.* 11:787–800.

Hull, D. L., 1973. *Darwin and His Critics.* Cambridge, MA: Harvard University Press.

Hull, D. L., 1983. Karl Popper and Plato's metaphor. In *Advances in Cladistics*, vol. 2, N. I. Platnick and V. A. Funk, eds., New York: Columbia University Press.

Jaki, S. L., 1966. *The Relevance of Physics*. Chicago: University of Chicago Press.

Jamieson, I. G., 1986. The functional approach to behavior: is it useful? *Amer. Nat.* 127:195–208.

Kettlewell, H. B. D., 1955. Selection experiments on industrial melanism in the Lepidoptera. *Heredity* 9:323–342.

Kettlewell, H. B. D., 1961. Geographical melanism in the Lepidoptera of Shetland. *Heredity* 16:393–402.

Kettlewell, H. B. D., 1965. Insect survival and selection for pattern. *Science* 148:1290–1296.

Kimura, M., and T. Ohta, 1971. *Theoretical Aspects of Population Genetics*. Princeton: Princeton University Press.

King, J. L., and T. H. Jukes, 1969. Non-Darwinian evolution: random fixation of selectively neutral mechanisms. *Science* 164:788–798.

Lagerspetz, K., 1959. Teleological explanations and terms in biology. *Ann. Zool. Soc. Vanamo* 19:1–73.

Lauder, G. V., 1981. Form and function: structural analysis in evolutionary morphology. *Paleobiol.* 7:430–442.

Lauder, G. V., 1982. Historical biology and the problem of design. *J. Theor. Biol.* 97:57–67.

Lewontin, R. C., 1980. Adaptation. *Encyclopedia Einaudi*. Milan. (Reprinted 1984 in *Conceptual Issues in Evolutionary Biology*, E. Sober, ed., Cambridge, MA: MIT Press.)

MacLeod, R. B., 1957. Teleology and theory of human behavior. *Science* 125:477.

Maynard Smith, J., R. Burian, S. Kauffman, P. Alberch, J. Campbell, B. Goodwin, R. Lande, D. Raup, and L. Wolpert, 1985. Developmental constraints and evolution. *Quart. Rev. Biol.* 60:265–287.

Mayr, E., 1961. Cause and effect in biology. *Science* 134:1501–1506.

Mayr, E., 1974. Teleological and teleonomic, a new analysis. In *Methodological and Historical Essays in the Natural and Social Sciences*, vol. 14, R. S. Cohen and M. W. Wartofsky, eds., Boston: Reidel.

Mitter, C., and D. R. Brooks, 1983. Phylogenetic aspects of coevolution. In *Coevolution*, D. J. Futuyma and M. Slatkin, eds., Sunderland, MA: Sinauer Associates.

O'Grady, R. T., 1984. Evolutionary theory and teleology. *J. Theor. Biol.* 107:563–578.

O'Grady, R. T., 1986. Historical processes, evolutionary explanations, and problems with teleology. *Can. J. Zool.* 64:1010–1020.

Paterson, H. E. H., 1980. A comment on "mate recognition systems." *Evolution* 34:330–331.

Paterson, H. E. H., 1981. The continuing search for the unknown and unknowable: a critique of contemporary ideas on speciation. *South African J. Sci.* 77:113–119.

Paterson, H. E. H., 1982. Perspective on speciation by reinforcement. *South African J. Sci.* 78:53–57.

Petersen, A. F., 1983. On downward causation in biological and behavioural systems. *History and Philosophy of the Life Sciences* 5:69–86.

Pittendrigh, C. S., 1958. Adaptation, natural selection and behavior. In *Behavior and Evolution*, A. Roe and G. G. Simpson, eds., New Haven: Yale University Press.

Quinn, J. F., and A. E. Dunham, 1983. On hypothesis testing in ecology and evolution. *Amer. Nat.* 122:602–617.

Roughgarden, J., 1983. Competition and theory in community ecology. *Amer. Nat.* 122: 583–601.

Russell, E. S., 1916. *Form and Function*. London: John Murray. (Republished 1982, Chicago: University of Chicago Press.)

Simberloff, D., 1983. Competition theory, hypothesis-testing, and other community ecological buzzwords. *Amer. Nat.* 122:626–635.

Simpson, G. G., 1958. Behavior and evolution. In *Behavior and Evolution*, A. Roe and G. G. Simpson, eds., New Haven: Yale University Press.

Smith, R. J., 1982. On the mechanical reduction of function and morphology. *J. Theor. Biol.* 96:99–106.

Stebbins, G. L., Jr., 1950. *Variation and Evolution in Plants*. New York: Columbia University Press.

Strong, D. R., 1983. Natural variability and the manifold mechanisms of ecological communities. *Amer. Nat.* 122:636–660.

Thompson, D'Arcy, 1917. *On Growth and Form*. Cambridge: Cambridge University Press.

van der Steen, W. J., 1983. Methodological problems in evolutionary biology II. Appraisal of arguments against adaptationism. *Acta Biotheoretica* 32:217–222.

van der Steen, W. J., and B. Voorzanger, 1984. Methodological problems in evolutionary biology III. Selection and levels of organization. *Acta Biotheoretica* 33:203–213.

von Bertalanffy, L., 1962. *Modern Theories of Development*. New York: Harper.

Vrba, E. S., and N. Eldredge, 1984. Individuals, hierarchies and processes: towards a more complete evolutionary theory. *Paleobiol.* 10:146–171.

Webster, G. C., and B. C. Goodwin, 1982a. History and structure in biology. In *Towards a Liberatory Biology*, S. Rose, ed., London: Allison and Busby.

Webster, G. C., and B. C. Goodwin, 1982b. The origin of species: a structuralist approach. *J. Social Biol. Struct.* 5:15–47.

Wicken, J. S., 1981a. Causal explanations in classical and statistical thermodynamics. *Phil. Sci.* 48:65–77.

Wicken, J. S., 1981b. Evolutionary self-organization and the entropy principle: teleology and mechanism. *Nature and System* 3:129–141.

Wicken, J. S., 1985. Thermodynamics and the conceptual structure of evolutionary theory. *J. Theor. Biol.* 117:363–383.

Williams, G. C., 1966. *Adaptation and Natural Selection*. Princeton: Princeton University Press.

15

Consequences of Nonequilibrium Thermodynamics for the Darwinian Tradition

David J. Depew and Bruce H. Weber

15.1 Introduction

The neo-Darwinian or Synthetic Theory of Evolution restored the Darwinian tradition in evolutionary biology to primacy after its eclipse, and near demise, in the last decades of the nineteenth and the first decades of the twentieth centuries. Actually, neo-Darwinism has been rightly construed more as a treaty than a theory, because it laid down terms that allowed evolutionists and practitioners of the new science of genetics (and more generally molecular biology) to work together under common presuppositions. Evolutionists, in repudiation of their earlier flirtations with Lamarckism, accepted Weismannism; while geneticists, abandoning stress on macromutations, accepted the gradualist assumptions of the Darwinian tradition (Mayr and Provine, 1980). What made these agreements possible was a common analytical framework based on the amplification of Mendel's Rules to the level of populations by way of the Hardy-Weinberg Equilibrium Formula, according to which gene frequencies could be presumed to remain the same over successive generations unless and until exogenous forces caused one genetic variant to be preferred to another.

Within this framework many different explanatory scenarios were available. For, among other things, the forces that cause gene frequency changes were, at first, thought to be many and various. Eventually, however, most neo-Darwinists came to believe that natural selection was the preeminent cause of the spread of variants through populations. Neglect of such forces as genetic drift (and, in Sewell Wright's work, its complex interactive relationship with natural selection) led to what Stephen Jay Gould has perspicuously called "the hardening of the modern synthesis" into its markedly adaptationist canonical form by the 1950s (Gould, 1983).

In the last decade, however, neo-Darwinism, especially of the 'hardened' sort, has come under stress. It appears to be facing anomalies at a faster rate than it can absorb them, revealing in the process the inherent fragility of the Synthesis itself, and raising the spectre that the entire Darwinian tradition may be becoming what Lakatos has called a "degenerating research programme" (Lakatos, 1970).

In the following pages we shall review some of these anomalies, and how neo-Darwinists have responded to the challenges posed by them. These responses divide, roughly, into the conservative and progressive. Conservatives argue that new results are *consistent* with neo-Darwinist principles and so call for no conceptual innovations to accommodate new empirical findings. Progressives have asked for an 'expanded synthesis' that attempts to reaccommodate a wide variety of evolutionary processes into a new conceptual framework. This framework is to be based on the idea that there is a plurality of biological units and levels at which and between which such processes can act (cf. Eldredge, 1985). In Lakatos' language, this conceptual revision attempts to preserve the 'core' of the Darwinian tradition by abandoning or modifying certain assumptions hitherto associated with it, but only contingently—notably its preference for gradualism, its stress on natural selection to the exclusion of other processes, its tendency to restrict selection to the level of the individual organism, its Malthusianism, and its penchant for adaptationist arguments.

While we applaud the innovations suggested by proponents of the expanded synthesis, our own concern is to propose that these advances can best be understood, and further advances fostered, by seeing them in terms of what we shall call 'background assumptions' deriving from nonequilibrium thermodynamics and information theory. We thus recommend taking some distance from the Darwinian tradition's historical reliance, at tacit levels of its conceptual structure, on equilibrium models of systems-dynamics. Our view is (a) that nonequilibrium models can provide a set of principles showing why the evolution of biological systems is something to be expected, rather than something that needs to be explained against a theoretical background that does not strongly anticipate it; (b) that such systems will naturally organize themselves into a complex pattern of 'units' and 'levels' of selection as they evolve toward enhanced and more efficient energy flows through them; and (c) that as biological systems evolve they will tend to form the diachronic branching patterns that are observed in phylogeny.

It would certainly be wrong to think that the full power of the nonequilibrium approach to evolutionary theory has been realized by those whose work already reflects this perspective. Still, that body of work is already significant and suggestive enough to permit a provisional review of its results, and to allow us to ask what the larger implications would be if it were successfully pursued further. It is worth asking, for example, whether its results would be continuous in an important way with the Darwinian tradition, or would render that tradition a historical relic. It is also worth inquiring how such an approach would affect relations between physical theory and biology, on the one hand, and biology and social theory on the other. We close with a few reflections on these issues.

15.2 Neo-Darwinism and Its Anomalies

As they come to be developed and articulated in and through a sequence of related research programs and their associated theories, research traditions encounter anomalies. In a familiar but limited sense an anomaly arises when an empirical fact fails to be deducible or predictable from an accepted system of theoretical relationships, together with what appears to be a reasonable set of auxiliary hypotheses. In a slightly wider sense, which we shall employ, anomalies are any results at odds with and unexpected by current understanding. Thus understood, anomalies arise not only when empirical data are at variance with received conceptual structures and auxiliary assumptions, but also when internal difficulties emerge within those conceptual structures and when there exists inadequate coherence between a given research program or theory and other relevant programs, theories, and assumptions within its milieu.[1]

When a research tradition has been and continues to be successful in articulating theories that organize a significant amount of information about the world, in generating and solving new research puzzles, and in resolving and absorbing significant anomalies by revised theorizing, there is little anxiety about the occurrence of anomalies, especially of the conceptual sort. There is faith that they will be successfully dealt with or can be safely ignored as irrelevant. That a program enters a 'degenerating' phase means just that its fecundity in the problem solving activities that Kuhn calls 'normal science,' and its ability to generate improved theoretical structures, fails to keep pace with the rate at which new anomalies appear. Attention is then, at first quite reluctantly, drawn to conceptual choices and to background assumptions deeply, but sometimes contingently, associated with the tradition, as well as to the cultural milieu within which the tradition is set, where these conceptual difficulties are thought to have their origin. If new developments and explanatory models drawn from fields earlier thought to be irrelevant come to be regarded as having a bearing on these problems, and if these developments and models are themselves thought to be less affected by problematic conceptual commitments, they may lead, eventually, to the abandonment not only of specific theories and research programs, but, in extreme cases, of an entire tradition of scientific thought.

In the last twenty years, neo-Darwinism has come under increasing pressure from a variety of anomalies arising both in fields that have been deeply affected by the Synthesis, such as systematics, biogeography, and paleontology, and in fields, such as developmental biology and molecular genetics, that were never fully integrated into the Synthesis. Relatedly, a new flurry of philosophical activity has raised concerns about conceptual difficulties in the neo-Darwinian research program. In our brief review, we shall concentrate on the following classes of anomalies: (1) the relation of theories of the origin of life to neo-Darwinism; (2) neutral molecular evolution; (3) the degree of polymorphism in populations; (4) the complex structure of the genome; (5) multilevel selection; (6) the punctuated pattern of the paleontological record; and (7) certain conceptual difficulties that have continued to plague Darwinism over the years.

To the extent that neo-Darwinism has concerned itself with the origin of life, it has envisioned the fundamental problem as discovering how reliable replicators could evolve without requiring already evolved enzymatic machinery, and how such machinery develops given the prior existence of replicators. Eigen's (Eigen and Schuster, 1979, 1982) concept of a 'hypercycle' has been suggestive in organizing research programs in this area, but where external selective forces are thought to be needed to get greater replicative fidelity among 'naked replicators' the problem can become intractable. For what seems required are catalytic agents whose existence depends on the very replicators whose fidelity is in question. Elaborate 'bootstrapping' mechanisms have been postulated to overcome this difficulty, but none with sufficient persuasiveness.

Findings from molecular genetics have produced even more problematical anomalies. Contrary to expectations, extensive variation has been observed in sequences of proteins and nucleic acids. Much of that variation is plausibly interpretable as synonymous and selectively neutral (Kimura, 1983) and as consistent with a 'molecular clock' that fixes variation on a schedule not well correlated with environmental change (Li et al., 1985). In that case, much evolution *at the molecular level* would appear to represent stable, predictable rates of fixation of neutral mutations rather than the action of natural selection in accord with environmental contingencies.

Electrophoretic studies (Lewontin, 1974; Selander and Whittam, 1983) have, moreover, shown extensive enzyme polymorphism in natural populations to a degree unanticipated by neo-Darwinism and not readily explainable in terms of selectionist or adaptationist principles.

Further, structural and molecular genetic studies have shown in recent years that the genome is not just a string of independently assorting genes. Genes have a complex internal structure. They are, for example, often arranged in 'multigene families' that give rise to a variety of non-Mendelian phenomena (Campbell, 1982, 1985). For instance, genes can exhibit 'molecular drive' (Dover, 1982), ramifying copies of themselves throughout the genome in defiance of Mendel's Laws, resulting in the spread and persistence of traits for which there has been no selection.

The complex regulatory patterns of gene expression in development—a field more or less marginalized by the Synthesis—seem reflective of similar endogenous imperatives. Developmental stability restricts the hand of variation and thus biases its subsequent pattern of distribution (Maynard Smith et al., 1985). Regulatory gene systems seem, moreover, to maintain generic patterns over phylogenetic time that are buffered from selective pressures (Kauffman, 1985). In view of these facts, explanations bearing on the evolution of the regulation of gene expression might sometimes be more informatively given by noting such biases and constraints rather than by citing whatever selective processes, if any, are in operation.

More generally, once it is admitted from a philosophical point of view that successful explanations are relative both to the kind of question asked (Brandon, 1981), and to a determinate space of alternative possibilities (Garfinkel, 1981), the existence of nonselective processes for fixing variants, as well as patterns of internal constraint, suggest that evolutionary explanations cannot always be ascribed solely, or even preferably, to summing over a large number of independent selective events. Sometimes citing background pattern is more properly explanatory than citing a foreground of selective events treated as antecedent efficient causes (Goodwin, 1984; Webster, 1984).

These new developments have affected debate about the idea that selection might operate on biological entities other than individual organisms, such as demes and even species. Lewontin and Dunn (1960) presented empirical evidence some time ago for group selection of this sort in at least one case. Since then a number of theorists, including philosophers interested in the logic of evolutionary arguments, have defended the conceptual possibility of multilevel selection, especially if the objects on which selection works are treated as 'individual' systems and not as classes (Hull, 1976, 1978; cf. Brandon and Burian, 1984, for a review of the literature). Bound together by genetic linkages rather than by a list of necessary and sufficient properties, species in this sense might function as entities on which selective pressures and other evolutionary 'forces' can be brought to bear, and hence as 'units of selection.'

Revelation of the complex internal structure of the genome has begun to suggest *how and why* selection might occur at and across any number of biological levels. Where functional stability is assured by internal constraints, the dominant action of selection can be shifted to a different level. At levels protected by constraints, variation can accumulate unimpeded; selection, meanwhile, will operate wherever a source of variation is open to its action. The interanimation of the 'units of selection' theme with the discovery of endogenous genomic constraints constitutes the heart of the call for an expanded synthesis (Gould, 1982a; Eldredge, 1985).

Meanwhile, paleontologists have presented neo-Darwinism with another set of anomalies. 'Punctuated equilibrium' is a term used to describe patterns of long 'stasis' and 'sudden' change observed in the fossil record (Eldredge and Gould, 1972; Gould and Eldredge, 1977). Not only are such patterns unanticipated by the gradualist assumptions of neo-Darwinism, but neo-Darwinians have been inclined to explain them away as due to imperfections in the fossil record. However, the new molecular genetics continues to draw attention to the idea of punctuated equilibrium because, with its stress on internal constraints, molecular genetics keeps adducing results that seem consistent on their face with the expectation that there might well be, in many cases, an alternation between periods of stability and of sudden change.

In this context, it was inevitable that conceptual difficulties in the Darwinian tradition would once more come into view. Complaints about the tautological emptiness of the concept of fitness have been raised again. They have been plausibly answered by appealing to the relative adaptedness of traits in relation to a specified environment as the cause of differential fitness (Brandon, 1978). Yet this defense has become attractive to neo-Darwinians at the very time when the role of nonadaptationist constraints is also coming to the fore, and when eminent neo-Darwinians themselves have grown suspicious of the sort of adaptationist arguments that are common in sociobiology. This puts a great, and potentially unsustainable, burden on adaptationist arguments to be more than "'just so' stories." If they cannot be, the threat of explanatory emptiness raises its head once more (Gould and Lewontin, 1979).

When a strongly adaptationist approach is taken, it is inevitable that differences between evolutionary explanations and explanations in the physical sciences will be stressed (cf. Mayr, 1985; Brandon, 1978). For adaptationist arguments do not figure at all in the 'teleomatic' fields explored by physics and chemistry. Yet adaptationist-inspired defenses of the 'autonomy' of evolutionary biology, such as those offered by Mayr, seem to conflict with the expectation that as sciences progress their links with one another will grow increasingly close—even if it is well conceded that these links do not move in the reductionistic direction once anticipated by the positivist *conception* of the unity of science (cf. Darden and Maull, 1977). Thus the 'autonomy of biology' stance no longer has the attractiveness it once had in the light of continued revelations from molecular biology—and, as contributors to this volume suggest, from the study of systems operating far from thermodynamic equilibrium. (Cf. Rosenberg, 1985, for a view in which facts coming from molecular biology lead to a considerably chastened autonomism.)

In the light of these general considerations, yet another question acquires particular importance. How is it that the inherently reversible processes leading to changed gene frequencies lead not only to irreversible speciation, but also to the ordered complexification of life forms over geological time, as manifested in such regularities as Dollo's Law? Are not constraints at and perhaps above the species level the source of such phylogenetic patterns? And might not the explanatory role of constraint and stable structure rest ultimately on the operation of physical laws at the macroevolutionary scale rather than on the accumulation of small, inherently reversible microevolutionary changes in populations?

15.3 Conservative Responses to Neo-Darwinism's Anomalies

Neo-Darwinians are not incapable of making reasoned responses to these new developments. With respect to the alleged molecular clock, for example, it can and has been argued that the phenomenon of regularity is only apparent—an artifact, in effect, of measuring over inappropriate time frames (Stebbins and Ayala, 1981). Similar arguments have been deployed against those who would draw radical conclusions from an alleged fact of punctuated equilibrium: A paleontologist's evolutionary instants may be quite enough time to accommodate a population geneticist's gradualism (Ayala, 1985).

Arguments such as these are 'conservative' in the sense that they do not acknowledge the validity of apparently anomalous findings. Increasingly, however, arguments of this sort have been replaced by acknowledging the phenomena in question and then accommodating them to the received theory. The simplest way to do this is to postulate selectionist forces to account for apparently nonselectionist phenomena. For example, the existence of an unanticipated degree of genetic polymorphism can be accommodated by postulating mechanisms such as 'balancing selection,' in which polymorphism is retained in an evolutionary strategy that is stable over changing environments (Ayala, 1982; Stebbins and Ayala, 1985).

But there are risks in doing this. For explanations that have an open-ended recourse to auxiliary hypotheses in order to square new facts with old theories (such as those that arose in profusion during the last phases of the Ptolemaic tradition in astronomy) can easily appear jury-rigged and cumbersome. When this perception is current, almost any rival research program that emerges can gain support if it appears to reduce what we wish to call the 'explanatory burden' that is borne by any theory relying heavily on the use of new auxiliary assumptions to square the theory with facts not initially predicted by it. In the absence of independent empirical proofs in their favor—proofs that rebut a strong presumption against them—such arguments will be judged ad hoc, ex post facto, and ultimately question-begging.[2]

In the present case, mechanisms like 'balancing selection' constitute auxiliary hypotheses that are certainly consistent with the theoretical assumptions of the neo-Darwinian research program, but do not flow naturally from these assumptions, were not anticipated from them, and have been invoked only after anomalous facts have made their appearance. Such devices neither add new confirmations to the theory to which they are added, showing its fecundity, nor explain anything more than the mere *possibility* that the phenomena in question are the result of selection. Arguments with this low a degree of modal strength will be acceptable only *faut de mieux*. They thus bear a 'high explanatory burden' that will lead workers to prefer rival accounts when these do not appear to rest so heavily on arbitrary assumptions.

Recently defenders of the adequacy of the current neo-Darwinian scheme have been inclined to admit both the existence of certain apparently anomalous phenomena and the fact that they may not be *directly* due to selective forces. They stress that the Synthesis had been prepared to acknowledge such phenomena from the outset (Stebbins and Ayala, 1985). Arguments employing this strategy get their power by appropriating weapons forged originally by their opponents: The 'hardened' version of the Synthesis, it is now said, was either a misunderstanding or a deviation, as proponents of an expanded synthesis had maintained, and its original plasticity is capable of accommodating new empirical findings without requiring conceptual revision. All that is insisted on is that natural selection has a *heuristic or presumptive* primacy in evolutionary explanations: Alternative explanations can be admitted only when selectionist arguments fail, and only after it has been inquired whether the phenomena in question might play an indirect role in selection.

Arguments of this sort often prove successful. But they receive a potential challenge from the discovery of internal structure within the genome. Internal structure allows for the accumulation of noncoding DNA and for the proliferation of gene copies through the genome, independently of selection. Moreover, it puts severe constraints on the production of variation, biasing its distribution from the outset. It also constricts the pathways down which and around which natural selection can operate. Until recently, neo-Darwinians professed to be indifferent to such facts because they treated the internal structure of the genetic system as a 'black box,' whose precise mechanisms it was left to biochemists to discover. The results of these inquiries, they were convinced, could not call into question already established principles (Ayala, 1985). Recent developments, however, make that no longer a tenable position. Defenders of the adequacy of the Synthesis are now inclined to affirm, therefore, that these phenomena are real. However, their presumption that the effects of internal structure are in most cases secondary or peripheral—a presumption that underlies the belief that 'heuristic' primacy should still be accorded to natural selection—no longer appears, in the light of these admissions, to have sufficient force. For admitting the facts revealed by molecular genetics entails that an indefinite number of evolutionary explanations depend on combining pathway constraints with variation driven by means that escape sorting into Mendelian ratios, with little or no reference to selection. If it can be shown that important facts about evolution flow naturally from combinations of such processes, then the primacy of selection, even if it is merely heuristic, appears not only an empty insistence, but a procedural recommendation that might actually retard fruitful inquiry. For a strong presumption in favor of the primacy of selection can, in fact, give rise to at least one serious sort of conceptual error. Once constraints are admitted on selectionist processes, one can *always* ascribe what one actually sees, as distinct from what one would have predicted on selectionist criteria alone, to deviations caused by these very constraints. Arguments like these appear to succeed without any independent checks: All observed effects are (always) the result of selection doing the best it can. But such explanations are actually empty and give, therefore, false comfort. (Cf. Schwartz, 1986, for a summary of this objection in the case of sociobiology.)

15.4 Radical Responses to Neo-Darwinism's Anomalies

One radical way of defending selectionist and adaptationist accounts in the face of the anomalies we have been discussing has been proposed by Richard Dawkins (1976, 1982). In Dawkins' theory, stress on maximization of the individual's interests in a world of scarcity—an idea deeply associated with traditional Darwinian thinking but threatened by current findings—is preserved by making one major conceptual revision in current theory: The level at which selection occurs is not that of the individual organism but that of particular stretches of genetic material. 'Selfish genes' in this sense can be presumed to spread themselves through the genome and to persist there in the absence of competition. Those that flourish are those whose mere persistence and multiplication is consistent with an internal drive toward self-proliferation, or, more frequently, those that code for phenotypic properties enhancing their proliferation. In this view, organisms are merely the means genes use to perpetuate copies of themselves when that tendency would otherwise be threatened. All higher level biological structures presumably bear the same utilitarian relationship to their genes at ever further removes.

This theory can account on its face for the proliferation of noncoding DNA within the genome and for extensive polymorphism without having to invoke any special auxiliary hypotheses. Thus part of its appeal is its capacity to reduce the explanatory burden borne by orthodox neo-Darwinism in relation to several classes of anomalies. It also provides foundations for the appeal to 'kin selection' that sociobiologists rely on to account for phenomena such as altruism, which is difficult to explain on the basis of classical Darwinian organismic selection.

Dawkins' approach is, however, less successful in dealing with evolutionary constraints on selection. Its basic principles involve a radical affirmation of the preference for atomistic and reductionistic ontological assumptions that has characterized much of the Darwinian tradition. Higher level structures are assumed, in that tradition, to have few or no constraining effects on lower levels. On the contrary, they are presumed to take hold only insofar as they facilitate and enhance the autonomous activity of lower level entities. Dawkins' theory features an appeal to this conceptual assumption stronger even than Williams' use of it to undo certain versions of group selection (Williams, 1966). But these very assumptions have been rendered dubious in the light of the existence of internal constraints, the possibility of multilevel selection, and doubts that have been cast on 'just so' adaptationist stories—against temptations to which Dawkins' proposal, no less than the version of sociobiology that sometimes relies on it, has few easy defenses. Thus even if Dawkins' theory proves to be internally coherent (cf. Brandon, 1985, for a strong argument that it is not) and modestly fecund, a cost will have been paid for retaining aspects of traditional Darwinian thinking—its stress on atomistic self-interest, on Malthusian competition, and on treating organisms merely as decomposible collections of traits—which grow increasingly anomalous in the light of current discoveries about genome complexity and constraint. It is hard, in the end, to escape the conclusion that the conceptual revision proposed by Dawkins invites us to maintain a particular world-view more surely than it proposes a hypothesis aimed at reducing the explanatory burdens currently borne by neo-Darwinism.

Contrasting, but no less radical, conceptual revisions have been proposed by a number of eminent paleontologists, including Niles Eldredge, Stephen Jay Gould, and Stephen Stanley. These advocates of a punctuated macroevolutionary pattern have sought to find an explanation for phylogenetic pattern in genetic changes with large effects. Even if they were to concede what Ayala and Stebbins have long maintained, and what others appear to have confirmed—that the mathematical models of standard population genetics can be made to accommodate such phenomena—these workers argue that what is required in evolutionary theory is an explanation of these phenomena that goes beyond the mere affirmation of consistency with current theory. They demand to know precisely *why* this pattern of speciation and phylogeny might have been *expected* in the light of new facts and more powerful theorizing. These demands put constraints on the range of means that can be used legitimately to reduce explanatory burdens. Realistic causal mechanisms are called for rather than appearance-saving auxiliary hypotheses.

The paleontologists' proposed account is based, in the first instance, on their sympathetic view of the hypothesis that selection can, *in principle*, act at a number of levels and on and for the sake of a wide variety of units or 'individuals' within the biological hierarchy—on demes and species as well as on organisms, and even (as Dawkins has proposed) on and for the sake of autonomously replicating genes. Gould (1983) has, for example, tried to show that in the early days of the Synthesis, it was possible for Sewell Wright to postulate interdemic selection, but that as the Synthesis hardened this essentially hierarchical notion was abandoned in favor of the individual organism as the privileged unit and beneficiary of selection. In arguing for a renewal of these inspired beginnings, Gould (1982a,b,c) assigns a key role to genomic constraints, particularly on the developmental sequences conrolled by regulatory genes.

Constraints can allow variation at a lower level—for example, the level of amino acid substitutions in protein evolution—to accumulate without immediately affecting higher level structure or function. Such a view can account for the prevalence of neutralism at functional levels deeply embedded within stable structures. At a higher level, this approach might also render less problematic the greater degree of polymorphism found among populations than can be accommodated by standard neo-Darwinism. Populations might have a relative ontological autonomy that protects individual organisms from selective pressures and thus allows polymorphism to accumulate. In this event, what Dawkins ascribes to the selfishness of genes would be due rather to a tolerance for the accumulation of variation in gene pools permitted by higher level structures. Genomic constraints would presumably also explain the persistence of *Bauplaene* over phylogenetic time, and hence the stasis that these paleontologists find in the fossil record.

To this general picture is added a preferred mechanism for initiating change that comes from recent work in developmental genetics. Speciation would occur as a result largely of sudden changes in the timing of regulatory genetic systems (Gould, 1982c). Lewontin's description of evolution as a way in which natural selection must find devious ways around constraints is then invoked to suggest that natural selection might be deflected onto the level of species. Relatively common and directionless with respect to phylogenetic pattern, speciation can be treated as a source of variation, the ultimate fate of which is determined by characteristics properly ascribable to the clade within which these speciation events occur. The pattern of macroevolution would be greatly affected, then, by the relative success of some lineages in fostering greater rates of speciation or lower extinction rates—and not, as in classical and modern Darwinism, because of the greater selective advantage possessed by individual organisms over a long period of time.

The strength of this program lies in the fact that it validates the increasingly accepted principle that the biological world is both complex and, in some sense, hierarchical. Its weakness, however, is that it does not give a fully satisfactory account of *why* we might have *expected* the biological world to be structured this way, *why* selection operates on and across all levels, and *why* we might have *presumed* that such systems will evolve over time in the pattern and tempo that they do. The result of this failure to meet its own criterion of success is that the expanded synthesis is no more immune to potentially question-begging arguments than are the programs it has criticized, and so carries with it a rather explanatory burden of its own. The greater range of possible evolutionary scenarios that its more complex general hypothesis allows must, Gould has acknowledged, be brought to the study of particular cases in a pragmatic, rather than a hypothetical-deductive, spirit. But perhaps this very openness allows the investigator to move too easily from one hypothesis to another when difficulties arise, just as rigid adaptationists can move from one 'just so' story to another. The fact that the investigator acknowledges that the search must be for 'robust theorems' (Levins, 1966) that are not artifacts of the modeling process itself is no guarantee that this will occur in practice.

This situation would be improved considerably if a set of principles could be adduced that show why we might have expected, *on highly general grounds,* the biological world to look and behave the way proponents of an expanded synthesis say it does. For such principles might at the same time suggest a series of *general* constraints to which all evolutionary processes must conform. Revelation of such constraints would go a long way toward limiting and providing checks on the potentially empty proliferation of evolutionary scenarios that has thus far haunted the Darwinian tradition. Our own hypothesis is that a highly relevant set of such principles and constraints can be found in the thermodynamics of complex, far-from-equilibrium systems, among which we count all biological systems, from the ecological to the organismic level. Locating many of the insistences of the expanded synthesis within such a perspective will reduce considerably the explanatory burden currently borne by that program, and will provide a new way of looking at the Darwinian tradition as a whole.

15.5 Equilibrium versus Nonequilibrium Background Assumptions

The fact that nonequilibrium thermodynamical principles have not hitherto been invoked as an appropriate backing for an expanded synthesis is due in large measure, we believe, to a historically contingent preference of the Darwinian tradition for background assumptions deriving from models of systems dynamics in which impinging 'forces' disturb an assumed equilibrium in order to account for change. Our first task, therefore, will be to give a brief exegesis of the notion of 'background assumption.' We shall go on to contrast equilibrium and nonequilibrium background assumptions. We shall then return to our main theme—why, and to some degree how, nonequilibrium assumptions provide theoretical backing for an expanded evolutionary synthesis and thereby lower the explanatory burden borne by its proposals.

The role of background assumptions in theories derives from the now commonly acknowledged fact that theories are underdetermined by evidence. No theory, however powerful, can attain the ideal once proposed by Logical Empiricists: that there would be nothing in its conceptual structure except the definitions and logical operations required correctly to deduce and predict the data in the domain of the theory. Rather, connections between facts and generalizations are mediated by several sorts of *interpretive schemata*. These include both models and what we are calling background assumptions. Models allow particular ranges of data to be interpreted in terms of a theory by specifying initial and boundary conditions. Background assumptions operate further up in the structure of the theory, serving to provide interpretive schemata to the theoretical structure itself by giving general characterizations of the system whose type the theory is presumed to exemplify. Background assumptions enable us to "explain … empirical problems by 'reducing' them to the ontology of the research tradition" (Laudan, 1977, p. 79). For the fact is that not every conceptual commitment of a scientific theory is fully explicit. Behind its more overt assumptions often lie tacit commitments to highly generalized pictures of 'the way things are.' We call such commitments background assumptions.

A theory, having proven successful in one domain of inquiry, often spreads to others, and eventually to a whole culture, forming its peculiar kind of 'common sense' and coming therefore to constrain the sorts of explanations that that culture regards as plausible. When a theory that has proven fruitful in one domain is extended to another, this is accomplished by showing that background assumptions obtaining in the first domain also successfully characterize the second—that is, that entities in the new domain have the general characteristics of those in the primary one, and therefore that the laws governing both classes are either materially the same or formally similar. In the first case we may speak of a 'reduction' of the second to the first theory. This is a comparatively rare achievement. More frequently, laws similar to those obtaining in the first domain can be devised for the new one on the assumption that both systems are of the same *type* and thus have the same background assumptions at a higher logical level. A simple example is the transfer of the background assumptions of Newtonian mechanics to market economics, with the result that the laws of economics were rendered more or less analogous to those of Newtonian physics.

That Adam Smith accomplished this extension of Newtonian background assumptions to economics is well known. It has been less frequently acknowledged, however, that Darwin accomplished something like the same thing for evolutionary biology. Darwin's work, on its theoretical side, is perspicuously, though imperfectly, describable as an attempt to extend the Newtonian paradigm from Lyell's uniformitarian geology to evolutionary biology with a little help from the Malthusian version of Smithean economics. The work of these pioneers in both economics and evolutionary biology has been articulated into powerful, operational tools in the present century—in the first instance in neoclassical micro-economics, based on the principle of marginal utility, and in the second in neo-Darwinism. As reconstructed recently by Elliott Sober (1984), neo-Darwinism is based on defining the inertial motion of a gene pool by generalizing Mendel's Laws to the populational level by way of the Hardy-Weinberg Equilibrium Formula, and then ascribing deviations from these expectations as due to a ranked series of impinging 'forces,' preeminently natural selection.[3] It is important, then, for the purposes that inform this paper to get clear on the general properties of Newtonian systems.

The basic characteristic of a Newtonian system, formulated at the most general level, is that each entity in the system is assumed to possess—indeed is identified by its possession of—an inherent inertial motion whose assumed direction is deviated from only under the influence of impressed forces, forces exerted by the other entities within the system. At each instant a Newtonian system will tend to an equilibrium between inertial motion and impressed force. The following are conceptual presuppositions of such systems: they are closed, deterministic, reversible, and atomistic or decomposable.

They are closed because if extrasystemic inputs are permitted as a source of change, none of the laws that govern the behavior of the system can be assumed to hold. Any state change can be ascribed either to spontaneity or to the action of an extrasystemic input. Thus no resulting motion would be predictable. (Extrasystematicity is what natural theology claimed, and creationists still claim, about the origins of functional organic traits. It is precisely what Darwin contested by showing how functional features could emerge by way of natural law within a system of Malthusian closure conditions.)

They are deterministic because, given the initial position of an entity in the system, the set of forces operating on it, and stable closure conditions, every subsequent position of every entity in the system is in principle specifiable.

Our very notion of natural law, and hence of scientific method, has been tailored to this specification. A law, as now commonly understood, tells us how, given a closed system and an inertial or zero point against which state changes can be measured, the imposition of quantifiable forces results in a determinate, and hence predictable, pattern of instantaneous changes in the motion of the entity affected as it moves from an initial to a terminal state.

This is what must be presupposed if laws are to support counterfactual claims—to tell us what would have happened were it not for some interfering force or event—and if explanations are to be regarded as deductions from laws.

Newtonian systems are also reversible—from a formal point of view because the laws specifying their motions can be calculated in both directions; and materially, because every state of the system is in principle recoverable. There is no inherent arrow of time in a Newtonian system.

Finally, if such a system is to be reversible, and successive states of the system recoverable, it must also be atomistic: If the entities are to retain their identity—that is their definition as independent centers of inertial motion—through successive state changes, larger units must be regarded as additive composites or aggregates of stable least units.

What plays the role of inertia in the Smithean case is the tendency toward self-preservation, which is thought to manifest itself in the tendency of each economic agent to maximize command over scarce resources. The operation of law-governed relationships in a system composed of such agents is underwritten by the physical limits that cause scarcity, thus providing conditions for system closure. Competition is the force that all the interacting members exert on each other. Its dynamics can be explicated in terms of laws of supply and demand. Equilibrium is reached when there is a balance between supply and demand. This equilibrium will be a dynamic one, constantly threatened and constantly being restored.

Admittedly, Darwin's case looks somewhat different from this, even though he was influenced by the grim Malthusian conclusion that economic equilibrium will tend to occur at a point below that where exchanges are correlated with the biological survival of all agents who would otherwise exist. For one thing, it is not the self that is preserved in Darwinian evolution, but descendants—Dawkins' fantasy about the genes notwithstanding. Inertial motion is ascribable only to the hereditary machinery itself. Second, there will be no evolution unless there is a source of variation that can be shaped by competitive pressures. This variation comes from an endogenous propensity toward errors in the hereditary machinery. This has no parallel in a strictly Newtonian system. We may, in fact, readily envision this situation as one in which probability space at the level of heredity expands over time. Macrostates are selected that are more well-adapted to their environment—in equilibrium with it—than would be possible in a strict Malthusian world. Indeed, it was just this affinity to his own, implicitly non-Newtonian world-view that led Boltzmann to call the nineteenth century "The Century of Darwin" (cf. Prigogine and Stengers, 1984). Current efforts to link thermodynamics and evolutionary theory more closely will doubtless do a great deal to develop this side of the Darwinian picture.

Nonetheless, several circumstances have hitherto prevented these affinities from flowering. First, Darwin's own skirmishes with thermodynamics, such as his unfortunate set-to with Kelvin, led evolutionists to distance their work from physics. Second, Darwin's preoccupation, in his own cultural circumstances, with natural theology led to a stress on external (environmental) pressures and closure conditions as the cause of evolution (and to variation as a mere presupposition of it.) For Darwin's task, as even the structure of the *Origin of Species* shows, was to refute the standing presumption, associated with Paley, that no natural law could account for functional organic traits. By envisioning the *environment* as a *closed* Malthusian space defined by intense competition, Darwin provided the 'pressures' and 'forces' that could cause this effect, with no need to invoke any extrasystemic cause, least of all a divine one. In this way, Darwin's theory was understood as delivering up the biological world to the same Newtonian framework that had already captured the physical and chemical worlds.

One consequence of this interpretation was that evolution was assigned only a weak arrow of time. For when 'chance variation' is understood merely as a necessary presupposition for evolution and not a causal-explanatory agent, there is nothing that *in principle* prevents recurrence of an earlier state of the system—it is *in principle* reversible. It is merely asserted that this is unlikely on a factual basis because initial conditions in the environment will seldom actually be the same. Another implication is that Darwinism is given a distinctly atomistic bias. Organisms are fractioned into separate traits, each of which is molded by 'selection pressure' and then assembled into a whole that is only the sum of its parts (Gould and Lewontin, 1979).

These ways of looking at evolution are almost exclusively the (nonempirical) result of interpreting the Darwinian tradition in terms of equilibrium background assumptions. Nor, it should be added, has this culturally contingent interpretive tendency been alleviated in the present century. For, while it is no longer pressing to interpret Darwin's theory materially along Newtonian lines, in order to undercut widely held theological views, neo-Darwinism's legitimacy as a mature scientific theory has had to be secured by showing that it conforms (more or less) to the formal requirements of positivist philosophy of science. The positivist model of a mature science and of explanation brings with it, as we have already suggested, a highly abstract commitment to Newtonian assumptions. These are manifest in the neo-Darwinian case in the central role played by the Hardy-Weinberg Equilibrium Formula as the inertial baseline for all evolutionary computations (cf. Depew and Weber, 1985; Dyke, 1987).

We may, however, imagine systems quite different from, indeed with precisely opposed characteristics to, Newtonian systems. Such systems may be (1) constantly open to inputs from beyond the system, indeed retaining their identity as distinct systems just because this is so; (2) open, therefore, to changes, including spontaneous self-organization and non-deterministic bifurcations, that are not, or are not entirely, the result of predictable and measurable impressed forces operating against an inertial default drive; (3) irreversible not just in fact, but in principle, because, lacking inertial states to which they would tend to return when forces are removed, the entities in the system are defined historically—in terms of the entire sequence of their interactions over a series of irreversible changes, even if statistical changes at the microsystemic level are independently reversible; (4) only partially decomposable, because composed of complex modules arising historically and irreversibly across the micro-macro divide, thus precluding treating relations among the components of the system as entirely additive or aggregative.

Rather than tending inevitably and instantaneously toward equilibrium, systems of this type can maintain themselves far from equilibrium as long as appropriate boundary conditions are maintained. Such systems are physically instantiated. Following Prigogine we shall call them 'dissipative structures,' because their most salient characteristic derives from (1) above: They pull energy and matter into themselves and export it in degraded forms to an external sink as a condition of maintaining a changing pattern of internal self-organization, which they continue to exhibit until and unless the flow of energy and matter falls below a crucial threshold.

Prigogine has shown that these systems and their behavior can be analytically understood by dividing their entropy production into two parts (Prigogine, 1980; Prigogine et al., 1972). The entropy produced by interactions within the system—a cost of maintaining structure—can be measured separately from the entropy produced by interactions between the system and the environment. Between the two parts there is, of course, mutual conditioning: Influxes of matter and energy are required to sustain the building of internal structure, and the structures thus built lead to more efficient interactions between the system and the environment. But by noting and measuring the different components, various possible states of systems can be defined—including that important state in which small increases in internal entropy can be accompanied by decrease in specific interactive entropy by deflecting it to components of the containing system, the environment. It is precisely the self-organized internal structure that spontaneously arises in far-from-equilibrium conditions that creates this capacity to deflect entropic debt beyond the system itself to the environment.

It should be clear, moreover, that there will be differential survival rates between such systems in proportion as they increase their efficiency. This will enable us to view natural selection in a light that considerably lessens any contrast between it and known physical principles and that does not rely on invoking an external force to contravene an inertial drive. It is simply the case that endogenous increase in internal complexity leads to increased efficiency of energy dissipation and utilization, while decreasing specific entropy production. Meanwhile, overall entropy for the system and the environment increases. Since at least some kinds of 'dissipative structures' thus exhibit thermodynamically irreversible behavior in the very process of evolving *by means of natural selection*, they can also be said in an appropriate sense to evolve through, even by means of, entropy production. This analysis provides new insights into the dynamics of those 'negentropic' systems that Schroedinger had spoken of, in which complexification only appears to contravene the second law.

Prigogine himself has applied these analytical tools to investigate self-organization and irreversibility within dissipative physical and chemical systems, in which self-organization occurs by way of chemical autocatalysis and in which competition and selection are not primary factors (Prigogine and Stengers, 1984). He has not been indifferent, however, to the extension of such analysis to nascent and realized biological systems and their evolution. While acknowledging that his work can lead to an improved analysis of natural selection, he does not appear to think, however, that this new analysis necessitates any revision of standing evolutionary theory, but on the contrary provides it with deepened physical foundations (Prigogine et al., 1972). Others, however, including most of the contributors to this volume, believe that the consequences of this new analysis are much greater, particularly as they bear on contemporary disputes within evolutionary theory. Much of the work in these pages is an attempt to see how far down this path we are at present able to travel. In the next section we shall review, for the most part favorably, some of these results, showing in the process how they provide an improved backing for many of the speculations advocated by proponents of an expanded synthesis.

15.6 Nonequilibrium Thermodynamics and the Dynamics of Living Systems

The most accessible point of intersection between the study of contemporary thermodynamics and biology is ecology. For, to the extent that an ecological system has a relative autonomy within at least one sort of biological hierarchy, and is not simply regarded as a product of dynamics operating at lower levels, that autonomy is provided by regimes of energy flow through the system. Patterns of energy flow partition the environment into potential 'niches,' whose exploitation stabilizes the system as whole, provides matrices for community structure and population dynamics, and endogenously generates complexifying tendencies that irreversibly drive the evolution of the system itself. What Schneider (this volume) calls 'expanded thermodynamics,' therefore, breathes new life into our understanding of known ecological dynamics.

Consider, for example, how these concepts throw light on Lotka's principle that "natural selection will so operate as to increase the total mass of the organic system, and to increase the total energy flux through the system so long as there is presented an unutilized residue of matter and available energy" (Lotka, 1922, p. 148). In addition to enabling us to understand how and why ecological systems maximize energy flows, the concepts of expanded thermodynamics also illuminate other important principles of ecological dynamics: that, for instance, complex organization will enable systems to hold energy (Morowitz, 1968) and to decrease specific entropy production "as the elaboration of mutualistic networks under selection increases biomass/throughput ratios" (Wicken, 1986; cf. Schneider, this volume).

To investigate these principles and their consequences by using the analytical tools of nonequilibrium thermodynamics has the effect of renewing a tradition in ecology that had been stultified by being taken from its original, energetics-based context and pressed into the service, on its mathematical side, of neo-Darwinian populational ecology. Some of Lotka's work, for example, has been integrated into neo-Darwinism in a way that renders ecological change *merely* the *outcome* of population dynamics, at lower levels, thus denying the autonomy of ecological dynamics, and their status as context, constraint, and even cause of population-genetical change and evolution at lower levels. This 'bottom-up' strategy has thus severed evolution from thermodynamics at their most natural point of intersection. The work of Schneider and Johnson (this volume) is intended to redress this situation by setting classical ecology against the more perspicuous background of nonequilibrium thermodynamics. These writers concentrate on stability, succession, and evolution in ecosystems considered as relatively autonomous units of selection (cf. also Ulanowitz, 1986).

The work of Jeffrey Wicken concentrates on how, within ecological systems thus construed, biological evolution, as distinct from ecological succession, occurs. Wicken (1984) approaches evolutionary problems, from the origin of life to phylogeny, from a 'top-down' perspective. This means that he views life within a strongly ecological context. Biological systems and units are defined relationally to whole ecosystems. Thus part-whole relations, from a philosophical point of view, become more important than linear cause-effect relations. This approach contrasts with the atomism of neo-Darwinians, who analyze higher units by summing over cause-effect relations at lower levels. The top-down perspective is governed by dynamical laws deriving from the fact that the wholes and parts in question are dissipative structures. Accordingly, Wicken universalizes Lotka's expanded flow principle by proposing that, *for any evolving system*, innovations and strategies that focus resources into the system, while at the same time stabilizing the web of energetic interconnections of that system, will be selected for (Wicken, 1986). This process will in all cases produce increased biomass/throughput ratios and decreased specific entropy production.

Wicken's most sustained application of this approach is to the question of the origin of life (Wicken, 1984, 1985a, 1987). The 'prebiosphere' is treated as a nonisolated, closed system in which energy sources (solar and geothermal) create thermodynamic gradients that give rise to thermodynamic flows cycling a relatively constant supply of elements through the system. If there were a mechanism to capture some of this energy, then the prebiosphere would become charged with chemical potential. Thermodynamic flows would at the same time be more efficiently dissipated through the appearance of 'negentropic' structures within the system. Thus while the prebiosphere was being charged, it was also dissipating energy through the formation of ever more complex chemical structures, through which thermal energy moved from densely packed translational modes to less densely packed vibrational modes associated with chemical bonds. This increase in structural complexity is associated, in this far-from-equilibrium situation, with increased dissipation through the system.

If the molecules so produced develop autocatalytic properties, then these will even more efficiently deflect energy and resources through the system. The most likely scenario, in Wicken's view, is that spontaneously forming proteinoid microspheres, which possess some catalytic properties in their nonrandomly formed peptide chains (Nakashima et al., 1977; Fox, 1980, 1984), provided the milieu within which proteins and nucleic acids coevolved through mutual stabilization and through interlocking autocatalytic cycles to produce a primitive mechanism for the replication and translation of nucleic acids and proteins. Initially the sequences would be expected to be generic, with only slight specificities or functions. But greater thermodynamic efficiency would have soon obtained as certain sequences and functions became stabilized. Thus the relational molecular ecology of the proteinoid spheres under thermodynamic flows would lead us to expect the emergence of biological information and its replication (Wicken, 1985a).

Once there were informed autocatalytic systems capable of reproduction, biological evolution properly so-called began. Over time, the pace of biological evolution overwhelmed that of physical evolution, especially after the emergence of metabolism and biological membranes, which allowed more efficient pathways for energy utilization. It is clear, in any event, that replicating molecules were a particularly powerful component of autocatalytic systems, and that systems utilizing them would have been favored by natural selection over other autocatalytic systems. This consideration leads to Wicken's definition of living beings as 'informed autocatalytic systems' (Wicken, 1984). Such self-replicating macromolecules would become ever more efficient contributors to the process of energy utilization and dissipation as specific sequences came to be favored for their functions within the systems within which they arose—and not because 'naked replicators' somehow found means to build a system around themselves.

To see how this occurred, it is important to recognize that information theory and thermodynamics (whose relations are, of course, anything but harmonious) nonetheless concur in postulating that every replicating system will generate 'mistakes' as an inevitable, and potentially calculable, consequence of its very structure. Some of these variants will permit the growth of further internal structure, and with it the more efficient creation and exploitation of still further ecological niches. This in turn will further enhance the overall quantity and efficiency of energy utilization in ecological space as a whole, providing a platform for yet further growth and utilization of informational complexity. As a result of this physically driven feedback system, ecological dynamics can be rederived in such a way as to include, both as cause and effect, the growth of informational complexity. We are now within sight of a general theory of organic evolution (Wicken, 1987).

Wicken's proposal for coupling environmental efficiency and the growth of informational complexity utilizes and extends the scope of Prigogine's analytical principles for studying the dynamics of dissipative structures. Like Prigogine, his theory is based on sustaining, rather than questioning, the role of natural selection. But on Wicken's analysis natural selection is reconceived in ways that seem to call for a more radical conceptual revision than Prigogine's. What has changed is that natural selection is not seen as an external force acting upon a system that needs to be jarred out of rest by an exogenous force if it is to move at all. Rather, selection is treated as a self-generating process in which the properties of macromolecules along kinetic pathways differ in dissipative efficiency and in which the more successful are accumulated in proportion as they facilitate both the processes in which they are immediately involved and the efficiency of the entire structure of systems and subsystems. While limiting resources are always a factor in such processes, there is no need to speak of scarcity as a cause without which such a sorting out process would not occur at all.

Another important conceptual point emerges from these considerations. It is an essential property, as we have seen, of dissipative structures, when proper kinetic pathways are available, to self-organize and, when initial and boundary conditions are specified, to evolve over time toward greater complexity. This means that such structures, and systems composed of such structures, have a history derived from the path of the bifurcations that they undergo. But biological systems have a particular advantage over other dissipative structures because genetic information not only ensures proper functioning, but also encodes the history of the system into the macromolecules in a way not available to other systems. Organisms take their own history with them as they move through their careers. This historicity is, moreover, inseparable from irreversibility. Thus if we grant that biological systems are constrained by the same physical laws that made their emergence possible, we can expect that such systems—organisms, populations, species, clades, ecosystems, and the biosphere as a whole—will evolve, and evolve toward greater complexity (in accord with Dollo's Law).

On this view of the matter, there is a deep, structural *expectation* of the *fact* of evolution once biological systems are seen as dissipative structures. This fact, meanwhile, is not so strongly anticipated in the Darwinian tradition, as it has thus far been articulated, because that tradition has been affected by equilibrium background assumptions. These require additional assumptions to account for evolution itself—such as more or less complete system closure, adaptationist imperatives driven by maximization and optimization rules, and the decomposability of organic entities into collections of independent traits so that the latter can be specifically and precisely molded by exogenous forces.

Given these general principles, we may now go on to suggest that many of the ideas insisted upon by proponents of an expanded synthesis can be given a deeper intuitive appeal and theoretical backing. First, we may expect from this point of view that the biological world would be hierarchically arranged. Any ecosystem will be thermodynamically rewarded as it becomes more efficient in both dissipating and utilizing energy, which it does by increasing overall flow through the system and decreasing specific entropy production in the ever more complex parts. These effects are achieved by irreversible processes in which the increasing complexity of informed autocatalytic cycles, and of the structures that manifest this complexity, are accompanied by increasing efficiency in system-environment interactions. The type of complex structure that is both kinetically available from simpler modular units and has reasonable stability in the face of informational errors is a hierarchical relationship of integrated modular units. Such a hierarchical structure will be more stable and efficient than a system consisting of, and reducible to, mere interactions at one level. Thus a nonequilibrium thermodynamical approach to evolution also leads to the *expectation* of increasing modular, and in this sense 'hierarchical,' organization and to the idea that selection, as defined above, can and will act at various levels. A group, moreover, such as a deme or a species, can be considered as an 'individual' all the more readily when it is recalled that it is actually a system that facilitates a certain pattern or regime of energy flow, thus maintaining itself within a tightly structured ecological whole and contributing to its stability. While each level of this series of informed autocatalytic cycles provides constraints on other levels and is in turn constrained by them, each can and will also be a site where the accumulation of increased flow and decreased specific entropy will occur and will be rewarded. Heuristic primacy in the investigation of these dynamics will be given to the ecological system as a whole, with attention moving to smaller subsystems as required. This is precisely the opposite investigative pathway from that commended by traditional 'bottom-up' versions of Darwinism.

This approach to the central insistence of the expanded synthesis has an additional advantage over the original version. When the ideal of multilevel selection is presented against equilibrium background assumptions, it can reasonably be asked what inertial tendencies at other levels play the role that the Hardy-Weinberg Equilibrium plays at the populational level. Since there is no clear answer to this question, the population level remains primary. Multilevel selection backed by nonequilibrium assumptions does not, however, require that an inertial tendency and an external force be postulated as a necessary condition for natural selection. On the contrary, whatever inertial tendencies exist, such as the Hardy-Weinberg Equilibrium, will be regarded as homeostatic constraints within a wider framework of endogenous change. Thus Beatty's correct claim (Beatty, 1980) that the Hardy-Weinberg Equilibrium cannot be a universal law of nature, because it is the product of the evolutionary development of meiotic mechanisms, need occasion no worry. The Hardy-Weinberg Equilibrium merely specifies a set of boundary conditions within which a number of specific evolutionary problems and their solutions can be worked out.

It should not be surprising in view of these facts that the structure of the genome would have proven more complex than previously thought. Certainly, in the absence of sufficient mechanistic and historical information, it is not possible to predict in what ways a genome will become complex, but it is possible to expect that increasing complexity over all lineages would occur as the biological world matures into a more complex system of systems. For complexity, viewed as integrated modular organization, serves to enhance the efficiency with which a system handles its entropic debt. A system that operates at the level of "bean bag genetics" would not be expected to be efficient in this sense, and hence would not be maintained without change (as if that were possible) as the biological world moves toward more complex systems and interrelations.

Another consideration follows from this. Not relying on an instant-by-instant need for maximum efficiency to preserve the individual in the face of withering atomistic competition unprotected by hierarchical structure and constraint, organic function within a relational field of flow and structure can be maintained while stochastic processes continue to occur at lower levels in the system. Thus many mutations can occur at the level of individual amino acids for a given protein so long as the higher level tertiary and quaternary structure necessary for function is unaltered. This process, being stochastic, should in the absence of any other factors be fairly constant over time. In other words, we would expect to see at some evolutionary levels neutral molecular evolution and at least an approximate molecular clock.

These mutations arise from that important aspect of entropic increase that manifests itself as a tendency toward configurational disorder or expansion in probability space. While kinetics provides information about the kinds of mechanisms by which such configurational disorder can be produced, the expectation of this entropy increase itself is provided by the thermodynamic principles within which we are now working. Indeed, we would expect that not only point mutations, but chromosomal rearrangements and sexual recombination should also provide mechanisms for increased configurational disorder within this general framework. Extended to populations of organisms, we would expect that polymorphisms would be commonplace and that they would arise stochastically rather than by balancing selection, where constraints at higher levels permit. This aspect of entropy—increased disorder within a system—accords well enough with the principles of traditional thermodynamics, and is also a background concept for neo-Darwinism. What is different in a nonequilibrium thermodynamic view of evolution is that this disordering aspect of entropy is coupled with that aspect of entropic dissipation in which it serves as an organizing principle.

The empirical studies of molecular geneticists (Wilson et al., 1977; MacIntyre, 1982; Laurie-Ahlberg, 1985; Paigen, 1986) have shown that changes in the ontogenetic program, rather than in structural genes, correlate with organismic evolution. It is readily apparent why speciation and subsequent phylogenetic processes are likely to manifest themselves by way of changes in the ontogenetic program of the genome. Constraints that protect the integrity of an organism will hardly be overcome by accumulations of point mutations and the mere distribution of variant structural gene products through populations. Nonetheless, given these important facts, speciation through the breakdown and reorganizing of ontogenetic programs might well be expected to be subject to the constraints of a teleomatic process in which entropy, in the form of configurational disorder, increases in populations that have a common ontogenetic program. Such an increase in information in a previously stable ontogenetic regime can, moreover, under some conditions reduce reproductive cohesion within and between the component populations of a species. The general behavior of dissipative structures is suggestive, even if not determining, in this connection. As a system composed of dissipative structures evolves over time, it reaches a point where a threshold is exceeded and the system becomes unstable. The system ultimately makes a discontinuous transition to a new state, the choice of which is determined by internal fluctuations as well as by external forces acting upon the restricted set of kinetic pathways available at that point in time. In this way, a species can, and from a certain point of view inevitably will, come apart at the seams.

We thus arrive at a consideration of how the new thermodynamics might apply to macroevolutionary problems, and especially to the dynamics that underlie phylogeny. Brooks and Wiley (1986) have given an account of this process based on nonequilibrium principles, influenced by Layzer's ideas about the cosmological growth of entropy (Layzer, 1975, and this volume) and Gatlin's extension of information theory to biological systems (Gatlin, 1972).

Brooks and Wiley (1986; Brooks et al., this volume; Wiley, this volume) suggest that a type of 'entropy' can be calculated from empirical data from systematics and that this 'entropy', or perhaps more perspicuously this informational 'complexity,' can be more or less isomorphically mapped onto phylogeny. At the heart of this proposal is a notion of 'information dissipation' in populations that have built up enough variation to threaten gene linkages in and between populations. Brooks and Wiley are inclined to treat this process as an inference from a single, overarching formulation of the second law, expressed in information-theoretical terms, which generalizes and deepens the Boltzmann analysis of entropy just as surely as Boltzmann deepened the physically limited version that comes from Carnot. On their view, therefore, the lawlike status of this physical-informational principle leads to the *necessity* of phylogenetic branching, and to the suggestion that branching can be treated as an informational analogue of bifurcations in the history of nonequilibrium thermodynamical systems. Because the object on which this process works is the species, considered by Brooks and Wiley as an individual sharing an ontogenetic program,[4] phylogenetic branching is not, properly speaking, caused by processes going on at levels below that of species, or indeed because of interactions between species and their environment. Rather, it is an inevitable and autonomous consequence of the working of the second law and would not otherwise occur.

This does not, however, mean that natural selection plays no role. On Brooks and Wiley's account, natural selection acts primarily as a negative and pruning factor controlling the rate at which this branching process occurs. Speciation, considered as change in an ontogenetic program, is expected to be a constantly occurring event in view of the inevitable increase in informational entropy or configurational disorder, but its frequency can be constrained by selection, especially if that selective constraint is not seen as coming so much from the environment as from the internal requirements for a coherent ontogenetic program that will tie populations together through reproductive cohesion. In other words, 'negative' natural selection serves to answer a question that arises from conceptual sources in Brooks and Wiley's scheme: Why are there not more species than there are? Note that a precisely opposite question arises from the background assumptions within which Darwinians have worked: Why are there any new species at all in a world governed by equilibria?

One of the most attractive features of the Brooks and Wiley program, in addition, is that there is a strong sense in which evolution is tied to developmental biology, the stepchild of the neo-Darwinian Synthesis and a rallying point for proponents of an expanded synthesis. In this connection it is worth noting too that Brooks and Wiley's focus on entropic changes in the nonetheless deeply constrained ontogenetic program leads to a possibility that the pattern in organismic evolution could be one of stasis over significant time and much environmental change, due to the imperative of maintaining a specific ontogenetic sequence of events, followed by rapid evolutionary change, due in turn to a 'phase-transition' to a new ontogenetic regime.

It would appear that Brooks and Wiley's work has a solid biological base and that their methods are of value in a number of empirical applications. What is not so clear is the validity of generalizing the concept of entropy to include biological informational entropies, as has been pointed out in several of the contributions to this volume and elsewhere (Bookstein, 1983; Løvtrup, 1983; Wicken, 1983, 1985b; defenses of the use of the Shannon H are given in Wiley and Brooks, 1983, 1986, and this volume; Collier, 1986 and this volume).

Clearly there is a Dollo's Law operating in the biological world. Equally clearly, it must have some connection to the fact that the biosphere is subject to nonequilibrium energy flows and has an irreversibility that parallels the irreversibility of complex physical systems. But the careful analysis of Denbigh and Denbigh (1985) demonstrates that there are many pitfalls in equating the entropy concept with that of informational complexity. In their view, what is fundamental and telling in the second law of thermodynamics is the concept of irreversibility—the fact that at the macroscopic level time has a directionality even though the physics of the microscopic realm is in principle time-reversible. This implies, as Wicken has insisted, that any application of nonequilibrium thermodynamics and the concept of a dissipative structure to biological processes and problems must rest on a firm grasp of the micro-macro distinction. To say that the second law is applicable to the dynamics of speciation and phylogeny does not immediately allow one to infer what kinetic pathways the process will take, or to ascribe explanatory force to the second law itself.

One potential infelicity in the way Brooks and Wiley have conceived the problem is that natural selection and informational-thermodynamic necessity are set up as rival causal processes, when in fact we should think, with Wicken, that nonequilibrium background assumptions actually serve to show *how* natural selection should be conceived and how it comes to be causal and explanatory. It is only a deductivist metascience that leads one to fail to distinguish between causality and deducibility. We tend to think, in fact, that Brooks and Wiley's best ideas are somewhat obscured by a hypothetical-deductivist model of scientific method that applies readily only where, as in a closed Newtonian system, one can deductively infer from a law and a set of initial conditions what the behavior of a system will be (Depew, 1986). In the essentially complex world of open, historical systems investigative pathways must carefully respect the setting up of local boundary conditions in order to generate causal stories, while relying on a clearly stated set of background conditions to constrain the choice of possible stories and to provide backing for robust explanations (cf. Dyke, in press).

In sum, the relationship between informational complexity and thermodynamic entropy still needs clarification. The 'phylogenetic hierarchy'—the branching of lineages over time that yields the mappings of systematics—should be linked informatively to causal processes at work in what Salthé (1985) and Eldredge (1985) have called the 'ecological hierarchy'—the system of molecules, cells, colonies, organisms, populations, species, and ecosystems whose definition and dynamics have been explored by Wicken and others from the perspective of energy flows. Working out how the phylogenetic and ecological hierarchies are linked remains a major challenge for the program of viewing evolution in the context of background assumptions drawn from nonequilibrium thermodynamics.

15.7 Some Wider Implications

We have distinguished between a scientific tradition and the succession of research programs and attendant theories by which a tradition comes to be articulated. We may well ask, then, whether the proposed change to nonequilibrium background assumptions would end or would continue the Darwinian tradition. Naturally, the answer to this question depends a great deal on what principles constitute the core of the Darwinian tradition. Our view is the most obvious one: Natural selection is at the core of the Darwinian tradition. The most general formula for the principle of natural selection has been well expressed by Lewontin (1980): Any entities that combine heritable variation with differential reproduction will evolve.

In both the original Darwinian program and its neo-Darwinist successor, this general scheme has been interpreted, as we have seen, in terms of analogues of Newtonian dynamics: An initial condition of equilibrium is disturbed by exogenous forces and is bent in a certain direction under conditions of Malthusian or semi-Malthusian constraint. Although variation is viewed as the result of stochastic processes in neo-Darwinism, the fixation of traits is most commonly ascribed to selective forces. Our understanding of natural selection has been so affected by this set of background assumptions that it is difficult to think of it in any other way, or to imagine the continuity of the Darwinian tradition without it. Yet, as we have suggested above, and as Wicken and others have shown in more detail, it is perfectly possible to express nontrivialized interpretations of evolution by natural selection in terms of background assumptions and models derived from the thermodynamics of complex systems.

Indeed, evolution becomes *more* intuitively explicable on these terms than in earlier versions of Darwinism because of the commitment to irreversibility present in the new theoretical background. Because of this commitment, moreover, the explanatory role of constraints in evolution is made clearer: If it is assumed that all systems of a certain type will evolve, what really needs to be explained is not the fact of evolution against a background that does not strongly predict it, but rather the path that a system will take as its presumed evolution unfolds. What properly explains that path is the set of constraints, both internal and external, that determine evolutionary tempo and mode. Brooks and Wiley have stressed the role of internalized constraints in explaining phylogenetic pathways by favoring such explanations over explanations by natural selection. We suspect that they may be misconstrued by those assuming that natural selection is inherently tied to Newtonian assumptions, who may fail to see that, with the relevant change in background assumptions, natural selection and evolutionary constraints are inextricably tied together. Greater understanding of this relation will serve to renew and continue the Darwinian tradition by freeing it from assumptions, deriving from the prestige of the Newtonian paradigm, that are no longer helpful in formulating or evaluating concrete research programs and by reinforcing the inherent affinity between Darwinism and thermodynamics, the two great nineteenth century theories about temporal processes. It may well be the case that no science has become mature without, at one stage or another, conforming itself to the Newtonian paradigm. But the history of science in the twentieth century also assures us that no truly mature science has continued to develop without abandoning that framework. Our view is that evolutionary biology has reached that stage.

It also seems clear on its face that as sciences mature their links to other developed sciences should grow tighter. An increased integration between biological and physical sciences can, moreover, be as devoutly wished for by antireductionists as by reductionists, on the general ground that progress in science is measured in part by the progressive coherence of the entire fabric or web of our beliefs. What needs to be recognized is that there is no longer any need heuristically to assume that the steady advance to a few powerful principles that apply across fields is correlated to a preference for explanations couched in terms of the independent behavior of the atomic constituents of systems. Theory reduction (if that is any longer a proper name for it) is no longer reliably correlated with entity or ontological reduction. For progress in many sciences, and especially in those that link nonliving systems to living, now depends on understanding the behavior of systems that are not mere aggregates and are not strongly decomposable.

As long as the physical sciences had not understood this, biologists may have been justified in rejecting calls to radical reductionism and in taking up the autonomist stance that has been, especially through the efforts of Ernst Mayr, so prevalent in evolutionary biology. Resistance to linking evolution to thermodynamic laws, for example, was justified so long as the thermodynamics in question was that of the nineteenth century study of closed and isolated systems. Under such conditions, an apparent clash between a biological world moving toward greater order and complexity and a physical world moving toward heat death was rendered artificially persuasive. This circumstance suggested that, in order to be free enough to develop in relative peace from both its scientistic and its religious opponents, evolutionary biology should insulate itself from physics, except by acknowledging that all biological systems are subject, as physical systems, to physical laws but are not, as specifically biological systems, adequately explained by such laws.

The development, however, of nonequilibrium thermodynamics and the study of dissipative structures underscores earlier repudiations of any conflict between biology and physics. We may now call for closer, positive links between thermodynamics and evolutionary theory. Just as an earlier generation was able to move beyond an alleged contradiction between physics and biology to affirm their compatibility, the present generation is in a position to move beyond mere consistency toward a positive affirmation of the relevance of physical principles to biological systems and their history. This affirmation is expressed, somewhat imprecisely, in the notion that evolution is 'driven' by entropy.

This perspective has, we feel, certain implications for the vexed relation among natural selection, adaption, and teleology. In both classical and modern Darwinism a preference for Newtonian background assumptions in the interpretation of natural selection sustains, we believe, the puzzles attending teleological explanation. Equilibrium between organisms and environments is established, in the classical Darwinian view, by the exogenous force of natural selection molding separate traits to maximum utility in specific environmental conditions. Arguments establishing such adaptations presuppose that organic systems are highly decomposable assemblages of traits and employ optimization and maximization assumptions as criteria for regarding products of these forces as genuinely adaptive. One effect of the central role played by arguments of this sort in evolutionary thinking is that both chance effects and internal constraints are seen as limitations on adaptationist arguments, giving rise to a projection onto nature of an interpretative and explanatory scheme whose primacy, even if only heuristic, is ours more than nature's, and ours only at a specific point in the development of science. More important in the present context, however, is the fact that where background assumptions do not strongly imply evolution at all as a teleomatic process, explanations of particular events must bear the *double load* of showing that evolution has occurred, where it would not otherwise be expected, and of showing its rationale in a particular case. Adaptationist arguments bear this double load because they seem to provide a rationale as coherent to us as intentional explanations based on craftsmanship.

The risk of slipping into an illegitimate teleology in making such arguments is very high. It is of course true that the teleological element in adaptationist arguments can be distinguished from creationist arguments, as Robert Brandon (1978) and Larry Wright (1973) have shown; and in this sense it is false to treat such arguments as relying on a disguised teleology of the 'design' sort. It remains the case, however, that arguments of this type have a *deeper* resemblance to those cherished by natural theologians. Such arguments assume that nature has been able to achieve the same *kind* of effect that an engineer-god could attain by 'using' different 'means.' This manner of representation borders continually on being a category mistake. If, however, the fact of evolution is expected, and in no need of any special explanation, as it is in any articulation of the nonequilibrium paradigm, some of the explanatory burden could be taken off these arguments. In that case, as O'Grady and Brooks (this volume), and from a different perspective Wicken (this volume), have argued, teleonomy and what is distinctive about evolutionary teleology would be anchored in fundamental teleomatic processes, and their distinction from intentionist and purposive forms of teleology would be more clearly marked. Maximization criteria would lose their *a priori*, as opposed to their empirical, utility. Moreover, on this view the clear distinction between natural selection and adaptationism, which advanced neo-Darwinists such as Lewontin (1980) have been trying to express, would be more easily drawn. Freed from the postulate of strong decomposability, the integrity of the organism, so mitigated by Newtonian-Cartesian biology, would be restored.

There is another good reason to try to find ways to eliminate the conflation of evolutionary and intentional-technical teleology. An insufficiently clear distinction between these forms of argument tends to keep alive the intelligibility of creationist arguments in a scientific and cultural milieu that should be able to forget them. As long as creationist thinking forms the shadow logic of evolutionary reasoning, standards of adequacy in scientific reasoning itself tend to be lowered. In Darwin's day, to show that species could have arisen by the working of a natural law met its proper explanatory burden, against a cultural background that strongly inclined to think, with natural theologians, that functionally organized entities, unlike simple physical systems, could not be given naturalistic explanations. Similarly low burdens of proof still characterize the work of social scientists, who must rebut the standing cultural presumption that human actions and practices cannot be subsumed under natural laws. The inherent ambiguity of teleological arguments based on the assembly of traits into systems that efficiently maximize their self-interest, or trade off goods for overall success, allows creationist arguments to receive more attention than they actually deserve, given the actual state of the development of evolutionary science. To refute creationists, therefore, evolutionary biologists and their philosophical allies often deploy arguments showing merely that the facts of organic structure and function are *consistent* with natural law or are plausibly explicated by natural law (Ruse, 1982; Dawkins, 1986). Neo-Darwinist arguments serve this purpose well. But if arguments of this reassuring sort were not seemingly required, evolutionary science could be pursued and presented in a light much more impressive to other scientists. Conservative arguments showing once again that this or that new discovery does not after all portend the imminent refutation of evolution itself, because the new discovery is, after all, consistent with acknowledged principles, would not have the prestige that they now so wrongly enjoy. If then as we have suggested, a switch from equilibrium to nonequilibrium assumptions reduces the tendency to conflate natural selection and design, the maturity of evolutionary science might make itself more apparent. For with the greater distance thus revealed between selectionist and design arguments, representatives of the latter tradition would gain no initial foothold and time would not be wasted rebutting them with inadequate theories. Meanwhile the closer linkage between physics and biology that is a desideratum of progress in evolutionary biology would be free to proceed apace.

Just as rapprochement with physics constitutes one conceptual constraint on the adequacy of new evolutionary thinking, so too successful new evolutionary work must better bridge the gap between nature and human culture than the Darwinian tradition has been able to manage. This is a field where the Darwinian tradition has failed deeply, allowing gaps to be filled with ideological nonsense. The most recent case in point is sociobiology of the sort advocated by E. O. Wilson (1975), which purports to overcome previous Darwinian failures by liberal use of the theory of kin selection, backed by genic selectionism of the sort most stridently articulated by Dawkins (1976, 1982). As Gould and Lewontin (1979) have argued, this view depends on a strongly adaptationist interpretation of natural selection, and a quasi-teleological deployment of adaptationism that fails to keep itself free of disguised design arguments. Once again, such arguments rest on a strongly atomistic conception of organisms and on the role of external forces in molding traits to environments.

The proper response to these difficulties, however, is not to abandon the general notion of sociobiology, and to regress to an affirmation of the old position that social science is irreducible to natural science on the (false) ground that culture interrupts and transcends nature (Sahlins, 1976). Rather, sociobiologists should take advantage of developments in the natural sciences that allow culture to be treated as a specification of nature without depriving cultural phenomena of their unique properties.

Our view is that an evolutionary theory based on nonequilibrium thermodynamics will advance the study of human society considerably. In an important sense, as Marx had already pointed out, all human societies are economies before they are anything else. But economies are modes of organizing ecological space for greater flow, enhanced dissipation, and complexity. What is not true is that economies in this sense are generally explicable in terms of Newtonian equilibrium assumptions, despite a long history that parallels and informs Darwinism. In any case, the predictive reliability of equilibrium models in economics grows ever weaker, especially in the very advanced capitalist economies that, at less complex stages of their development, seemed to confirm the universal applicability of such models. As long, then, as both evolutionary science and economics are limited to Newtonian framework, this false and ideologically distorted universalization, combined with increasing predictive failure, will continue to provoke countermovements insisting that culture begins only where nature, and the science of nature, ends.

A way out of this impasse is to develop an ecologically, and hence thermodynamically based, economic science that is at home with irreversibility and complexity (Wicken, 1986). R. Adams has pioneered in this field by attempting an explanation of certain stretches of British history in terms of energy flows, on the explicit assumption that a national economy is a dissipative structure (Adams, 1981). The investigation of cities as dissipative structures conducted by C. Dyke (this volume) suggests where such an evolutionary and ecologically based social science might begin to take us. If the revisions of biological theory recommended there, and in the other contributions to this volume, increase the prospects for an improved social science in the very act of improving the link between physics and biology, no reasonable scientific mind will resist exploring the avenues thus opened up.

Acknowledgments

We wish to thank the following for helpful comments on an earlier draft: Mike Bloxham, Richard Burian, Joel Cracraft, Chuck Dyke, Jim Hofmann, John Jungck, John Olmsted, Yasuyuki Owada, Jeff Wicken.

Notes

1. This account of scientific change is more indebted to Laudan (1977) than to any other single source. We have written elsewhere about a certain "hermeneutic" dimension in the development of research traditions to which Laudan may well be unsympathetic. Cf. Depew and Weber (1985).

2. We invoke the notion of 'explanatory burden' and its alleviation informally. The principle that no fact used in the construction of a theory can also be used to support it—a principle developed by John Worrall (1978) on the basis of Lakatos' work—exemplifies a similarly strong suspicion of emptiness and circularity in its manifold forms. The best cases of low explanatory burden are those in which novel facts flow naturally from axioms that were in no way designed to account for them.

3. Elliott Sober's *The Nature of Selection* (1984) provides an interpretation of neo-Darwinism that makes extremely strong use of a Newtonian interpretive framework. Our suspicion is that his (admirable) scientific realism leads to a slight hypostatization of 'forces' that 'disturb' the Hardy-Weinberg Equilibrium. Although our interpretation of neo-Darwinism can be seen as relying on something like Sober's account, it should be remembered that it is far from the only recent reconstruction of the logic of neo-Darwinism, and that in other accounts Newtonianism is much more recessive. It is hidden for the most part in the formal structure of the theory, for instance, in Rosenberg (1985). Reconstructions of the theory based on model-building or problem-solving (Beatty, 1980; Brandon, 1978; Lloyd, 1984; Thompson, 1986) can be realistic without being overtly Newtonian.

4. It is a misreading of Brooks and Wiley to say that a species can be defined by a single shared ontogenetic program. Clearly (Brooks and Wiley, 1986), with a species there are variations in the ontogenetic program. They follow the more perspicuous approach of Kauffman (1985), in which the ontogenetic program of a species is viewed as a statistical ensemble with an (in principle) calculable centroid that would indeed characterize a single species.

References

Adams, R. N., 1981. *Paradoxical Harvest: Energy and Explanation in British History, 1870–1914.* Cambridge: Cambridge University Press.

Ayala, F. J., 1982. The genetic structure of species. In *Perspectives on Evolution*, R. Milkman, ed., Sunderland, MA: Sinauer, pp. 60–82.

Ayala, F. J., 1985. Reduction in biology. In *Evolution at a Crossroads: The New Biology and the*

New Philosophy of Science, D. J. Depew and B. H. Weber, eds., Cambridge, MA: MIT Press, pp. 65–79.

Beatty, J. H., 1980. What's wrong with the received view of evolutionary theory? In *PSA 1980*, vol. 2, P. Asquith and R. Giere, eds., East Lansing, MI: Philosophy of Science Association, pp. 397–426.

Bookstein, F., 1983. Comment on a "nonequilibrium" approach to evolution. *Syst. Zool.* 32:291–300.

Brandon, R., 1978. Adaptation and evolutionary theory. *Studies in the History and Philosophy of Science* 9:181–206. [Reprinted in E. Sober, *Conceptual Issues in Evolutionary Biology*. Cambridge, MA: MIT Press.]

Brandon, R., 1981. Biological teleology: questions and answers. *Studies in the History and Philosophy of Science* 12:91–105.

Brandon, R. N., 1985. Adaptation explanations: are adaptations for the good of replicators or interactors? In *Evolution at a Crossroads: The New Biology and the New Philosophy of Science*, D. J. Depew and B. H. Weber, eds., Cambridge, MA: MIT Press, pp. 81–96.

Brandon, R. N., and R. M. Burian, 1984. *Genes, Organisms, Populations: Controversies over the Units of Selection*. Cambridge, MA: MIT Press.

Brooks, D., and E. Wiley, 1986. *Evolution as Entropy: Toward a Unified Theory of Biology*. Chicago: University of Chicago Press.

Campbell, J. H., 1982. Autonomy in evolution. In *Perspectives on Evolution*, R. Milkman, ed., Sunderland, MA: Sinauer, pp. 190–200.

Campbell, J. H., 1985. An organizational interpretation of evolution. In *Evolution at a Crossroads: The New Biology and the New Philosophy of Science*, D. J. Depew and B. H. Weber, eds., Cambridge, MA: MIT Press, pp. 133–167.

Collier, J., 1986. Entropy in evolution. *Biology and Philosophy* 1:5–24.

Darden, L., and N. Maull, 1977. Interfield theories. *Phil. Sci.* 44:43–64.

Dawkins, R., 1976. *The Selfish Gene*. Oxford: Oxford University Press.

Dawkins, R., 1982. *The Extended Phenotype*. San Francisco: Freeman.

Dawkins, R., 1986. *The Blind Watch Maker*. New York: Norton.

Denbigh, K. G., and J. S. Denbigh, 1985. *Entropy in Relation to Incomplete Knowledge*. Cambridge: Cambridge University Press.

Depew, D. J., 1986. Nonequilibrium thermodynamics and evolution: a philosophical perspective. *Philosophica* 37:27–58.

Depew, D. J., and B. H. Weber, 1985. Innovation and tradition in evolutionary theory. In *Evolution at a Crossroads: The New Biology and the New Philosophy of Science*, Cambridge, MA: MIT Press, pp. 227–260.

Dover, G., 1982. Molecular drive: a cohesive mode of species evolution. *Nature* 299:111–117.

Dyke, C., in press. *Pathways through the Possible: the Evolutionary Dynamics of Complex Systems*. Oxford: Oxford University Press.

Eigen, M., and P. Schuster, 1979. *The Hypercycle.* Berlin: Springer-Verlag.

Eigen, M., and P. Schuster, 1982. Stages of emerging life—five principles of early organization. *J. Mol. Biol.* 19:47–61.

Eldredge, N., 1985. *Unfinished Synthesis: Biological Hierarchies and Modern Evolutionary Thought.* Oxford: Oxford University Press.

Eldredge, N., and S. J. Gould, 1972. Punctuated equilibria: an alternative to phyletic gradualism. In *Models in Paleobiology,* T. J. M. Schopf, ed. San Francisco: Freeman, Cooper, pp. 82–115.

Fox, S., 1980. Metabolic microspheres. *Naturwissenschaften* 67:378–383.

Fox, S., 1984. Proteinoid experiments and evolutionary theory. In *Beyond Neo-Darwinism: An Introduction to the New Evolutionary Paradigm,* M.-W. Ho and P. T. Saunders, eds. London: Academic Press, pp. 15–60.

Garfinkel, A., 1981. *Forms of Explanation.* New Haven: Yale University Press.

Gatlin, L., 1972. *Information Theory and the Living System.* New York: Columbia University Press.

Goodwin, B. C., 1984. A relational or field theory of reproduction and its evolutionary implications. In *Beyond Neo-Darwinism: An Introduction to the New Evolutionary Paradigm,* M.-W. Ho and P. T. Saunders, eds., London: Academic Press, pp. 219–241.

Gould, S. J., 1982a. Changes in developmental timing as a mechanism of macroevolution. In *Evolution and Development,* J. T. Bonner, ed., Heidelberg: Springer-Verlag, pp. 333–346.

Gould, S. J., 1982b. Darwinism and the expansion of evolutionary theory. *Science* 216: 380–387.

Gould, S. J., 1982c. The meaning of punctuated evolution and its role in validating a hierarchical approach to macroevolution. In *Perspectives on Evolution,* R. Milkman, ed. Sunderland, MA: Sinauer, pp. 83–104.

Gould, S. J., 1983. The hardening of the modern synthesis. In *Dimensions of Darwinism,* M. Grene, ed. Cambridge: Cambridge University Press, pp. 71–93.

Gould, S. J., and N. Eldredge, 1977. Punctuated equilibria: the tempo and mode of evolution reconsidered. *Paleobiology* 3:115–151.

Gould, S. J., and R. C. Lewontin, 1979. The spandrels of San Marco and the panglossian paradigm: a critique of the adaptationist programme. *Proc. Royal Soc. London* B 205:581–598; reprinted in *Conceptual Issues in Evolutionary Biology,* E. Sober, ed. Cambridge, MA: MIT Press.

Hesse, M., 1965. The explanatory function of metaphor. In *Logic, Method and Philosophy of Science,* Y. Bar-Hillel, ed. Amsterdam: North Holland; reprinted in M. Hesse, 1980, *Revolutions and Reconstructions in the Philosophy of Science,* Bloomington: Indiana University Press.

Hull, D. L., 1976. Are species really individuals? *Syst. Zool.* 25:174–191.

Hull, D. L., 1978. A matter of individuality. *Phil. Sci.* 45:335–360; reprinted in E. Sober, 1984, *Conceptual Issues in Evolutionary Biology,* Cambridge, MA: MIT Press.

Kauffman, S. A., 1985. Self-organization, selective adaptation, and its limits: a new pattern of inference in evolution and development. In *Evolution at a Crossroads: The New Biology and the New Philosophy of Science*, D. J. Depew and B. H. Weber, eds., Cambridge, MA: MIT Press, pp. 169–207.

Kimura, M., 1983. *The Neutral Theory of Molecular Evolution*. Cambridge: Cambridge University Press.

Lakatos, I., 1970. Falsification and the methodology of scientific research programmes. In *Criticism and the Growth of Knowledge*, I. Lakatos and A. Musgrave, eds., Cambridge: Cambridge University Press, pp. 91–195.

Laudan, L., 1977. *Progress and Its Problems: Towards a Theory of Scientific Growth*. Berkeley: University of California Press.

Laurie-Ahlberg, C. C., 1985. Genetic variation affecting the expression of enzyme coding genes in Drosophila: an evolutionary perspective. *Isozymes: Current Topics in Biology and Medical Research* 12:37–88.

Layzer, D., 1975. The arrow of time. *Sci. Amer.* 223:56–59.

Levins, R., 1966. The stategy of model building in population biology. *Amer. Sci.* 54: 421–431.

Lewontin, R. C., 1974. *The Genetic Basis of Change*. New York: Columbia University Press.

Lewontin, R. C., 1980. Adaptation. In *The Encyclopedia Einandi*; reprinted in *Conceptual Issues in Evolutionary Biology*, 1984, E. Sober, ed., Cambridge, MA: MIT Press.

Lewontin, R. C., and R. Dunn, 1960. The evolutionary dynamics of a polymorphism in the House Mouse. *Genetics* 45:705–722.

Li, W.-H., C.-C. Luo, and C.-I. Wu, 1985. Evolution of DNA sequences. In *Molecular Evolutionary Genetics*, R. J. MacIntyre, ed., New York: Plenum, pp. 1–94.

Lloyd, E., 1984. A semantic approach to the structure of population genetics. *Phil. Sci.* 51:242–264.

Lotka, A. J., 1922. Contribution to the energetics of evolution. *Proc. Nat. Acad. Sci. USA* 8:148–154.

Løvtrup, S., 1983. Victims of ambition: comments on the Wiley and Brooks approach to evolution. *Syst. Zool.* 32:90–96.

MacIntyre, R. J., 1982. Regulatory genes and adaptation—past, present and future. *Evol. Biol.* 15:247–285.

Maynard Smith, J., R. Burian, S. Kauffman, P. Alberch, J. Campbell, B. Goodwin, R. Laude, D. Raup, and L. Wolpert, 1985. Developmental constraints and evolution. *Quart. Rev. Biol.* 60:265–287.

Mayr, E., 1985. How biology differs from the physical sciences. In *Evolution at a Crossroads: The New Biology and the New Philosophy of Science*, D. J. Depew and B. H. Weber, eds., Cambridge, MA: MIT Press, pp. 43–63.

Mayr, E., and W. B. Provine, 1980. *The Evolutionary Synthesis: Perspectives on the Unification of Biology*. Cambridge, MA: Harvard University Press.

Morowitz, H. J., 1968. *Energy Flow in Biology: Biological Organization as a Problem in Thermal Physics*. New York: Academic Press.

Nakashima, T., J. R. Jungck, S. W. Fox, E. Kederer, and B. C. Das, 1977. A test for randomness in peptides isolated from a thermal polyamino acid. *Int. J. Quantum Chem.* QBS4:65–72.

Nicolis, G., and I. Prigogine, 1977. *Self-Organization in Nonequilibrium Systems: From Dissipative Structures to Order through Fluctuations*. New York: Wiley-Interscience.

Paigen, K., 1986. Gene regulation and its role in evolutionary processes. In *Evolutionary Process and Theory*, S. Karlin and E. Nevo, eds., Orlando: Academic Press, pp. 3–36.

Prigogine, I., 1980. *From Being to Becoming: Time and Complexity in the Physical Sciences*. San Francisco: Freeman.

Prigogine, I., G. Nicolis, and A. Babloyantz, 1972. Thermodynamics of evolution. *Physics Today* 25(11):23–27; 25(12):38–44.

Prigogine, I., and I. Stengers, 1984. *Order Out of Chaos*. New York: Plenum.

Rosenberg, A., 1985. *The Structure of Biological Science*. Cambridge: Cambridge University Press.

Ruse, M., 1982. *Darwinism Defended: A Guide to the Evolution Controversies*. Reading, MA: Addison-Wesley.

Sahlins, M., 1976. *The Use and Abuse of Biology*. Ann Arbor: Michigan University Press.

Salthé, S., 1985. *Evolving Hierarchical Systems*. New York: Columbia University Press.

Schwartz, B., 1986. *The Battle for Human Nature*. New York: Norton.

Selander, R. K., and T. S. Whittam, 1983. Protein polymorphism and the genetic structure of populations. In *Evolution of Genes and Proteins*, M. Nei and R. K. Kochn, eds., Sunderland, MA: Sinauer, pp. 89–114.

Sober, E., 1984. *The Nature of Selection: Evolutionary Theory in Philosophical Focus*. Cambridge, MA: MIT Press.

Stebbins, G. L., and F. J. Ayala, 1981. Is a new evolutionary synthesis necessary? *Science* 213:967–971.

Stebbins, G. L., and F. J. Ayala, 1985. The evolution of Darwinism. *Sci. Amer.* 253(1):72–82.

Ulanowicz, R. E., 1986. *Growth and Development: Ecosystem Phenomenology*. New York: Springer-Verlag.

Webster, G., 1984. The relations of natural forms. In *Beyond Neo-Darwinism: An Introduction to the New Evolutionary Paradigm*, M.-W. Ho and P. T. Saunders, eds., London: Academic Press, pp. 193–217.

Wicken, J. S., 1983. Entropy, information and nonequilibrium evolution. *Syst. Zool.* 32:438–442.

Wicken, J. S., 1984. Autocatalytic cycling and self-organization in the ecology of evolution. *Nature and System* 6:119–135.

Wicken, J. S., 1985a. An organismic critique of molecular darwinism. *J. Theor. Biol.* 117:545–561.

Wicken, J. S., 1985b. Thermodynamics and the conceptual structure of evolutionary theory. *J. Theor. Biol.* 117:363–383.

Wicken, J. S., 1986. Evolutionary self-organization and entropic dissipation in biological and socioeconomic systems. *J. Social Biol. Struct.* 9:261–273.

Wicken, J. S., 1987. *Evolution, Information, and Thermodynamics: Extending the Darwinian Program.* Oxford: Oxford University Press.

Wiley, E. O., and D. R. Brooks, 1983. Nonequilibrium thermodynamics and evolution: a response to Løvtrup. *Syst. Zool.* 32:209–219.

Williams, G. C., 1966. *Adaptation and Natural Selection.* Princeton: Princeton University Press.

Wilson, A. C., S. S. Carlsen, and T. J. White, 1977. Biochemical evolution. *Ann. Rev. Biochem.* 46:573–639.

Wilson, E. O., 1975. *Sociobiology: The New Synthesis.* Cambridge, MA: Harvard University Press.

Worrall, J., 1978. The ways in which the methodology of scientific research programmes improves on Popper's methodology. In *Progress and Rationality in Science*, G. Radnitzky and G. A. Anderson, eds., Dordrecht: Reidel, pp. 45–70.

Wright, L., 1973. Functions. *Philosophical Review* 82:139–168. [Reprinted in *Conceptual Issues in Evolutionary Biology*, 1984, E. Sober, ed., Cambridge, MA: MIT Press.]

16

Cities as Dissipative Structures

C. Dyke

Recently there have been several interesting attempts to extend the methods and models of nonequilibrium thermodynamics (NET) from ecosystems to economic systems——as particular sorts of ecosystems.[1] The results seem to offer promise that such extensions will prove useful. So far the attempts have been made by people more familiar with the biology of ecosystems than with the economics of social systems. Consequently, the style and language of the most interesting work may not yet be such as to allow social scientists to appreciate the potential of NET models. Here I shall lay out an account of cities as dissipative structures that makes more direct contact with the language and concerns of economic theory. My intent is to offer a specimen exploration of the techniques of NET sufficiently plausible to tempt further explorations by others. In particular, my discussion will be far more qualitative than quantitative, while my view is that we have to move quite quickly to the point of seeking analytical results. At the end I shall discuss some of the methodological issues central to the achievement of such results.

My approach to the extension of NET techniques is a conservative one. Every step must be examined with critical care. Terminological and epistemological issues must be noted as they arise. So I must begin by saying that the claim that economic systems in the large are dissipative structures has, for me, only the following potential meanings.

1. If we keep the books of an economic system in terms of the entropy measures suggested by NET we get a useful picture of what is going on as the system participates in the complex of systems from organism to natural and social environment.
2. Issues of environmental engineering, resource utilization, waste management, etc., are better considered in the systematic context provided by NET than they are in the more standard contexts.
3. There seem to me to be many reasons for questioning the concept of economic equilibrium, and the possibility of challenging that concept with the concept of far-from-equilibrium stability is an attractive one.

It might seem that the greater wisdom would be to treat economic systems as if they mere *analogues* to the dissipative structures normally discussed in the literature of NET. But I do not think that this would be right. I think we can say right off that economic systems *are* dissipative structures. In order to see why, we have to look at the way dissipative structures are identified in the first place. According to Brooks and Wiley, the following identify dissipative structures: they are seen as "(1) exhibiting finite information and cohesion, (2) maintaining themselves through irreversible dissipation of matter and energy, and (3) existing in an open energy system" (Brooks and Wiley, 1986). In addition, I would say, perhaps equivalently, that we have a dissipative structure wherever the methods of NET get results. This apparently offhand way of identifying dissipative structures is not careless or trivial, but I shall not stop to discuss the epistemological issues at this point.

The main criterion of dissipative structures is their time dependence. This criterion surely must be met. Quite evidently, economic systems meet the criterion; but we have to be careful to see clearly *how* they do so. For, much of classical, neoclassical, orthodox economic theory—in fact— makes use of techniques that play down or obscure the essential time dependence of economic processes. In particular, equilibrium analyses treat the process of economic exchange as if it were reversible. Indeed this is the heart of orthodox price theory and its accounting system. Yet, in another sense—still within orthodox theory—the processes of trading *cannot* be reversible. The path to the bargaining locus cannot be retraversed by rational traders. But in any case it is an illusion to think that orthodox economics is about trading. Nowhere does orthodox economics examine the process of trading. It examines only the logical consequences of a set of assumptions: e.g., that the bargaining system contains only rational economic men, defined by the standard process of abstraction; that initial assets are such and such for each of them; and that there are no exogenous constraints on the results of trading. We have to ask seriously how idealizations can engage in causal processes. The answer we usually get is that they do not enter into the processes, but that real beings closely approximating the idealizations do, with their behavior, *ceteris paribus*, conforming to the ideal. I have discussed this claim at length elsewhere (Dyke, 1981). Here it is enough to say that the insistence upon the bookkeeping of abstractions sets up insuperable impediments to our inquiring about the processes underlying that bookkeeping.

Two particular impediments need to be mentioned. First, many of the processes we would like to look at, and processes we would like to include in our calculations as we try to understand economies, turn out to be unavailable to us—by accident, as it were—if we confine ourselves to the bookkeeping of market equilibrium. For nothing enters market calculations that has not somehow been internalized in the market, has not found an equilibrium price. In the primary instances, the participants in the market have control over the items that enter the market and get prices attached to them. Secondarily, government at all levels forces market participants to recognize items not otherwise included in the market by taxing, licensing, etc. But the items taxed, licensed, and otherwise controlled are likewise historical artifacts, those items that come to public attention in the normal course of political life. As our concerns become better informed, we find, not surprisingly, that a lot of the things we would like to know about have never come to the attention of the market system, let alone become internalized in it.

Second, we have to look at the concept of efficiency associated with the standard equilibrium models. Again, the concept is given in micro theory, and then (if ever) imported into macro accounts. In particular the equilibrium claim to efficiency is that for a given set of resources as inputs the free operation of the market will yield an equilibrium result that can be shown to be optimally efficient in the sense that no participant in the market can be made better off by a redistribution without some other participant being made worse off. Now, this conception of efficiency has been the subject of extensive and intensive criticism in its own right; but I shall not go into that here. Rather, I shall point out that whatever concept of efficiency we may eventually want for our deliberations about comprehensive economic policy, this is among the last to recommend itself. In the first place, the "efficient" equilibrium is a function of the short range interests and perceptions of a population of the moment. Since any long range economic policy would *budget* resources over a long period of time, either the momentary equilibrium is irrelevant, since on the usual assumptions market participants have no reason to aim at long run efficiency, or we have to suppose that the long range budget is serendipitously in accord with the short range budgets of the participants in the market equilibrium. The latter supposition is bizarre.

As an example, we can think of decisions with respect to the utilization of land. Land use issues normally have the following structure: firms, in the normal course of their business, attempt to exploit land for whatever resources it offers to the normal course of their activity. Usually firms will compete for given land. Either the competition will be between two similar firms for the same resource, e.g., minerals of a certain sort, or it will be between two dissimilar firms for different resources, e.g., a mining company and a hotel chain may both become interested in a particular piece of ground.

In the former cases the price of the land may exclusively represent the estimate of its worth in terms of a single resource. In the latter case the price of the land will represent the marginal benefits of its use in one way over its use in another way—where we can imagine that often the two uses are flatly incompatible. In both cases the land will be internalized in the market at a determinate price, but there is no need for that price to be a figure that makes sense in terms of the long run socioeconomic concerns we have. The price simply represents the more or less short term calculations of one or more firms that have one or another interest in the land. The use of this price for long term planning is ludicrous. Yet the price is the only legitimated figure that the equilibrium calculations of the market can yield.

There is no doubt, of course, that equilibrium models offer us more comfort than models of stability far from equilibrium. In the first place, equilibrium models make it seem as if the perpetuation of the status quo were up to us; and if we were just careful enough to behave in the proper way we could be sure that we had our lives in our own hands. Talk of stability far from equilibrium is disconcerting, since it has the sound of a situation on the ragged edge of collapse. But, everything we learn from the natural sciences indicates that everything that lives could well be on the ragged edge with respect to key components of its ecosystem. If this were not so, whatever would happen to the theory of natural selection? Are we somehow exempt?

As we know from reading Prigogine and others, one of the major tasks in dealing with NET phenomena is setting up the criteria for the systems to be dealt with—their boundaries and the background conditions within which they arise and are sustained. Any dissipative structure consists of a system with enough internal coherence to utilize a background flow of matter and energy to *sustain, maintain, and reproduce* this very internal coherence. As the work of Brooks and Wiley suggests, this internal coherence, under the right conditions, can even become more elaborate and differentiated over the course of the history of the dissipative structure. So we know that if human institutions and systems are dissipative structures we have to identify structures and relate their ability to sustain, maintain, and reproduce themselves according to the resources (material and energy) available to them. These resources, so to speak, flow by and through the systems, and the successful systems find ways of organizing themselves to be able to utilize the available resource flow. The first question is, "What are the appropriate systems to look at?" In the modern world we seem to have a lot of choices, all the way from families to nation states. From an economic point of view, families, villages, cities, regions, provinces, states, etc., all the way up to nations seem to be prospective candidates for investigation as dissipative structures. Furthermore, economic accounts are kept at each of these levels; and decisions are made on the basis of calculations of the future behavior of these accounts.

Such thinking quite naturally leads us to think of increased interdependence of institutions, and their increased differentiation as a consequence of what each has to contribute to the sustenance of the whole. A familiar story. But each increment of interdependence requires new devices for establishing the internal coherence of the larger system. And each of these new devices has its cost; its "entropic debt." The larger system may indeed be able to balance its internal accounts in the manner of economic equilibrium theory, but the mere balancing of the accounts does not tell us anything about the relative costs of sustaining the new larger system as opposed to the old smaller ones.

What *NET* does, then, is to show us that there are interrelations between the social structures we have and the rate of material flow required to sustain them.[2] Or, in other words, it tells us that the entropy debt incurred by our elaborate organization can be paid in several ways: that the information content of our social system is necessarily connected to the rate of material flow needed to sustain it. For example, just to fix ideas, the standard line (since Hume) has it that economic systems have moderate scarcity as their condition. But scarcity is not the primary condition for an economy. What economies rest on are gradients. They depend on finding ways of keeping material flow at a suitable rate. Sometimes this is recognized by economists themselves, as in the concept of comparative advantage in discussions of international trade. More often, however, the need for gradients is *misrecognized*.

At this stage we need something a bit more concrete to work with. Among a number of sources I could have chosen from, I choose to discuss a theme from Jane Jacobs' recent *Cities and the Wealth of Nations* (1984). Her analysis raises very convenient sorts of questions for my present purposes. In addition, it gives us a clear set of structures and issues to work with before we have to treat the vexing problems of measure and measurement that eventually have to be confronted by NET.

Jacobs argues that despite the bifurcated emphasis on individuals and nations as the important constituents of economic systems (in micro- and macroeconomics, respectively), the dominant structural components of economic life are import-replacing cities and their associated regions. She gives no general account of the rise of such cities. Perhaps there *is* no general account. But once in place these cities organize an economy that prospers over a significantly long run. These import-replacing cities are to be contrasted with other cities that *do not* organize viable economies. Economic life in and around the latter is very different from that around the favored cities.

Now, no one acquainted with NET and reading Jacobs' book could fail to note the resemblance of these favored cities to dissipative structures. The lack of a general account of their genesis is itself indicative of the failure of linear causal models to account for them. The import-replacing cities look for all the world like strange attractors—structures that emerge from economic flux, and then begin to organize that flux. This model, of course, is consistent with a wide range of explanations for why a favored city arose here or there, at this time or that. But the explanation need not be "economic" in the same sense that would be appropriate to an account of its continuing stability once established.

We may be able to see this in terms of one of the dominant themes in NET, namely, the recurring theme that a stable structure far from equilibrium must succeed in altering flux rates sufficiently to create clear-cut phase separation. That is, internal order must be created that is far more efficient in utilizing energy for organization and maintenance than the background system within which the primary flux occurs. Lionel Johnson's study of the subarctic lakes can serve as a reference point here (Johnson, 1981, and this volume).

When we weave this theme into Jacobs' analysis we get some illuminating results. First of all, we are led to notice that there are two importantly different sorts of trade, where the dominant theories of economic analysis give us only one. In one sort of trade the mutual flow of material and energy simply tracks gradients. The trading *process* is simply a gate through which flow takes place. *This* sort of trading does indeed tend to lead to equilibrium—in the classic Boltzmannian sense. The redistribution resulting from trade tends to eliminate the gradients. Depending on the time-dependent fate of the traded material, equilibrium may actually be reached, approached, or never reached.

Examples of this sort of trade are extremely common, of course. Historically there are even some conspicuous cases in which this sort of trade persisted virtually by itself for relatively long periods. The Islamic traders both in Africa and on the Indian Ocean provided the gates for such trade. Much of the trade of Venice and Genoa *in their early days* was of this sort. The Dutch replaced local merchants as the gatekeepers of such trade in the Malaysian Archipelago (Braudel, 1984; Cipolla, 1980).

As we think of examples of gradient-tracking trade, we are bound to notice that in some favorable circumstances stable identifiable structures emerged, fueled by this trade. These identifiable structures can initially and typically be called markets, if we remain prepared to accommodate future complexities that convert them into fully formed economies. When I talk of markets as identifiable structures I do not mean simply that phenomena arise susceptible to bookkeeping of a certain sort. This is the trap that must be avoided. Nearly every human activity (and many nonhuman ones) can be squashed into the Procrustean bed of orthodox economic bookkeeping. This obscures nearly every feature of institutions and practices we need to know in order to get a satisfactory account of their historical dynamics.

When I talk of markets, I mean established spatiotemporal entities organized within the flux of gradient-tracking trade.

Not surprisingly, these entities grow up at the gates. They start out as stable, reliable managers of the gradient-tracking flux. But in favorable circumstances these market centers begin to use their advantage as gatekeepers to divert part of the flux to the creation, elaboration, and sophistication of their own internal organization. The part of the flux they internalize fuels an internal division of labor and a consequent differentiation of social function that allows space and time to be cleared for the activities that eventually result in what we would recognize as developed civilization and culture. In other words, the coalescence of these structures —first markets, then economies—results in just what we would expect in NET terms, the development of an internal economy. With this development there arises a second sort of trade: organization-promoting trade.

Organization-promoting trade is constituted by the allocation and distribution of material and energy (including human energy) *within* an economy. It is utilized to produce and reproduce the structures necessary to achieve the efficiencies in energy and materials utilization that result in, and are promoted by, phase separation.

Now that we have both sorts of trade preliminarily in view, let us pause for a moment to examine their relationship at a next stage of clarity. I mentioned above that the gradients necessary for economic activity are often misrecognized. We can now see better why this is so. Every economic system sophisticated enough to be available for analysis is already fairly complexly organized, and generally (but not always) has adopted a medium of exchange that tends to obscure the distinction between the two sorts of trade. In other words, the accounts tend to be kept in a uniform accounting system. This is what, in the end, allows us to keep *national* accounts, despite the fact that, as Jacobs points out, these accounts are tremendously misleading as a picture of the health or sickness of the regional economies added together in a national lump. Given the uniform accounting system, it is hard to see that there are two different sorts of trade at work.

But we have to remember Jacobs' key concept of import-replacement. For it can be understood precisely in terms of converting gradient-tracking trade into organization-promoting trade. Part of the gradient-traded material and energy is diverted to internal organization. This, in fact, is what distinguishes an economy from a market. The initial organization of a market consists simply in the establishment of a determinate place for a gradient-tracking trade gate. In addition, the market becomes organized in terms of rules of access and trading procedure. At a next stage, systems of credit can develop—the first internal division of labor and function. The crucial change from market to economy takes place when those who are associated in the market organize themselves in such a way that they can change the flux qualitatively. What used to be imported is now manufactured internally, for example, and the imports tend to consist of more primary material. The nascent economy is now differentiated at least into a manufacturing and a mercantile sector. But soon, under favorable conditions, the differentiation becomes very much more complex.

Notice that the distinction between gradient-tracking trade and organization-promoting trade does not reduce precisely to the distinction between external trade and internal circulation. The reduction is blocked when we recognize the ways in which organization-promoting trade generates and maintains structure. This structure generation need not be performed by internal circulation within a social system that has been unable to constitute itself as an economy. Jacobs gives a number of examples of such social systems; many more are available in the broader historical accounts provided by Fernand Braudel and others. Furthermore, economies are normally constituted by subsystems of various sorts, and some trade internal to the economy as a whole is gradient-tracking with respect to the subsystems. Last, it ought to be obvious that organization-promoting trade is gradient creating. It generates new differential needs.

Not all flux promoting gates become markets. Not all markets become economies. Just so, of course, not all dissipative structures arising out of chemical flux achieve a degree of internal coherence allowing them to become lasting and stable phase separated systems. This leads to the obvious question of why some evolutionary pathways succeed, and some fail. I leave this question as it arises in the biological realm to others. In the economic sphere it is useful to keep some of the following considerations in mind.

Geographic location is a crucial variable in the rise of economies as dissipative structures. But no one set of rules will define the nature of the geographic variable for all time. The development of economies generates new efficiencies in the management of energy and material flow. Some of these efficiencies are explicitly transportational and/or concerned with information management and dispersal. Geographic variables are importantly transportational and informational variables, so developments in transportation and communication redefine the geographic base of viable economic structures.

Second, economic structures are interpenetrated by other social structures—e.g., political and military structures—which can have a semiautonomous history with respect to any given economy. For example, a military capability may develop within the marauding seminomadic way of life of an essentially rootless people. However, if this capacity is attracted and trapped by a market it may function as one of the material conditions needed for this market to develop into a fully articulated economy. Military capacity can temporarily provide sealing off from buffeting flux and allow phase separation to be secured within the system the military strength has "artificially" sealed off. Eventually, of course, the internal structure of the system must become efficient enough to provide the surplus upon which the military depends. (Alternatively, the military can return periodically to marauding.) In the modern world, when an economy is weak and incapable of sustaining its own organization, military and police power, fueled from outside the economy, become a permanent, dominant feature of life.

Finally, we can think of an extreme situation ecologists often encounter: a species adapting itself to one dimension of its environment, rigidly committing itself to maximal efficiency within that environment at the expense of the capacity to react effectively to environmental change. Such species are always in grave danger of being evolutionary dead ends, because environmental change destroys the narrowly circumscribed conditions for their survival. (Notice, by the way, how wrong it would be to attribute this process to "natural selection." Without an account of the material conditions embedded in the ancestral genome, including the ability of that genome to generate variability, the natural selection explanation would be totally adventitious—truly tautological.)

Similarly, we can think of the "one product" city: for instance, the mining town. It is extremely vulnerable to changes in, let us say, the economic climate. Organized rigidly for one purpose as it is, if the lode dries up, or if the market changes, etc., it will take enormous effort to reorganize for success in the new environment. *Here is where the entropy debt is paid!* This may be called the mining town/ghost town phenomenon. Ghost towns, always single resource towns, find it impossible to marshall the resources to reorganize their economies for success after significant changes in the economic climate for their single resource: the vein runs out or new technologies and social conditions alter the demand for their resource, and they die.

If, on the other hand, there are reasons why the city in such circumstances cannot be allowed to die (as, for example, in the case of Montevideo—Jacobs, 1984), the cost of keeping them alive is enormous. Typically the cost is paid by people who live in poverty and squalor, and, eventually, the cost of maintaining order is paid for by those who support and equip military and paramilitary organizations that keep the city "intact" by brute force.

All the while that the single resource city is functioning successfully, its economic accounts are satisfactorily balanced. In fact, it could well be thought to be a healthy, growing, thriving place. The entropy debt that is piling up is hidden until the sustaining flux is interrupted. *It enters the economic accounts only when crisis occurs.*

The general point here is that the material conditions for the emergence of an economy as a dissipative structure are potentially many dimensional, and no one-track account of the rise and solidification of an economy is to be expected. To put the same point in other terms, an unstable, temporary looking structure arisen out of the flux of one gradient-tracking trade could be all it takes to ground the stability of a long lived structure in the flux provided by a newly arisen gradient-tracking trade.

Those wedded to free enterprise may take superficial comfort in the view that dissipative structures arise "spontaneously" without centralized manipulative control. But this is shallow. The order-out-of-chaos of the market is most like a simple dissipative structure in the relatively spontaneous appearance of small local markets operating in terms of barter and extended barter. Thus it is clear why these small markets are always invoked as the intuitive entrée to theories of the market. But these small markets are extremely modest entropy producers. And the small entropy debt is paid largely by the market participants themselves, and the beasts of burden (wives, etc.) who truck the produce to market. The rise of complex fully developed economies is entirely another matter. For example, in contrast, the modern capitalist economy, when looked at in these terms, is a strategy premised on an infinite bankroll.

When we say that an economy is not an equilibrium system, but a system stabilized far from equilibrium by material and energy flux, we recommend a modified accounting system—one that insists on examining the flow requirements for, say, a city, and considers the sources of that flow and the consequences of dependence on these sources. Our accounting insists that the internal stability—the viability—of the city is directly linked with the available resources, and with the ability of the city to generate some of these resources itself. And we also insist that the important consequences of this interdependence will not show up in the normal equilibrium calculations unless circumstances change significantly. So if someone can argue that circumstances will always be pretty much the same—the necessary material and energy flow that sustains the city will always be reliably present—then he can argue that the equilibrium calculations are enough, and, for example, land use decisions can be made on the basis of the marginal product of the land under present market conditions.

Or, in short, capitalism and its ideology are and always have been ahistorical. And if we think history—as any serious structural change—can be prevented, we can be comfortable with equilibrium bookkeeping. Evolutionary theory in biology, on the other hand, is a theory that has to be historical. The fossil record and everything else we know about the biota of the earth force this. Equilibrium bookkeeping will not work in evolutionary biology. But then, this means it will not work in ecology; and if it will not work in ecology, then eventually it will not work in economics either. For the second law of thermodynamics insists that we cannot stop ecological change, and that we cannot seal ourselves off from the changes except temporarily and at extremely high cost.

We are used to thinking of the material and energy flow from nature through our economy as one we ourselves initiate (by exploiting the resources of nature), and then cause to circulate in such a way that the benefit is distributed among us. Since we seem to see ourselves getting more and more wealthy, as individuals and collectively, over the course of time, it is hard to think of the flow in NET terms—e.g., as requiring a sink as well as a source. Trash, soot, and sludge seem an annoying and inconvenient by-product of our lives and activities rather than a necessary feature of them. But without a gradient down which material flow can cascade, no dissipative structure can remain stable. Genuine economic equilibrium looms as the heat death of our civilization.

Naturally I am far from arguing that in order to maintain a stable existence of the form of life we love we ought to promote the wholesale production of waste. *Far* from it. But what I am saying is that our existence as dissipative structures defines a space of possibilities for us, and does so rather tightly. We know from the standard thermodynamic analyses of human life that if we conserve and recycle we can lengthen the course that materials follow as they run through our hands. We know that if we use sunlight (and its immediate and inevitable correlates such as wind) we can select a composition of the material flow that gives us a longer thermodynamic horizon. Of course we do not need the resources of NET to tell us that. But within the frame of standard economics the pattern of decisions concerning resource utilization is set one way, and within the frame of NET the pattern is set another way.

The difference is the following: Within standard economics the decisions are all framable as cost/benefit decisions. The costs and benefits are cast as resource allocations, including the allocation of our own time and energy, all within the framework of "equilibrium" efficiency. We *never*, except in the most superficial ways, examine the relationships between our patterns of social organization and the rate of material flow needed to sustain them. This optimal efficiency is never satisfactorily connected to the time dependent thermodynamic conditions that really matter.

Now for some important *caveats*: In order to make it worth our while to construct economic models and theories in analogy to NET models in chemistry and biology, we ought to be dissatisfied until we have entropy measures that give us measurements, and until we have identity criteria for structures and systems to which the measures can be applied. In other words, we must be dissatisfied until we can proceed analytically as well as phenomenologically. Fortunately, this is more easily done in economic systems than in many other sorts of systems, if we are modest enough to recall a few important points.

We must remember that entropy calculations are contextual, and use great care in specifying spatial, temporal, and other "localities" such as technological capacity. The insistence on locality may seem strange to physicists—at least initially—but I have to point out that exactly analogous locality-establishing conditions are involved in *every* calculative use of the concept of entropy. That is, if entropy bookkeeping is to be useful in tracking physical, chemical, or biological processes, then the initial, boundary, and closure conditions have to be set in order for the books to be opened, inscribed, and closed.

Furthermore, in multidimensional systems such as social systems, there are varieties of ways of creating and maintaining order—sublocalities of one sort organized one way, those of another sort organized another way or allowed to drift; some organized by rules, others by the fixing of systems variables (inventory management, for example), still others by devices that are "internal" to individuals (moralities, etc.). In other words, filters of all sorts are available, and can be used in all sorts of combinations. So there will not, in general, be any simple way (e.g., Shannon-type bookkeeping) to keep internal entropic books and assess their significance vis-à-vis flow requirements. A sophisticated *combination* of techniques will have to be found.

A possible irony in working toward the utilization of NET techniques in economics is that NET does not yield deterministic theory—which means, I am still convinced, that precise predictions are unavailable using NET techniques. But I do not think the situation is as anomalous as it can be made to seem. NET *can* give us predicted ranges. It can give us clear accounts of the limits and constraints within which we work. And, in fact, that is all any science can do. As I, and others, have argued elsewhere, the apparent determinism and predictive sufficiency of even Newtonian science is a combination of hope, and luck in establishing abstractions stable for normal purposes. What we have to substitute for the metaphysics of determinism is the intelligence of sophisticated heuristic problem solving strategies. And *that*, in the end, is the challenge made by NET to economic theory.

Notes

1. In my judgment, the current most solid source is by Jeffrey Wicken (Wicken, 1986). This paper contains the most useful conceptual structure to date, is free of the outlandish claims that tend to infect the literature, and canvases previous contributions in a productive way. The most important earlier contributions are, in addition to the key works developing NET in strictly biological contexts, Adams (1982), Boulding (1970), Odum (1971), and Proops (1983). Wicken provides a clear progranatic statement to which I subscribe:

All natural organizations ... are products of evolutionary history. Since the functional referents of their operations are perpetuation and propagation, existence and operation are inseparable. This coupling requires that all natural organizations be *informed dissipative structures*, the integrity of whose organizational relationships depends on degrading free energy and dissipating entropy to a sink of some sort. The natural organization is inseparable from nature's overall dynamics.

Socioeconomic systems belong to this class of organizations. While planning and design are essential to socioeconomic development, this development is of an evolutionary nature—bound by the hand of history on one hand, and the ecological-societal tolerances of what can work in sustaining organization on the other.

2. These interrelationships may be far from simple. Multidimensionality makes the job of, for example, determining information measures of organization a very complex one. See Prigogine (1955), Proops (1983), and Wicken (1986).

References

Adams, R. N., 1982. *Paradoxical Harvest*. Cambridge: Cambridge University Press.

Boulding, K. E., 1970. *Economics as a Social Science*. London: McGraw-Hill.

Boulding, K. E., 1981. *Evolutionary Economics*. Beverly Hills: Sage Publications.

Brooks, D. R., and E. O. Wiley, 1986. *Evolution as Entropy: Toward a Unified Theory of Biology*. Chicago: University of Chicago Press.

Braudel, Fernand, 1984. *The Perspective of the World*. New York: Harper and Row.

Cipolla, Carlo M., 1980. *Before the Industrial Revolution*. New York: Norton.

Dyke, C., 1981. *Philosophy of Economics*. Englewood Cliffs: Prentice-Hall.

Georgescu-Roegen, Nicholas, 1971. *The Entropy Law and the Economic Process*. Cambridge, MA: Harvard University Press.

Jacobs, Jane, 1984. *Cities and the Wealth of Nations*. New York: Random House.

Johnson, L., 1981. Thermodynamic origin of ecosystems. *Can. J. Fish. Aquat. Sci.* 38: 571–590.

Odum, H. T., 1971. *Environment, Power, and Society*. New York: Wiley.

Odum, H. T., and Elisabeth S. Odum, 1976. *Energy Basis for Man and Nature*. New York: McGraw-Hill.

Prigogine, I., 1955. *Introduction to the Thermodynamics of Irreversible Processes*. New York: Wiley.

Proops, J. L. R., 1983. *J. Soc. Biol. Str.* 6:353.

Wicken, J. S., 1986. Evolutionary self-organization and entropic dissipation in biological and socioeconomic systems. *J. Soc. Biol. Str.* 9:261–273.

Index